# THE CORRUPTION OF ANGELS

# THE CORRUPTION OF ANGELS

## THE GREAT INQUISITION OF 1245–1246

*Mark Gregory Pegg*

PRINCETON UNIVERSITY PRESS

PRINCETON AND OXFORD

PUBLISHED BY PRINCETON UNIVERSITY PRESS, 41 WILLIAM STREET,

PRINCETON, NEW JERSEY 08540

IN THE UNITED KINGDOM: PRINCETON UNIVERSITY PRESS,

3 MARKET PLACE, WOODSTOCK, OXFORDSHIRE OX20 1SY

*LIBRARY OF CONGRESS CATALOGING-IN-PUBLICATION DATA*

PEGG, MARK GREGORY, 1963–

THE CORRUPTION OF ANGELS : THE GREAT INQUISITION OF

1245–1246 / MARK GREGORY PEGG.

P. CM.

INCLUDES BIBLIOGRAPHICAL REFERENCES AND INDEX.

ISBN 0-691-00656-3 (ALK. PAPER)

1. ALBIGENSES. 2. LAURAGAIS (FRANCE)—CHURCH HISTORY.

3. INQUISITION—FRANCE—LAURAGAIS. 4. FRANCE—CHURCH

HISTORY—987–1515. I. TITLE.

DC83.3.P44 2001

272′.2′0944736—DC21        00-057462

THIS BOOK HAS BEEN COMPOSED IN BASKERVILLE TYPEFACE

PRINTED ON ACID-FREE PAPER. ∞

WWW.PUP.PRINCETON.EDU

PRINTED IN THE UNITED STATES OF AMERICA

1   3   5   7   9   10   8   6   4   2

*To My Mother*

# CONTENTS

# ACKNOWLEDGMENTS

T HE STAFF, librarians, and archivists of Olin Library at Washington University in St. Louis, Firestone Library at Princeton University, Speer Library at Princeton Theological Seminary, Rare Books at Columbia University in New York, the Bibliothèque nationale in Paris, the departmental archives of the Tarn-et-Garonne in Montauban, the departmental archives of the Haute-Garonne, the Bibliothèque méridionale of the Institute d'études méridionales, and the Bibliothèque municipale, these last three all in Toulouse, were invaluable throughout the writing of this book. Almost all of the research was undertaken with fellowships, grants, and funds from the Andrew W. Mellon Foundation, the History Department at Princeton University, the Center for Human Values at Princeton University, The Group for the Study of Late Antiquity at Princeton University, the School of Historical Studies at the Institute for Advanced Study in Princeton, and the History Department at Washington University in St. Louis. Also, vital to the life of this book were the participants of the seminars and lectures where chapters, often quite shaggy and unshaven, were heard and discussed: the University Center for Human Values at Princeton University, the Institute for Advanced Study in Princeton, the Centre for Medieval Studies at the University of Sydney, the Quodlibet Conference at the Centre for Medieval Studies at the University of York, and the History Department of Washington University in St. Louis.

More personally, my thanks (occasionally belated) go to Beatrice Casèau, Ivona Percec, Elspeth Carruthers, Emily Rose, Barbara Krauthamer, Christopher Brest (for his excellent map), Mark Spencer, John Mundy, William Stoneman, Michael Stoller, David d'Avray, John Ward, Teófilo Ruiz, James Given, Susan Reynolds, Robert Moore, Jacques Le Goff, George Kateb, Pierre Bonnaisse, Maurice Berthe, Claire Péquignot, Claire Vernon, Alison MacDonald, Sunjoo Moon, Anja Belz, Peter Biller, John Arnold, Caterina Bruschi, Sean McWilliams, Sara Lloyd, Bette Marbs, Sheryl Peltz, Amanda Hingst, Henry Berger, Joseph Schraibman, David Konig, Hillel Kieval, Léopold Delisle, Elora Shehabudin, Victor Bolden, Roy Seckold, Graham Knowles, Andrew Knowles, and Victoria Knowles. This study, in a number of past guises, was read with great intelligence, care, and friendship by Peter Brown, Edward Peters, Malcolm Barber, John Pryor, David Nirenberg, Derek Hirst, Giles Constable, and Anthony Grafton. My editor Brigitta van Rheinberg was, when things looked a bit bleak, forever hopeful, always encouraging, and extremely patient. Lauren Lepow improved my writing (and so my ideas) with wonderful skill and insight. William Jordan, my remarkable adviser at Princeton, knows how much I owe to him, and I can only say, along with some rather cute little iron goats . . . well, he knows. Ussama Makdisi is a great friend and scholar; my work now, and in the future, will always be the richer thanks to him. Anthony Peck, a mate all too similar to myself, has helped my research, and me, in ways he does not even realize. Nicole Jacobs, in her concern that I finally finish this book, will always be my friend. Jennifer Baszile, more than anyone else, has given my scholarship, and life, a clarity when I frequently felt lost—I could not have finished this study without her.

This book is a small gift to five women. First, my late grandmother Lillian Pegg. Second, Mary Douglas. Third, the late Dianne Lim for all her remembered faith in me. Fourth, my sister, Trescha Knowles, without whom my life would be incomplete. Finally, above all others, my mother, Veronica Seckold, who, in so many moments of wisdom and forgiveness, understanding and worry, humor and love—whether in Woy Woy, or on the telephone to Princeton and St. Louis, or even to a lonely, chilly *téléphone* box at the foot of the Pyrénées—never doubted that I would finish this book, this thing I had to do, now lovingly dedicated to her.

# THE CORRUPTION OF ANGELS

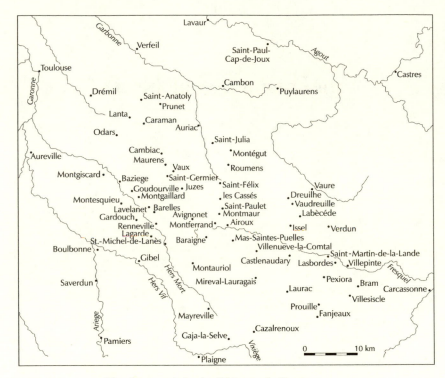

The Lauragais in the Thirteenth Century

# 1

## TWO HUNDRED AND ONE DAYS

IN two hundred and one days, between the first of May 1245 and the first of August 1246, five thousand four hundred and seventy-one men and women from the Lauragais were questioned in Toulouse about the heresies of the "good men," the "good women," and the Waldensians. Nobles and diviners, butchers and monks, concubines and physicians, blacksmiths and pregnant girls, the leprous and the cruel, the literate and the drunk, the deceitful and the aged—in short, all men over fourteen and all women over twelve were summoned (through their parish priests) by the Dominican inquisitors Bernart de Caux and Jean de Saint-Pierre. They traveled from their villages in the fertile corridor between the Ariège and Agout rivers to the Romanesque cloister of the Abbey of Saint-Sernin. There, before scribes and witnesses, sworn to the truth, individuals (sometimes almost two hundred in a day) confessed whether they, or anyone else, had ever seen, heard, helped, or sought salvation through the heretics.

Some of the confessions were long and rambling; most were short and sharp—all, without exception, were translated into Latin, then attested. Memories, as old as half a century or as young as the week before last, recalled the mundane and the wonderful: two cobblers knew that all visible things were made by the Devil; widows spoke of houses for heretics; a sum of twelve shillings passed through thirteen hands; notaries read the Gospel of John in *roman*; a monk whined about a *crezen* pissing on his head; a *bon ome* healed a sick child; a *faidit* had a leper for a concubine; an old woman was stuffed in a wine barrel; three knights venerated two holy boys; *bonas femnas* refused to eat meat; cowherds wanted to be scholars; friar-inquisitors were murdered; angels fell to earth; and very few (only forty-one) had ever seen a Waldensian.

This inquisiton into heretical depravity in the Lauragais was, without a doubt, the single largest investigation, in the shortest possible time, in the entire European Middle Ages. One can, through reading the surviving manuscript of the Lauragais interrogations, in that twist of fate whereby the luck of the historian rests upon the efficiency of persecutors, grasp, however tentatively, something of the vibrant rhythms by which thousands of medieval men and women lived their lives. All that follows, from angels to adoration, from parchment to paper, from crusades to chestnuts, derives its inspiration from this extraordinary manuscript, whose leaves allow for the passionate evocation of the Lauragais in the years before, as well as during, the great inquisition of Bernart de Caux and Jean de Saint-Pierre.

# 2

## THE DEATH OF ONE CISTERCIAN

THIRTY-SEVEN years before the inquisition of Bernart de Caux and Jean de Saint-Pierre a papal legate was murdered in the cool haze of a Provençal dawn. The murder happened on Monday, 14 January 1208, just where the Rhône divides (into *le petit* and *le grand*) before it enters the Mediterranean. The Cistercian Peire de Castelnau, legate of Pope Innocent III and a virulent denouncer of heresy in Languedoc, was about to cross the Rhône (from the right bank to the left) when an anonymous "evil-hearted" squire galloped up behind him and punctured his ribs with a swiftly thrown lance.[1] Peire de Castelnau fell from his pacing mule, briefly raised his arms to heaven, forgave his murderer, and died just as the sun finished rising. The unknown assassin comfortably escaped on a fast horse to nearby Beaucaire.[2] The abrupt killing of Peire de Castelnau was the immediate cause of twenty-one years of sporadic warfare, indiscriminate butchery, and bloody conquest known as the Albigensian Crusade.[3]

It took only two months for Innocent III to accuse Raimon VI, the count of Toulouse, in a belligerent (and rhetorically bludgeoning) letter, dated Monday, 10 March 1208, of complicity in the assassination of the papal legate.[4] After all, less than a year earlier, Peire de Castelnau had excommunicated the count of Toulouse (at the end of a nasty and bitter quarrel) for refusing to publicly suppress heresy.[5] Innocent III, at the time, took up this excommunication, confirmed it, and then, amplifying the anger of his legate in a letter of more than thirteen thousand words, told the count of Toulouse, in one overwrought metaphor after another, that his lands deserved to be confiscated because he was so strongly suspected of heresy.[6] Now, a year later, Innocent III, convinced that Raimon VI had rewarded and protected Peire de Castelnau's murderer, proclaimed a crusade, with the same indulgences as would be granted for an expedition to Palestine, against the count and the heretics of Languedoc. "Attack the followers of heresy," the pope commanded all potential *crucesignati*, "more fearlessly than even the Saracens," since perfidious heretics, "are more evil!"[7]

Yet, while there is no question that Raimon VI, like many Languedocian nobles, appreciated (without necessarily participating in) the holiness of the good men and the good women, it would be wrong to assume that the count of Toulouse knowingly sanctioned the murder of an apostolic envoy.[8] The troubadour Guilhem de Tudela in his *canso* about the Albigensian Crusade—which he started composing in 1210 and whose sympathies, unlike those of the anonymous poet who continued the song, were clearly with the crusaders—was probably closer to the truth when he sang that the unknown assassin had pierced the spine of the papal legate "hoping to win the count's approval."[9] Raimon VI and Peire de Castelnau certainly disagreed, but the count of Toulouse, well aware of the mischief Innocent III would cause in Languedoc if he had the chance, and lacking the thoughtless *ingénuité* of the legate's killer, would never have risked the county of Toulouse (which he held as a tenant-in-chief of the French crown), the marquisate of Provence (where he was a vassal of the Holy Roman emperor), the Agenais (whose overlord was the king of England), the counties of Gevaudan and Millau (purchased from King Pere II of Aragon in 1204), the Rouergue, the Querceynois, and the towns of Saint-Gilles, Nîmes, and Beaucaire upon the death of one Cistercian.[10]

Innocent III tried to coax and cajole the French king, Philip II Augustus, into leading the crusade against Raimon VI, in *litterae generales* and *litterae speciales*, but the French monarch refused.[11] Nevertheless, in May 1208, Philip II Augustus, in a halfhearted response to the irritating mandates of Innocent III, did allow the duke of Burgundy and the count of Nevers, with no more than five hundred knights between them, to take "the sign of the cross" against the heretics of the Midi.[12]

So, in the stifling heat of early July 1209, a large, essentially northern French, crusading army, with "gold-embroidered crosses and bands of silk" displayed on their right breasts, gathered at Lyon.[13] "If I started right now, not stopping 'till dark, not stopping 'till first light tomorrow," flourished Guilhem de Tudela with only a small portion of the crusading host in mind, "I couldn't even begin to tell you the names of those Provençaux who joined the *crozada*, let alone all the others who rushed to join, because no one in the world could do such reckoning," and, in an offhand codicil after such hyperbole, "none of this, by the bye, recalls the innumerable horsemen brought by the French."[14] In any event, it does seem that there were probably five thousand mounted *crucesignati* (nobles, bishops, knights, sergeants) and ten to fifteen thousand other pilgrims (an assortment of squires, foot-sergeants, crossbowmen, priests, siege engineers, kitchen boys, blacksmiths, mercenaries, prostitutes, monks, cooks, carpenters, servants, wives, meanderers, armorers, thieves, and child scavengers).[15]

Raimon VI—reviled as the "count of cunning" by the youthful Cistercian historian Pierre des Vaux-de-Cernay, writing a decade after the death of Peire de Castelnau[16]—managed on Sunday, 18 June 1209, with the *crucesignati* quickly descending upon Languedoc, to reconcile himself to the Church and even, four days later, to be indulged as a crusader.[17] At this point, with the count of Toulouse no longer the target of the crusade, a decision was taken by the leading "soldiers of Christ" that they should invade, instead, the heresy-infected lands of the twenty-four-year-old Raimon-Roger Trencavel, *vescomte* of Béziers, Carcassonne, Razès, and Albi, a youth whose overlord (as count of Barcelona) was King Pere II of Aragon rather than Raimon VI.[18]

This resolution decided upon, and with the count of Toulouse guiding them, the crusaders moved down the Mediterranean coast until they stopped on the warm evening of Tuesday, 21 July 1209, below the walls of Béziers and pitched their tents on the sandy west bank of the river Orb.[19] The next day, the feast of Saint Mary Magdalen, Raimon-Roger Trencavel having galloped away to Carcassonne, the men and women of Béziers, refusing to hand over any heretics, were completely surprised and overwhelmed when, in response to the death and dismemberment of a crusader by some Biterrois, thousands of frenzied servant boys from the crusaders' army, "with not a pair of shoes between them," leaping defensive ditches and scrambling over ramparts, finally succeeded after an hour or so, through sheer numbers and blood lust, in smashing open the city's gates.[20] Once inside Béziers, these vicious boys began to kill everyone they met, young and old, with wooden clubs.[21] Amidst all this killing a greedy search began for treasure, and it was only at this point in the massacre, according to Guilhem de Tudela, that the crusading nobility rode in and "drove the lads out with sticks, like dogs."[22] In revenge, these ragtag youths, these aroused *ribauds*, started shouting, "Burn it! Burn it!" and so Béziers, its population butchered, was burnt to the ground.[23]

Arnaud Amalric, the papal legate leading the crusaders, writing to Innocent III shortly after the cleansing of Béziers, joyfully told the pope "that our men [*nostri*] spared no one, irrespective of rank, sex, or age, and put to the sword almost [*fere*] 20,000 people," and—the final apocalyptic touch as he recalled the flames of burning Béziers—"divine vengeance raged miraculously."[24] As to the truth of Arnaud Amalric's triumphant death tally, his accounting was perhaps too high by only five or seven thousand.[25] Also, as Arnaud Amalric's obvious pleasure at the destruction of Béziers reveals, the cruelty of the servant boys is not to be seen as a tragic exercise in vulgar excitability; quite the opposite, the shoeless *ribauds* did nothing more than act out the extremely lucid intentions of the crusading nobility toward any town or village that did not immediately surrender.[26] Incidentally, Bernart de Caux, if not originally from Agen, was possibly born in the region of Béziers just before, or just after, the coming of the crusaders.[27]

The crusaders, after resting for three days by the smoldering ruins of Béziers, started a leisurely march through the valley of the Aude upon Carcassonne. They reached Carcassonne on Saturday, 1 August 1209, and, after encircling the entire city with their camp, vigorously attacked at dawn three days later, quickly storming the ring of thirty towers that made up the outer wall.[28] Raimon-Roger Trencavel retreated, with most of the inhabitants of Carcassonne, into his citadel, the *cité* proper, and, lacking food and water, prepared to fight and die.[29] The young *vescomte*, tormented by desperate thirst, suffocating heat, escalating fear, stinging flies, and the "crying and shrieking of the women and little children," finally surrendered, after a fortnight of such agonies, his city, goods, lands, everything he and the people of the Carcassès owned, to the crusaders on Saturday, 15 August 1209.[30] Simon, count of Montfort l'Amaury in the Ile-de-France, became, by common consent among the noble and ecclesiastical *crucesignati*, the new *vicomte* of Béziers, Carcassonne, Razès, and Albi.[31] In effect, Simon de Montfort also became the new lay leader of the crusade, undertaking the "sacred business of Jesus Christ in the fight against the infection of heresy,"[32] particularly as many of the crusader nobility, like the duke of Burgundy and the count of Nevers, left the army and returned north.[33] Raimon-Roger Trencavel was imprisoned by the crusaders and would die, probably from dysentery, three months later on Tuesday, 10 November 1209.[34]

Simon de Montfort, despite the retirement of many crusaders, so that he had "scarcely any companions," not only swiftly occupied villages, *castra*, in the southern Lauragais, like Fanjeaux and Montréal sitting upon their small strategic hills, but he also, without warning, swept into the territories of Count Raimon-Roger of Foix (whose suzerain, once more, was Pere II of Aragon), seizing Pamiers and Mirepoix.[35] Castres, on the Agout in the northeast of the Lauragais, and Albi, on the southern bank of the Tarn, were also hastily grabbed by the new *vicomte*.[36] In Castres one captured heretic, fastened to a wooden stake by heavy irons around his legs, stomach, and throat, was burnt in the village square. The death of this anonymous man, whom Pierre des Vaux-de-Cernay described as a "perfected heretic," was Simon de Montfort's (and so, in a sense, the Albigensian Crusade's) first, though far from last, deliberate incineration of an individual accused of heresy.[37]

In early September 1209, Raimon VI, having successfully diverted the crusaders away from his lands, which included most of the Lauragais, was, rather rudely, and certainly unexpectedly, sent a delegation from Simon de Montfort and Arnaud Amalric demanding that all heretics living in the city of Toulouse be handed over immediately for judgment. The count, and the consuls, of Toulouse refused.[38] Once more, Raimon VI was threatened with excommunication; once more, he appealed to

Innocent III; and, not quite believing his inability to shake off the crusaders, he also complained to his liege lords Philip II Augustus and the emperor Otto IV of Brunswick.[39] All this effort was wasted. On Sunday, 6 February 1211, a new sentence of excommunication was placed upon the count of Toulouse by a chorus of archbishops (Narbonne and Arles) and bishops (Avignon, Maguelonne, Toulouse, and Orange).[40] Innocent III confirmed the excommunication on Friday, 15 April 1211.[41]

While all this futile, and sometimes humiliating, diplomacy by Raimon VI was going on, Simon de Montfort, having lost a few *castra* during the chilly winter of 1209, campaigned aggressively, brutally, and victoriously, throughout the next year and a half, aided by an influx of new *crucesignati*. For instance, in the Lauragais, he attacked and easily overcame Bram, a *castrum* positioned, a little too candidly, in the middle of the flat cereal-rich fields that lay (and still lie) between Carcassonne and Castelnaudary. In revenge for the facial mutilation of some crusaders a few months earlier at Minerve,[42] a hundred of Bram's defenders had their noses sliced off and their eyes gouged out. These mutilated fellows were then made to traipse behind a one-eyed companion (whose cyclops condition was also the result of crusader surgery) throughout the Lauragais until, finally, thirty kilometers away, they found comfort in Cabaret.[43]

Lavaur, on the west bank of the Agout, caught in that fuzzy area of demarcation where the Trencavel lands in the Albigeois met those of the counts of Toulouse in the Lauragais, was, after a siege of five to six weeks, taken by the crusaders on Tuesday, 3 May 1211.[44] In the malevolent thrill of victory, four hundred townspeople, all condemned as heretics, were gathered in a meadow and burnt in a great funeral pyre. As this holocaust took place, eighty or so Lavaur knights were enthusiastically put to the sword when the initial idea of a mass hanging, with all the humiliation such a death meant for a *miles*, failed because the jerry-built gibbet toppled over. A coda to all this cruelty was the death of na (from *domna*, lady) Girauda, the dame-seigneur of Lavaur: this elegant and courtly woman was held over a deep well, shrieking and screaming, before her captors dropped her in and gleefully threw stones on top of her.[45]

Simon de Montfort, Lavaur in his possession, and secure in his right to sieze the territories of anyone punished with excommunication, now invaded the lands of the count of Toulouse.[46] Montgey, in the Vieilmorez to the north of the Lauragais, became the first *castrum* overwhelmed by the crusaders that lay, without any legal doubt, under the lordship of Raimon VI.[47] In the Lauragais itself, the village of les Cassés, close to the old Roman road from Carcassonne to Toulouse, was smoothly occupied, and, with brisk punctiliousness, sixty heretics were tossed into fires.[48] Toulouse, "the flower and rose of all cities,"[49] finally got to see the "French of France," *Frances de Fransa*, as Guilhem de Tudela and the anonymous *canso*-continuator invariably call the *langue du roi* crusaders,[50] when Simon de Montfort's army camped before the strong southeastern walls (between the Porte Narbonnaise and the Porte de Villeneuve) on Thursday, 16 June 1211.[51] Simon de Montfort, lacking men and resources, vainly tried a number of sorties against the defenses of Toulouse but, achieving nothing, abandoned the siege on Wednesday, 29 June 1211, and, retreating to Castelnaudary, started to raid the possessions of Raimon-Roger of Foix.[52]

Raimon VI, remarkably clumsy in warfare, could not dislodge Simon de Montfort from Castelnaudary.[53] So, when new *crucesignati* arrived in Languedoc from the Rhineland, Frisia, Saxony, Westphalia, even the Balkans, and, of course, northern France, Simon de Montfort managed, quite adroitly, to capture one *castrum* after another until, by the end of the summer of 1212, only the city of Toulouse itself remained unconquered.[54] Simon de Montfort ended the year by promulgating at Pamiers, before a council of his followers, a set of statutes reorganizing his conquests into a colonial regime that, though in the deep south of the Midi, would faithfully mirror the "good customs," the *bonos mores*, way to the north in Paris and the Ile-de-France.[55]

Pere II of Aragon, worried at the turn of events north of the Pyrénées, especially at the seemingly inexhaustible ambition and talent of Simon de Mortfort, decided to formally intervene on behalf of Raimon VI and arrange a truce, at the very least, among the pope, the crusaders, and the count of Toulouse.[56] The Argonese king did not fear any accusation of heresy—he was, after all, still bathed in an aura of Christian glory since his victory, with the kings of Castile and Navarre, over the Almohade Muslims at the battle of Las Navas de Tolosa in Andalusia on Saturday, 16 July 1212.[57] At first, Pere II of Aragon met with some sympathy from Innocent III, but, as with all attempts at reconciliation among the crusaders, the Languedocian prelates, and the count of Toulouse, nothing was achieved (except the continuation of violence at an even more feverish pitch).[58] The king of Aragon was, understandably, somewhat dismayed by his diplomatic failure, and so, in an ambitious riposte to such spiteful crusader intransigence, he proceeded on Sunday, 27 January 1213, to accept oaths of allegiance from Raimon VI, his son Raimon, the twenty-four consuls of Toulouse, Raimon-Roger of Foix, his son Roger-Bernart, Bernart of Comminges, his son Bernart, and Gaston de Béarn. These grand gestures of fealty completely altered the feudal map of Languedoc, theoretically tearing off the county of Toulouse from the *regnum* of France and making Pere II of Aragon the effective suzerain, protector, and arbitrator of all the territories occupied, or threatened, by the crusaders.[59]

In August 1213, Pere II of Aragon crossed the Pyrénées intending to destroy, once and for all, Simon de Montfort. Outside the little village of Muret, snug by the west bank of the Garonne and roughly twenty kilometers from Toulouse, the king of Aragon was joined by Raimon VI, Raimon-Roger of Foix, and Bernart of Comminges. Simon de Montfort's army, going through one of its habitual shrinkages because a large number of knights had left after completing their forty-day crusading vow, were trapped inside Muret. Nevertheless, because of a perfectly timed cavalry charge into the Aragonese host, Simon de Montfort was victorious. It was all over, bar the shouting, in less than an hour on the morning of Thursday, 12 September 1213. Pere II of Aragon was dead, his five-year-old son Jaume captured, and his knights either slaughtered in battle or drowned in the Garonne as they fled. A stunned Raimon VI simply rode away without unsheathing his sword, an exile, fleeing, soon after, to England.[60]

Simon de Montfort, despite renewed Languedocian defiance after Muret, and difficulties in having his conquests formally recognized, did, in the end, get named the new count of Toulouse by Innocent III at the Fourth Lateran Council in November 1215.[61] Eight months earlier, Philip II Augustus, confident after his spectacular victory over King John of England and the emperor Otto IV at Bouvines in Flanders on Sunday, 27 July, finally allowed his son Louis to become a *crucesignatus*.[62] Louis, staying no longer than his obligatory forty days, helped Simon de Montfort suppress all lingering dissent to rule by the "French," and, most important, the prince and the count dismantled the walls, towers, and other fortifications of Narbonne and Toulouse.[63] In April 1216, Philip II Augustus accepted Simon de Montfort's homage for the county of Toulouse, the duchy of Narbonne, and the *vicomtés* of Béziers and Carcassonne.[64]

Raimon VI, though stripped of all his possessions by the papacy, immediately began a vigorous resistance, largely undertaken by his talented son, so that, within a year, the two Raimons had retaken Avignon and Beaucaire.[65] The old count, hidden by a gray early morning mist, even managed to sneak (after a fashion, as he and his entourage still had their vibrant banners unfurled) into Toulouse on Wednesday, 13 September 1217.[66] The men and women of the city, "great and small, lords and ladies, wives and husbands," overcome with joy, mobbed Raimon VI, kissing his clothing, feet, legs, arms, and fingers.[67] After months of murmuring, "God, you have delivered us into the hands of Pharaoh,"[68] or so the anonymous *canso*-continuator had the Toulousains lament about Simon de Montfort's harsh rule, everyone started to say to each other, with rising excitment, "Now we have Jesus Christ!" and "This is our Lord who was lost!"[69] This joy, swiftly giving way to giddy violence, especially as each person started to feel "as brave as Oliver," caused the great and the small to run through the streets crying, "Toulouse!" as they grabbed apple-wood cudgels, pikes, and clubs, before clobbering to death all the "French" they could find.[70] Simon de Montfort's wife, Alice, withdrew with her surviving knights into the comital castle, the Château Narbonnais, saying, at least in the wicked deadpan irony of the anonymous *canso*-continuator, "And yesterday all was going so well!"[71]

Simon de Montfort, told of the trouble in the Toulousain by a "squire fluent in many dialects" whom his wife had instantly dispatched, hastily rode back from the Rhône valley where he was besieging rebellious *castra* and immediately assaulted the southern walls of Toulouse near the Porte Montoulieu (which was about five hundred meters east of the Château Narbonnais).[72] So, as the men, women, and children of Toulouse attacked the Château Narbonnais within the city, they themselves were being attacked by Simon de Montfort outside their newly rebuilt walls, moats, and ditches. The anonymous *canso*-continuator remembered an impromptu garden that "burst forth and blossomed" every day in the Montoulieu field. "It was sown with lilies," the poet softly sang about this *jardin*, "but the white and the red that budded and flowered were of flesh, blood, weapons, and splattered brains. Spirits and souls, sinners and saved, the freshly killed replenished hell and paradise."[73]

The siege went on for another nine months, each side reinforced by new recruits, especially mercenaries, each side building trebuchets, mangonels, and other catapults, each side flinging stones "like a snowstorm, like thunder and tempest," so that these rocks "shook the town, the river, and the riverbank."[74] Alice de Montfort escaped north and set about raising reinforcements. Meanwhile, "I want nothing that's in Toulouse, nothing," the anonymous *canso*-continuator has Simon de Montfort, frustrated by the Toulousain resistance, bitterly tell his followers, "except the destruction of the place and the people!"[75] Unfortunately, as far as Simon de Montfort was concerned, on Monday, 25 June 1218, a rock flung from a mangonel worked by little girls and men's wives struck him on his crystal-encrusted helmet, "shattering his eyes, brains, back teeth, forehead, and jaw." Simon de Montfort, "bleeding and black," fell to the ground dead.[76] Exactly a month later the crusaders, after one more lackluster assault on Toulouse, retreated with the body of Simon de Montfort to Carcassonne where it was buried *more gallico*.[77]

In the aftermath of Simon de Montfort's death, the energy needed to continue the crusade, to retake lost *castra*, just was not there. Aimery de Montfort, though acclaimed by his father's followers as count of Toulouse, steadily lost all crusading conquests to the triumphant campaigning of Raimon VI and his son, "the brave young count who paints the darkness with gold and brings green back to a dead world."[78] Pope

Honorius III, elected to the papal throne in 1216, tried, like his predecessor, to entice Philip II Augustus into becoming a participant in the Languedocian crusade.[79] The pope offered the French monarch papal protection, absolution from penance because of the English wars, even half of all crusading tithes—and yet, despite such gifts, Philip II Augustus was still wary.[80] Until, that is, the pope turned to the young and aggressive (and potentially rebellious) count of Champagne, Thibaut IV, for help in fighting the southern heretics. Philip II Augustus now provoked into action, but forever cautious about involvement in the south, eventually allowed his son Louis, after a year's preparation, to take a second expeditionary force into the Midi.[81]

Prince Louis marched into Languedoc in May 1219 with "cartloads of weapons" and, in the company of Aimery de Montfort, immediately captured the town of Marmande.[82] Five thousand men, women, and children were, with little more than a second thought, hacked to pieces by the crusaders. The ground was littered with arms and legs, lungs and livers, blood and brains, "as if they had rained down from the sky."[83] Louis was, apparently, annoyed by this improvised butchery; in any event, he made no attempt to stop it.[84] After this massacre, recalling the slaughter of Béziers a decade earlier, the royal *crucesignati* marched on Toulouse and started besieging it on Sunday, 16 June 1219. After six weeks of inconclusive warfare, Louis, his forty-day crusading commitment over, abruptly ended the siege on Thursday, 1 August 1219, and returned to France.[85]

Three years after this, during August 1222, Raimon VI, sixty-six years old and still an excommunicant, died at Toulouse.[86] Almost a year later, on Friday, 14 July 1223, Philip II Augustus, aged fifty-eight, died at Mantes.[87] Aimery de Montfort, seemingly abandoned (once more) by the French crown, endeavored throughout these years, in a number of truces with Raimon VII, to secure some sort of peace in Languedoc.[88] Nevertheless, in January 1224, Aimery de Montfort fled from the Midi, and, with this northern interloper gone, the counts of Toulouse and Foix recalled young Raimon Trencavel as *vescomte* of Béziers, Carcassonne, Razès, and Albi. After almost fifteen years of cruel and bitter fighting, Languedoc was, at least in feudal terms, close to what it been before the death of Peire de Castelnau.[89]

Such a situation could not last long. On Sunday, 30 November 1225, at Bourges, in a scenerio all too familiar, fourteen archbishops, one hundred and thirteen bishops, and one hundred and fifty abbots, all fretting about the persistence of heresy and the reinvigoration of the southern nobility, excommunicated Raimon VII and proclaimed the continuation of the crusade.[90] Aimery de Montfort had, by this time, ceded all his (somewhat brittle) rights to the king of France, Louis VIII.[91] So, with the financial and moral aid of the new papal legate to France, Roman Frangipani, Louis VIII prepared to invade the Midi for a third time. Royal prestige, and the efficient bureaucracy established by Philip II Augustus, sufficed to persuade enough barons of France to join their king at Lyon in June 1226 for what would be a majestic campaign of conquest. This royal host was easily twice the size of the crusading army of 1209.[92] The king captured Avignon in September 1226 after a three-month siege and then proceeded to march toward Toulouse.[93] Louis VIII, after his initial delay at Avignon, hastily occupied the possessions of the Trencavels along the Aude, but before he could strengthen his position, the thirty-nine-year-old king died (from an illness he caught during the Avignon siege) on Sunday, 8 November 1226, at Montpensier.[94] "Rome, you killed good King Louis," no question about it, so the Toulousain troubadour Guilhem Figueira sang in his bitter and angry *sirventes* (an overtly satirical *canso*) a few years later, "because, with your false preaching, you lured him away from Paris."[95]

The death of Louis VIII did not end the war in the south. The king had installed *sénéchaux* and *baillis*, royal administrators, in his newly acquired lands and had reorganized (along northern French lines) the territories ceded to him by Aimery de Montfort as the *sénéchaussées* of Beaucaire-Nîmes and Carcassonne-Béziers. All this royal domain was placed firmly under the control of his cousin Imbert de Beaujeu and protected by five hundred northern French knights. The crusade, as undertaken by Imbert de Beaujeu, became an exercise in the gradual exhaustion of Raimon VII and the county of Toulouse. It was a campaign of one small atrocity after another, of a vineyard burnt here, of a field destroyed there, of hamlets razed, of men and women murdered. The *castra* of the Toulousain and the Lauragais were especially hurt by Imbert de Beaujeu.[96] Finally, Raimon VII, badly in debt, starved of resources, and fighting a losing battle against the *éclat* of the French crown, was offered the chance for peace—which he gladly took in 1229.[97]

On Holy Thursday, 12 April 1229, the Peace of Paris, whose twenty-two articles had already been accepted by an ecclesiastical *concilium* at Meaux in January 1229, officially ended the Albigensian Crusade.[98] The thirty-one-year-old Raimon VII swore submission to the Church and to the not yet fifteen-year-old Louis IX.[99] He had to dismiss all mercenaries, remove any Jews in his service, and, from then on, confiscate the property of anyone who remained excommunicated for more than a year.[100] This last clause particularly affected the numerous southern nobles, knights, and other persons exiled from their properties whom the northern French called *faidits*—rebel, heretical sympathizer, fugitive, and criminal all at once.[101] The count of Toulouse, though no longer an excommunicant or *faidit* himself, forfeited to the French crown over two-thirds of the lands formerly held by his father. Raimon VII, as a vassal of the French king, was permitted to keep most of the diocese of Toulouse, including the Lauragais, the Albigeois north of the Tarn, the Rouergue, Quercy (but not Cahors), and the Agenais. The marquisate of Provence, east of the Rhône, however, was surrendered to the Church (though it would be returned to Raimon VII in 1234). In Toulouse itself the Château Narbonnais was to be occupied by the French crown for ten years.[102]

One qualification, which would have extreme future ramifications, was that Raimon VII had to hand over his nine-year-old daughter Joanna into the custody of Louis IX so that she could be married to one of the king's brothers. Joanna de Tolosa was quickly betrothed to the nine-year-old Alphonse de Poitiers in June 1229, and, with somewhat less haste, they married in 1236 (or 1237).[103] At the death of Raimon VII his daughter and her husband were to inherit his properties; in the unlikely event that they had no children, then the county of Toulouse would be completely absorbed into the *regnum* of France.[104] Another qualification, equally profound in its implications, especially for the medieval inquisition, was that the count of Toulouse and his local administrative officials, especially his *bayles*, promised to hunt down all heretics in Languedoc. Indeed, all the subjects of Raimon VII and of Louis IX in the south were required to take an oath to aid the Church in the pursuit of heresy. There was even a bounty of two marks (four *livres* of Paris) for any heretic captured in the next two years. After this, the prize for a good man, a good woman, or a Waldensian would be reduced to one mark.[105]

Whatever the anonymous assassin had in mind when he killed Peire de Castelnau, the consequences of his action, especially the long and bloody Albigensian Crusade, transformed an act of swift thuggery into an inescapable *avant-propos* by which all efforts at understanding the great inquisition of Bernart de Caux and Jean de Saint-Pierre, by which all attempts at comprehending what it was like to live in the thirteenth-century Lauragais, must always be prefaced.[106]

# 3

## WEDGED BETWEEN CATHA AND CATHAY

FREDERICK Conybeare, in the illustrious eleventh edition (1910) of the *Encyclopædia Britannica*, began his short history of the "Cathars" (two pages wedged between Catha and Cathay) with the vivid observation that these medieval heretics "were the débris of an early Christianity."[1] The Cathars were the direct descendants of fugitive Manichees, dualist refugees from late antiquity who, though invisible for most of the early Middle Ages, managed to scatter themselves from the Balkans to the Pyrénées between the tenth and fourteenth centuries. In eastern Europe this diaspora became the Paulicians and the Bogomils; in western Europe these itinerants were just about any heretical group with vaguely dualist tendencies—but, most especially, they were the good men and good women of Languedoc. No matter the time, no matter the place, all were one and the same heresy.[2] Conybeare lucidly, and quite elegantly, summarized what was thought about the *bons omes, bonas femnas*, and their believers in the century before him[3]—and, this is the surprise, what a great many have thought since.[4]

A powerful, and enduring, intellectualist bias is at work here. This prejudice assumes that heresy is basically a kind of thought, a distinctive attitude, a philosophy, a theory, a discourse.[5] The ideas of a Lauragais good man are perceived as something intellectually pure, uncontaminated by material existence or historical specificity.[6] Habits and behaviors, actions and practices, essentially anything that is not the stuff of thoughts, like so many bulls with so many rings in their noses, are assumed to follow ideas wherever they may go, sometimes kicking and screaming, sometimes mute and passive, either way it makes no difference, because the intellectualist bias takes it for granted that the world is made from theories, that cultures are hammered together from discourses, and that the elaboration of a philosophy is all the explanation a scholar need ever give.[7] No matter how many bits and pieces from other cultures might break off and adhere as a result of contact, no matter how many different societies might rise and fall through the decades, the original heresy stays recognizably the same.[8]

The learned medieval mind (awash with Augustine's descriptions of Manichaeism, fearful of the timeless nature of evil, convinced of enduring continuities, aware that the new is always revealed in the old) might classify a twelfth-century heresy as similar to a heterodox creed from the fourth, or adopt an ancient word to explain a thirteenth-century belief, or think that dualist errors had always lingered in the world, but these past efforts at explanation should not persuade twenty-first-century scholars to adopt almost identical approaches.[9] Admittedly, such notions about the origins of Catharism, though still lingering here and there, are far less common than they once were.[10] A variation on this theme has the *gnosis* of Mani sneaking back into medieval western Europe through the Byzantine Bogomils, who, it is tacitly understood, were undoubtedly influenced by this late antique heresy.[11]

As for there being any genuine intimacy between the Bogomils and the *bons omes*, it is neither obvious nor irrefutable that such a liaison ever existed, even though the assumption of such a connection between the two heresies has become a truism in almost all studies of medieval heterodoxy.[12] For a start, any argument which sees Bogomil preachers in Europe from the first millennium onward and posits that these Bosnian or Bulgarian seers were the cause of almost all eleventh-century heresy is simply untenable.[13] A more nuanced (and much more persuasive) vision imagines Balkan missionaries coming to Europe only in the twelfth century. Still, despite some allusions to wisdom arriving from the east in the twelfth and thirteenth centuries, as well as the small number of questionable references to heretical holy men journeying from the Byzantine Empire to northern France, Lombardy, Languedoc, and, in one instance, the Lauragais itself, the efforts to truly link the Bogomils and the *bons omes* remain unconvincing.[14] Paulician influence upon the good men and good women, whether through missionaries or through immigration, though popular with Conybeare and his contemporaries, has never been championed in the same way as Bogomilism.[15] All in all, arguments about the specific influence of the Bogomils upon the heresy of the *bons omes* and *bonas femnas* rely upon the detection of likeness, similarity, resemblance, between ideas, irrespective of time and place.[16]

Likewise, explanations that treat heresy as solely a manifestation of purely economic or material problems, as an expression of social or class discontent, not unlike something from the revolutions of the nineteenth and twentieth centuries, are just as limited as the more prevalent arguments from the similarity of ideas.[17] A peculiar irony about these theses— one that gives their somewhat dated (Victorian Romantic, Cold War Marxist-Leninist) approaches more than just curiosity value; in fact, an irony permeating much historical thinking and surprisingly common if the world under the microscope is a rural one—is that if the material world is thought to be unchanging, as physical existence in the medieval countryside is often thought to be, then the beliefs concerned with that world are assumed to be unchanging as well.[18] Rural communities, like those of the Lauragais, tied to the soil, trapped in the cyclical movement of the seasons, forever dwelling in an eternal present and so denied the virtues of linear time, never change the way they do things, never change the way they think things.[19]

"The most satisfactory answer" for stifling conversation with strangers, W. H. Auden dryly recommended, "satisfactory because it withers curiosity, is to say *Medieval Historian*."[20] A universal truth, perhaps, though not in southwestern France. There, whether on the 17.22 from Toulouse to Carcassonne, or in a quiet Lauragais *café*, or at the breezy summit of Montségur in the Pyrénées, such an answer will (nine times out of ten) instantly involve you in lively discussions with neo-Cathar mystics, English expatriates hunting for buried Albigensian treasure, or, and this is much more common than one might think, Californians motoring after heterodox enlightenment in the modern *départements* of the Aude (conveniently called the *pays du cathare* on road signs and tourist maps) and the Haute-Garonne. Histories, novels, plays, poems, red wine, television documentaries, troubadour CDs, travel guides, New Age manifestos, cream-filled pastries, academic conferences, www.you.name.it.and.the.cathars.com, redemptive philosophies, gaythers (gay neo-Cathars), snowflake domes, cassoulets, and pamphets on Occitan regionalism all celebrate the Cathar *bons hommes* and *bonnes femmes*. The Cathars, promiscuous in their friendships, influencing everything and anything, have been tied to the Holy Grail, to courtly love, to the hidden secrets of the Knights Templars, to the magical lodges of late-nineteenth-century mysticism, and even to the veracity of reincarnation.[21] Occasionally, these occult fantasies are grafted onto the related, and just as anachronistic, need to see the good men and good women as Protestants before their time.[22] Such esoteric desires affect, despite the most austere scholarly will in the world, all who think about the *bons omes* and *bonas femnas* of Languedoc. Such desires, it goes without saying, must be strongly resisted.

No one at Saint-Sernin, whether friar-inquisitor, petty noble, or aging widow, ever used the noun *Cathari* to describe heretics in the Lauragais. The word "Cathar," apparently, was first used in the middle of the twelfth century by a group of heretics from Cologne, or so Eckbert of Schönau wrote in his *Sermones contra Catharos* of 1163.[23] It is now assumed that *Cathari* derived from the Greek *katharos* (pure);[24] though there are other explanations which trace the name to derivations of *cattus* (cat) and to Augustine's *Catharistae* (a branch of the fourth-century Manichees).[25] This confusion of words, let alone centuries, gets glossed over way too quickly. Whatever the origin of the word, the heretics of southwestern Languedoc, unlike those of northern Italy, were hardly ever known as *Cathari*. The Tuscan pope Alexander III, to be sure, used the term at the Third Lateran Council in 1179 when he tried to launch a crusade against the heretics and mercenaries infecting the Toulousain and the Albigeois.[26] As did the Dominican inquisitor (and former "heresiarch" at Piacenza) Rainier Sacconi in his *Summa de Catharis et Pauperibus de Lugduno* of 1250 where, toward the end of a detailed analysis concerning the *Cathari* of Lombardy, he added a tiny section about the "Cathars of the Toulousain church, and those of Albi and Carcassonne," simply stressing that these *langue d'oc* heretics were obviously connected to the *langue de si* dualists.[27] In the end, despite the sometime medieval adoption of *Cathari* for certain heretics, it is only the scholarship of the last century that has justified the use of "Cathar" for heresies, whether in the Rhineland, England, northern France, Lombardy, Catalonia, or the Lauragais, whose connections with one another, though worth pondering, are at best problematic. Whatever was going on in the Lauragais, whatever Bernart de Caux and Jean de Saint-Pierre thought they would find there, whatever the thousands questioned thought heresy or holiness added up to in their lives, "Catharism," as understood in encyclopedias and textbooks, whether medieval or modern, has very little, if anything, to do with it.

"It should be understood," scoffed Pierre des Vaux-de-Cernay near the beginning of his history of the Albigensian Crusade, "that some of the heretics were called 'perfected' heretics or 'good men,' others 'believers of the heretics.' "[28] The use of *perfecti* and *perfecte*, like *Cathari*, is taken for granted by modern scholarship, and yet not once were these words uttered by the two friar-inquisitors, or the thousands they questioned, at Saint-Sernin. This does not necessarily invalidate Pierre des Vaux-de-Cernay's apparently firsthand knowledge, let alone the modern use of this terminology, but it does make a difference if we are to truly imagine what went on in, and outside of, Saint-Sernin. Certainly, *boni homines, probi homines, bone femine, bone domine, bonas mulieres, bons omes, prozomes, prodomes, bonas femnas, bonas domnas, bonas molhers, heretici, eretges, iretges,* Latin and Occitan, echoed throughout the verandas of Saint-Sernin, as did *credentes, crezedors,* or *crezens* for those who believed in the holiness of the heretics,[29] but Bernart de Caux and Jean de Saint-Pierre, like the men and women they interrogated, chose their words well, and, consequently, so must we. The *bons omes* and *bonas femnas* themselves, just to add one more term to the list, usually referred to each other as the "friends of God," *amici Dei, amicx de Dieu,* or so hundreds of testimonies recollected. Incidentally, the Waldensians, in the forty-one times they were mentioned at Saint-Sernin, were always called the *Valdenses.*[30]

Catholic chroniclers and Capetian bureaucrats complicate all this heretical terminology by frequently referring to the *bons omes, bonas femnas,* and *crezens* of Languedoc as the *Albigenses,* the "Albigensians."[31] This is not to be taken as a specific reference to the orthodox diocese of Albi, just north of the Lauragais, whose form, anyhow, was always *Albiensis;* it indicates merely that "Albigensian" was the term used, more often than not, by the northern French to denote heretics, who were not Waldensians, in the lands of the count of Toulouse.[32] Occasionally, *Albigensis*, or variations on the word, occurred elsewhere in Europe, as when the English merchant Arnold Fitz-Thedmar cryptically noted in his late-thirteenth-century chronicle that in 1210, when he was nine years old, "an Albigensian [*Ambigensis*] was burnt in London."[33] Such enigmatic references, though fascinating, do not suggest proselytizing Cathar missions; on the contrary, they demonstrate an imaginative historical shorthand whereby a long-dead individual, half remembered, laconically recorded, was instantly animated, instantly explained, by the tag of an insidious depravity known to have caused a crusade at the beginning of the thirteenth century.[34] In the end, *Albigenses* occurred in thirteenth-century chronicles, seventeenth-century polemic, and nineteenth-century scholarship only because of the famously violent warfare of the Albigensian Crusade. Yet, and this is crucial, the *heretici* were never called *Albigenses* in the registers of the thirteenth-century inquisition.[35]

Unlike, of course, the remarkable eleventh edition of the *Encyclopædia Britannica* where, despite Conybeare's Cathars, the "Albigenses" received their own graceful cameo (two pages caught between Albian and Albino) from Paul Alphandéry.[36] No mention was made of the Manichaeans, though the influence of the Bogomils and Paulicians was taken seriously, while the Albigensians, as Catharist heretics, first appeared in the Limousin between 1012 and 1020 before finally settling down in the Toulousain sometime in the early twelfth century.[37] Nevertheless, it was exceedingly difficult for Alphandéry, unlike the irrepressible Conybeare, "to form any very precise idea of the Albigensian doctrines, as our knowledge of them is derived from their opponents," especially the early friar-inquisitors.[38] A difficult problem, certainly, and a relentless question that still haunts the study of the *bons omes* and *bonas femnas*, but it is not insurmountable, and, most definitely, it is not solved by grand intellectualist gestures through time and space.

# 4

## PAPER AND PARCHMENT

THE ORIGINAL leaves studied by Bernart de Caux and Jean de Saint-Pierre are lost, perhaps to the pillaging of a *révolutionnaire* or, just as likely, to the bookbinding of a *relieur*.[1] Fortunately, for the modern historian if not the medieval heretic, two other Dominican inquisitors, Guilhem Bernart de Dax and Renaud de Chartres, had the Lauragais testimonies copied sometime after October 1258, though no later than August 1263, and this copy has survived as manuscript 609 in the Bibliothèque municipale of Toulouse, where it has lived since 1790.[2]

Only a handful of parchment fragments still exist of any inquisitorial *originalia* from the middle of the thirteenth century, and most of these scraps of skin were found by modern scholars in the bindings of seventeenth-century books.[3] Ironically, in 1667, at the same time that the records of the early inquisition were being scissored, glued, and wrapped around the odd *cahier*, Jean-Baptiste Colbert commissioned Jean de Doat, president of the Chambre des comptes of Navarre, to make transcriptions of original manuscripts from the archives of Béarn, Languedoc, and Guyenne. Doat's commission, whose purpose was simply to collect interesting things (political, legal, historical) for Colbert's library, eventually filled two hundred and fifty-eight volumes.[4] Among the many *curiosités* that Doat's scribes copied, such as the heretical (apocryphal, Bogomil) *Interrogatio Johannis* or extracts from the Dominican inquisitor Étienne de Bourbon's *Tractatus de diversis predicabilibus*, were numerous investigations by inquisitors from the thirteenth century that once existed in the archives of Carcassonne and Toulouse.[5] The Collection Doat, as this part of Colbert's library is cataloged today in the Bibliothèque nationale, though invaluable, is still a seventeenth-century copy written in a beautiful flourishing cursive with the Latin respelled *style classique* and the marginalia of the inquisitors left out.[6] The transcribed *registrum* of Bernart de Caux and Jean de Saint-Pierre—if for no other reason than the simple fact of survival, all other paleographic companions having fallen by the wayside—is the most substantial document still existing from the first twenty years of the medieval *inquisitiones heretice pravitatis*.[7]

The register or archival *thesaurus* comprises two hundred and sixty folios, though only two hundred and fifty-four are paginated, with each leaf measuring 291 millimeters high and 236 millimeters wide.[8] All the leaves were firmly protected sometime in the late thirteenth century by

wooden boards covered in parchment.[9] Twenty-two quires of twelve folia
were stitched together to produce the register.[10] A single leaf after folio
56 and a double folio from the nineteenth quire were lacking when the
quires were initially made; one more folio (the very last and known to
have been blank) simply fell out of the completed register over time.[11]
The folios were created (bifoliated) from seventy sheets of paper, probably 360 millimeters high and 480 millimeters wide before trimming, instead of sheep- or goatskin.[12] The paper undoubtedly came from Valencia, via Catalonia, has no watermark (they do not appear until the last
decade of the thirteenth century), and was made from linen and cotton
scraps, that is, from the rags of clothing.[13] The copy made for Guilhem
Bernart de Dax and Renaud de Chartres is one of the oldest paper manuscripts in Europe.[14]

The folios were created (bifoliated) manuscript minutiae, though somewhat tedious to read, are
important. Thirteenth-century inquisitorial *originalia* were never made
from paper, only from parchment.[15] This use of different materials was
not due to any overt moral theory about paper—in the way that Peter
the Venerable thought it ethically vile in the twelfth century, or Johannes
Trithemius felt nothing but contempt for its mortality (compared to the
immortality of parchment) in the fifteenth—it was because parchment
allowed for the quick scribbling of thousands of confessions, and the
scrawling of marginal notes, in a way that paper did not.[16] In the earliest
surviving record of expenses for the Languedocian inquisition, a roll of
five parchment membranes listing everything purchased between Thursday, 6 May 1255, and Sunday, 6 February 1256, for Jean de Saint-Pierre
and Renaud de Chartres, from shoes to saffron to special oilskin bags
for carrying their *registra, papirus* was bought only once (an unspecified
amount was obtained on Monday, 25 October, for 6 shillings, 8 pence),
while on the inquisitorial shopping list *pergaminum* was a constant item
for the production of registers, for the writing of letters, and for the
creation of *littere penitentiarum*.[17] Parchment is more durable; the ink does
not run so much, especially when the surface has been scratched by a
goat's tooth; mistakes are easily rubbed away with a pumice stone or a
small knife; and it can be reused as a palimpsest in a way that paper
cannot.[18]

The original loose quires and floating leaves of Bernart de Caux and
Jean de Saint-Pierre, with their marginalia, their scrubbed out words,
their edges curled from constant handling, their small wounds of
smudged ink, embodied the haste of the early friar-inquisitors. The
paper copy of the parchment register, which in turn had evolved from
all those loose and floating leaves, records the recording of this investigation. Yet, in this copying, a metamorphosis took place—that overpower-
ing sense of so much to do in so little time, that necessity to read and

judge quickly, had evaporated in the ten to fifteen years that separate the original and the copy. And, obviously, even if the copying had taken place immediately after the original was assembled, things would still not have been the same. Now, the copied confessions were to be perused, calmly and smoothly, for heretical precedents, for old crimes. Parchment and paper, flesh and fabric, meant two different types of reading, reflection, and detective work.

A startling feature of manuscript 609 is that it appears to be only two books out of an estimated ten that Bernart de Caux and Jean de Saint-Pierre originally compiled.[19] A small oblong of vellum neatly inserted between the two leaves of the flyleaf has this late-thirteenth-century caption: *Hic sunt duo volumina confessionum de libris fratis Bernardi de Cautio transcripta: scilicet de Lauraguesio et de multis aliis locis dyocesis Tholosani: per fratres Guillelmum Bernardi et Reginaldum de Carnoto inquisitores.* On the verso of the last folio of the flyleaf a mid-thirteenth-century scribe identified the two books: *Confessiones de V° libro Laurag— fratris Bernardi de Caucio transcripte in hoc libro usque ad CLXXIII folium. Item et deinceps de quarto libro.* Curiously, the fourth book comes after the fifth. Perhaps this ordering was a simple matter of how the quires were put together, or a scribal oddity as to what was copied first.[20] In the margin next to the confession of Bernart Amielh, from Montgaillard, is a note, written in the same hand as the main text, directing the reader to the missing *X libro.*[21]

The two hundred and fifty-four numbered folios actually end with the Roman numeral CCLV, the scribe having jumped in his numbering from folio CXC immediately to CXCII.[22] Nevertheless, the act of foliation, venerable but rare before the thirteenth century, reveals in its small way the scholastic and archival attitude of the friar-inquisitors in searching out heresy.[23] The folios average thirty-nine lines of dense thirteenth-century cursive minuscule.[24] The manuscript was written by at least two scribes with a penchant for abbreviations, like *t.j.* for *testis juratus, d.* for *dixit, he.* for *hereticus* or *hereticatio, ad.* for *adoravit* or *adoraverunt.*[25] The orthography is a little unstable, with *b* for *v, d* for *z, l* for *r.*[26] Occasionally a scribe wrote the same testimony twice or, in one case, got halfway through a confession, stopped, left what he had written, and rewrote it in full seventy folios later.[27] Relatively sophisticated punctuation in the form of the *punctus* (point) and *paragraphus* delineating the beginning of a new confession or, more often, a collection of confessions and abjurations from the same parish aimed for clarity and swiftness in reading: a necessary attribute when the folios, like all leaves of the inquisition, have no decoration or color and only limited rubrication.[28] Reference agility was also facilitated by a running title at the top of each folio with the name of the parish, such as *de Berreillas juxta Montem Gailhardum*,[29] from which a collection of testimonies came.[30]

Most important, the notarial protocol of the inquisitors has been recorded in the copying. The parchment trail of separate leaves, isolated quires, even little *aides-mémoires*, upon which testimonies were initially written by the scribe or notary, then witnessed by him and at least one other person, received legal authentication when all this material was rewritten by the same notary or scribe and marked with his *signum* (usually just his name).[31] An individual allowed his or her testimony to become a public instrument (*et concessit fieri publicum instrumentum*) when it was notarized. In this sense the inquisitorial register, original and copy, is no different from any other notarized register from thirteenth-century Toulouse. In both cases authenticity, of an action and of the document recording it, was sought in the formula of the notariate.[32]

Equally important, the frequent marginalia, sometimes indicated by a *signe de renvoi* in the text,[33] next to particular confessions seem to have been faithfully copied.[34] These glosses were made not only by Bernart de Caux and Jean de Saint-Pierre after they read the testimonies, but also by inquisitorial scribes and witnesses at the time when a particular testimony was given. One set of comments was very much after the fact, while the other, like stage prompts from the wings, aimed at influencing the deliberations of the inquisitive reader.[35] Consequently, some marginal notes seem to be nothing more than contemptuous asides whispered in the cloisters of Saint-Sernin. The snide graffito written beside the confession of the knight Bernart de Quiders—"It's said that he and his wife Saurimunda are worse than all the others in Mas-Saintes-Puelles"[36]—captures this sense of corridor-gossip among the functionaries of the inquisition. Beside the initial testimony of Bernart de Quiders' wife, na Saurimunda, a confession in which she denied any knowledge of heresy, is the curt end-of-the-day memorandum, "Let her be held in prison."[37] Twelve days later she changed her mind and admitted her association with some *bons omes*.[38] The scribe also made a point of adding after the names of the three witnesses to na Saurimunda's second testimony—in which she was sorry and penitent, *dolet et penitet*, for her earlier unwillingness to tell the truth—that Bernart de Caux, though not present for either court appearance, had read her recent change of heart.[39]

Confessions and abjurations are grouped throughout the register according to the thirty-nine Lauragais parishes from which individuals came, rather than by the day or days on which they were questioned at Saint-Sernin.[40] The four hundred and twenty testimonies of Mas-Saintes-Puelles, for example, are gathered in folios 1–30 and, with one hundred and one testimonies from Saint-Martin-de-la-Lande in between, 41v–42r;[41] the one hundred and eighty-nine testimonies heard from ten different parishes on Monday, 3 July 1245, are scattered throughout sixteen different folios.[42] This systematic sorting of testimonies by topography was not something performed by the copyists; rather it was the organization imposed upon the testimonies by Bernart de Caux and Jean de Saint-Pierre.[43] The friar-*enquêteurs* of Louis IX and of Alphonse de Poitiers organized their investigations into complaints against royal and comital officials in this way; mendicant philosophers, theologians, and librarians classified thoughts, angelic hierarchies, biblical *exempla*, and libraries similarly.[44]

It was not unusual for the inquisition in Languedoc to produce, and to use, copies of earlier inquiries, especially after the Dominican provincial chapter of Narbonne forbade the transportation of original inquisitorial registers from 1243 onward.[45] The well-known inquisition of Jacques Fournier, as bishop of Pamiers between 1318 and 1325, into the heresy of some small Pyrenean villages—a seven-year investigation into the guilt or innocence of sixty-six men and forty-eight women—can be read only in the parchment copy made for Fournier's private library.[46] This register is made of parchment and not paper, as with other copies from Languedoc, because it was for the bishop's personal use, rather than a record to be deposited in an inquisitorial or Dominican archive.[47] It is also from the early fourteenth century and so not alone in having survived up to the present; a number of inquisitorial manuscripts from the fourteenth century, copies and even some originals, have managed to sidestep revolutions, wars, and the book trade.[48] All that is left from the thirteenth-century inquisition to exemplify the implications of a copy and, once or twice removed, the intentions of an original, is manuscript 609. Nevertheless, the considerable activity devoted by the early friar-inquisitors to copying, and so to the making of archives, can be inferred from the variety of duplicated documents that Doat's scribes found and then copied themselves in seventeenth-century Toulouse and Carcassonne.[49]

Yet it would be a mistake to assume that the surviving paper leaves of Guilhem Bernart de Dax and Renaud de Chartres were an exact replica, or even an attempt at such cloning, of the missing parchment folios of Bernart de Caux and Jean de Saint-Pierre. The confessions and abjurations recorded in the register may be in the thousands, but many more are missing. The *castrum* of Castelnaudary, for instance, is represented by only thirty-eight testimonies;[50] whereas the hamlet of Mas-Saintes-Puelles has the already-mentioned four hundred and twenty, the largest number in the whole register.[51] Then there are confessions at the very end of manuscript 609 that have nothing to do with the inquisition of Bernart de Caux and Jean de Saint-Pierre. They still concern the Lauragais, and they were heard in Saint-Sernin, but they took place eight years later and involved the inquisitors Raimon Respland and

"Magister S."[52] There is also an isolated testimony from Monday, 28 October 1258, of Pons Garrigue, from Issel, before Guilhem Bernart de Dax himself.[53] This confession, however, is actually an addition to two testimonies (one long and one short) Pons Garrigue had made thirteen years earlier before Bernart de Caux.[54] Garrigue's later confession immediately follows his much earlier and slightly different testimony in manuscript 609.[55]

Leonard Boyle, in his reflections upon the historical uses of medieval inquisitorial registers, applies a none-too-gentle rap upon the knuckles of those who forget, for instance, that all they have are two books out of an estimated ten.[56] The missing registers of Bernart de Caux and Jean de Saint-Pierre, consequently, possess a quality not unlike that of phantom limbs. They seem so real, so tangible, so annoying, simply because their presence, or rather lack of presence, can never be forgotten. The rest of the testimonies from, say, Castelnaudary, or any number of other villages, are undoubtedly in one of the lost books. That the confessions and abjurations of women account for less than a third of all testimonies in manuscript 609 is not because their husbands or brothers answered questions for or about them, as men commonly did for women in customary law or before friar-*enquêteurs*, or due to some inherent quirk in the inquisitorial process; it is, once more, only because this is what books four and five contain.[57]

The most disturbing ghosts in the register are, however, the absent folios of punishments and condemnations that Bernart de Caux and Jean de Saint-Pierre pronounced between Sunday, 18 March, and Sunday, 22 July 1246, at Toulouse.[58] The late-seventeenth-century Dominican Jean-Jacques Percin casually observed in his *Monumenta conventus Tolosani ordinis F.F. Praedicatorum . . .* , an intriguing and occasionally eccentric history of the Friars Preachers in Toulouse, that these condemnations could be read between folios 45 and 169 in the lost first register of the two friar-inquisitors. The other nine volumes receive no mention, though it is possible that Percin may have read the fourth and fifth books that constitute manuscript 609, whose home, until its removal in 1790, was the Dominican convent in Toulouse.[59] Although the first register is no longer with us, a rough scribal draft—an *aide-mémoire* rather than a notarized instrument of *acta inquisitionis*[60]—of one hundred and ninety-seven condemnations survives in the Bibliothèque nationale as Latin manuscript 9992.[61] These twelve parchment folia, out of perhaps one hundred and sixty-two, were saved at the last minute by the abbé Magi in 1781 from a dismembered manuscript that was being used to bind school *alphabets*.[62] Apart from these condemnations, only ten punishments are suggested in the margins of manuscript 609, with, for example, the penalties of perpetual imprisonment or exile for Peire Barot of Saint-Anatoly, who confessed on Monday, 26 February 1246, and Estotz de Rocovila, who testified on Friday, 25 May 1246.[63] Fortunately, a few other documents reveal a little of what happened to some of those who testified in the verandas of Saint-Sernin.[64] Yet, for all intents and purposes, the known penalties of two hundred and seven must suggest the possible punishments for hundreds of others.

It should be stressed that what might appear to be sleight of hand in imagining books that do not exist, or folios once or thrice removed, is not quite the Borges-like exercise in fiction it seems. The transcription of Guilhem Bernart de Dax and Renaud de Chartres, while not replicating the form of the *originale* (pagination, *mise en page*) is, as Yves Dossat decided many years ago in what is still the most learned analysis of manuscript 609, a truthful copy of its content (testimonies, witnesses).[65] The Dominican obsession with *originalia*, with the authenticity of original sources, with the intrinsic authority of whole texts rather than mere extracts, guides the *registra* of the friar-inquisitors.[66]

The register of Bernart de Caux and Jean de Saint-Pierre has never been edited or published—though not for want of trying. In 1868 the first twelve folios appeared as an appendix to the *Revue Archéologique du Midi de la France*; unfortunately, this appendage is close to useless.[67] Austin Evans and Merriam Sherwood began a long and ultimately unfulfilled attempt at publishing an edition of the register in 1933 when they received $2,400 from Columbia University's Council on Research in the Humanities,[68] a substantial, indeed remarkable, amount when the United States of America was still suffering from the Depression and only just beginning the New Deal of Franklin Roosevelt.[69] Evans argued for the necessity of editing manuscript 609, known to the Council on Research in the Humanities as Project 62, because the inquest of Bernart de Caux and Jean de Saint-Pierre was easily the largest investigation by any two inquisitors in any part of Europe throughout the entire Middle Ages—and his opinion, all these decades later, is still correct.[70] Evans conservatively estimated for his generous patrons that the edition would fill five volumes and perhaps run to two thousand five hundred typed pages.[71] The register is, with no exaggeration, one of the foundation documents of what has been called, with some exaggeration, "the Columbia school of heresiology."[72] Unfortunately, not a single page of Evans' and Sherwood's project, which lingered in an editorial shadowland for almost thirty years, was ever published.[73]

Sherwood's correspondence with Evans in the early thirties also reveals the magnitude of the manuscript's restoration in 1952. In 1934 she lamented that some of the folios "literally crumble in my hand."[74] Today the manuscript is in quite good condition with only fourteen pages where either the ink has blurred or the paper dissolved into small holes from humidity.[75] Only two folios are completely unreadable owing to blurring.[76] In some places the scribe had pressed through to the other side, creating cuts in the paper, and there are occasional rips that tear a whole folio.[77] Fine translucent silk now holds these leaves together.

Georges Duby once wrote that he felt a peculiar, though often exquisite, pleasure when he touched the old skins of medieval documents.[78] He added to this palpable delight the evocative sensation of archival silence being filled, at that moment when a manuscript is opened or a charter flattened out, with "the fragrance of long-vanished lives."[79] Duby's peculiar pleasures illustrate one more difference between parchment and paper: the heavy varnished leaves of manuscript 609 are actually quite clinical to touch and, despite their warm amber sheen, completely without any perfume from the past.

# 5

## SPLITTING HEADS AND TEARING SKIN

I BELIEVED," the Avignonet knight Bertran de Quiders hesitantly replied when Bernart de Caux and Jean de Saint-Pierre questioned him on Tuesday, 6 February 1246, about the murder of the Dominican inquisitor Guilhem Arnaut and his Franciscan *socius* Esteve de [*Sant Tuberi*] Saint-Thibéry at Avignonet three years earlier, "and it was said by others, that the work of the inquisition would be destroyed and all the land would be free."[1] Raimon Alemon, from Mas-Saintes-Puelles, overheard na Austorga de Resengas, the *crezen* wife of the knight Peire de Resengas, say something very similar at Falgarde, a hamlet quite close to Avignonet, on Friday, 29 May 1242 (Ascension)—that is, the very next day after Guilhem Arnaut, Esteve de Saint-Thibéry, and their eight companions were chopped, hacked, and clubbed to death by axes, swords, and cudgels.[2] Bernart de Caux, within a day of Bertran de Quiders' confession, the Avignonet homicides clearly on his mind, managed to elicit from Crivessent Pelhicier, a Plaigne noblewoman, the horrid quotation "I cut out the tongue of the friar-inquisitor Guilhem Arnaut" that one of the Avignonet killers, Guilhem de Plaigne, had viciously boasted to her in the early summer of 1242.[3] Twelve months before Crivessent Pelhicier's testimony, one of her friends and the wife of Guilhem de Plaigne, na Faiz de Plaigne, recounted to the friar-inquisitor Ferrer most of the details behind the massacre at Avignonet—like the names of the ten or so assassins who did the killing, how the parchment inquisition registers were taken but not destroyed, that one of the murderers grabbed a tiny box of ginger as a souvenir, and the astonishing idea (which Raimon d'Alfar, the *bayle* of Avignonet, had led Guilhem de Plaigne to believe) that Raimon VII was involved in the conspiracy to kill Guilhem Arnaut and Esteve de Saint-Thibéry.[4]

Such hopes, such fantasies, such bloody braggadocio were not all that dissimilar to the expectations that Peire de Castelnau's killer must have had thirty-four years earlier, even down to thinking that the count of Toulouse would, somehow or other, be pleased with crude and reckless thuggery. This wishful thinking allied to desperate action, and only three years before the massive Lauragais inquisition at Saint-Sernin, reveals, with the clarity of hindsight, just how naïve the Avignonet assassins and their supporters actually were, just how simplistic their calculations of cause and effect, in thinking that a frenzied moment of brutality would completely reverse the recent history of their world.

Yet this same desire not to accept what was happening throughout Languedoc in the decade after the Peace of Meaux-Paris, a powerful and exhilarating assumption that violence could make things close to what men and women thought they were before the crusaders came, also led to a series of futile southern attempts at rebellion against the northern French, against the *Frances de Fransa*. Raimon Trencavel, the nominal *vescomte* of Béziers, attempted during the late summer and early autumn of 1240 a clumsy coup in the Carcassès against the *sénéchaux* and *baillis* of Louis IX. He failed miserably.[5] Two years later, Raimon VII, in alliance with Hugh de Lusignan, count of La Marche, and Henry III, king of England, began a loosely orchestrated group of campaigns against the French king.[6] This war, a serious continuation of the Albigensian Crusade rather than the artless military daydream of a young *faidit* nobleman, nevertheless quickly stumbled, tripped, and slid into complete victory for the French *regnum* by Monday, 20 October 1242, with the unconditional surrender of Raimon VII.[7]

Louis IX, as a consequence of these rebellions and wars, extracted from the Occitan rebels, throughout 1243 and 1244, meticulous pacts of submission, precise oaths of obedience, and definitive promises to accompany him on crusade to the Levant.[8] The count of Toulouse, despite swearing to become a *crucesignatus*,[9] was still excommunicated as a *faidit* and as a protector of heretics by Friar Ferrer and Guilhem Raimon on Friday, 6 June 1242, and, six weeks later, by the archbishop of Narbonne on Monday, 21 July.[10] At Toulouse, on Monday, 23 February 1243, one thousand and twenty-eight notable citizens swore to maintain the Peace of Meaux-Paris.[11] Finally, four months later, the newly appointed royal *sénéchal* of Carcassonne-Béziers, Hugues d'Acris, attacked the castle of Montségur, a little stone *castel* perched upon a sharp Pyrenean splinter three hundred meters high, whose lord, Peire-Roger de Mirepoix, had largely organized the assassinations at Avignonet. Hugues d'Acris captured the castle after a siege lasting almost a year. There was, despite modern romantic legends and laminated tourist guides, no great bonfire of four hundred good men and good women in a paddock below Montségur (now known as *prat dels cremaz,* "field of those who were burned," and marked by a memorial).[12]

Raimon VII was not formally accused of complicity in the murders at Avignonet, despite the assassins' having clearly derived inspiration from his hapless confederacy against Louis IX, yet the slaying of Guilhem Arnaut and Esteve de Saint-Thibéry did, once and for all, cause the count of Toulouse—and many of his local officials, especially the village *bayles*—to start systematically hunting, capturing, even incinerating, men and women known to be *bons omes, bonas femnas,* and *crezens.* After the deaths at Avignonet, to take a rather cruel example, the *crezen* Faure Raseire from Auriac was captured at Toulouse by comital officials: "I stayed in the Château Narbonnais for three weeks, and the sign of the cross [*crucesignatus*] was made on my forehead by a hot iron." Faure Raseire "first believed the heretics to be good men" around 1240, so he admitted to Bernart de Caux and Jean de Saint-Pierre at Saint-Sernin on Thursday, 1 March 1246, but he no longer held this belief after his capture and branding. Faure Raseire finished his testimony by observing that none of what he had just said at Saint-Sernin was told to Guilhem Arnaut and Esteve de Saint-Thibéry at Avignonet in 1242, even though he was summoned to appear before them, because "in the interim, the massacre of the inquisitors took place."[13] Similarly, Arnaut Peyre from Gaja-la-Selve testified at Saint-Sernin on Thursday, 16 November 1245, that when the *bona femna* Raimona de Bagnères was seized in his house sometime after the Avignonet killings, "I was branded on my forehead and everything I owned confiscated." Arnaut Peyre, like Faure Raseire, did not name the person who cauterized his brow, but there can be no doubt that it was one of the administrative officers of Raimon VII. Raimona de Bagnères was, incidentally, burnt at Laurac soon after her capture.[14]

"I fled the land for fear of the *bayles* of the count of Toulouse" were the final words of the nervous *crezen* Giraut Durant of Auriac when he confessed (with neither friar-inquisitor in attendance) at Saint-Sernin on Saturday, 30 June 1246. The *bayles* "wanted to grab me" in the summer of 1244, so Giraut Durant explained his fear of these comital men, because they had just caught three Auriac *bonas femnas* whom, though women heretics pursued by the Church, "I believed to be good women, to be truthful, to be the friends of God, to have good faith, and to have salvation through them."[15] The knight Peire Guiaraut, now living in Saint-Martin-de-la-Lande, and who was a *crezen* from 1220 to 1225 in Saint-Pons—a man who had once believed that "God didn't make visible things, that the sacred Host is not the body of Christ or the Lord, that marriage is prostitution, and that the flesh won't be resurrected"— ended his confession to Bernart de Caux on Friday, 15 December 1245, with the terse "I burnt two female heretics when I was the *bayle* of Laurac."[16] On Wednesday, 2 May 1246, all of the testimony of na Nomais of Scaupon, whose husband Guilhem de Roveret had been recently burnt as a heretic, was taken up by the awful memory of the *bayle* of Vaux, Bertran Amblart, grabbing, imprisoning, threatening, and beating her, until she confessed to having adored the heretics, "but it wasn't true," she pleaded to Bernart de Caux; "it was due to fear that I said so!" Na Nomais' bullying by the *bayle* seems to have happened only a few weeks or days before her confession, and, as her strident appeal to Bernart de Caux implied, Bertran Amblart intimidated her into lying only because he wanted to help the inquisition at Saint-Sernin.[17]

The *bayles,* always nobles in the Lauragais, holding positions that were sometimes appointed, sometimes inherited, deriving wealth usually from revenue farming (that often bordered on extortion), possessed only extremely localized jurisdiction within one village or, at most, a group of *castra.*[18] In a further administrative nuance, *bayles* and other officers were also appointed by some village lords, with the jurisdiction of the *bayles* of the count of Toulouse overlapping, intersecting, and dominating this layer of petty officialdom. All of these various *bayles,* comital or not, were remembered at Saint-Sernin mostly as sympathic, supportive, indifferent, complaisant, or custodial toward the *bons omes* and *bonas femnas* before, and during, the Albigensian Crusade. After these twenty-one years of war, a clear shift in administrative temperament slowly developed in fits and starts, first here and then there, until it was given a clarity of persecutory purpose after the failed rebellion of Raimon VII and the murders at Avignonet. This active change in the habits of local officials, feigned by some, genuine for others, affected lesser functionaries as well. Guilhem Cassaire, for instance, "huntsman of the lord count of Toulouse," deliberately sought, and caught, three good women in the d'Esquilhas wood near Montgaillard in 1243.[19]

Not only did Bernart de Caux and Jean de Saint-Pierre's inquisition depend upon this new atmosphere of comital approval (exemplified in Guilhem Cassaire) and communal fear (quivering in Giraut Durant), but it was through the goods confiscated from heretics and their believers that the friar-inquisitors derived virtually all their funds. Any penance imposed by the friar-inquisitors involving the confiscation of property did not go to the inquisition; rather it went to the lord of the condemned individual, and it was this lord who then endowed the *inquisitiones heretice pravitatis.*[20] Raimon VII was the beneficiary of these confiscations, and it was he who provided Bernart de Caux and Jean de Saint-Pierre with their monies.[21] The sum total for the expenses of Jean de Saint-Pierre and Renaud de Chartres between May 1255 and February 1256 was, paper and parchment included, 830 pounds, 10 shillings, 4 pence.[22] This was quite a substantial amount for two mendicants with a *familia* (scribes and other assistants) of only thirteen, especially when the wages of these inquisitorial helpers added up to a piddling 45 pounds, 9 shillings, 4 pence (6.7 percent) of the total.[23] Pope Innocent IV nevertheless complained that Jean de Saint-Pierre and Renaud de Chartres had too large a staff.[24] The financial burden to Raimon VII of Bernart de Caux and Jean de Saint-Pierre's Lauragais interrogations is unknown, but if these latter expenses are anything to go by, then, at the very least, something like 40 shillings were spent each week, that is, approximately the price of a tiny house in Toulouse. This rough estimate for the Saint-Sernin inquisition of 1245 and 1246 excludes occasional little extravagances, all bought a decade later, like three pounds of pepper and saffron for 13 shillings, tuppence on Monday, 10 May 1255; sweet rose essence and pomegranates for 5 shillings, 4 pence on Friday, 18 June 1255; a treatise on logic that Renaud de Chartres acquired for his nephew Thomas at 26 shillings on Tuesday, 20 July 1255; or the snug lambskin hat purchased by Jean de Saint-Pierre for threepence on Monday, 20 December 1255, to keep his tonsured head warm.[25]

Despite this new support from Raimon VII, it should never be forgotten that in 1235 he actually expelled the Dominicans from Toulouse because of their inquisitorial activities—not the least of which were the energetic investigations of Guilhem Arnaut.[26] The inquisition undertaken by Bernart de Caux and Jean de Saint-Pierre at Saint-Sernin, unthinkable without this new comital support, was nevertheless still an investigation into heresy by the two Dominicans as individual *inquisitores*. In the first months of their inquisition, Bernart de Caux and Jean de Saint-Pierre were totally dependent upon the coercive talents (or the realization that interference was pointless) of local comital officials, whether *bayles, viguiers*, sergeants, huntsmen, or anyone else working for the count of Toulouse. The fiscal aid and general tolerance of Raimon VII himself, along with the support of other churchmen in Toulouse, particularly the prior of Saint-Sernin, as well as local village clergy in the Lauragais, were indispensible throughout. At no time, however, and this must never be forgotten, were Bernart de Caux and Jean de Saint-Pierre ever representatives of a fully functioning self-perpetuating institutional "Inquisition."[27]

Sooner or later, especially when words start getting capitalized, let alone crowned with inverted commas, the use of torture by the medieval inquisition has to be addressed. Bernart de Caux and Jean de Saint-Pierre did not torture. No early inquisitor did.[28] Even when Innocent IV promulgated the bull *Ad extirpanda* of Sunday, 15 May 1252, in which he classified heretics as spiritual thieves, as murderers of the soul, and so, like ordinary criminals, deserving of torture, he was only authorizing secular officials in the Italian peninsula to use torture in getting accused heretics to confess.[29] This papal justification and recommendation for judicial torture by lay officials seems to have had no effect upon inquisitors within Languedoc and the Kingdom of France (which, from 1271 onward, included the county of Toulouse) until the last years of the thirteenth century.[30] And then what may have been more decisive in edging Languedocian inquisitors toward the use of torture was the bull *Ut negotium* of Friday, 7 July 1256, that Pope Alexander IV issued specifically for Toulouse, allowing inquisitors to absolve each other if they committed any irregularities in their investigations (which torture, no matter what the justification, would always be for a friar-inquisitor).[31]

So, when Peire de Vinhalet from Rieux-en-Minervois bragged, in words recollected by Peire Gaillard from Saint-Martin-de-la-Lande, that he would not confess to the inquisitors even "if they should split his head open,"[32] or when Fabrissa Artus told the fearful Girauda Artus that a great many people from their village, Auriac, had no intention of telling the truth at Saint-Sernin, "even if the friars should tear their skins off,"[33] one must be wary of confusing hyperbole (which is nevertheless revealing) for a hypothesis about the actual use of torture by the early inquisition.[34] Faure Raseire and Arnaut Peyre may have testified at Saint-Sernin with crosses branded into their foreheads by hot irons, but this brutal scarification was not the result of their having been tortured for the truth about heresy in the Lauragais. Finally, the tragic Raimona Jocglar ended her first testimony at Saint-Sernin on Saturday, 20 January 1246, with the harsh memory of how two and half years earlier, condemned to be burnt for heresy, and "led all the way to the flames, I converted to the Catholic faith in fear of the fire."[35] This grim recollection, though saying much about an individual's expectation of pain in this world and the next, is quite different from the memory of being deliberately hurt as part of the *formula interrogatorii.*[36]

None of this is to deny all those other forms of coercion that existed inside and outside the cloister of Saint-Sernin, nor is it an attempt to make the early friar-inquisitors appear soft and cuddly. Obviously, Bernart de Caux and Jean de Saint-Pierre's use of the Château Narbonnais as an inquisitorial gaol, and the ease with which they sent men and women there for a week or so as an inducement to confession, certainly qualifies as an overtly physical insistence on truthful answers to their questions. Nevertheless, imprisonment was not torture as a Dominican would have understood it in the middle of the thirteenth century.[37] Part of the problem when one thinks about the early inquisitors and their methods, and so the necessity of having to stress that torture was not one of them, is that a vicious mythical beast known as *The Inquisition* prowls the modern imagination.[38] Yet such mythologizing (or rather the unreflective acceptance of the fantasy for fact) is woefully misleading for a whole host of reasons. The most crucial error is that when one confuses the medieval inquisition with the Inquisition of the sixteenth and seventeenth centuries, especially the Spanish and Roman tribunals, and so makes a rather ordinary noun all too proper, a monolithic institution comes into being, a bureaucratic entity that lacks not only historical specificity but also historical reality.[39]

Naturally, an institution need not be larger than two men, or live longer than two hundred and one days, but the institutionalization that did not occur, in any way, shape, or form, was of the evolutionary kind that someone like Max Weber (or closer to home, Joseph Strayer) saw as heralding the modern state.[40] Certainly, what Bernart de Caux and Jean de Saint-Pierre did at Saint-Sernin went a long way in helping to formulate methods that, even though they might be reworked and rethought by later inquisitors, would eventually lead to clearly recognized regularities in procedure. Nevertheless, to jump from this to the notion that the two Dominicans were aware of the future institutional implications of their interrogations, or even that their registers were the start of a distinctive literary form, is simply a leap of faith.

The pathetic expectations of a man like Bertran de Quiders, all too cruelly realized at Avignonet—that the *inquisitiones* into the Toulousain and the Lauragais would end by killing individual friar-inquisitors— illustrate, more poignantly than any academic argument ever could, that the inquisitions into heretical depravity were still seen as something accidental, transient, dangerous but not immutable, to the predictable rhythms of the Lauragais. The great inquisition of Bernart de Caux and Jean de Saint-Pierre would, for good or ill, change all that.

# 6

## SUMMONED TO SAINT-SERNIN

A S a general thing," Henry James sketched in one of three prose-minatures he drew of late-nineteenth-century Toulouse, "I favour little the fashion of attributing moral qualities to buildings; I shrink from talking about tender cornices and sincere campanili," and yet, against his better judgment, he had to admit that "one can scarce get on without imputing some sort of morality to Saint-Sernin."[1] A pious fiction perhaps, but somehow appropriate for an abbey church in whose Romanesque cloister the inquisition had once held court.[2] Sadly, it cannot have been the cloister that prompted such thoughts in James, as this particular building, erected on the western side of the church in 1117,[3] had been torn down and sold off, stone by stone, column by column, between 1803 and 1808 by the mason Arnaud Traverse (who had acquired it in 1798).[4] Prosper Mérimée, traveling through the Midi half a century before James, as inspecteur-général of historical monuments for King Louis-Philippe, ignored the few remaining fragments of Saint-Sernin's porticoes,[5] though his report did eventually lead to the classification of the basilica itself as a national *monument historique* in 1838.[6] And when Eugène-Emmanuel Viollet-le-Duc, under Mérimée's patronage,[7] began to restore Saint-Sernin in 1845, to a condition rather more medieval than anything to which the Middle Ages could ever have aspired, he did not even consider rebuilding the *claustrum*.[8] Today, Saint-Sernin having undergone *dérestauration* from Viollet-le-Duc's vision,[9] the saucer-shaped *Place Saint-Sernin* occupies, as daily parking lot and weekend flea market, the space where the cloister would have been.[10]

Seven hundred years earlier, when the limestone verandas of Saint-Sernin were still intact, and Bernart de Caux and Jean de Saint-Pierre were about to begin their inquisition, an impressive town house lay directly opposite the cloister. In this grand stone hall (whose storerooms were demolished in 1240, after being purchased by the consuls of Toulouse, so that a large square for tournaments could be laid out) lived the widow Aurimunda de Capdenier.[11] Aurimunda's husband, Pons, had died sometime between October 1229 and March 1230, but not before this wealthy notable had given the Dominicans, in the last months of his life, a small garden on the city side of the Saracen wall (an old edifice that marked the border between the *civitas* of Toulouse and the *burgum* of Saint-Sernin) and a house, with a dovecote, on the bourg side.[12] The

first permanent buildings of the Friars Preachers in Toulouse, a little
convent and priory, were constructed upon this gift.[13] And it was within
this walled enclosure, after Pope Gregory IX had specifically called upon
the Dominicans to the *negotium fidei contra hereticos* throughout Languedoc in two bulls of Wednesday, 20, and Friday, 22 April 1233, that the
Friars Preachers launched the first *inquisitiones heritice pravitatis* into the
heresies of the good men and good women.[14]

To stroll from the wide patios of Saint-Sernin to the small rooms near
the Saracen wall, from Aurimunda de Capdenier's town house to her
husband's bequest, all of a ten-minute walk at most, and one which Bernart de Caux and Jean de Saint-Pierre would have undertaken each day
of their great inquisition, reveals the significant investigative change that
had happened since the two previous and quite limited inquiries into
heresy in the Lauragais. The first had been undertaken by Guilhem Arnaut and Esteve de Saint-Thibéry between Thursday, 17 October 1241,
and Thursday, 28 May 1242, while Friar Ferrer undertook the second
from the middle of 1243 to around Christmas 1244, and though each
friar-inquisitor had started out from the Dominican convent in Toulouse,
all their tribunals had been itinerant and provisional.[15] The records of
these inquisitions have survived, for the most part, only as bits and pieces
in the Collection Doat.

The first inquiry had stopped at Saint-Paul-Cap-de-Joux, Lavaur, La-
bruguière, Auriac, Saint-Félix, Labécède, Castelnaudary, Laurac, and,
tragically, Avignonet.[16] Admittedly, sometimes a few communities that
were close to the villages where the friar-inquisitors had set up their provisional courts would be summoned, like the inhabitants of tiny Saint-
Martin-de-la-Lande who were called to Castelnaudary for questioning by
Guilhem Arnaut.[17] But the fact remains that individuals were questioned
close to their homes, in spaces which were familiar to them and not
necessarily as familiar to the wandering friar-inquisitors.

Bernart de Caux and Jean de Saint-Pierre reversed these transient
methods; instead of traveling through the numerous Lauragais parishes,
which made up the archdeaconries of Lanta and Vieilmorez in the diocese of Toulouse, they made the inhabitants of these rural communities
come to them at Saint-Sernin.[18] Thousands converged on a fixed tribunal
that was, in most cases, somewhere between a few hours to a good day's
walk from their villages. It was also a court that could recall witnesses as
many times as the friar-inquisitors thought necessary. One violent incident provoked this change: the assassination of Guilhem Arnaut and
Esteve de Saint-Thibéry at Avignonet by that group of *faidits* and heretical
sympathizers during the night (Ascension Eve) of Thursday, 28 May
1242. The inquisition at Saint-Sernin happened in the way that it did
three years later, and Bernart de Caux and Jean de Saint-Pierre followed

certain forensic paths rather than others, because journeying through the Lauragais in the middle of the thirteenth century had become an unacceptable risk—despite the sustained pursuit of heretics by Raimon VII since 1243 and the total destruction of Montségur in 1244.[19] The murder of a cleric and an inquisitorial courier, and the burning of the inquisition registers they were carrying, at Caunes (near Narbonne) toward the end of 1247 would seem to lend credibility to this fear.[20]

Apart from their Lauragais investigations, Bernart de Caux and Jean de Saint-Pierre undertook *inquisitiones* at Agen from Monday, 30 November 1243, to Thursday, 10 March 1244,[21] and at Cahors on Wednesday, 18 May 1244 (and they returned to Cahors once more on Wednesday, 22 February 1245).[22] After the inquisition at Saint-Sernin, the two Dominicans made inquiries at Pamiers, in the county of Foix, from Thursday, 18 October 1246, until Saturday, 20 April 1247.[23] The friar-inquisitors were again at Saint-Sernin from Thursday, 22 August, to Tuesday, 10 December 1247, to hear testimonies from four Franciscans about what they had overheard a certain Peire Garcias say about the cosmology of the *boni homines*.[24] This singular inquisition stands out from other surviving early-thirteenth-century inquiries, the Lauragais investigations included, because it contains the most elaborate account of what a very chatty and opinionated *credens* was remembered as having said about his heretical beliefs. Bernart de Caux and Jean de Saint-Pierre remained in Toulouse until September 1248, when they traveled to Carcassonne.[25] Eventually, Bernart de Caux retired as an inquisitor sometime toward the end of 1249 and proceeded to found a Dominican convent at Agen, where he died on Tuesday, 26 November 1252.[26] Jean de Saint-Pierre continued as an inquisitor at Toulouse, though now with Renaud de Chartres as his *socius*, until May 1257, when Guilhem Bernart de Dax took over.[27]

Two years after their inquisition at Saint-Sernin, when Bernart de Caux and Jean de Saint-Pierre were briefly assigned to Carcassonne, the two Dominicans jotted down their procedural reflections, their methodological afterthoughts, in a small pamphlet now known from one surviving manuscript in Madrid as the *Processus inquisitionis*.[28] This deceptively simple book, commissioned by Innocent IV and the archbishop of Narbonne as a guide to help other inquisitors, became the first manual, certainly for Languedoc, on how to conduct an inquisition.[29] Moreover, this synopsis on nascent inquisitorial technique could not have been written in the way that it was, especially with the confidence in which it set forth a system of detection, without the extraordinary experience of the Lauragais investigations. The *Processus*, then, is also something of a mémoire on the procedures tried and tested in those two hundred and one days at Saint-Sernin.[30]

Bernart de Caux and Jean de Saint-Pierre's manual stressed, at the very beginning, that one must first choose a suitable place at which the inquisition of other localities could be made.[31] Suitability was not explicitly defined, except that this was somehow a rather obvious quality, which, in a sense, it was by the time the *Processus* was written. The Council of Béziers in 1246, and Innocent IV in 1247, had clearly expressed, with the murders of Avignonet in mind, the necessity for safety as the deciding factor in determining where an inquisitor should hold his inquiries.[32] The friar-inquisitors would then give a general sermon at this apt place, before an assembly of clergy and other people, and read out the letters from the pope and their provincial prior authorizing them to inquire into heresy.[33] Apart from the reading out of the letters, the content of the sermons is not suggested, though they were obviously expected to be much more than just bureaucratic recitations. Indeed, they could apparently be moments of revelation for those in the audience. On Tuesday, 5 June 1246, Arnaut Durant, from Montégut, confessed to Bernart de Caux that he had been a *crezen* as recently as the previous month, and that his conversion had happened—and here, perhaps, flattery and fear enhanced the truth—only because he heard the general sermon the inquisitor had given on Thursday, 17 May 1246, in the cloister at Saint-Sernin.[34]

After the sermon, a general summons was issued, either orally to those present or by letter to those who were absent, in this form:

> The inquisitors of heretical depravity [*inquisitores heretice pravitatis*], greetings in the Lord to so and so, parish priest. We enjoin and strictly instruct you, in virtue of the authority we wield, to summon in our name and by our authority all the parishioners of such and such church or the inhabitants of such and such place, men from the age of fourteen, women from the age of twelve, or younger if perchance they shall be guilty of an offense, to appear before us on such a day at such a place to answer for acts that they may have committed against the faith and to abjure heresy.[35]

A summons to a particular individual had this formula:

> In our name and by our authority, you [the parish priest] are to issue a summary citation to so and so, once and for all, to appear on such a day at such a place to answer for his [or her] faith (or for such and such an offense or to receive sentence of imprisonment or, more simply, penance for acts committed or to defend a deceased parent, or to hear sentence in his [or her] own case or, in the case of a deceased person, whose heir he [or she] is).[36]

Along with the first summons there also came "a time of grace or indulgence," *tempus gratie sive indulgentie,* a window of tolerance that Innocent IV had first demanded of the inquisitors in 1243, and which the Council of Béziers had codified in 1246.[37] That is, if there had been no previous inquisition in a parish, or a village, then those who voluntarily presented themselves before the inquisitors within a specified time and told the truth about themselves and about others would escape imprisonment. This indulgence, however, would not be given to persons who had already received it or to a particular individual who had been summoned by name.[38]

That the two friar-inquisitors chose fourteen for men and twelve for women as the minimum ages for interrogation was nothing more than an acknowledgment of the wider acceptance, certainly in the Toulousain and the Lauragais, that these were the ages when boys and girls reached their majority, that is to say, a threshold at which they could marry, a threshold at which they could enter into new and crucial relationships not only with society but also with the Church.[39] The age of emancipation— when a young person was no longer under familial authority and so was able to act independently of the *patria potestas*—was, however, twenty-five for both men and women.[40] Theoretically, a girl or a boy under twelve or fourteen, as a minor, could not be tried for a criminal offense or enact a legal document without the consent of a parent.[41] This technicality was hardly a worry for Bernart de Caux and Jean de Saint-Pierre because, as their general summons made clear, they could question girls and boys of any age if the inquisition thought a child guilty of some heretical crime. Either way, as far the two Dominicans were concerned, boys at fourteen and girls at twelve had reached a point in their lives (and, perhaps more important, a point in the lives of other men and women) when their adolescent memories and youthful confessions were indispensable in the search for heresy in the Lauragais.

The date when Bernart de Caux and Jean de Saint-Pierre must have given their *predicatio generalis* at Saint-Sernin, and so inaugurated their Lauragais inquisition, is unknown. It was obviously preached before the earliest testimony recorded in manuscript 609, that of na Dias, from Saint-Germier, on Monday, 1 May 1245, and, as the year began for all notarized documents in Toulouse on 1 April, it must have happened sometime after this date.[42] As for an immediate reaction to being summoned, Girauda Artus from Auriac remembered that when she first heard the friar-inquisitors' citation, she told a relative, Fabrissa Artus, that the friar-inquisitors frightened her very much, and even though she intended to tell them the truth, she expected the worst from the two Dominicans and hoped "that, God willing, they would impose a good penance on me."[43] Despite such fears, or rather because of the uncertainty that went with such anxieties, only two people came forward during the *tempus gratie* to test this fleeting mood of inquisitorial indulgence: Sabdalina de Goudourville and Peire de Valères from Saint-Félix.[44] Even more unusual were two men, Arnaut Faber and Guilhem Gasc, who apparently made the journey to Saint-Sernin without even waiting to be summoned.[45]

This lack of response to the *tempus gratie* is all the more surprising because in a judgment they gave in the house of the abbot of Saint-Sernin on Sunday, 29 September 1247, Bernart de Caux and Jean de Saint-Pierre condemned the noblewoman Algaia de Villeneuve-la-Comptal to perpetual imprisonment because, among other things, "she did not come before the other inquisitors during the period of grace for the purpose of making her confession of heresy."[46] The *miles* Bernart de Rocovila from les Cassés, however, did go and confess to the late Guilhem Arnaut during the *tempus gratie* of that inquisitor, but, as he shamefully admitted at Saint-Sernin on Sunday, 24 June 1246, with Bernart de Caux and Jean de Saint-Pierre listening, "I know that I've been bad because, in that period of grace, I denied the truth about believing and adoring heretics."[47]

The Lauragais was undoubtedly perceived by Bernart de Caux and Jean de Saint-Pierre as (in the disease metaphor they, and other clerics, frequently used to describe heterodoxy)[48] a region so widely infected with heresy that it could be cured, according to the *Processus*, only by a general inquisition of all persons, no exceptions, "even of those who insist they know nothing about other people and have committed no crime, so that if they have lied or if subsequently they commit an offense, as is often found true of a number of persons, it is on record that they have abjured and have been interrogated in detail."[49] Among the five thousand four hundred and seventy-one men and women interrogated by the two Dominicans, only seven hundred and fifty-eight had, apparently, ever confessed to a friar-inquisitor before.[50] Some, like Bernarta Trebolha of Saint-Paul-Cap-de-Joux, initially feigned forgetfulness about having ever spoken to previous friar-inquisitors, but, when their old testimonies were inconveniently read back to them, they soon remembered their earlier confessions.[51] Nevertheless, even if we take into account individuals who chose to hide former inquisitorial questioning, and whose selective recollection was not discovered, the sheer numbers who came to Saint-Sernin to be interrogated should never be forgotten. No other investigation in the Middle Ages, inquisitorial or not, coerced so many into making such a journey.[52]

Yet, as observed earlier, Bernart de Caux and Jean de Saint-Pierre could not hear all the testimonies, especially on a particularly busy day, so numerous interrogations were undertaken, when a friar-inquisitor was not available, by one or more of the witnesses listed at the end of each confession.[53] There were typically two witnesses to every deposition, though on three occasions there was only one.[54] All in all, there were one hundred and seventy-six different witnesses to the Lauragais testimonies, and most of these individuals, largely parish clergy, heard only one or two confessions. Nevertheless, the names of a few men do occur over and over again, and it is these men, asking questions and listening to answers, who essentially functioned as de facto inquisitors.[55] One name, for example, that frequently witnessed a testimony was that of Arnaut Auriol, the prior of Saint-Sernin. Indeed, he was present for one hundred and fifty-seven days out of the inquisition's two hundred and one.[56] During that long Monday of 3 July 1245, when one hundred and eighty-nine depositions were heard from ten parishes, Arnaut Auriol witnessed every single testimony.[57]

An interesting conclusion that can also be drawn from a look at the witnesses to various testimonies is that the men and women who came to Toulouse were, in almost every case, accompanied by their local priest on this journey and then watched, perhaps even questioned, by him in Saint-Sernin's verandas.[58] A great many of the marginal comments in manuscript 609 probably derive from such village clergy.[59] A scribal gloss that explicitly illustrates this, and in the process captures not only a listener helping to clarify a testimony for other listeners but also a listener aware that his clarification will aid a later reader, is the interjection next to the testimony of the leper Guilhem Rigaut at the exact point (about halfway through the confession) when he talks about the *miles* Raimon Barth, a *crezen* who had threatened him: "The archpriest of the Lauragais says that the knight, Raimon Barth, hanged two of his sergeants because they captured the mother of the said Raimon and six other female heretics."[60] Neither friar-inquisitor heard this testimony, but Esteve, the archpriest of Laurac (and so the Lauragais), did.[61]

The two friar-inquisitors allowed no excuse for anyone's not coming before them at Saint-Sernin. And yet, only a few years earlier, a friar-inquisitor would have made a point of personally visiting individuals who, because of some physical disability, could not come before his provisional tribunal. The noble widow na Blanca de Montesquieu, for one, remembered how Esteve de Saint-Thibéry, on the orders of Guilhem Arnaut, had traveled to her village three years earlier (and to whom she had confessed everything she was now telling Bernart de Caux and Jean de Saint-Pierre) specifically to hear the confessions of "the pregnant women and the infirm."[62]

After Avignonet, however, the sick and pregnant mingled with the healthy in the corridors of Saint-Sernin. For instance, the leper Peire Vidal (*leprosus* was written in margin of manuscript 609) from Mas-Saintes-Puelles, the already-mentioned leper Guilhem Rigaut from Laurac, and the leper Guilhema de Cumiés traveled to Toulouse and confessed with everyone else from their villages.[63] The blind Guilhem

Raimon (*cecus* was another marginal notation) walked all the way from the hamlet of Gasca; indeed, he even remembered seeing heretics when he still had his sight, though this memory, of course, could simply be formulaic answering to equally formulaic questioning.[64] The young and noble na Marqueza, wife of the knight Peire Raimon Gros, was in the advanced stages of her pregnancy (*prope partum est* was the diagnostic opinion scribbled, once more, in the margin) when she presented herself for questioning on Friday, 8 June 1246.[65] Numerous relatively older men and women in their fifties, sixties, and even seventies also came before the friar-inquisitors and remembered the sins of their long-dead mothers and fathers.[66]

Unfortunately, only one person had cause to mention his actual journey from the Lauragais to Saint-Sernin. This was Arnaut Godera, formerly of Montferrand, now living eight kilometers south of Toulouse in the parish of Auzeville-Tolosane, who told the inquisition on Monday, 30 October 1245, with Bernart de Caux listening, how earlier in the day, when he was still on his way to Saint-Sernin, two men from his old village stopped him on a road outside Toulouse and asked him not to tell the truth about heresy in Montferrand.[67] Apart from an insight into the potential for false testimony, a factor that must be added to the evaluation of any confession, Arnaut Godera's brief allusion to his journey reveals what must have been the common itinerary of those summoned to Saint-Sernin: travel, confession, return, all in the space of a day. Four hundred and thirty-three years later, John Locke, fascinated by the Languedocian inquisition, galloped from Toulouse to Castelnaudary one Sunday morning, roughly fifty-two kilometers, stayed the night at an inn called the Three Pigeons, and, before midday the next day, 10 October 1678, made it to Carcassonne. Locke had ridden the length of the Lauragais, close to ninety kilometers, fourteen seventeenth-century leagues, in less than a day.[68]

Arnaut Godera's and John Locke's journeys, different centuries but the same roads (even the same month), remind one that traveling to Toulouse from the Lauragais would have been a familiar experience for a great many people testifying at Saint-Sernin. The noble de Rocovila family, all of whom believed in the holiness of the *bons omes* and *bonas femnas*, not only owned properties and little seignories from Montgiscard through les Cassés to Mas-Saintes-Puelles but leased two town houses in Toulouse, one near the Saint-Étienne Gate and other near the Croix-Baragnon (and known as the *domus dels Rochovilas*).[69] More modestly, Terren Faber, a blacksmith from Laurac, owned a house in Toulouse at the time of the Peace of Paris-Meaux, that is to say, 1229.[70] Peire Roger recalled the time, around 1230, when his brother Pons left their village of les Cassés to go and live in Toulouse, forty kilometers away. Pons Roger's original intention had been to learn the art of leather work at Toulouse; unfortunately, as far as his brother and the inquisition were concerned, he also became a *bon ome*.[71]

As to any specific effect that the pilgrimage of so many people into Toulouse for questioning by the inquisitors had upon the bourg and the city, whose total population in the middle of the thirteenth century was roughly twenty-five thousand, no individual or even institutional memory has survived.[72] Yet only a decade earlier, as the Dominican Guilhem Pelhisson emphasized with singular passion in his chronicle of the early years of the Friars Preachers in Toulouse, the Dominicans had been expelled from Toulouse for four months by Raimon VII, from November 1235 to February 1236, because of their inquisitorial activities and the turmoil these investigations had caused in the city and the bourg.[73] Significantly, Guilhem Pelhisson, who had been an inquisitor himself, actually composed his chronicle at the same time as he was assisting Bernart de Caux and Jean de Saint-Pierre with their Lauragais inquisition.[74] Guilhem Pelhisson's reflection upon the immediate past, which, curiously, he "wrote on paper with his own hand" rather than on parchment,[75] coincided with his witnessing, and so listening to and questioning, hundreds of other reflections upon those same decades.

As to the effect Toulouse may have had on those coming to Saint-Sernin, the streets and alleyways of the bourg and the city possessed numerous physical examples of the consequences of someone's having been judged sinful. Near the Château Narbonnais, the comital gaol used by the friar-inquisitors, and only a fifteen-minute walk from Saint-Sernin, a wooden coffin sat above the ground in the precincts of the Hospitalers. In this box lay the slowly decaying body of Raimon VI. He had been excommunicated in 1207 by Innocent III and his legate Peire de Castelnau. Two years later, the pope repeated the excommunication after Peire de Castelnau was murdered by that "evil-hearted" squire. The old count, despite the frequent protests of his son Raimon VII, would remain unburied for centuries to come.[76]

Slightly less poignant, though no less evocative, and visible to anyone coming or going to Saint-Sernin, were some weathered foundations lying right next to Aurimunda de Capdenier's hall. These ruins had once been a town house belonging to the de la Claustra family, but sometime between March 1216 and September 1217, that brief period when Simon de Montfort occupied Toulouse during the Albigensian Crusade, the house was condemned as a punishment against two de la Claustra brothers, Guilhem and Aycard, who had fought against the crusaders and were consequently labeled by the northern French as *faidits*.[77] Forty years later, Toulouse was riddled with similar empty spaces where houses had once stood, though now such *destructio domorum* recalled not just the crusaders but also the more recent history of the friar-inquisitors and their penalties for heresy.[78] Raimon VII, angered at the ubiquity of these architectural and ethical scars inflicted upon his town by the friar-inquisitors, complained to Gregory IX in a letter of 1236 that such "a noble city should not be deformed by ruins, especially as it is men who sin and not things."[79]

Bernart de Caux and Jean de Saint-Pierre, by contrast, knew that a man's or a woman's sins could smoothly flow into (and through) objects like houses, a dish of chestnuts, a recently built wall, wooden tables, an old fur pelisse, a sack of wriggling eels, cornices, stones, even a Romanesque cloister. All that a friar-inquisitor needed to trace these moral pathways, to know where heresy had left its mark, to be able to separate good from evil, were the right questions.

# 7

## QUESTIONS ABOUT QUESTIONS

EVERY person questioned at Saint-Sernin began by first abjuring all heresy and then taking an oath that he or she would "tell the full and exact truth about oneself and about others, living and dead, in the matter of the fact or crime of heresy [that is, the heresy of the good men and the good women] or Waldensianism."[1] The questions that Bernart de Caux and Jean de Saint-Pierre considered fundamental in arriving at the truth, and that everyone from the Lauragais was asked in one form or another, can be inferred from the answers recorded in manuscript 609 and from the *formula interrogatorii* listed in the *Processus*. These questions were blunt, cumulative, almost cascading, in effect, and driven by a concern for what an individual might have done rather than what he or she might have thought.

"Did you see a heretic [a good man or a good woman] or a Waldensian?" was, invariably, the first question. The answer "No" might end the inquisition then and there. "Yes," however, immediately led to other queries. "If so, then where and when, how often and with whom, and who were the others present?" "Did you listen to the preaching or exhortation of heretics?" "Did you give heretics lodging or arrange shelter for them?" "Did you lead heretics from place to place or otherwise consort with them or arrange for them to be guided or escorted?" "Did you eat or drink with the heretics or eat bread blessed by them?" "Did you give or send anything to the heretics?" "Did you act as the financial agent [*questor*] or messenger [*nuncius*] or assistant [*minister*] of the heretics?" "Did you hold any deposit or anything for a heretic?" "Did you receive the peace from a heretic's book, mouth, shoulder, or elbow?" "Did you adore a heretic or bow your head or genuflect and say 'bless us' before the heretics?" "Did you participate, or were you present at their *consolamentum* or *apparellamentum* [*consolamen* and *aparelhamen* in Occitan]?" "Did you ever confess to another inquisitor?"[2] "Did you believe the heretics to be good men and good women, to have a good faith, to be truthful, to be the friends of God?" "Did you hear, or do you know, the errors of the heretics?" "Did you hear them say that God had not made all visible things, that there was no salvation in baptism, that marriage was worthless, that the Host was not the body of Christ, and that the flesh would never be resurrected?"[3] "If you did believe these errors, and also believed the heretics to be good, then how long have you persisted in these beliefs?" "And when did you first begin to believe in the heretics and their errors?" "Did you leave the sect of the heretics?" "How long ago did you leave and did you ever see the heretics after this time?"[4] "Did you ever agree to keep silent about all these things?" "Did you ever hide the truth?" usually concluded the interrogation.

Eighty years after these questions were asked at Saint-Sernin, the Dominican Bernard Gui, who resided in Toulouse as inquisitor from 1307 to 1324, had to justify, explain, elaborate, and dissect, over and over again in his *Practica inquisitionis heretice pravitatis*, why these particular questions, rather than others, would help worm out the truth about the heresy of the "Manichaeans"—as this long and learned manual now classified the heresy of the *boni homines*.[5] Still, after all Bernard Gui's flourishes and digressions, insights and swirls, the impression remains that the pursuit of the good men, as opposed to the Waldensians, for example, had lost that certainty of touch, that obviousness of method, which may be said to have characterized an inquisitor in the middle of the thirteenth century. This is all the more fascinating since Bernard Gui had undoubtedly read the manual of the two earlier Dominicans, as well as their registers, and was certainly aware that his *formula interrogatorii* possessed some continuity with the methods of earlier inquisitors.[6] Yet Bernard Gui's fine-tuned questions eventually came to focus much more upon what a suspected heretic thought than upon what he or she might have done. The apparent sophistication of the *Practica* (and this observation is perhaps justified only with regard to the errors of the good men and good women) is nothing more than the demonstration of inquisitorial abstraction about heretical habits that, apart from the born-again dualism of some tiny Pyrenean villages, no longer existed.[7]

This is not to suggest that Bernard Gui was making it all up, or that he did not think the *boni homines* were still a threat, or that the method of questioning he suggested was not the one he used in his own interrogations, but it is to argue that what can only be called the reality of heresy for Bernart de Caux and Jean de Saint-Pierre, and so their cut-and-dried detective manner with its concentration on the evidence of actions rather than ideas, had come to mean something very different to an inquisitor by the turn of the fourteenth century. Significantly, while *heresis* meant only the good men and the good women to Bernart de Caux and Jean de Saint-Pierre, the word meant a great deal more to Bernard Gui. The *boni homines* as "Manichaeans" were now one of five heretical sects—the Waldensians, the Beguines, the pseudo-Apostles, and "Jews who have been converted to the faith of Christ and have returned to the vomit of Judaism."[8] And, most important to Bernard Gui, these various heresies demanded equally various investigative techniques, because as "different and specific medicines exist for particular diseases, so neither is the same method of questioning, investigation, and examination to be employed for all heretics."[9]

Consequently, not only did Bernard Gui think it necessary to smother his Manichee-detecting questions with justifications and explanations, but he also felt it expedient to preface these questions with a description of the way of life, the customs, and the behavior of the dualists, culled not just from his own experience but from other sources, especially the Pyrenean inquisition of Jacques Fournier.[10] Bernart de Caux and Jean de Saint-Pierre may have questioned, and read, their way through the Lauragais, but they never implied in their manual or in the records of their investigations that one needed to undertake secondary reading in heresy in order to know what to look for, in order to understand a clue, in the way that Bernard Gui did.

This brief glance at the early fourteenth century helps to emphasize the deliberateness, the specificity, of the particular questions that Bernart de Caux and Jean de Saint-Pierre used in their inquisition at Saint-Sernin. The reason why this rather obvious point must be made—basically, that questions have their historical meanings as much as anything else—is due to the implicit assumption that the early friar-inquisitors were somehow less inquisitive than those who conducted later investigations, and that this is due to a certain crudeness in their style of detection.[11] Essentially, the fault of Bernart de Caux and Jean de Saint-Pierre, as opposed to, say, Jacques Fournier or Bernard Gui, is that they were bad ethnographers, to use the interesting but ultimately misleading analogy of the inquisitor as anthropologist, because they did not ask the sort of questions that modern scholars wished they had asked.[12]

The questions asked by Bernart de Caux and Jean de Saint-Pierre determined the angle of perspective, the palette, the style of the picture that they drew (so very quickly) of heresy in the Lauragais. These inquisitorial questions framed the way in which the testimonies were to be understood. The principles of analysis that the two Dominicans used to detect good men, good women, and heretical believers, were embodied in their questions. As a result, the confessions heard at Saint-Sernin were judged as responses to whatever these analytic principles were expected to yield; which, at least for the friar-inquisitors, was meant to be a truthful evocation of heresy in the Lauragais. Therefore, the ability to select the right questions was as much a test of the friar-inquisitors, in their search for the truth, as giving the right answers was a test of those being interrogated, in their ability to confess, or conceal, this truth.[13]

This necessity for right questions, and the effort involved in their selection, leads to the intriguing and far from whimsical problem of why inquisitors need bother with questions at all, a point that Arnaut del Faget and Guilhem Vezat, cowherds from Maurens, actually stressed for

Bernart de Caux in their testimonies of Tuesday, 16 January 1246. Three years earlier, these two cowherds had come across a couple of unknown men in the woods around Maurens and immediately "knew in their hearts" that these strangers were heretics.[14] Clearly, by the middle of the thirteenth century it was no great feat to suspect two anonymous men in a Lauragais wood of being *bons omes*, and for such suspicions to be more often than not correct, but that is to miss the lesson here, which is that Bernart de Caux and Jean de Saint-Pierre would never have hunted for heretics through heartfelt knowledge, through intuition, alone.

Neither did the two friar-inquisitors rely upon demonic or heavenly revelations, such as miracles, to discern a *bonus homo* in the way that Dominic Guzman was said to have done in the Lauragais only a few decades earlier. Once, during a sermon against the *boni homines* that the founder of the Dominicans was preaching at Fanjeaux, a grotesque and intolerably smelly cat leapt into the congregation and identified a heretic.[15] By the time this anecdote was told to Étienne de Bourbon by the Dominician Romeu de Llivia, sometime around 1261, complete faith in miraculous clues, like putting too much trust in an intuitive truth, merely demonstrated that one did not know how to go about investigating the origins of anything.[16]

Wondrous evidence can help and be the sign of a saint, just as a lucky guess can work for a cowherd, but their conflation of cause and effect, so that the past history of a present crime never had to explained, were both judgments about the world without the necessity of having to understand the world being judged. To forgo tracing great waves back to small ripples, to ignore the continuity of evil in a gift much given, simply left all the whys and wherefores of heresy, all the work of detecting heretics, and so all the work of punishing them, up to God.

Which is exactly what the fiery Cistercian abbot Arnaud Amalric apparently did when the crusaders captured Béziers in 1209. The crusaders had a problem about how one could precisely distinguish Catholic from heretic, the good from the bad, among the people of Béziers. "Kill them!" was Arnaud Amalric's judicious solution. "Truly," the legate concluded, "God will know his own."[17] Whether or not this anecdote about Arnaud Amalric is true, and all we have to go by is the word of Caesarius of Heisterbach, it still evokes an approach virtually unthinkable for two Dominican inquisitors in the middle of the thirteenth century. To Bernart de Caux and Jean de Saint-Pierre, there was nothing inherently miraculous or demonic about why heretics did what they did. Heretical thoughts and habits were not to be explained by reference to anything outside the usual course of nature. So, like any human whose motives were less than supernatural, less than holy, a heretic could be, indeed had to be, judged and punished through profane procedures.[18]

In this way the inquisition at Saint-Sernin, as a procedure for discovering the truth about heresy, was markedly different from the judicial ordeal. The use of fire and water as reliable tools in judging veracity, though not the only methods of proof before the thirteenth century,[19] were certainly the specific practices that men like Bernart de Caux and Jean de Saint-Pierre saw themselves as abandoning, as no longer tolerating, in their need to collect true and systematic evidence[20]—especially as Innocent III in the eighteenth canon of the Fourth Lateran Council had forbidden clergy to participate in the ordeal.[21] While the legal plumbing behind the ordeal was, relatively speaking, simple and well-hidden, the investigative formula adopted at Saint-Sernin could not help but reveal much of its legal and moral structure. As such, the basic inquisitorial design used at Saint-Sernin was not unlike the Roman-inspired and canon-regulated *ordo iudiciarius*, those rules of procedure built upon written and oral evidence that had been developing since the middle of the twelfth century, and which all ecclesiastical courts (and many secular) had adopted by the thirteenth.[22] If the ordeal may be characterized as letting God be the judge of a person's guilt or innocence, so that the evidence which caused a man or a woman to be accused in the first place was either confirmed or dismissed through divine judgment, then the ordeal was a style of judging that no ordinary person could ever truly imitate.[23] Inquisitorial method, on the other hand, was a system made to be imitated.

In the middle of the thirteenth century, as God the Judge became Christ the Savior, as He became more "human" and His servants more "divine," as men and women undertook the *imitatio Christi* (replicating the divine way of life rather than the divine way of thinking), individuals like Bernart de Caux and Jean de Saint-Pierre could trust themselves, and be trusted by others, to judge innocence and guilt.[24] The judicial ordeal expected no individual confession, no testimonial about a life lived over the years, no scribal record for reading and reflection.[25] The ordeal asked only one question, that being whether an accused person was guilty or innocent, and it was a query put to God. Arnaud Amalric's bloody method at Béziers was essentially the ordeal taken to its logical conclusion. The friar-inquisitors, through carefully formulating questions, all of which were clearly earthbound rather than heaven-sent, allowed the causes of heresy to be just as carefully formulated. The right questions allowed the inquisitors to accumulate answers about individual lives, to stockpile evidence about past deeds, and, more important, it allowed them to discover the truth without having to rely upon heartfelt insight or wondrous miracles.[26]

In one sense, what the friar-inquisitors did at Saint-Sernin was not dissimilar to the *quaestio disputata* that all mendicants would have learned at Paris.[27] Indeed, as a *studium generale* had been established near Saint-Sernin as a requirement of the Peace of Meaux-Paris, with Parisian masters of theology and philosophy specifically dispatched to train local Dominicans and Franciscans in the fight against the heretical *boni homines*, such intellectual techniques were taught at Toulouse.[28] Scholars endeavored to ask the right questions, within the constraints of a consciously stylized dialogue form, in their Aristotelian processions to the truth.[29] Nevertheless, despite this rhetorical similarity, what went on in Saint-Sernin was not a dialectic as practiced by mendicant *litterati* in the thirteenth century. The Lauragais interrogations were spoken dialogues only insomuch as they involved someone's asking questions and someone's giving answers. So, apart from this likeness to the procedures of finding truth learned in the *studia* of Paris and Toulouse, which is still worth noting, the ability to question the questioner did not really exist.

"Now they've made themselves into inquisitors, and they judge just as it suits them," the Toulousain *trobador* Guilhem de Montanhagol sarcastically sang about the Dominicans in 1233 or 1234—that is, immediately after Gregory IX had called upon them to eliminate heresy in Languedoc through *inquisitiones* and a year before the count of Toulouse expelled the Friars Preachers from his city.[30] "But," Guilhem de Montanhagol instantly added, tongue in cheek, orthodoxy in tow, "I've nothing against the inquisition; far from it, I like those who pursue errors and who, with their charming delightful words, devoid of anger, restore to the faith those who have strayed and turned away."[31] The clever manipulation of questions, the smart play with words, and so the ability to mislead and confuse someone into saying anything that might imply guilt, was a criticism leveled at Friar Ferrer in 1235 during his inquisition at Narbonne.[32] Friar Ferrer, that same year, also managed to cause a riot in the bourg of Narbonne after he accused most of the town of being heretics during a general sermon.[33] As for Bernart de Caux and Jean de Saint-Pierre, no one overtly mocked them in song or openly accused them of tricking people with their questions, of judging as they pleased.

Bernart de Caux and Jean de Saint-Pierre's concentration on habits rather than beliefs, with the implication that this realm would provide more clues about heresy than the realm of ideas, though occasionally making for some dull and repetitive reading in their register, clearly reveals the model that the two friar-inquisitors had for what constituted a person in the middle of the thirteenth century or, at the very least, what made a person a heretic. Instead of a theory whereby a person existed as a separate entity before coming into contact with other people, a man or a woman to the friar-inquisitors existed as a person only through the relationships that individual had, or was anticipated to have, with other people. This is not to say that the friar-inquisitors imagined an individual as a person-shaped hole surrounded by a swirl of relations with other people-shaped indentions, as this would be to still think of men and women as having the ability to separate themselves from the context, from the complicity, of others. On the contrary, what made men and women, what revealed the lives they had lived and would go on to live, were their relationships with other men and women.

An aspect of this model, and something that relates specifically to the fact that some people at Saint-Sernin remembered things from well in their past, is that though the friar-inquisitors' definition of individuality depended upon perceived continuities of relations through time, there was no temporal limit placed upon the repetition of habits classified as heretical. As such, a relationship with a heretic from, say, 1210, even if it never happened again, could still be the cause of something yet to occur. People could never divorce themselves from the old habits and the antici-pated relationships that made them—even in death, as the inquisition sought out the graves of good men, good women, and their believers. No relationship, action, or thought could ever be contingent or accidental. There could be no separation of cause and effect in the narrative of an individual life. It was a vision where no one received the benefit of a doubt, and where women, for instance, were not seen as any more sus-ceptible to heresy than men. The universe of Saint-Sernin, at least for those two hundred and one days of questioning, was decidedly determin-istic. As observers, readers, listeners, interrogators, and finally judges, everything was implicated in everything else to the friar-inquisitors.

Finally, none of this detective theorizing should be seen as lessening the sense of religious purpose felt by the friar-inquisitors, the holiness embodied in their questions, procedures, and punishments. Their way of understanding all those people interrogated at Saint-Sernin, of defining heresy within the life of an individual, arose from a profound clarity of spiritual mission and a deep penitential impulse to punish justly, whether those punishments took the form of two large yellow crosses stitched to the outside of clothing or perpetual imprisonment. To be an inquisitor, as Guilhem Pelhisson remembered a prior of the Dominican house in Toulouse once saying, was to be like one of the holy martyrs.[34]

# 8

## FOUR EAVESDROPPING FRIARS

FOUR Franciscans, on Thursday, 22 August 1247, eagerly confessed to Bernart de Caux and Jean de Saint-Pierre in the cloisters of Saint-Sernin everything they had heard someone else say about the heresy of the *boni homines*. The testimonies of Guilhem Cogot, Déodat de Rodez, Friar Imbert, and Guilhem Garcias were all concerned with what a *credens*, Peire Garcias, had told his relative, the aforementioned Guilhem Garcias, in the common room of the Franciscan convent in Toulouse.[1] Peire Garcias had, during the previous Lent, frequently wandered over from his house in the Bourguet-Nau quarter of Toulouse and engaged Guilhem Garcias in seemingly friendly, though lively, debate about heresy and holiness.[2] On at least two of these visits, however, a handful of Franciscans had hidden themselves above the common room and eavesdropped.[3] Guilhem Garcias, apparently, was well aware that his fellow friars were lurking overhead (he could even see them); Peire Garcias, who trusted his kinsman, was completely ignorant of the trap that had been set for him.[4]

Bernart de Caux and Jean de Saint-Pierre did not use the *formula interrogatorii* of their Lauragais inquisition, or of their manual, with the four gossipy Franciscans. Indeed, the friar-inquisitors seem to have asked no methodical questions of the Friars Minor at all, except for some points of clarification. The Dominican inquisitors still verified the testimonies, but the recorded confessions of what the Franciscans had to say about Peire Garcias demonstrate, along with much else, how inquisitorial questions, or lack of them, clearly determined the nature of recorded evidence. These testimonies also reveal that Bernart de Caux and Jean de Saint-Pierre could easily have followed very different investigative paths in their Lauragais interrogations, roads full of ideas rather than habits. During the Lauragais interrogations, the two Dominicans heard nothing that even came close to what the four Franciscans told them about the thoughts of Peire Garcias. This reason alone makes it worth devoting a little time to this rather singular *inquisitio*. Further, by noticing how the use of a different interrogation technique can produce vividly different results, one moves a little closer to comprehending why the friar-inquisitors did what they did with the thousands from the Lauragais.

Guilhem Garcias would always begin his chats with Peire Garcias in the same way, or so four different memories suggested, by asking whether his relative believed in one compassionate God who had created all things as in Scripture or in two Gods.[5] Peire Garcias would always reply, with slight variations, by saying that there was no singular benevolent Creator. On the contrary, the universe had, according to Peire Garcias, in words recollected by Déodat de Rodez, "one benign God, who created all incorruptible things and things that will endure, and another God, who was evil, who made all corruptible and transitory things."[6] Guilhem Cogot, oddly enough, seemed to have forgotten statements such as this; instead, he told the inquisitors that he recalled Peire Garcias to have expressed, at the end of an inconclusive debate, uncertainty about whether there were two Gods or one.[7] Guilhem Garcias, on the other hand, had, like Déodat de Rodez, no doubts concerning the dualism of Peire Garcias. "Two Gods?" the Franciscan never failed to query the *credens*. "Yes," would come the immediate answer, "one good and one bad!"[8]

Peire Garcias was then asked by Guilhem Garcias, and here everybody's recollections were essentially similar, what he thought of the Apostle Paul's observation about the "God that justifies circumcision."[9] Déodat de Rodez testified that he heard Peire Garcias' riposte: "The law of Moses was nothing but shadow and vanity; and that the God who gave that law was a bastard!"[10] Then, Guilhem Garcias continued, what about the Apostle John's reflection that "[w]ithout Him, nothing was made."[11] Peire Garcias explained—and Guilhem Cogot's memory, as far as the following exegesis is concerned, was the sharpest—"that the word 'nothing' was used to designate visible things, which are nothing";[12] and, as an afterthought, he added, "that man was sin and nothing."[13] Guilhem Garcias stayed on this point about the perception of things and wondered whether it were possible for "He who hung on the cross" to create these visible things.[14] "No!" protested Peire Garcias, "for He was the best, and nothing of these visible things is good. *Ergo*, He made none of them."[15] In that case, Guilhem Garcias wanted to know, what had the Apostle Paul meant when he told the Colossians, "In Him were all things created in heaven and on earth, visible and invisible"?[16] Peire Garcias replied that the Pauline text should be understood as follows: "Visible to the heart and invisible to eyes of the flesh."[17]

Guilhem Garcias, at this point in the Franciscans' testimonies, including his own, stopped asking questions and just listened. Peire Garcias, in the silence left by his relative, and, it would appear, confident that he had explained the sources of good and evil in the universe, shifted the conversation by bluntly stating, "All the angels who fell from heaven, and they alone, will be saved."[18] Each of the eavesdroppers repeated the words of this non sequitur exactly to Bernart de Caux and Jean de Saint-Pierre; yet only Guilhem Garcias provided some shred of meaning, some hint of where the *credens* was taking his argument, by not forgetting that Peire Garcias had appended this endnote to his sophistry: "All who were not heretics, the Devil had made in body and soul."[19] Those tumbling angels, created from the same incorruptible stuff as the good God's heaven (rather than Satan's corruptible muck), were the *heretici*—which is to say, they were the holy *bons omes* and *bonas femnas*, the good men and good women.

Peire Garcias' cosmic causitry became clearer as he elaborated more and more aspects of what he believed. As he did this, emphasizing a notion here, dismissing an idea there, the depositions of the four Franciscans, largely in tempo until now, start to follow surprisingly individual tangents. For instance, Peire Garcias was remembered as having uttered the boozy oath "May he die of gout!" in two very different circumstances in three separate recollections (those of Guilhem Garcias, Déodat de Rodez, and Friar Imbert). In the memory of Guilhem Garcias, the oath seems nothing more than a pub curse, with the scribe even recording Guilhem Garcias' use of the earthy Occitan word *caja* for gout, upon anyone silly enough to believe that a nonexistent God created the eternal spirit anew in each person.[20] In the other two recollections, the oath was a bitter malediction at the end of a long angry tirade against the nonexistent God of the Roman Church. This was the completely Latin deposition of Déodat de Rodez: "Peire also said that if he could get hold of that God who would save only one out of a thousand men created by Him and would damn all the others, he would break Him in pieces, and rend Him with nails and teeth as perfidious. Peire believed that God to be false and perfidious and would spit in His face. Peire then added, 'May He die of gout [*gadat*]!' "[21]

Peire Garcias, once more in Déodat de Rodez's hindsight, instantly contrasted the previous unfair lottery of salvation with the guaranteed spiritual luck of the *bons omes* and *bonas femnas*: "All the angels who fell are to be saved, not just all the leaders and their assistants, but also the ordinary folk, so that not one out of a thousand will be damned."[22] The good men and good women would be saved, but so would a *crezen* like Peire Garcias—that is, if he received the heretical *consolamen* at his deathbed. It was a ritual, almost, but not quite, a form of penance, that essentially transformed a man into a *bon ome* and a woman into a *bona femna*. The unbearable burden of having fallen from heaven, of always feeling the gravity of corruption, was finally arrested and reversed. Now, it is enough to know that the four Franciscans never said the word *consolamentum* and used *hereticatio* only in relation to Peire Garcias' mother. So, when Déodat de Rodez reviewed Peire Garcias' concern about salvation, he worded it this way: "Peire said that there was no purgatory, and that alms given by the living are no help to the dead, and that no one is saved unless he does perfect penance [*perfectam penitentiam*] before death, and that a spirit which had not been asked to do penance in one body, if it was to be saved, will pass into another body to complete penance."[23]

Guilhem Garcias, according to his own testimony and that of Guilhem Cogot, showed his hand to Peire Garcais on one occasion and, returning to the question of the body and salvation, asked, "Will the flesh rise again?" Peire Garcias retorted, "The flesh will not rise again, except as a wooden post," and, rather theatrically, whacked a wooden post to underscore his point.[24] The body was nothing but a tragic reminder of the fall from heaven. It was made by the evil God; it was steeped in corruption; it was prey to the ravages of time; it was a prison of the soul. Consequently, for the *crezen*, Christ's descent from heaven, unlike the fall of the angels, never caused Him to possess flesh.[25] The same fleshlessness was also true for the Virgin Mary and the Apostle John, whom Christ, in His journey from the invisible to the visible world, had brought *in testimonium*.[26] Matrimony, as an encouragement to procreate and so to the making of more flesh, was therefore nothing but prostitution; the only true marriage was that of the soul with God.[27] Peire Garcias, adopting this austere conclusion, had not slept with his wife Ayma for two years.[28] (Ayma, by the way, originally came from Mas-Saintes-Puelles in the Lauragais.)[29] Guilhem Garcias was curious (or rather, Déodat de Rodez and Friar Imbert remembered his curiosity for him) about whether Ayma agreed with her husband's faith. "No!" snapped Peire Garcias; "she's a moron, just like you!"[30]

A few other things that Peire Garcias told his kinsman were as follows: no miracle which can be seen by the eyes is of any worth;[31] he had a "Passion, written in *roman*, as it actually occurred [*sicut fuerat in re*]";[32] John the Baptist was one of the greatest devils there ever was;[33] Christ led no one out of hell;[34] up until the time of Pope Sylvester, the Church had owned no property and had celebrated no Mass;[35] chanting in church was just singing in an unintelligible manner to deceive simple people;[36] the Roman Church was a harlot who gives out poison and the power to poison to all who believe her;[37] the Roman Church would pass away in twenty years;[38] he hated every mendicant order, except the Franciscans, but even they were worthless because they preached the crusade;[39] it was not good for crusaders to march against the emperor Frederick II, the Saracens, or a castle (that opposed the Roman Church) like Montségur;[40] his father and mother had taught him everything he believed;[41] justice should never be carried out through a death sentence;[42] and any official who judged a heretic and then put him or her to death was a murderer.[43]

Peire Garcias, when asked by Guilhem Garcias whether he really believed everything he had said in their discussions, swore on his faith that he honestly believed everything that he had said.[44] Bernart de Caux and

Jean de Saint-Pierre, however, still had to confirm the truth of all that they had been told about Peire Garcias. Consequently, the two Dominicans took short statements from two more Franciscans (Peire de Sant-Barti on Monday, 26 August, and Arnaut Daitz on Tuesday, 10 December 1247), one priest (R. Ferrières on Monday, 26 August 1247), and two laymen (Guilhem de Montoti and Bernart Prima also on Monday, 26 August 1247). These further depositions did not contradict the longer testimonies of Guilhem Cogot, Déodat de Rodez, Friar Imbert, and Guilhem Garcias.

Bernart de Caux and Jean de Saint-Pierre summoned Peire Garcias on Sunday, 2 February 1248, to come before them and to confirm or deny the charge of heresy. He did not appear, although he had been informed that he was suspected of heresy, and that the inquisitors had issued an individual summons calling him before them at Saint-Sernin. Therefore, Peire Garcias was excommunicated as a contumacious heretic.[45] That was the last anyone ever heard of him.

A final observation has to be made about Piere Garcias and the eavesdropping friars, in that the lucidity of heretical thought reported back to Bernart de Caux and Jean de Saint-Pierre may, in fact, be nothing more than the creation of four heresiologically learned mendicants trying to make sense of what they thought a *credens* had actually said, or, rather, what a heretic should have said. Perhaps, and this is the irony, Peire Garcias was less the dualist, less the theologian, less the believer in heresy than the men who interpreted, remembered, and repeated his thoughts.[46]

# 9

## THE MEMORY OF WHAT WAS HEARD

AS the men and women of the Lauragais answered the questions they were asked in the verandas of Saint-Sernin, their responses were instantaneously translated from the vernacular into Latin by the scribes and notaries employed by the friar-inquisitors. These quick translators did not use a form of shorthand, nor did they attempt to create a literal word-for-word transcription of what was said. Instead they used a form of tachygraphy: a style of rapid writing whereby the scribe quickly selected, abstracted, and translated from the testimony he was hearing those words and phrases he thought essential to the investigative needs of the friar-inquisitors.[1]

This translating also involved shifting all confessions from the first person to the third. A notable exception to this rule occurred when the scribe or notary allowed the memory of a past conversation to be recorded in its recollected first-person form.[2] One presupposition that arises from this, and which the two inquisitors never mention in their manual, is that the interrogation, the asking of the questions, must have been undertaken in the vernacular.[3] Further, there must have been a constant interplay among scribes, friar-inquisitors, inquisitorial assistants, even those testifying, in this fast reporting—as has already been revealed in the marginal comments of manuscript 609—in which quick decisions were made about what needed recording and what did not. The Lauragais testimonies, though frequently full of Occitan nouns where the scribe had no alternative Latin word immediately at his fingertips, were all translations from one language to another, from first person to third, and from the spoken word to the written.[4]

While Latin sat at the top of the medieval linguistic ladder, the vernacular languages, though not necessarily at the very bottom by the thirteenth century, dwelt in significantly lower lexical positions.[5] Now—the moral implications of this distinction aside, for the moment—the transcription and translation of testimonies into Latin by the inquisition was also immensely practical. Latin was the only language that had a fully developed method of reporting speech, the only language with simplified versions of itself, so that the spoken word, whether heard in a sermon, lecture, or courtroom, could be easily represented for *litterati* like two Dominican inquisitors.[6] In this sense, Latin was a pragmatic choice on the part of the inquisition, no different from similar choices made by other judicial tribunals, like the friar-*enquêteurs* of Louis IX and Alphonse de Poitiers, throughout thirteenth-century Europe.

A result of such hastily written Latin was that a great deal of a person's testimony was often rendered as abbreviations or in stock phrases. *Anno et die predictis Petrus Maria testis juratus dixit idem quod Johannes Fabri*: "Aforesaid year and day, Peire Maria, sworn as a witness, said the same as that of Joan Fabre."[7] These thirteen pithy Latin words were the sum total of Peire Maria's confession on Friday, 9 June 1245, before Esteve, archpriest of Laurac; *magister* Peire de Caraman; Silurus, priest of Verfeil; and Bernart de Caux. *Anno et die predictis, Johannes Fabri, testis juratus, dixit quod nunquam vidit hereticos nisi captos, nec credidit, nec adoravit, nec dedit, nec misit* were the words that made up Joan Fabre's testimony, and which, apparently, resembled what Peire Maria had said.[8] Joan Fabre's alliterative confession was, clearly, a ready-made response to a set of ready-made questions, though this time, unlike the bland scribal summary of Peire Maria's talk at Saint-Sernin, the prefabricated quality of the Latin, the safe template into which an innocent life could neatly fit, was equally convenient to those confessing (in that they could prepare themselves accordingly) and to those interrogating.

Thousands of confessions in manuscript 609 duplicate exactly, or very closely, the twenty-three words of Joan Fabre's testimony and the corresponding baker's dozen of Peire Maria. Ocasionally, as in the confession of Izarn Niger—a squire from Issel, who testified eight days before Peire Maria and Joan Fabre—a laundry list of innocence was breathlessly recited. "I never saw heretics except caught," this youthful Issel nobleman told Guilhem Pelhisson and Bernart de Caux, "nor believed, nor adored, nor gave, nor sent, nor received, nor led, nor caused to be led, nor heard the preaching of them."[9] In a wonderful reversal of such rolling declarations, Jean de Saint-Pierre himself, when questioning the Auriac widow Alazaïs (also known as Flors) den Pata on Monday, 26 June 1246, ended the interrogation with "[D]id you believe the heretics to be good men, or adore them, or give them anything, or send them anything, or receive them, or get the peace from the heretics, or from a book of theirs, or participate in the *apparellamentum* or the *consolamentum* of the heretics?" "No," was Alazaïs den Pata's deliciously dull answer after such a spiel.[10] An unresolvable aspect of this discriminating recording process, in which the answers to a series of questions were not necessarily taken down, in which numerous testimonies were drastically reduced when written on parchment leaves, and perhaps further condensed in the paper copy, is that one can never know how long an individual interrogation lasted beneath the porticoes of Saint-Sernin. The length of a testimony in manuscript 609 provides no scale, along the lines of half a folio equals half an hour, by which to measure such things.

Bernart Durant of Issel, interrogated directly after Peire Maria, short-ened his time at Saint-Sernin considerably because, instead of answering all the usual questions, he submitted a written confession to the inquisi-tion about all he had ever done with the *bons omes*, or seen anyone else ever do, or knew that anyone else had ever done. This document was presumbly in Latin and authenticated by a notary. Bernart Durant also admitted that his confession was composed in collaboration with the sometime *crezen* Pons Garrigue, who had already testified twice at Saint-Sernin in 1245, on Tuesday, 30 May, and Saturday, 16 December, and would confess again thirteen years later on Monday, 28 October 1258, to Guilhem Bernart de Dax. Bernart Durant's testimony, thought out and written in advance, was the only one offered at Saint-Sernin. Sadly, it was not copied into the two books that form manuscript 609, if indeed it was ever inserted or transcribed into the original register, so there is no way of knowing what it said or the form that it took. Nor can it be determined whether anyone ever systematically questioned Bernart Durant on the content, though the latter did emphasize, obviously in response to a question, that the document contained all that he knew, and that he believed everything in it to be true.[11] As to whether Bernart Durant might have used a local scribe or notary to write up and authenticate his testi-mony, a number of the villages in the Lauragais appear to have had resi-dent *scriptores* and *notarii publici*.[12] For example, Avignonet and Auriac each had a public notary, while Saint-Michel-de-Lanès and Baziège each had a *scriptor*.[13] There was even at Vaudreuille, near Castelnaudary, an elderly lawyer, *chausidicus*, named Raimon de Venercha.[14]

Equally important in trying to get a sense of the way in which men and women confessed at Saint-Sernin, and how these spoken testimonies differed from what was recorded on parchment, is the fact that though the "heretics" were almost always the *bons omes* and *bonas femnas* to those confessing, the scribes of the inquisition would occasionally translate these references to the "good men" and "good women" as simply *heretici*. This was unlike the situation with the Waldensians, who, as already noted, were always called, and transcribed as, the *Valdenses*. Occasionally, a per-son confessing at Saint-Sernin intentionally damned the good men and good women as heretics, as in the case of the worried mother of the Montgaillard knight Gardoz Vidal who, when her boy lay gravely wounded in a house at Toulouse, gently questioned him, "Son, it's been said to me that you gave yourself to the *bons omes*, that is, the heretics."[15] Despite the concerns of his mother, "I was never hereticated," confessed Gardoz Vidal.[16] Then there were men like Artau d'En Artigad, from Avi-gnonet, who, with Arnaut Auriol, Guilhem Pelhisson, and Bernart de Caux listening, self-consciously described the *bons omes* as "the good men who are called heretics": *boni homines qui vocantur heretici*.[17]

So, even without scribal editing, a man like Artau d'En Artigad knew what he had to say at Saint-Sernin, knew, whether he believed it or not, that the good men were *heretici* for the inquisition. How all this self-correction, this conscious relabeling a *bon ome* as a heretic, or hearing one's confession read back and recognizing that references to the *bons omes* and *bonas femnas* were sometimes reworded as *eretges*, actually affected an individual once he or she left Saint-Sernin's cloister is open to speculation. However, there can be no doubt that such a process, in its own small way, emphasized, for those still unsure, what constituted the two friar-inquisitors' vision of the world.

The necessity for men and women to verify the truth of what they had just confessed before the inquisition—or, more precisely, to confirm the truth of what a scribe had recorded of their confession, because such verification was a step in the process of legal authentication that turned a testimony into a notarized public instrument—leads to the curious problem of why an individual thought that a far-from-literal Latin version of what he or she had just said actually resembled what he or she had just said.[18] Moreover, there were numerous instances when men and women referred to older confessions they had given to other friar inquisitors, and how they remembered the truth contained in these former testimonies as also resembling what had been recorded by an inquisitorial scribe.[19] Undoubtedly, the coercive atmosphere permeating Saint-Sernin must have caused a number of individuals to hastily agree that the truth they had recently revealed out loud was indeed similiar to the truth quickly copied out on parchment, whether they really believed this or not.[20]

Nevertheless, it should never be assumed that the men and women of the Lauragais, even the most humble, would have found this problem of how one language could truthfully resemble another, let alone how words on parchment could honestly resemble a confessed life, as outside of their ordinary experience in the world. Latin was a language that all Lauragais men and women heard, looked at, and had translated to them, on a regular basis. Charters, wills, oaths, bequests, deeds, debts, accounts, contracts, letters—all acts of existence that needed notarized authentication were, more often than not, written in Latin, even if an individual could not read the language. A somewhat banal observation about the Toulousain and the Lauragais, perhaps, but one that is often forgotten because, in this sense, Latin was a vigorously alive language, in that so much depended on its ability to faithfully resemble the wishes of a dying man, the size of a house being sold, the length of a vineyard, or the freedom of a manumitted woman.[21] It also means that most people knew a smattering of Latin, or at least enough to recognize a few words, or at least enough to recognize the look and, owing to parchment, the feel of a Latin document. The work of the inquisition into heretical depravity must have enhanced all the assumptions Lauragais men and women ever had about the relationship of Latin and the vernacular. Latin was not just a language that gave legal verisimilitude to existence; it was now an explosive collection of words, abbreviations, and pen strokes that could potentially destroy a person or a community.

Soon after the massacre at Avignonet, the *miles* Bertran de Quiders sold, by his own admission, one of the assassinated Guilhem Arnaut's parchment inquisitorial registers to the *bon ome* Bertran de Maireville for eight shillings.[22] As to why this "friend of God" wanted the book, perhaps he was curious to read, or have translated for him, what the inquisition may have found out about the *bons omes* and their sympathizers, or, like so much else stolen from Avignonet that bloody night, the good man simply wanted a keepsake to remind him of how the inquisition was now destroyed and the land made free. Whatever Bertran de Maireville's reasons were, and he paid a fair price for the register, which perhaps was only a quire or two, there can be no doubt that the good man clearly understood that a book full of abbreviated Latin testimonies resembled, if to no one else except a friar-inqusitor, something very close to the truth about *bons omes*, *bonas femnas*, and *crezens* in the Lauragais. It was due to this profound idea about the similarity of a particular text to a specific life, and the possibility of Latin words' altering communal and individual existence, that inquisitorial registers were stolen or burnt. Manuscript 609 exists only because of the friar-inquisitor's fear about the theft and immolation of original parchment records.

The interesting thing here is that the good men, good women, and their believers used the New Testament, or at least the Gospel of John, only in Occitan. This text was essential during the *consolamen*, the transformation of a *crezen* into an *amic de Dieu*, because it was held over the believer's head.[23] This use of parchment or paper was one of the reasons why the friar-inquisitors were always willing to hear, and individuals ready to tell, about any books that had passed through the hands of *bons omes*, *bonas femnas*, and *crezens*. These tomes did not necessarily have to be the vaguely defined *libros hereticorum*, "books of the heretics"; any book, quire, or leaf, whether in *latin* or *roman*, no matter the content, was suspicious to the inquisition. Included were such items as the loose Latin charters, remembered by Saurimunda Peyre, that her brother-in-law, the *bon ome* Raimon Peyre, stole from her husband Bernart in 1214 after breaking open a chest to get at them.[24] Or the anonymous book written in both Latin and Occitan that the knight Arnaut de Miglos, *bayle* of Quié, felt compelled to tell Bernart de Caux about on Saturday, 15 December 1246, when the friar-inquisitor was at Pamiers.[25] By a strange irony, as hundreds swore to the truth of Latin testimonies read back to them in the vernacular, knowing full well that these confessions lived a Latin life on parchment, they nevertheless thought of Occitan outside Saint-Sernin as resembling biblical reality, gospel truth, better than Latin.

Ever since Innocent III had called upon Christians in the twenty-first canon, *Omnis utriusque*, of the Fourth Lateran Council to confess all their sins once a year to a priest, truthfully, faithfully, and not publicly but alone, confessions were meant to be uttered, to be heard, to be the result of questions asked and answers given.[26] Yet it would be wrong to see the early confessional and the early inquisition as possessing so close an affinity that medieval men and women might confuse the two procedures or imagine them to be one and the same thing.[27] For a start, the very act of immediately recording testimonies makes the friar-inquisitor different from the priest-confessor; though, it has to be admitted, an early inquisitor such as Guilhem Arnaut did not always bother to record the testimonies he heard.[28] In any case, and this is perhaps more crucial, confessing to a friar-inquisitor, or even to a friar-*enquêteur*, was probably a more common experience for someone living in southwestern Languedoc in the middle of the thirteenth century than was confession to a priest, which, since the Council of Toulouse in 1229, was meant to occur three times a year (Easter, Pentecost, and Christmas).[29]

Despite some arguments to the effect that the written word (whether in Latin or the vernacular) became inherently more "truthful" than the spoken word in the early thirteenth century, the truthfulness of the testimonies recorded in Bernart de Caux and Jean de Saint-Pierre's register, as well as the truth of a copy like manuscript 609, derived from the ability of ink on parchment to resemble the original oral confessions.[30] This symmetry was not just a necessity for two men who had to read what they could not hear; it was a necessity brought about by the wider thirteenth-century notion that a written confession was less efficacious than a spoken one. This would explain why Bernart Durant's written statement was the only one of its kind given at Saint-Sernin.[31] Guilhem Pelhisson took it for granted that a confession was not only something an individual had to say but something an inquisitor had to hear, and that an inquisitorial book was of little use unless it had truly "preserved the memory of what was heard."[32] The scribes and notaries at Saint-Sernin in their rapid recording—and here the aural connotations that go with this word are not inappropriate—endeavored to capture this orality, to snare this particular kind of confessed truth, not to replace it.

# 10

## LIES

AIMERSENT Viguier had made up her mind to tell Bernart de Caux and Jean de Saint-Pierre the truth about heresy in the village of Cambiac. In late May or early June 1245, just a few weeks before Aimersent Viguier's interrogation, some men from Cambiac took her aside for a quiet word. One of these bullies was her own husband, Guilhem Viguier, while another was the lord of Cambiac, Guilhem Sais. All of the men warned Aimersent Viguier not to say anything to the inquisitors that could harm *crezens* such as themselves. Aimersent Viguier listened to their threats, calmly stated that she no longer liked the *bons omes*, and repeated her intention to confess the truth. Guilhem Sais, exasperated by Aimersent Viguier's stubbornness, gave up on words and proceeded to stuff her inside a wine tun. Aimersent Viguier's youthful son gripped her hand. "Boy!" screamed the lord of Cambiac as he shoved Aimersent Viguier into the barrel, "do you want to help this old bag destroy us all?" Guilhem Sais, taking the lad's understandable confusion for defiance, proceeded to squeeze Viguier *junior* into the barrel as well. Aimersent Viguier and her son stayed inside the wine tun all night and were freed the next morning only after the mother paid Guilhem Sais 3 shillings and 7 pence.[1] When Bernart de Caux questioned Aimersent Viguier on Friday, 23 June 1245, straight after interrogating her husband, she was, one might say, somewhat careful with the truth, in that she denied having had any familiarity with the heretics and their believers. The only hint that she knew more than she was saying, and added almost as an afterthought to her testimony, was a throwaway line about how she and her husband had never allowed any books of the heretics to come into their house.[2]

Six months later, however, on Friday, 22 December 1245, when Bernart de Caux called Aimersent Viguier back for further questioning, she told him everything she knew about the *bons omes* and their believers in Cambiac, including not only her imprisonment in the wine barrel but also how she had once refused to let her husband bring a heretic's book into their house.[3] Indeed, later that same chilly Friday, Aimersent Viguier was interrogated two more times by Bernart de Caux (with the assistance of Guilhem Pelhisson and two other Dominicans).[4] And almost a year after her first confession, on Thursday, 21 June 1246, Aimersent Viguier returned to Saint-Sernin and told the inquisition a few more things about the *crezens* of her village—like the fact that Guilhem Sais and some other men from Cambiac (though not Guilhem Viguier) had all sworn an oath to hide from Bernart de Caux and Jean de Saint-Pierre the incriminating evidence of grain once given as a gift to a large group of heretics.[5]

Aimersent Viguier's experience at the hands of a man like Guilhem Sais, though somewhat extreme concerning the cruelty of the wine tun, was nevertheless all too common. Quite a few men and women were bullied into telling lies to the inquisitors—at least at first, as with Aimersent Viguier, until a second or third interrogation revealed the truth. Raimon Dauri from Saint-Julia, for instance, confessed during his second testimony that he had lied when he was first questioned by Bernart de Caux because he feared violent reprisals from the *crezens* of his village if he told the truth. Raimon Dauri's fear, largely induced by his sister, that something bad might happen to him if he were honest about the little he knew, and he really did only know a fragment, was serious enough for him to have also lied to Guilhem Arnaut and Friar Ferrer.[6] Peire Terren (also known as Peire de Tolosa), though confessing truthfully in his first testimony at Saint-Sernin, did admit to Bernart de Caux that he had lied to Friar Ferrer the previous year at Fanjeaux about four *crezens* he knew, two men and two women, because one of these believers had warned him, in no uncertain terms, that if he named any of them, he would "lose his head."[7] Peire Terren's new willingness to confess the truth was undoubtedly helped by the knowledge that the *crezen* who had threatened him was now safely immured in prison.[8]

Slightly more ambiguous, though still painfully explicit, were the fears of another person from Fanjeaux, Raimona Autier. She admitted hiding from Guilhem Arnaut, though not from Friar Ferrer, the fact that her mother had been made a *bona femna* just before dying. "Why?" asked Bernart de Caux. "Fear of death," replied Raimona Autier.[9] Similarly, when Fabrissa Artus heard that her sister-in-law was going to tell the friar-inquisitors the truth about heresy at Auriac, "You're dead," was her matter-of-fact epitaph upon such a plan.[10] The slight ambiguity here, despite the morbid bluntness of both women, is whether Raimona Autier and Fabrissa Artus were expressing concern about what their fellow villagers would do, or about what Guilhem Arnaut and Bernart de Caux would.

Now, a man like Arnaut Godera, intercepted by two *crezens* on the morning of his second interrogation outside Toulouse and asked to conceal what he knew about heresy at Montferrand, does not appear to have been threatened with any overt violence.[11] Similarly, Guilhem Aimeri from Cazalrenoux made no mention of physical coercion when three men wanted him to lie to Bernart de Caux and Jean de Saint-Pierre.[12] Unlike Aimersent Viguier's experience of having a group of *crezens* gang up on her, what seems to be the case with Arnaut Godera and Guilhem

Aimeri, at least at first, is that both men were being asked to participate in wider and more mutual conspiracies of silence.

Twelve villagers in Saint-Félix took just such an oath to say nothing about heresy before the inquisition at Saint-Sernin.[13] At Barelles, nine people decided not to reveal that they had once adored the good man Raimon Gros in the woods below their hamlet.[14] A number of other parishes had similar groups of men and women bound together by agreements (*pactum de non revelando heresim*) to conceal evidence that they thought would incriminate them as *credentes* (or, in some cases, as former good men and good women).[15] This determination to collectively resist the truth that the inquisition was after, to answer all or some of the friar-inquisitors' questions by deliberately lying, was frequently remembered as corrupting not just individual confessions but the testimonies that entire communities had given to earlier inquisitors.

Pons Aigra, for one, recalled on Saturday, 16 December 1245, how Guilhem Gras, the *bayle* of Montauriol, gathered all the people of this village during Lent of 1244 and gave them some friendly advice about what should be said to Friar Ferrer and the inquisition at Conques. "Beware," Guilhem Gras admonished the men and women of Montauriol, "that you say nothing bad about any of us, because if I learn that someone has, I'll get whoever did it and confiscate all their goods." The people of Montauriol were suitably impressed and told Friar Ferrer nothing about the heretics.[16] Likewise, Arnaut de Clètenx recollected on Saturday, 11 November 1245, that when the inquisitor Guilhem Arnaut was at Saint-Félix three years earlier, and was about to make inquiries into neighboring les Cassés, the lords of this village, Raimon and Bernart de Rocovila, gathered together twenty or so men, once more quite openly, and told this crowd that they should lie to the inquisition. The men of les Cassés agreed that this was a good idea, and so they lied to Guilhem Arnaut.[17] The first any friar-inquisitor knew of these communal deceptions were the testimonies of Pons Aigra and Arnaut de Clètenx before Bernart de Caux.

Certainly, there is a recognition here by the lords and *bayle* of two small villages that all it took was one (even vaguely) truthful testimony for the friar-inquisitors to suspect the guilt of not just other individuals but also entire communities. None of this local speculation about who would inform on a neighbor was helped by the friar-inquisitors' policy of never releasing the names of those who had pointedly accused others of heresy.[18] The inquisitorial argument for not revealing the identity of an accuser, first outlined by Gregory IX and then reiterated by Innocent IV, was that it would remove the danger of violent reprisals against such men and women, and so might encourage others to confess truthfully.[19] While no individuals at Saint-Sernin requested, at least formally during their interrogation, knowledge of possible accusations that had been made against them, a man questioned by the inquisition at Villalier in 1250, and a woman interrogated at Carcassonne the same year, did; moreover, these two people—Peire de Garda, from Conques, and Alazaïs Barrau, from Moussoulens—did not just want to know what had been said against them; they wanted to see these accusations in writing.[20]

In Mas-Saintes-Puelles, despite the supposed anonymity of heresy whistle-blowers, the peasant Bernart Cogota was well known among the *crezens* of his village to be a risky man in confession. Admittedly, Bernart Cogota had drawn attention to himself a few years earlier when, without even waiting to be summoned, he went off to Toulouse and testified before Guilhem Arnaut.[21] Such an open provocation, though initially ignored by the men and women of Mas-Saintes-Puelles, whether *crezens* or not, did eventually cause the *crezen* Peire Gauta to publicly denounce Bernart Cogota before one of the lords of the village, the knight Bernart de Quiders. "Bernart of Mas-Saintes-Puelles," Peire Gauta sarcastically quizzed his lord, "is it good that someone who might've betrayed you should walk alive on this earth?" Such moral severity was not lost on Bernart de Quiders, or rather the need to be seen to do something did not go unrealized, because Bernart Cogota had to immediately leave Mas-Saintes-Puelles with his family.[22]

Bernart Cogota, rather foolishly, returned to Mas-Saintes-Puelles. And if he thought his confessional tendencies had been forgotten, the new inquisitorial summons to Saint-Sernin instantly revived memories and fears about him. "Soon, it'll be obvious," the squire Jordan de Quiders insinuated to Bernart Cogota, "who'll be swiftly dispatched." This far-from-subtle threat, with its allusions to expulsion and death, seems to have been lost on the earnest (or just plain simple) Bernart Cogota, so the young nobleman spelled it out for him. "You!" exclaimed Jordan de Quiders, "who went to other inquisitors in confession!"[23]

Yet the incentive to forget the local history of a village when questioned by the friar-inquisitors, to think and act as though certain incidents had never happened, did not have to be as physically explicit as that endured by Aimersent Viguier or as verbally allusive as that suggested to Bernart Cogota. Forgetfulness, selective or total, was an obvious reaction by many, *crezens* or not, to the common fear that an individual confession had to reveal only a little bit of the communal reality for Bernart de Caux and Jean de Saint-Pierre to immediately see criminal potential. Peire de Mazerolis, the lord of Gaja-la-Selve, remembered the terrible sense of impending catastrophe that people felt in his village during 1241 after the *bon ome* Bernart dels Plas was burnt, because the good man had obviously said something before he died and so "destroyed the *vila* of Gaja-la-Selve."[24] Such fears led some men and women to attempt to stay one step ahead of the two Dominicans during the inquisition at Saint-Sernin. "I've suffered before the betrayers [*proditores*]" was how Peire Baussa described to Guilhem Padet his interrogation by Bernart de Caux and Jean de Saint-Pierre. "I had to be on my guard," he recalled; "otherwise, I might've said something about my neighbors."[25]

Peire Baussa was not a *crezen*, unlike Guilhem Padet who was, but his condemnation of the friar-inquisitors as men who betrayed what was said in confession, as men who knowingly broke the confessional seal, certainly shows a man deeply contemptuous of inquisitorial tricks of the trade. It is not apparent that Peire Baussa actually disagreed with confession as a necessity of being a good Christian, but like many people in the thirteenth century, and after, he clearly detested clerics who were betrayers of confessions. The disgust and fear that Peire Baussa felt toward the inquisitors, and so his advice about the necessity of being on your guard when questioned by them, reveal a man keenly aware of the difference between the priest-confessor and the friar-inquisitor. Peire Baussa simply knew that an inquisitor, unlike a confessor, could never be anything but a *proditor confessionum.*[26]

"Why are you so terribly frightened?" was the first thing Girauda Artus asked an obviously agitated Alazaïs d'Auri when, as arranged, both women rendezvoused at Auriac's spring. "The heretic Arnaut Garriga, imprisoned in the Château Narbonnais, converted," was Alazaïs d'Auri's cryptic answer. "Why are you frightened by this?" wondered Girauda Artus, no stranger to fear herself in the weeks leading up to the inquisition at Saint-Sernin, yet somehow not quite seeing the danger that Alazaïs d'Auri saw in Arnaut Garriga's conversion, especially as her friend had never been a *crezen*. "I saw him in the house of Giraud Artus," was Alazaïs d'Auri's reply.[27] That was it, nothing more, nothing less, except that Girauda Artus, who had been in her brother's house that day, immediately understood the other woman's fear. Alazaïs d'Auri was scared because she had seen a *bon ome* four years earlier, never reported it, and as this good man was now a Catholic, he was sure to remember her visual indiscretion to Bernart de Caux and Jean de Saint-Pierre. Alazaïs d'Auri's imagination was set racing by what a possible confession might contain. Alazaïs d'Auri envisioned her life destroyed by a misplaced glance.

Alazaïs d'Auri's misery was the despair of a woman who lived in a world of inescapable intimacy with her neighbors; she simply could not help seeing, from one day to the next, what was going on in someone else's house. The walled villages of the Lauragais, resting at the top of steep sunburnt hills, like Fanjeaux, or nestled into the sides of tame grassy slopes, like Mas-Saintes-Puelles, with all the houses radiating outward from the castle or *forcia* (fortified farm) of a local lord, and no more than a hundred meters from one end to the other, were difficult places in which to do anything unseen or unheard.[28] The ears of Arnaut Godera from Auzeville-Tolosane were testaments to this oppressive familiarity. At the beginning of his second testimony at Saint-Sernin he remembered the heretication, four years earlier in 1242, of Peireta Rei. At the time he was living at Montferrand, and his house happened to be right next door to *domo d'En Peireta*. He did not see Peireta Rei die, but he heard from within his own house, in truly astonishing detail, everything that five people, including one good man (*probus homo*), said at the deathbed.[29]

Houses in the Lauragais, and the surrounding regions, were usually constructed from local rubble, rocks, and stones, chipped into angular interlocking shapes that were deftly dry-built or held together by lime mortar.[30] Sandstone, limestone, shale, schist, and other carbonates, all relatively easy to collect in the Lauragais, were the most commonly used materials. Such sedimentary rocks, all very malleable for masons, are not, as Guilhem de Tudela pointed out, useful in war, because when Raimon VI set up a trebuchet in the autumn of 1211 outside Castelnaudary to beseige Simon de Montfort, "neither on road or path could [the crew of the catapult] find stones that didn't shatter on impact."[31] As difficult as it is to estimate the precise size of a typical Lauragais house (*domus, casal, ostal*) in the middle of the thirteenth century, such dwellings were, based on measurements recorded by Bernard Gui about similar structures in Toulouse between 1248 and 1263, probably no larger than four meters wide and twenty-one meters long.[32] Indeed, a house in Montesquieu, Auriac, or Saint-Martin-de-la-Lande was probably a great deal smaller, and easily more irregular in shape, than a humble *domus parve* of Toulouse. The height of a village house varied between one to two meters and four to five meters.[33] A little *domus* commonly had one room, *camera*, with some sort of internal partition, not unlike the stone wall that took Peire Serni, of Mas-Saintes-Puelles, three days to build inside the Laurac house of the good woman Laura in 1216.[34]

The width of an average wall, inside or out, lay somewhere between 60 and 70 centimeters, while an outside wall that contained a door, and so was built more sturdily, usually possessed a girth between 80 centimeters and just over a meter.[35] Also—remember Arnaut Godera's ears— more than one house frequently shared the same wall. All doors, almost always situated at the side of a *domus* where two walls met, opened onto streets, squares, or some other communal space. Lintels, rarely arched, were timber or stone.[36] Doorways were usually no higher, as at Cabaret, than a head-bending 150 centimeters, and though the mean was probably an uncomfortable 100, there were entrances at Calberte, a village in the Cévennes, as low as a back-aching 55 centimeters.[37] Doors themselves were made of wood or cloth or skin. It should be noted that such entrances would have required most men and women to bow, to awkwardly genuflect, every time they entered a house, because a thirteenth-century skeleton older than fifty, sex unknown, excavated at Lasbordes, a *castrum* in the middle of the Lauragais, was a good 169 centimeters tall.[38]

Windows were few, often only a meter from the ground, quite narrow (roughly 20 by 50 centimeters), uncovered, and sometimes incorporated into the space where the wall and roof met.[39] Jean de Saint-Pierre and Renaud de Chartres had to buy some fabric, worth five shillings of Cahors, to cover an exposed window, more for privacy than to keep out late summer breezes, when they were at Montauban in September 1255.[40] Floors were earthen or, at best, stone, and wooden if a house had more than one floor. Roofs, with rafters and beams of rough branches or crafted timber, generally at a sharp pitch, were covered by thatched vegetable matter, curved clay tiles, or slices of green-gray schist.[41]

The castle or farm of some village lords, by contrast, with cellars, staircases, halls, towers, little courtyards, stables, and more than one floor, could be four or five times as large as the tiny houses around them, even though these larger structures were frequently called *domus* as well.[42] Arnaut de Bonahac, a servant of the Lanta noble and *crezen* Peire de Resengas *junior,* enhanced his confession with some structural details about his lord's *domus* when, on Friday, 23 February 1246, before Bernart de Caux, he recalled that last Easter his wife Raimona de Bonahac happened, quite by chance, to peer through an opening in the de Resengas cellar and see four unknown men come out of one underground room and go into another. Arnaut de Bonahac and his wife Raimona instantly "knew in their hearts," because the de Resengas family were all *crezens,* that these men simply had to be heretics. Arnaut de Bonahac, gripped by this revelation, rushed to the *bayle* of Caraman, Peire Dellac, and reported what his wife had seen through the hole in Peire de Resengas' cellar. Peire Dellac told Arnaut de Bonahac that, after some consultation with his brother Arnaut Dellac, he would seize the four men, and "he'd give me one silver mark and all the salary that I was owed by Peire de Resengas." On Easter Saturday, 2 April 1244, Peire Dellac checked with Arnaut de Bonahac on whether the four unidentified men were still in Peire de Resengas' *domus.* "No," replied the frustrated servant, "they left the house on Good Friday."[43]

All houses in the Lauragais, large or small, must have had similar cavities and eyelets in their walls, apart from windows, and they clearly seem to have been, and were understood to be, aurally porous and optically explicit. Hundreds of testimonies at Saint-Sernin confirm this deep village transparency. The inquisition not only played upon what everyone in the Lauragais had always lived with; it now added a new intensity to this anguish through confession to a friar-inquisitor. Raimona de

Bonahac's peek into a cellar, much less offhand than her husband implied, emphasizes that no one, noble or servile, living in a large *domus* or not, could ever physically escape the burden of nearness, closeness, perpetual immediacy, that so agonized Alazaïs d'Auri.[44]

The Lauragais was (as it still is) an incredibly fertile region, with all the land under cultivation, roughly 90 percent in the thirteenth century and largely devoted to cereals (as it still is), fragmented into literally thousands of little parcels of soil, wood, marshland, garden, and mountain slope.[45] According to the *Liber Reddituum Serenissimi Domini Regis Francie*, compiled in 1272 or 1273—that is, after the county of Toulouse had been absorbed into the Kingdom of France—the hamlet of Mas-Saintes-Puelles, for instance, was surrounded by a parquet pattern of two hundred and ninety-three minuscule plots of land, fifty-two vineyards, six gardens, and two meadows.[46] The land around Saint-Martin-de-la-Lande was splintered into five hundred and eighty-eight cultivated shards of soil, sixty-seven vineyards, thirty meadows, forty-one gardens, three *ferragines* (tiny plots of land where leguminous plants were grown for fodder), and one orchard.[47] Although it is difficult to calculate the actual size of all these pieces of terrain, since the scribes of the *Liber Reddituum* never precisely state the measurements they used, one can still imagine the smallness of scale going on here by recalling that for both *castra*, Mas-Saintes-Puelles and Saint-Martin-de-la-Lande, these petty holdings extended no further than five to seven hundred meters from the village walls.[48]

The importance of all this fragmentation, and of the fact that almost every person in a village possessed one or two of these holdings, often without any service owed to someone above them, was that most men and women in the Lauragais, nobility included, very rarely owning more than a handful of these properties at any one time, were quite impoverished.[49] This impoverishment and splintering of land was, in part, caused by the custom of the Toulousain and the Lauragais, written down and formalized in 1286, whereby all the male children of a married couple were the equal heirs of any property. In practice, sometimes one son, usually the oldest, was favored, with younger children being relatively underendowed. Occasionally even the daughters or widows of bakers, gardeners, or knights were the major heirs of an estate, rather than the surviving sons. It was for this reason that so many Lauragais villages had so many coseigneurs, so many related nobles of varying degrees of wealth, so many ordinary men sharing small houses and little vineyards with brothers—in short, so many men deserving, wanting, needing, honor and respect.[50]

Also, it was as if the spatial intimacy of the Lauragais village, that inescapable sense of always being within someone else's line of sight, within another's earshot, had been transferred onto the very terrain of the Lauragais itself. No piece of land was ever large enough for an individual not to be able to see or hear what was going on in a field or vineyard next to him or her. Woods, mentioned so many times at Saint-Sernin, essentially existed at the interstices of these fields and vines, and though never very big themelves, and always separated from one another by exposed distances, they were the only physical thing, apart from the setting sun, that allowed some secrecy in the Lauragais landscape. Laurence Sterne, exaggerating only slighty, still felt the pain of these open spaces in the Lauragais and Toulousain five hundred years later when, on Saturday, 14 August 1762, he wrote to a friend in Paris that, "on the hottest day and hour of it," after a back wheel of his Paris coach had broken into ten thousand pieces on the road outside Toulouse, he was a searing "four miles from either tree or shrub which could cast a shade of the size of one of Eve's fig-leaves."[51] Indeed, as most villages in the Lauragais sat (as they still do) upon small hills, with those paltry parcels of land collected below them, a man or a woman need not even leave a village street to know what was happening in, say, a field of wheat somewhere in the middle distance. This panoramic intensity becomes even more powerful when it is also remembered that virtually every village can easily see the nearest two or three *castra*. It was no effort at all (nor is it now) to stand in the village square of Fanjeaux and pick out the bleached limestone walls of Laurac, Montréal, or Pexiora.

"I'm aware that I did evil," a contrite Arnaut Godera went on to say at the end of his second testimony at Saint-Sernin, because in his first appearance before Bernart de Caux, *in judicio constitutus*, he had lied about once believing the *bons omes* to be the "friends of God."[52] "I'm sorry and penitent," were the opening words of Sapdalina de Barelles' second confession on Sunday, 8 July 1246, eleven days after her first visit to Saint-Sernin, because she too, *in judicio constitutus*, had lied; though this time it had been to both friar-inquisitors and was not only about having once thought the good men to be *amicx de Dieu*, but, more important, she had omitted to mention the oath of secrecy that nine *crezens* (excluding herself) had taken at Barelles.[53] Such confessional regrets were voiced, with similar phrasing, by many Lauragais individuals, especially if it was, as in the cases of Arnaut Godera and Sapdalina de Barelles, their second or third visit to Saint-Sernin.[54] Interestingly, the legal formula *in judicio constitutus* did not appear in any notarized testimonies before March 1246.[55] What is so fascinating about Sapdalina de Barelles' and Arnaut Godera's small acts of contrition, and those of all the other men and women who mouthed similar apologies, is that they remind us of something all too easily forgotten, namely, that there was a ritual to telling the truth at Saint-Sernin. People were well aware, when they stepped inside the cloister, walked the sunlit verandas, took their oaths before two or more witnesses, and watched as their testimonies were quickly recorded by scribes, that they had entered a special place constituted, however briefly, to elicit the truth.

But this did not prevent four Cambiac men from attempting a blatant piece of subterfuge beneath Saint-Sernin's porticoes. According to Marti de Cesalles, formerly the priest of Auriac, in his testimony of Saturday, 25 November 1245, four *crezens*, four months earlier, had given four false names. Peire Arnaut pretended to be Peire Gitbert, Raimon Vassar renamed himself Raimon Sicart, Guilhem de Mas became Guilhem Esteve, and Peire Viguier decided upon Peire Marti. Afterward, to top it all off for Marti de Cesalles, these men had openly joked in Auriac about fooling Bernart de Caux. Not surprisingly, these fellows were called back for further questioning.[56] Marti de Cesalles also admitted, by way of verifying his information, that he knew of this chicanery only because a woman from Cambiac, one Aimersent Viguier, had told him all about it.[57]

Truth, "the conformity of meaning with things," was how the Dominican Thomas Aquinas, thinking and writing in the middle years of the thirteenth century, once characterized this slippery prize his fellow friars were attempting to grasp as inquisitors.[58] This formula neatly captures something already observed about Bernart de Caux and Jean de Saint-Pierre, and most noticeable in their questions, which is that it was only through reflecting upon the fit between thoughts and habits, meaning and things, that the friar-inquisitors would find the truth they were after. In essence, heresy in the Lauragais would be truthfully evoked in the imaginations of the friar-inquisitors because of a simple, but powerful, equation which stated that a man who had given bread to a *bona femna* must, by definition, have understood the good woman's heresy. No idea or practice was inherently innocent to the inquisition.

Lying, as a way of trying to confound inquisitorial logic, was, unless an individual expressed sorrow mixed with hard evidence, severely punished. For instance, Peire Babau, one of those nine oath-takers from Barelles, was sentenced to life imprisonment on Monday, 28 May 1246, because, as Bernart de Caux and Jean de Saint-Pierre decided, he had, among other things, "conspired to conceal heresy, and denied the truth from the other inquisitors against his sworn oath."[59] Likewise, Esclarmonte Bret from Goudourville was also condemned to life imprisonment by the two Dominicans because, along with the familiar crimes of a *credens*, she had "denied the truth to the other inquisitors, and afterward denied the truth in our presence while under oath."[60] Incidentally, Peire Babau's deception was found out thanks only to Sapdalina de Barelles' sorrowful and penitent second testimony at Saint-Sernin.

The ability to lie, let alone be honest, presupposes a conscious attempt by the men and women of the Lauragais to try to work out what the friar-inquisitors wanted when the inquisition swore them to the truth. The effort taken by *bayles*, lords, and *crezens* to keep people quiet about what they knew, and the consequent individual and communual mendacity, would appear to support this assessment. This does not mean that the truth wanted by the friar-inquisitors in any way resembled the truth perceived by a *crezen* or even a Catholic. It does mean, however, that ordinary people looked at their lives and extracted, or concealed, old doings and old chatter which they knew would be used by the friar-inquisitors to constitute a true picture of heresy in the Lauragais. Lying may be a form of resistance to a truth desired by somebody else, but for the lie to work, even to be imagined in the first place, the truth that a liar wishes to cripple must be, in some sense, understood.[61]

## NOW ARE YOU WILLING TO PUT

## THAT IN WRITING?

SIBILIA Joan and Guilhema de Tournefeuille, two married women from Montesquieu, were walking to Toulouse one day in 1230 when, all of a sudden, Guilhema de Tournefeuille tripped and fell. "Damned is the master who made this bodily thing!" she cursed, having evidently hurt herself. "Isn't it God that made it?" asked Sibilia Joan with some surprise at her friend's apparent hatred not so much of the flesh as of its Creator. "Go on!" Guilhema de Tournefeuille scoffed at Sibilia Joan's naïveté, then, rather more playfully, "[N]ow are you willing to put that in writing for me?"[1] Bernart de Caux, Guilhem Pelhisson, and Arnaut Auriol heard about Guilhema de Tournefeuille's tumble, and so her roadside malediction, from Sibilia Joan on Thursday, 23 November 1245. Despite never having listened to the preaching of the *bons omes*, so she confessed, Sibilia Joan was apparently aware of what the heretics taught, and so what a *crezen* was supposed to believe, because she now realized, with inquisition-induced hindsight, that her friend had been cursing the Devil as the *magister* who crafted bodies and so must have been, in the past if not the present, a heretical believer.[2]

Aimersent Viguier's last day as a *crezen* happened in 1223 when she was very young and very pregnant. She had been taken to Auriac by her aunt, Girauda de Cabuer, to hear two noble "good ladies," *bonas domnas*, preach in the house of the knight Guilhem Aldric and his wife na Esquiva. Aimersent Viguier, following the instructions of na Esquiva Aldric, not only genuflected three times but also, along with Guilhem Aldric, his son Guilhem, and Girauda de Cabuer, solemnly repeated, "Bless us, good ladies [*bone domine*], pray God for these sinners." Soon afterward, Raimon de Auriac and some others from the village came to Guilhem Aldric's house, and, clearly waiting for these *crezens* to arrive, the *bonas domnas* then preached a long sermon. Once this homily was over, *cortesia* was again performed through adoration, but, Aimersent Viguier painfully recalled for Bernart de Caux and Guilhem Pelisson, the "good ladies" then rudely pointed to her swollen adolescent body and, in front of everyone, declared "that I was carrying a demon in my belly." The *bonas domnas* and their noble believers all laughed at Aimersent Viguier's embarrassment.[3] Guilhem Viguier, in the days that followed this incident, constantly bullied his wife about the need to love these "good ladies," just as he and everyone else in Auriac did, but "I didn't want to love them," Aimersent Viguier stressed for Bernart de Caux and Guilhem Pelisson, "after they'd told me that I was pregnant with a demon."[4]

In a field outside Maurens known as lo bosc Donat, na Pagana Torrier came across two anonymous fellows in 1226 who, at least to this noblewoman, looked like servile peasants. "Whose men are you?" she asked with evident disdain. "We are the 'friends of God,'" they replied. "Tell me why I should destroy all my sons," na Pagana Torrier instantly spat at these *amicx de Dieu*, angered, clearly for some time, by what she thought she knew of the good men's disgust for procreation. "All your sons are demons!" was the vindictive, and equally pompous, answer of the *bons omes*, who, clearly offended by the lady's manner, did not even bother to set her straight about their beliefs. "Consequently," piqued by the heretics' response, na Pagana Torrier told the inquisition rather superciliously, "I didn't wish to listen to them."[5]

An old man from Baziège, Pons Estotz, while confessing that he first believed in the faith of the *bons omes* in 1215, managed, somehow or other, not to listen to a word the good men said, or even what anyone else might have said about them, until 1233, when, much to his surprise, he finally heard the good men say "that God did not make visible things, that the sacred Host is not the body of Christ, that baptism, like marriage, is no salvation, and that the bodies of the dead will not be resurrected." Now, despite his eighteen years as a *crezen*, Pons Estotz swore that "when I heard the heretics saying these errors, I left their faith at once."[6] Sadly, no friar-inquisitor asked Pons Estotz what he actually did believe during those years when he thought of himself as a sincere *credens*.

Certainly, most Lauragais men and women, whether ardent *crezen* or not, thought they had some understanding about what made one idea more heretical than another, whether from actually hearing the preaching of the good men, or deducing their errors from the pointed questions of the friar-inquisitors, or, as many confessed, from hearing clerics conveniently explain the beliefs of the *bons omes* and the *bonas femnas*.[7] Indeed, swearing that one knew what the heretics taught only because a priest, a monk, or even the bishop of Toulouse had described those teachings was sometimes a falsehood behind which a *crezen* hoped to hide.[8] Guilhem de Castilho, a knight from Gardouch, tried this in his first testimony on Monday, 8 May 1245.[9] Unfortunately, he was called back the next day, and, though he said his memory was a bit sketchy, he now recalled having heard the *bon ome* Guilhem de Solier give a sermon twenty-five years earlier in a house before an audience of twenty people; he finally confessed after a few more incriminating memories, "I believed in the heretics and in their faith and in their works."[10]

In any case, no person at Saint-Sernin ever discussed the ideas of the good men and good women at any length during the Lauragais inquisition, and certainly not in the way those four eavesdropping Franciscans would, a year later, rattle on about the supposed thoughts of Peire Garcias, because, as has already been pointed out, Bernart de Caux and Jean de Saint-Pierre did not ask for, or want, philosophical or theological discussions. A confession only had to acknowledge having heard heretical ideas, as well as telling where and when. It was an irrelevancy as to whether an individual had understood what he or she heard, because, and this takes us right back to the detective model derived from the friar-inquisitors' questions, determining complicity through ideas, especially when priests were publicly explaining them, would have got the two Dominicans nowhere. Indeed, the friar-inquisitors' method of understanding what constituted a person in the middle of the thirteenth century, and so what determined individual intention, was undoubtedly an attempt at overcoming this problem of how to discern the complicity and the responsibility of ordinary men and women in the heretical thoughts of the *bons omes* and *bonas femnas*. As far as Bernart de Caux and Jean de Saint-Pierre were concerned, it was being in the right place at the right time to hear that the Devil made the world, or that sex kept evil circulating on earth, rather than just knowing these errors, let alone understanding them, which led the friar-inquisitors to be suspicious about the day-to-day habits of an individual life.

"Errors?" Bernart de Caux quizzed Guilhema de Dezine, a noblewoman from Montgiscard, on Sunday, 15 July 1246. "Well," she remembered, "I heard the heretics saying that all visible things were made through the will and wish of God."[11] This was, if anything, nothing more than a statement about divine nonchalance, because, as Paul Vidal from Mas-Saintes-Puelles had already confessed to the friar-inquisitor on Sunday, 27 May 1246, it was "the Devil that made the visible world."[12] Twenty days earlier at Saint-Sernin, the young Jordan de Quiders recalled an even more blasé and distant image of divinity when he told the inquisition about once hearing the *bons omes* say "that God didn't make heaven and earth."[13] Eight days earlier again, a woman from Avignonet, na Mateuz Esteve, tied all these notions of the universality of the Devil's handiwork and the complacency of God, and so the problem of good and evil, back to what lay behind the teasing of Aimersent Viguier and the disgust of na Pagana Torrier, by telling the friar-inquisitors that the most disturbing idea she had picked up from the *bons omes* was that "a man, having done it with his wife, couldn't be saved."[14]

Similarly, Peire Alboara of Laurac, though a *crezen* for only eighteen months around 1240, recalled the good men telling him that sex with his wife was just as sinful as, and therefore no different from, sleeping with any other woman. Moreover, he even admitted accepting this notion when he first heard it.[15] Peire Guiaraut, the former *bayle* of Laurac, now living in Saint-Martin-de-la-Lande, and who was a *crezen* from 1220 to 1225, testified to once believing that "marriage is prostitution," *matrimonium est lupanar*, just as the *bons omes* had brusquely told him.[16] No Lauragais testimony approached the deliberations about marriage that Peire Garcias supposedly outlined to his Franciscan relative, but the statements that were transcribed do give a sense that sex, marriage, and so procreation were all known to be condemned by the good men and good women as sinful habits, as manifestations of the Devil's work, as practices that allowed for the continuation of evil.

"When I was ten or twelve," reflected Covinens Mairanel, with some of the above issues in mind, "my brother, Peire Coloma, who was a believer of the *bons omes*, gave me to them." The girl then lived as a *bona femna* in a house for good women at Fanjeaux. Two years passed during which she unthinkingly adored the good men and good women, as she saw others do, "but when I finally understood them," and, by implication, herself, "I didn't want to be with the heretics." So "I left the heretics' sect, took a husband, and stayed in the Catholic faith from then on, just like a good Christian," and, as she proudly ended her testimony, "I was reconciled by Saint Dominic." All this happened to Covinens Mairanel sometime around 1212.[17] Among the many insights held within this reminiscence, not the least of which is a person's acknowledgment of a profound moment of awareness in her life, is that the act of marriage appears as a clear demonstration of orthodoxy, of being a good Christian, and so a sharp denial of any heretical habits, or ideas, that may have been adopted in the past. Also, marrying so soon after she left the "house of heretics" stressed for the friar-inquisitors, and probably for herself, just how young she was when given to the *bonas femnas*, and so her inability to question, or even understand, the intentions of her brother. Similarly, the twice-married Pictavina Izarn de Alborens pointed out for her interrogators that, though her first husband Guilhem Peire de Marval was made a good man at death, "I didn't see it because I was young and didn't yet live with him."[18] Covinens Mairanel never spoke about any beliefs that went with her sojourn as a *bona femna*, and there is no reason to assume that she knew what she was meant to know as a good woman, yet it must have been obvious to her, and to other villagers at Fanjeaux, that taking a husband shattered whatever thoughts supposedly went with her life as girl *bona femna*.

Though becoming a "friend of God" always meant living a celibate existence, marriage—or sexual relations in general, for that matter—did not prevent men and women from believing in the *bons omes* and *bonas femnas*. A married life seems to have been the familiar routine for most *crezens* in the Lauragais. Further, no one confessing at Saint-Sernin admitted, as Peire Garcias apparently did, to deliberately ending all sexual relations with a spouse, even if he or she believed what the good men and good women preached about the corrupting body. Quite possibly a fervent *crezen* like Guilhem Sais' wife, Orbria, did abstain from sexual intercourse because, according to servant gossip in the noble houses of Lanta and Cambiac, she loved the good men so much, and was so deeply convinced by their warnings about marriage, that she wanted to leave her husband and become a *bona femna.* Orbria, incidentally, was the sister of Peire de Resengas *junior* of Lanta, and it was this nobleman's resentful servant Arnaut de Bonahac, and his spying wife Raimona, who informed the inquisition not only of what they saw through openings in walls but also of what they heard about the de Resengas family, especially Orbria, from two maids: Finas, the *ancilla* of Peire de Resengas' mother, na Austorga, and Jordana, *ancilla domus.*[19]

Guilhem Sais, though very much a believer in the *bons omes* and the *bonas femnas,* took a slightly more temperate attitude toward the flesh than did his wife, in that he had a concubine in Cambiac named Valencia, the wife of a certain Peire Valencii.[20] Now, whether this relationship directly arose because of Orbria Sais' chaste yearnings, regrettably, the tattletales of servants can only be taken so far. Of course, it probably helped that Guilhem Sais' elderly father Jordan also had a local concubine, Guilhema Torneria (who, coincidentally, was a friend of Valencia Valencii's).[21] Such relationships seem to have been relatively common in the Lauragais.[22] Indeed, Guilhema Companha from Mas-Saintes-Puelles, who had been the *concubina* and *amasia* (lover) of the *crezen* knight Arnaut Maiestre fourteen years earlier, unashamedly described this *miles* as her *concubinarius* to Bernart de Caux.[23] On a more modest level, the Laurac cutler Peire Fabre had a concubine at Vitbran and a wife in Cazalrenoux, both called Guilhema (unless, that is, it was actually the same woman).[24]

On Wednesday, 12 July 1245, the leper Guilhem Rigaut testified at Saint-Sernin that the *faidit* Raimon Bart had, three years earlier, hidden himself with his leprous concubine Bernarta in the *domus leprosorum* at Laurac. Moreover, because Bernarta was very ill at the time, Raimon Bart secretly led two *bons omes* into the leperhouse, and these good men, whom Guilhem Rigaut tagged as *faidits* rather than heretics, "hereticated the sick woman, although she had first received the body of our Lord."[25] And, if this were not proof enough of Raimon Bart's heretical ways, Guilhem Rigaut reported how he, his wife Raimona, his son Izarn, and another leper named Aumenzs all heard the *faidit* frequently recite the errors of the heretics, particularly how one should believe only in the New Testament.[26] The concubine Bernarta's fascinating mix of Host and heresy, with the importance of one ritual's coming before the other, does not reveal a confusion of thought within the dying leper; on the contrary, it shows a clarity of vision, in that, as both rituals were realizations of the holy, they possessed a sameness for her and so an easy compatibility. Despite this insight into Bernarta's last moments, what seems to have really annoyed Guilhem Riguat, and so formed the crux of his testimony, was that the *faidit* Raimon Bart had "lived daily in the leperhouse and wickedly dissipated all its goods against the wishes of those of us who lived there."[27]

An important observation should be made here, considering the tendency among scholars to emphasize the persecution of lepers in the Middle Ages, and that is, although leprosaria and hospitals existed in a number of Lauragais villages, Bernart de Caux and Jean de Saint-Pierre never assumed, despite a fondness for disease metaphors in their manual, that leprosy in itself was a sign marking someone out as a heretic.[28] Indeed, only one leper interrogated at Saint-Sernin was, at least in the documents that have survived, punished by the two friar-inquisitors for heresy. It was Peire Vidal, and he was only made to wear two yellow crosses, or so a marginal note in manuscript 609 tells the inquisitive reader.[29] Seventy years later, around 1321, this would not be the case, as lepers throughout the Lauragais and the Toulousain were accused of plotting the overthrow of Christendom and were viciously attacked by local municipal authorities.[30] Jacques Fournier, whose Pyrenean inquisitions happened around the same time as these fourteenth-century accusations, never doubted that leprosy and heresy went together.[31]

If, for a moment, one discounts possible disingenuousness on the part of a man like Pons Estotz, then, as with the confessions of Sibilia Joan, Aimersent Viguier, na Pagana Torrier, Paul Vidal, or Guilhem Rigaut's memory of the leper Bernarta, a curious sensation of vagueness about what the good men and good women taught, and so what a *crezen* was meant to believe, takes hold of the imagination. No systematic dualist philosophy comes through the confessed thoughts of all these men and women; rather, instead of valid generalizations, a collection of vague generalities appear to have been recorded at Saint-Sernin. Yet this in no way denies these vagaries' profound meaning to Lauragais men and women, or their influence upon individual and communal habits. Agnes de Beaupuy, a Catholic nun of Brie, secretly chose in 1242 to die a good woman, having decided in her last moments that heresy was a more truthful path to the holy than orthodoxy, or so Arnaut Benedict, the prior of Brie, had heard tell.[32] The truth of these thoughts was not lessened by their being understood as contingent, as constantly being tested in one situation after another, as coming into play only during specific instances like the mockery of a pregnant girl or a woman's falling over.

The mistake would be to assume that the men and women of the Lauragais, whether *crezens* or not, necessarily went through life with strict dualist structures shaping their minds, determining their actions, to the exclusion of all else.[33] The ideas of the *bons omes*, as far as they were understood, and the beliefs of priests or mendicants, as far as these were understood, frequently lived together, sometimes rudely, sometimes amicably, in the thoughts of Lauragais men and women. All paths to salvation were forever on trial, forever tested through daily existence, forever needing to be verified through one circumstance after another. "I didn't strongly believe the heretics to be 'good men,'" reflected na Flors dels Mas about the contingent nature of holiness in the Lauragais; "on the contrary, I thought them 'good' as frequently as I didn't."[34] It is this seeming paradox that makes the thinking of so many ordinary medieval people appear, at least to modern eyes, as often shallow, equivocal, and incoherent.

Though invisible inside a woman, the demon that dwelt in Aimersent Viguier's womb was, so the teasing of the *bonas domnas* suggested, the physical exemplification of what was so corruptible, so temporal, about the visible world. Aimersent Viguier's swollen belly, as the consequence of her prior sexual relations with Guilhem Viguier, embodied the anticipated replication of such relationships, not only by herself, by her husband, and by others, but also eventually by her child. The growth that went with pregnancy, the passing of time revealed by a woman's body, was also the anticipation of decay. Interestingly, this meant that for the good women a fetus was not corporeally continuous with the mother, in that the unborn child already possessed individual social and moral relations in the world, all of them as yet unfulfilled in the future, but nevertheless still existing. An unborn child was already burdened with that oppressiveness which men and women thought, felt, heard, and saw as the terrible quality by which mundane existence was defined in the Lauragais village. Baptism could never reverse such a burden; it was, if anything, simply a damp confirmation of the demonic creative process that a mother's pregnancy had already advertised.

If understood this way, the beliefs of the *amicx de Dieu*, in and of themselves, did not cause the "friends of God" to detest women; rather, it was the resemblance of that specific aspect of the feminine, namely, pregnancy, to the perpetual cycles of life and death, to the rhythms that only demons tapped out, which made the youthful Aimersent Viguier exemplify everything the good men and good women hated.[35] The lives that men, women, and children lived—where all things were forever the consequence of other people's cumulative dealings, where everything had anticipated outcomes—were lives defined by constant movement and creation; in other words, terrestrial existence was shaped by an energetic Devil rather than a nonchalant God.

It was for this reason that the good men and good women would not eat meat, eggs, or any other food they thought derived from sexual intercourse.[36] These particular foods were all exemplifications of what, for instance, a *bona femna* or a *bon ome* would have recognized in Aimersent Viguier's pregnancy. Vegetables, grain, and fish, however, were acceptable, because, even though God did not make them grow or spawn, they were perceived as asexual, and so, to paraphrase what Sabdalina de Goudourville heard the *bons omes* say about flowers and wheat, they came into existence all by themselves, visible things as the result of no prior relationships.[37] Olive oil, bread, chestnuts, or salmon, unlike cheese, meat, poultry, or eggs, lacked, so to speak, any connection to past, present, or future. In this sense, the faith of the "friends of God" was not at all nature-oriented; the good men and good women saw nothing but evil, the flow of time through growth and decay, when they looked out upon the landscape. The awful anxiety that shaped so much of village life, that sense of always being swamped by time, sight, and sound, was, quite clearly, reflected, reiterated, and reinforced in the growing, the rushing, and the decomposition of woods, streams, flowers, and animals.[38]

Na Mateuz Esteve, complicating this picture slightly, did remember once sending "bread, wine, meat, and other foods" to Alamant de Roaix, after the Peace of Meaux-Paris, when this man was condemned for heresy; though, in this particular instance, na Mateuz Esteve was quite careful in her words, because she never called Alamant de Roaix a *bon ome* or an *eretge*, only someone accused of heresy, and so a man who could eat meat.[39] Moreover, the intriguing thing about the fact that the holiness of the *bons omes* and *bonas femnas* was so accountable through what they ate, or rather what they chose not to eat, was that such dietary restrictions did not seem to make them look any different to other men and women in the Lauragais. No one at Saint-Sernin confessed to knowing a heretic when he or she smelt the odor of a rigid diet, or saw a person's flesh, in the way that so many other people throughout the thirteenth century sensed divinity in the fasting bodies of other more orthodox religious women and men.[40] Bertran de Quiders, for example, had no idea that a certain Raimon Hymbert, from Moissac, whom he met in Lombardy around 1242, was a good man until they actually sat down to eat.[41]

This power that specific foods had, through their entrenchment of particular habits, the remarkable ability of chestnuts and grapes to keep holiness permanently humming in the very being of a good man or a good woman, also meant that particular foods could destroy the holy. Thus men like Bernart de Quiders and his brother Guilhem Palazis, the prior of Mas-Saintes-Puelles, tried to stop their mother, Garzen, and sister, Galharta, from being heretics by force-feeding them meat around 1233 or 1235. It worked for a short time, as it should, but these women chose to become *bonas femnas* again—though not for long, as they were burnt soon after.[42]

All these implications from a woman's tumble on a road outside Toulouse, the derision of a pregnant girl, a leper's concubine, or the eating of an egg, while certainly intimations of a tendency toward dualism, are much more clearly those of a culture in which individual lives were so tightly wrapped within communal relationships that to be *bons omes* or *bonas femnas* was to simply escape from such oppressive intimacy. Holiness in such a world was, in a very generalized way, the ability of men or women to divorce themselves from such particular and collective relations as exemplified in food or sex, to become, in short, as socially blasé about the rhythms of a Lauragais village as God was about the tempo of the universe.

# 12

## BEFORE THE CRUSADERS CAME

ONE DAY, sometime in 1242, Amielh Bernart *junior*, a schoolboy from Mireval, happened to be wandering down the street in front of the hospital at Laurac when he heard two tramps debating, good-humoredly if somewhat crudely, about the Eucharist. "It's just as good to have communion with the leaves of a tree, or an ass turd, as through the body of Christ," declared one of these vagabond-theologians, "as long as it's made in good faith." The other tramp, so the *scolaris* told both friar-inquisitors, vehemently disagreed. Amielh Bernart then embellished his picaresque evidence by saying how Peire Aldalbert, another lad from Mireval, had told him that Joan Aldalbert, Peire's father, took communion with a certain leaf of a plant each sunset or during an eclipse. Amielh Bernart, as if to emphasize the truth of all he had said, stressed that he had narrated the vagabonds' banter to three other Mireval *scolares* in exactly the same way as he was now recalling it before the inquisition at Saint-Sernin.[1] These vivid and slightly overdone memories, at once showy and uncertain, were those of a boy not much older than fourteen desperately searching his brief past for information he assumed an inquisitor would want to hear. The problem for the schoolboy, and so a sign of his adolescence, was that he had never knowingly seen a heretic. Consequently, the memory of two disputing tramps was the best Amielh Bernart could do in response to the friar-inquisitors' questions.

Forty years earlier, around 1208, two learned heretics had disputed the nature of holiness in Laurac's public square (*platea, plasa*) before all the people of the village. One of the debaters was Izarn de Castres, a deacon of the *bons omes*, while the other, interestingly, was the Waldensian Bernart Prima. The notary Pons Ameli *senex* had been in the audience as a young man visiting from Mireval, and now, as an old man interrogated at Saint-Sernin, he cast his mind back and told Bernart de Caux and Guilhem Pelhisson about this ancient debate.[2] Pons Ameli spoke of a lost world where *bons omes* freely preached and, before audiences of Catholics, *crezens*, and even Waldensians, loudly debated the problem of how to live a holy life. The teenage Amielh Bernart, by contrast, though still living in a culture where even beggars noisily wrangled about individual faith, was simply too young to have ever heard the good men publicly preach.

The elderly Michel Verger of Avignonet complemented Pons Ameli's memories with another fragment of local history. In 1221, Michel Verger recollected for Bernart de Caux, Arnaut Auriol, and Guassias, priest of Roquecézière, that when "the Waldensians persecuted the heretics" living at Avignonet, "and I frequently gave alms to these Waldensians," it was "because the Church then supported the Waldensians." Not quite the odd statement it sounds, as Guilhem de Puylaurens in his *chronica*, composed less than a decade after the inquisition at Saint-Sernin, lamented that ignorant Lauragais priests had once allowed the Waldensians of Lyon to publicly preach against the "Manichaeans."[3] Michel Verger went on to justify his past affection for the followers of Valdés by describing churches full of Waldensians and Catholic clerics singing and reading together.[4]

"At Montmaur, Mirepoix, Laurac, and many other places throughout the land, I saw heretics not only dwelling openly, just like other men, but also openly preaching," said the very old Guilhem de la Gras, also from Avignonet, as he remembered his childhood fifty years earlier in 1195. "And truly," the aged noble continued, "nearly all men throughout the land would gather together and go hear, and adore, the heretics."[5] Twenty years later, in 1215, it was not unusual to see heretics publicly disputing with clerics throughout Toulouse, or so Girauda Faber from Renneville recalled.[6] Similarily, a monk named Peire remembered arguing about the resurrection of the flesh with two heretics in the square of Vitrac in 1220 (and, three years later, he also spotted two heretics in the *platea publica* in front of his mill at Auriac).[7] In 1228 at Lagarde, according to Guilhem de Rival, not only did the *bon ome* Guilhem de Solier loudly preach in the *plasa* of Lagarde, but his sermon provoked a great dispute between Catholics and *crezens* in the village.[8] That same year, so Pons Faber de Paugberta remembered, two *bons omes* also preached in Avignonet's square, and, once more, everyone from the village gathered to listen, though unlike nearby Lagarde, the community was not torn by violent argument.[9] Almost every testimony given at Saint-Sernin by a man or a woman older than twenty recollected much the same thing about these years. After this time, however, no good men were seen or heard giving sermons, or engaging in open debate, in the squares and streets of the Lauragais.

The preaching of the *bon omes* within the houses of *crezens* to relatively large audiences of believers and doubters alike, just as common in the first decades of the thirteenth century as sermons *en plein air*, and frequently remembered at Saint-Sernin, also seems to have faded from the predictable routine of Lauragais village life around 1230. In this year at Mas-Saintes-Puelles, for instance, more than forty people assembled in the house of the knight Peire Cap-de-Porc and listened to the preaching of two good men.[10] Ten years earlier, the knight Guilhem de Castilho was one of over twenty men and women who had crowded into his mother's house at Gardouch to hear a sermon from the *bon ome* Guilhem de Solier.[11] While around 1232, in the house of the *miles* Arnaut Caldeira at Labécède, at least eleven people (most of them knights) gathered to hear two good men preach. This particular sermon, Guilhem de Castilho remembered, consisted largely of an exegesis upon a passage that the two *bons omes* had first read from a book.[12] In the knight Peire de Sant-Michel's memory of this gathering of heretics and their believers at Labécède, which he swore happened in 1235, some interesting details were also added, in that "not only did the heretics explain the Passion of Christ, but Guilhem Raimon, notary of Labécède, read the Passion."[13] The local notary, known as a man who turned spoken words into written documents, and vice versa, perhaps gave a touch of authentication to an Occitan *liber hereticorum*. Less likely, though still a possibility, Guilhem Raimon was actually extemporizing a vernacular translation from a Latin book.

Peire Symon of Castelnaudary, testifying on Monday, 7 May 1246, about the financial and moral dealings of his brother Guilhem Symon thirty-seven years earlier, recalled how "the abbot of Saint-Papoul placed a certain Bible with him as a pledge for 100 Toulousain shillings," but then "Guilhem was made a heretic and," moving to Laurac, "Guilhem took the Bible with him."[14] Guilhem Symon as a new good man, and clearly somewhat literate in Occitan and Latin, now possessed and undoubtedly read the abbot of Saint-Papoul's Latin Bible—even if such a book was held only on extended loan, did not evoke biblical reality as well as *roman*, and happened to contain the useless laws of Moses. The abbot of Saint-Papoul, though, wanted the Bible back—it must have been quite magnificient, after all—and knowing that Guilhem Symon had moved to Laurac, came up with the money and then harassed Peire Symon to go and get it. Peire Symon, accordingly, went to Laurac, and, what is so surprising, not only had Guilhem Symon not sold the pledge, which suggests that he did not think of the book as simply a useful pile of parchment to sell, but the *bon ome* instantly returned the Bible once the debt was paid.[15] Guilhem Symon may have become a good man, but this did not break his contract with the abbot, and, importantly, neither did the abbot consider the contract broken even though his moneylender was transformed into a heretic. Lastly, Peire Symon's family, and so the man himself, must have seemed deeply heretical to the two friar-inquisitors, as both his deceased mother and sister, though never good women, had been Waldensians.[16]

Raimon Bru, a man of decidedly argumentative tendencies, ended his testimony before Bernart de Caux with the recollection of a debate he,

Esteve de Boscenac, and the priest Guilhem Peire had with two *bons omes* and eleven *crezens* in a house at Avignonet in 1235.[17] Twenty-four years before this quarrel, and the memory that opened Raimon Bru's confession, this contentious Catholic recalled disputing about personal faith with some *bons omes* and *bonas femnas* in a "house of heretics" that then existed in his village. In that distant year, he also remembered arguing about Mosaic law with some good men and an acquaintance who, though not an ardent *crezen*, favored the side of the heretics.[18] A woman from Mas-Saintes-Puelles, Pitrella Petrona, testifying before her own village priest at Saint-Sernin rather than one of the friar-inquisitors, confessed that her son Arnaut had been fond of disputing with the good men and their believers when he was a youth. Yet, unlike the disputes of Raimon Bru, which seem to have been governed by a certain debating etiquette, the heated disputations of Arnaut Petrona had, at least for his mother, a very dangerous edge to them. In 1221, so Pitrella Petrona remembered, she had to extract Arnaut from what must have been a rather vicious argument he was having with a large group of *bons omes, bonas femnas,* and *crezens,* because she feared that her son might be killed.[19]

There is very little evidence of the good women preaching, or participating in disputes, in the Lauragais. In the two hundred and one days of questioning at Saint-Sernin, among the three hundred and eighteen *bonas femnas* that Bernart de Caux and Jean de Saint-Pierre heard (and read) about, only eleven were remembered as preaching.[20] Moreover, whether it was a sermon given as long ago as 1205 at Castelnaudary, as the elderly Dulcia Faber testified, or as recently as 1242 at Laurac, so the young Guilhema Garrona confessed, not a single oration by a good woman was preached out in the open; rather, they were all given before small audiences, mostly consisting of other women, often only noble women, in *domus hereticorum* or in the houses of *crezens.*[21]

"Indeed," observed the cobbler Arnaut Picoc as his thoughts went back thirty years to what Montesquieu was like in 1215, "there were six houses in the village [*vila*], both for male heretics as for female heretics, existing quite publicly."[22] The noble Bernart Mir (also surnamed Arezat) counted, in his mind's eye, ten houses for heretics at Saint-Martin-de-la-Lande in the same year. "And I saw," he added, still confessing what he had known and seen as a ten-year-old boy, "that most of the men of the village [*castrum*] would go to the preaching of the heretics."[23] Bernarta Verziana, when eight years old, lived for all of 1206 with her aunt at a house for *bonas femnas* in Villeneuve-la-Comptal.[24] The twice-widowed Maurina de Bosquet testified that at the age of seven she also stayed with an aunt, Carcassona Martina, though only from Lent to August 1210, in a "house of female heretics," at the village of Cabaret. "I saw heretics openly staying at Cabaret," she remembered, "openly coming and going through the streets."[25]

Significantly, Maurina de Bosquet dated all her memories for Bernart de Caux not just by adding up the decades, or noting how young she was at the time, but also by saying that everything she recalled from those early years had happened *in primo adventu crucesignatorum*, "when the crusaders first came."[26] By contrast, the young Sibilia Joan from Montesquieu, likewise confessing that she had seen heretics living quite openly *in domibus propriis hereticorum*, would date her testimony as *ante pacem*, that is, before the Peace of Paris-Meaux in 1229, when the crusade officially ended[27]—or, as Bernart de Quiders put it, when "the count [of Toulouse, Raimon VII] made peace with the Church."[28] Sibilia Joan, though not even born when the crusaders first invaded Languedoc in 1208, still placed her confession within what must have been a commonly understood time line of the war. So, while it may be true that the *bonas femnas* did not publicly preach or dispute, that they freely existed in their own houses and wandered through Lauragais villages in full view was nevertheless common knowledge before—and, it even seems, during—the Albigensian Crusade.[29]

*Ante adventum crucesignatorum* was written, with occasional variations like Maurina de Bosquet's, over and over again by the scribes at Saint-Sernin.[30] The Albigensian Crusade was the one inescapable event through which thousands of Lauragais men and women had lived, and through which they now sorted and cataloged their memories of the past. Yet when a person's reflections did touch upon the war, the coming of the crusaders and the Peace of Paris-Meaux were almost the only events mentioned. Twenty-one years of cruel and sporadic warfare were largely skipped, with only the beginning and the end of the conflict utilized as the temporal reference points around which a man or a woman might plot an individual testimony. So, while the crusade functioned as a way of keeping time within confessions, and perhaps within a person's life outside Saint-Sernin, the inquisitorial scribes recorded very few actual memories of the war. Admittedly, Peire Maurelli from Gaja-la-Selve did date a gift of wheat he once gave to some good men as happening at some otherwise unspecified moment during "the time of the count's war," and Alazaïs de Cales from the same village did confess that she had adored some *bons omes* when Carcassonne was besieged in August 1209, but, for all intents and purposes, the violence of the Albigensian Crusade was rarely mentioned in the verandas of Saint-Sernin.[31]

Then again, Bernart de Caux and Jean de Saint-Pierre never asked about the war. The crusade did not interest them, one way or the other, unless it related very specifically to their investigations into heresy.[32] Consequently, the noble Peire Guilhem de Rocovila's treacherous wartime reminiscence of how, during Simon de Montfort's seige of Toulouse in 1218, he had captured three foot soldiers whom he knew to be *faiditi de Tholosa* like himself—that is to say, men who were not crusaders, and whom, after two nights of imprisonment, he brazenly sold back to the citizens of Toulouse—was a memory that really had very little to do with the war itself. Instead, it was a narrative that had everything to do with how one of the foot soldiers went on to become a *bon ome*, or so it was rumored, and how the friend who had helped capture the three *faidits* went on to participate, twenty-four years later, in the murders of Guilhem Arnaut and Esteve de Saint-Thibéry.[33]

Peire Guilhem de Rocovila's roundabout way of answering the friar-inquisitors' questions on Thursday, 1 March 1246, and why he felt it necessary to travel back three decades as part of his response, was a deliberate exercise in trying to splinter those specific continuities that he knew an inquisitor would impose upon a man who had once come into contact with a soldier fated to be a heretic and a friend destined to be an assassin. As everything was implicated in everything else to the friar-inquisitors, their style of questioning assumed as much, it was the sequence of individual actions, and so times of transition like the Albigensian Crusade, that mattered to Peire Guilhem de Rocovila. The connections that this knight had with heresy and with the deaths at Avignonet were coincidences buried in his past, given value only through hindsight, and so unrelated to the here and now, except, ironically, as memories prompted by the inquisition. Peire Guilhem de Rocovila (*qui vocatur Tres Eminas*, so the scribe wrote after his name) was not denying his petty treachery during the crusade—he acknowledged this continuity about himself; indeed he probably thought it made him look good before the inquisition—but he used the war as a form of temporal shorthand, as thousands of others did, to emphasize that the history of the Lauragais, for communities and for individuals alike, had a distinct before and after, a clear break in time, and that all inquisitorial judgments about a person's moral virtue had to take this into account.[34]

Peire Guilhem de Rocovila, despite these arguments about how his life should be interpreted and judged, was sentenced by Bernart de Caux and Jean de Saint-Pierre to perpetual imprisonment on Monday, 28 May 1246.[35] The troubadour Guilhem de Tudela would, no doubt, have been pleased with Peire Guilhem de Rocovila's punishment because, when Simon de Montfort captured les Cassés in the summer of 1211, ninety-four heretics, "fools and traitors," were apparently discovered in a tower, having been "hidden away there by their friends the de Rocovilas," that is, Peire Guilhem Rocovila's brothers Raimon and Bernart, the lords of les Cassés. The de Rocovilas did this, the *trobador* stressed, "in spite of their *senhor*," the count of Toulouse, Raimon VI. "I was told all this," as a matter of interest, Guilhem de Tudela sang, "by my lord Izarn, archdeacon of the whole Vieilmorez and all that land."[36]

Similarly, confessing that one had only crossed paths with the good men and women "when the heretics were dwelling openly thoughout the terrain of the Lauragais," as Bernart Mir Arezat put it in his second testimony at Saint-Sernin,[37] was a plea of innocence based upon the argument that even though a person might have numerous memories of good men and good women from this time, he or she should not be punished, despite such recollections, for what had once been unavoidable. "I never saw the heretics except in public," was Bernart Mir Arezat's simple reassertion of this thesis at the end of both his confessions.[38] The blameless past, that time when heretics walked and talked in public spaces, was characterized in most testimonies at Saint-Sernin as an experience so obviously collective, so clearly lived without any awareness of future implications, especially if one were only a child, that no specific action could, or should, be pinpointed as making one person more guilty than another. Despite all this, and it does seem to have had some effect upon the friar-inquisitors, a man like Bernart Mir Arezat was still punished, albeit relatively leniently, by Bernart de Caux and Jean de Saint-Pierre with the penance of wearing two yellow crosses.[39]

"And, because they were cobblers," Arnaut Picoc began his explanation of how and why he knew the Montesquieu *bons omes* Pons de Grazac and Arnaut Cabosz in 1215, "they had a workshop there," that is, in the village, "and so they labored there publicly, and all the men and women of the *vila* went and bought there publicly." Now, Arnaut Picoc offered what he thought was a reasonable argument to the inquisition: "[B]ecause I was a cobbler, I was employed with them, and so I worked with, and was accustomed to, these heretics." Arnaut Picoc swore that he never adored Pons de Grazac and Arnaut Cabosz or heard them preach or believed his fellow cobblers to be *amicx de Dieu*. "Did you hear them saying errors?" Bernart de Caux still had to ask of a man who had made shoes in the same workshop as two heretics. "I did hear them saying," Arnaut Picoc remembered all these years later, "that nothing about that which God had created will corrupt or pass away."[40]

Even Guilhem Sais, the persecutor of Aimersent Viguier, tried in his first confession at Saint-Sernin on Sunday, 23 July 1245, to mask his guilt by admitting that in 1220 "during the time of the war" he saw three heretics openly staying on his father's fortified farm (*forcia*), but he never saw anyone adore them or go to their sermons.[41] Moreover, "I never believed the heretics to be good men or heard their errors," he lied.[42] Five months later during his second interrogation on Sunday, 10 December, he reiterated that the only heretics whom he knew by name were the three men from his last confession, now identifiable as his *homines proprii*, and, attempting once more to emphasize the inevitability of this acquaintance, he stated how these three peasant *bons omes* from Auriac all "dwelt publicly in their own houses."[43] That same year, 1220, so Guilhem Sais now recalled, he happened to visit ten villages in the Lauragais where, of course, he could not help but see many heretics living publicly. After this date, "I neither saw nor believed the heretics," he lied again.[44] Regrettably, the punishment that Guilhem Sais undoubtedly received is lost, though his father—Jordan Sais, the old lord of Cambiac—was, like Bernart Mir Arezat, given the penance of yellow crosses.[45]

An interesting speculation that arises from all this, especially as the modern historical image of the *bons omes* and *bonas femnas* essentially comes (or should come) from the early inquisition, is that the extensive familiarity of the good men and the good women among the people of the Lauragais, though undeniable, was perhaps sometimes enhanced by individual confessions at Saint-Sernin, and elsewhere, by those who wished to demonstrate the inescapable nature of heresy in Languedoc before the crusaders came. The more widespread heretical behavior was in the past, the less guilty an individual who had lived through those decades should be in the present—or, more precisely, in the presence of a friar-inquisitor.

"Otherwise, I never saw the heretics again," stated Peire Gairaut de Sant-Esteve, from Cazalrenoux, after he admitted seeing two unknown *bons omes* in 1240 in the woods near his village, "aside from those captured."[46] This assertion, this alibi, was the ubiquitous catchphrase repeated at Saint-Sernin by thousands of men and women when they described their encounters with the good men and good women after 1230. Raimon Garrig of Mas-Saintes-Puelles, for example, succinctly defended himself by saying that he had seen only heretics "seized or in public."[47] Then there were people like Bernarta Durant, a young married woman, not much older than the boy Amielh Bernart, who had lived her whole life in Mas-Saintes-Puelles, never once having seen a heretic, let alone, she felt compelled to point out, a captured one.[48] "I've never seen the heretics," a very young lad named Uc from Montesquieu eagerly confessed, "either caught or," he morbidly added, "burnt."[49]

Equally common in memories no older than a decade was the admission that when a heretic was seen unfettered, or heard preaching, or observed undertaking some holy function, this had occurred in a wood, a vineyard, an isolated field, or some other secret (it was hoped) place, and, more often than not, at night.[50] As to what caused this transformation of a highly visible, and for many unavoidable, way of living into a clandestine sect, and how this secrecy manifested itself through nighttime trysts in woods and vineyards, will have to wait for now, yet enough has been said to reveal why Amielh Bernart's search for something to say turned up only the rather childish memory of the two vagabond-theologians. The villages of the Lauragais—outside of the occasional sermons delivered by Dominicans or Franciscans, which in January 1247 Raimon VII commanded that every person had to attend[51]—seem to have become by 1230, as far as public preaching and debates about faith were concerned, if not totally silent, then places somewhat wary of open disputation.

This need for conversational wariness, on the part of heretic and skeptic alike, is demonstrated by the doubts, and subsequent deductions, of a knight from Montferrand, Pons de Soricinio, when two anonymous men started disputing with, of all people, the querulous Raimon Bru in an Avignonet house in 1235. Immediately, "I knew them to be heretics," Pons de Soricinio proudly told Bernart de Caux. This revelation came about not because of what the two strangers actually said—Pons de Soricinio had no recollection of any doctrinal errors—but owing to the fact that they were arguing so passionately with a Catholic like Raimon Bru.[52] A willingness to openly dispute, once a Lauragais commonplace, especially before the crusaders came, had become, at least for those with the inquisition in mind, a telltale sign that an individual, unknown but opinionated, was clearly one of the good men.

# 13

## WORDS AND NODS

QUITE FREQUENTLY, when Lauragais men, women, and children, whether they were *crezens* or not, met a *bon ome* or *bona femna* in the street, a house, the woods, in the morning, late at night, on the way out of a door, before a *consolamen*, after an *aparelhamen*, basically, in any situation involving a "friend of God," the first and last words to be uttered were "Bless us, good men [or good women], pray God for us."[1] A person, while reciting this polite prayer, lowered his or her head, and, bending at the knees, genuflected three times.[2] Sometimes individuals said only *benezion*, "bless us," as they bowed, with the good men and good women replying, "God bless you."[3] Another variation, which Esteve Rozenge remembered reciting before some Mas-Saintes-Puelles *bons omes* in 1227, had the introductory blessing followed by "Lords, pray God for this sinner, that it might make me a good Christian and may lead me to a good end."[4] The friar-inquisitors classified all this pious *cortesia* as heretical "adoration," *adoratio*. In many Lauragais villages, though not all, these benedictions were known as *melhoramen* (and transcribed *melioramentum* at Saint-Sernin). Each testimony at Saint-Sernin recounted, acknowledged, or denied these courtesies. Bernart de Caux and Jean de Saint-Pierre accumulated confessed acts of adoration, as they formalized these relationships, because such evidence allowed them to imagine, to reconstruct, the civilities that went into, and helped shape, the habitual relations among good men, good women, *crezens*, and everyone else in the Lauragais.

Ermengart Boer, an elderly Mas-Saintes-Puelles matron, was made a *bona molher* when a child in 1205 by the *bon ome* Izarn de Castres. She lived, like all other girls made into good women in these years, in a *domus hereticorum*, and, despite Dominic Guzman's removing her from this house, as well her eventual marriage to Peire Boer, she seems to have kept her faith in the *bonas molhers* all her life, constantly believing the "female heretics to be good women [*bonas mulieres*], and that, through them, I'd have salvation."[5] As a girl, in "any one week, I adored the female heretics in three or more exchanges," and, though she tallied up her regular benedictions for the inquisition, Ermengart Boer never described where or when this recurrent politeness took place.[6] Still, Ermengart Boer's interrogators, the prior of Mas-Saintes-Puelles and the chaplain of Verfeil, thought she knew more than she was saying, and so one of them helpfully scribbled in the margin next to her testimony, "She's suspected and could say a lot," for when Bernart de Caux and Jean de Saint-Pierre had time to read and reflect upon this guarded confession.[7]

Esteve de Vilanova, around 1231, allowed the *bons omes* Raimon Sans and Guilhem Quideira into his house at Avignonet on two separate occasions. During each of these brief visits, he also allowed a handful of local *crezens* to come into his house and talk with these good men. Yet, even amid such a gathering of believers, no one ever adored the *bons omes* in the de Vilanova *domus*. "Nevertheless," recalled Esteve de Vilanova, "I adored the heretics when they first entered my house."[8] As to why only adoration at the threshold of his *domus*, Esteve de Vilanova offered no further explanation to the friar-inquisitors, though he did confess to leading Raimon Sans and Guilhem Quideira from his own house to Blanca de Quiders' for the transformation of her sick son Bertran into a "friend of God." Despite the atmosphere of an ill man about to give himself to the good men, no one adored the *bons omes* within the de Quiders' house. Bertran de Quiders, in any event, was not made a good man, and so, still acting as a guide, Esteve de Vilanova kindly led the *bons omes* to the Avignonet house of Peire Quideira. As he left this *domus*, "I adored the heretics," he confessed. All of this is made even more intriguing because Esteve de Vilanova ended his testimony at Saint-Sernin with the rather unambiguous "I never believed the heretics to be good men, to have good faith, to be truthful, or to be the friends of God."[9]

Similarly, Raimon Capel, while denying having any faith in the heretics, conceded to having once adored two nameless *bons omes* in a field near Fanjeaux in 1234. "Still," this benediction was flawed, and so not truly heretical in Raimon Capel's view, because "I didn't say 'bless us.' "[10] He even divulged having met two more *bons omes*, whom he also did not know to be heretics at first, three years later during a nighttime stroll outside Fanjeaux. In this instance, however, there was no act of adoration.[11] "Why didn't you tell me about the aforesaid heretics?" questioned Fanjeaux's priest Raimon at Saint-Sernin, as neither friar-inquisitor participated in this interrogation. "Fear," pleaded Raimon Capel.[12]

Marti de Verazelh, another man who never thought the heretics were good men, nevertheless adored two nameless *bons omes* in the Saint-Martin-de-la-Lande house of his nephew Guilhem Faure in 1241. In the house were Guilhem Faure, whose grave illness was the reason for the visit of the *bons omes*, and seven other people, mostly relatives.[13] "And everyone there adored the heretics, genuflecting three times, saying 'bless us,' " Marti de Verazelh reported, "except me, who didn't bend the knee." Yet the overwhelming need to be seen to be polite, whether a *crezen* or not, was such that, as Marti de Verazelh confessed, "[N]evertheless, I did incline my head."[14] This concession to the etiquette of others bothered him so much, because he knew that even this small gesture of respect would be seen as compromising to a friar-inquisitor, that he lied about it to an earlier inquisition.[15]

Guilhem de Rival also confessed to having once given the *bon ome* Guilhem Ricart a respectful nod in the Bos Gontron woods near Lagarde in 1241. The interesting thing about this clandestine incident is that Guilhem Rival recalled three Avignonet men—Pons Faure, Peire Brun, and the public notary Michel—ardently disputing with Guilhem Ricart one moment and then adoring the *bon ome* the next.[16] Likewise, even though the sometime *crezen* Pons Estotz may have argued with the good man Raimon Imbert and his companion in a house near Saint-Sernin's cloister in 1216, this wrangling did not necessarily preclude his being civil toward the *bons omes*, because, as he had to admit, "I can't recollect whether I adored them there or not."[17]

Guilhema Esteve from Pexiora, though a *crezen* for only a month in 1226, nevertheless testified before the inquisition to routinely adoring the good men and good women throughout her life.[18] As recently as 1244, only a year and half before her interrogation at Saint-Sernin, she happened to be in a house at Pexiora where she could hear and speak with, but not see, two anonymous heretics. Guilhema Esteve's habitual politeness to the *bons omes* meant that not only did she give these two invisible heretics a loaf of bread, but, along with her friend Gualharda Pagesa, she inclined her head toward the wall hiding the *bons omes* and said, "[B]less us." Now, so that the friar-inquisitors would have no doubts about Guilhema Esteve's actions when they read her confession— because a woman's asking two unseen heretics for a blessing was, even for Bernart de Caux and Jean de Saint-Pierre, a little odd—she conveniently noted that her actions were clearly performed "with the intention of adoration."[19] The rather shy manners of the *bons omes*, their apparent need for secrecy and anonymity, especially before a woman who, though courteous, had not been a *crezen* for many years, is quite understandable in the middle of the thirteenth century. Guilhema Esteve's behavior, however, is rather more surprising in its perpetuation of an etiquette that was now patently dangerous following the Peace of Paris-Meaux and the coming of the friar-inquisitors.

Esteve de Vilanova's acts of adoration seem to be ordinary expressions of village politeness, a couple of courteous hellos and goodbyes performed in a style he knew to be correct when in the presence of the *bons omes* and their believers. By contrast, Raimon Capel and Marti de Verazelh's sly civilities, with a dropped word here and half-bow there (deceits obviously stressed for the benefit of the friar-inquisitors), are nevertheless examples of two men so constrained by a specific situation, and this singularity is important, that they adored more out of esteem for family and friends than as an acknowledgment of genuine belief in the *bons omes*. "On account of the familiarity that my parents had with heretics," the knight Guilhem Garsias of Fanjeaux explained, "I did those things that it is right to do with the heretics, not owing to any faith or belief I had in them."[20] As for Guilhema Esteve's desire to worship two men she not could see, eighteen years after she had supposedly stopped believing in the *bons omes*, this curious woman from Pexiora was apparently motivated by an enduring notion that the good men deserved such honors whether you continued to believe in their holiness or not.

In all these cases the act of adoration was very much a mark of respect for men and women known to be holy, known to be respected in a village, and not necessarily an admission of actual faith in the *bons omes* and the *bonas femnas*. Indeed, the good men knew themselves to be worthy of such honor, or rather they expected others to honor them, because na Saurimunda de Quiders was once expressly told by the *bon ome* Bernart Marti that she had to adore him in Guilhem Vidal's house at Mas-Saintes-Puelles in 1225.[21] The courtesy of the *melhoramen* was also an affirmation that the habits of relatives, friends, or the majority of a village frequently determined where and when a man, woman, or child adored. It was the recognition of the viewpoints of others and so a confirmation of them. None of this denies that, as Raimon Capel implied, numerous people must have adored the good men in fear of village *crezens* as a group or, like Alazaïs de Cales, who was compelled to adore in 1209 by her friend Aimergarda de Maserol,[22] through the rough intimidation of a single believer. Still, the regular civilities (or cruelties) of individual *domus* and communal *castra* seem to have had more influence on the routine *cortesia* toward the good men and good women than some predictable specialized regime undertaken in the same way in all places.

What is so intriguing about the epithet "good man," *bon ome*, belonging to a person deserving of honor, and transcribed at Saint-Sernin as *bonus homo* or less frequently *probus homo*, is that "good man" was the title adopted by any Lauragais man in situations circumscribed by courtesy. Nobles, knights, artisans, tradesmen, millworkers, even simple peasant farmers were described in charters, wills, oaths, communal decisions, court appearances, in everything and anything, as *boni homines* and *probi homines* in Latin, while in Occitan they were *bons omes*, *prozomes*, or *prodomes*. The designation was frequently applied to fathers with sons (signifying *senior* over *junior*) and uncles whose nephews had the same Christian and last names. *Dominus*, though sometimes just a polite general word for any man, was used by the inquisitorial scribes at Saint-Sernin only to indicate the lords of villages. In the Toulousain and Lauragais, at least, *bonus homo* also does not seem to have ever been explicitly used for Catholic prelates and monks; *dominus* or *dompnus* was used instead. Occasionally, in this play of courtesy and nomenclature, even the heretical good men were, like priests, addressed as *domini*.[23]

*Bons omes*, even with scribal contortions like *bononios* or *bonozios*, was also never a synonym for "Bosnians," as some modern scholars have desperately (and bizarrely) wanted the Occitan to mean.[24] Despite such attempts at discerning a Bogomil presence in the Toulousain and the Lauragais, no one at Saint-Sernin, whether speaking in the vernacular or writing in Latin, remembered or recorded any Balkan acquaintances. On this point about the adoption, and adaptation, of familiar terminology by the good men and their believers, far too much has been made of the fact that some *bons omes* were named deacons, like Izarn de Castres, or bishops, like Bernart Marti.[25] These titles do reveal a limited sense of hierarchy on the part of some good men, good women, and their believers, but it is a very long jump to start building elaborate ecclesiastical structures, heretical dioceses, systematic protocols—in short, a Church—out of words that, if anything, were simply used to help differentiate a person deserving even more respect than that accorded the day-to-day *boni homines* of any Lauragais village, whether the intimate "friends of God" or not.

That "good man" was an inescapably common term of respect must have made the interrogations at Saint-Sernin even more tense and confusing for many people (the friar-inquisitors and the transcribing scribes included) who thought nothing of saying *bon ome* in the customary etiquette of the Lauragais (and, it should not be forgotten, this must have caused terrible confusion during the Albignesian Crusade). An example is the testimony of Michel Verger, who, when trying to describe his youthful politeness toward the Waldensians twenty-five years earlier at Avignonet, could think of no other way of expressing it than the familiar "I believed them to be *bons omes*."[26] The Fanjeaux leather-worker Peire de Garmassia, by sharp contrast, deliberately used *bonus homo*, and all that it commonly meant to him, when he told Bernart de Caux, with some moral exactitude, "I never believed that the heretics were 'good men,' " that is, like other more orthodox village *prodomes*; "nevertheless, I believed that their works were good, even if their faith was bad."[27]

The same cannot quite be said for the designation "good woman," *bona femina, bona femna*: even though all older or married women, no matter who they were, did receive the blanket title of *domine* in notarial documents, in manuscript 609 only noblewomen were called *domina, domna, na*, "lady."[28] This exceptional specificity on the part of the scribes at Saint-Sernin allows us to hear when noblewomen who wished their nobility to be known, and transcribed, were confessing. This testimonial and scribal precision also lets us see and hear, particularly in acts of adoration remembered by women, when the "good ladies" themselves chose to stress their own nobility. The importance of noble good women's emphasizing their nobility, seemingly more frequently than did the good men, and the fact that this quality was a distinct part of their specific holiness, certainly motivated the good woman na Berengaira de Seguerville when the *castelan* Arnaut de Auriac caught her in the wood of Seguerville in 1233, because she was instantly released, so her son testified at Saint-Sernin, on account of her noble birth.[29] The use of the commonplace name "good woman," *bona femna, bona molher,* throughout the Lauragais to mean a holy woman, as contrasted with the socially revealing use of *bona domna,* was a deliberate exercise in adopting, imitating, very masculine notions of respect and holiness, at least as understood in documentary and daily discourse.

Yet the very use of "good man" and "good woman" to designate a person who was a "friend of God" takes us straight into the way in which villages in the Lauragais understood holiness, the *bons omes,* and the *bonas femnas.* The holy was to be understood and embraced as something decidedly ordinary, as something accessible to any man or woman, as something capable of being switched on, felt, enjoyed, admired—even something by which some might be repulsed—in the most simple nods and the most familiar of words. Routinely polite actions, like unavoidable head-bobbing as one entered the low doorway of a *domus,* and the most common forms of address, like *bon ome,* when said and done at particular times and places, instantly transformed, pierced, relieved the burden of, even if only for a moment, the oppressive visible world of the Lauragais village. It was always within the watched, heard, and unavoidable activity of the ordinary that a silent, passive, and invisible extraordinary dwelt.

The *dominus* of Cambiac, Jordan Sais, revealed to Bernart de Caux on Monday, 11 December 1245, that he had adored two of his *homines proprii,* Peire Gausbert and Arnaut Faure, in 1220. "I genuflected thrice, saying 'bless us,'" Jordan Sais remembered about this old *cortesia* to his serfs. This noble, through simple behavior, through simple words, briefly evoked a sensation of otherworldliness, of something outside the norm, in a relationship where it might be least expected, that of a lord adoring servile peasants. Jordan Sais knew that the holiness of a good man possessed a decided passivity, a perpetual sense of waiting to be acknowledged, in that it needed to be activated by the manners of *crezen.* Jordan Sais never forgot that Peire Gausbert and Arnaut Faure were his men, just as they never forgot that he was their lord. The world of Cambiac was not turned upside down; indeed, it was entrenched, reinforced, through such acts. Similarly, the noble Raimon de Rocovila, one of the lords of les Cassés, admitted adoring the *bon ome* Raimon Sirvens, "my *rusticus,*" his serf, in 1229.[30] In the same way, na Richa n'Azalbert's adoration of her own son Raimon in Arnaut Godalh's house at Mas-Saintes-Puelles in 1240 does not suggest, at least for the mother (who had stopped being a faithful *crezen* only in 1243), that being made a *bon ome* severed all maternal bonds.[31] The holiness of Peire Gausbert and Arnaut Faure could exist only through their being intimately part of Cambiac, as men accepting that they were caught within the familar petty rhythms of the village and yet stood outside of it, as accessible doorways to God momentarily opened through adoration, as *bons omes* whose very mundane existence was always suggesting, evoking, and proving that there was a transcendent reality beyond these visible constraints.[32]

It was as an intensification of this phenomenon evoked by adoration that the *aparelhamen* of the good men should be understood. This union, this coming together, of *crezens* around some good men, usually once a month, was about the precise and regulated activation of that shimmering connection with the divine that truly made some humans, especially some men, into the "friends of God." All those adoring village courtesies which momentarily proved that the holy could be glimpsed in ordinary rituals of respect found final proof in the vibrant excitable atmosphere of the *aparelhamen*. The good men, as always, remained determinedly passive, essentially motionless, while the *crezens*, in marked contrast, created a mood of feverish worship as they genuflected and bowed until a sustained sensation of holiness permeated the space in which everyone stood. It was when that reticent, insouciant, fluctuating divinity of the spirit stabilized for the duration of the *aparelhamen*, when the time of the physical world slowed or stopped, that the good men could offer their peace, could genuinely raise their hands in blessing and, having smothered the harsh immediacy of village life, discuss and confess things without the strain of consequence or repercussion.[33]

In such an atmosphere of the holy, sustained for the duration of the *aparelhamen*, not only could the good men give their peace, but they were able to bless bread and, it seems, through a physical kiss or touch, transfer some of their usually reticent sanctity into their believers. The holiness that the *bons omes* possessed was, for a moment, truly visible in something felt or eaten. Guilhem Bobis of Fanjeaux, confessing on Friday, 2 March 1246, with Fanjeaux's priest listening, remembered an "*aparelhamen* of heretics" where he accepted the peace from the good men, "and I ate twice with them at the same table and of bread blessed by them."[34] Guilhem Bobis' specificity about eating twice at the same table as the good men was a frequent admission of heretical culpability and of attendance at an *aparelhamen*. A discernable feeling of spatial accuracy suffused the ceremony, so that nearness to the good men (whether through kissing, touching, eating blessed bread, or just sitting at the same table) became vital to believers in the *bons omes*. Such tactile and finite intimacy was an empirical, and quite sensual, proof that the good men and their *crezens* were participating in a realization of the holy.

Na Alazaïs, widow of Roger de Turre, the late lord of Mireval, though letting two good men stay and eat in her house for two days in 1230, as well as adoring them, nevertheless stressed for the inquisition that "I didn't eat with them at the same table."[35] Bernart de Quiders remembered that when he and his *bona femna* sister Galharta stayed in a Mas-Saintes-Puelles house in 1222, though they had their meals in the same *domus*, "there was a wall in the middle."[36] Rixenda Calveta was a good woman living openly at Montmaur in 1221 when her daughter Guilhema Morlana and her son-in-law Raimon Morlana, a weaver at Saint-Martin-de-la-Lande, stayed two or three days in her house, "but we didn't eat there," Guilhema Morlana confessed about herself and her husband on Thursday, 20 July 1245, "because we ate outside the house."[37] This fascinating obsession about where a person was eating while a heretic ate, so that fractions of physical closeness were crucial when it came to acknowledging guilt or innocence at Saint-Sernin, helps emphasize the sensation of spatial and physical exactitude always involved in experiencing, and thinking about, existence in the Lauragais. In this way, the *aparelhamen* clearly possessed, and was understood to possess, a very localized potency in a room or around a table. This intense experience of sanctity, unlike fleeting benedictions in a street or a doorway, could last, at the very least, for the length of a meal, the eating of some bread, the lingering feel of a kiss.

An explicit, and rather humorous, memory of the intensity felt at an *aparelhamen* was recalled for Bernart de Caux and Jean de Saint-Pierre on Saturday, 10 March 1246, by that knight from Fanjeaux, Guilhem Garsias. The particular *aparelhamen* he described, with at least eight knights and noble ladies from Fanjeaux gathered before two *bons omes*, happened around 1234 in the house of the *miles* Bernart Ugon. Almost immediately the *aparelhamen* began, "a great laughter rose up among myself and several others who were there," an uncontrollable giggling precipitated by a lady's toppling over during the downswing of an especially passionate bow, and, unable to regain their composure, "I had to leave the house with some others, because we couldn't refrain from laughing." Guilhem Garsias also mentioned that he did not adore the good men once he went outside Bernart Ugon's house, though he was certain those who remained within did.[38] This amusing anecdote succinctly captures the serious excitement of the *aparelhamen*, the giddy tenseness felt by all participating in it, and the sheer physical movement, by one woman in particular, that was necessary to transform the visible world around some good men and their believers into a steady perceptible bubble of the invisibly holy. It also, by implication, shows that the genuflection of the *melhoramen*, although resembling the ritual of the *aparelhamen*, and obviously appreciated as being similar, was still considered distinct. The good men throughout all this falling over and silly laughter were, as they should be, silent embodiments of passivity and nonchalance.

This question of who was adored by whom, whether peasant by knight or son by mother, and the passiveness of good men in contrast to the eagerness of *crezens*, is made all the more fascinating by a memory the Gardouch knight Guilhem de Castilho had of an encounter with two *bons omes* in 1227. One day, "I saw at Montesquieu that Guilhem Peire del Lutz was seeking me out in the village square," so Guilhem de Castilho began his incriminating tale at Saint-Sernin on Tuesday, 9 May 1245, "and he told me that I should go with him up to his house, because he had two boys he wanted to show me." Guilhem de Castilho followed his friend to the house where the children were waiting, and, once inside, "I adored the heretics," as did Guilhem Peire del Lutz and another Montesquieu *miles*, Peire Raimon Gros.[39] Guilhem de Castilho was well aware that the act he performed before the children qualified as adoration because, earlier in his testimony, he recollected meeting two good women in 1220 secretly hidden in the house of Arnaut Marti, a man originally from Fanjeaux but now *claviger*, "key-keeper," head servant, for the *dominus* Jordan de Lanta. "As I left the house," Guilhem de Castilho recalled, "I wished them well, but I didn't adore them."[40]

As for the child *amicx de Dieu*, "I didn't know those heretics," Guilhem de Castilho conceded, but it did not matter to him, because the age of the anonymous *bons omes*, and thus what these two lads knew about the world, was irrelevant. These boys were still good men, staying in Guilhem Peire del Lutz's house, and three youthful adult knights were willing to pay their respects to them. The three knights saw past the silent little bodies, if only for the duration of the *melhoramen*, and felt the quiet holiness they were meant to venerate. The act of adoration briefly turned on the boys' link with heaven. In all the other recollections of boy *bons omes*, of which there are few, and girl *bonas femnas*, of which there are many more, no one seems to have adored small children. This incident at Montesquieu really does suggest two "friends of God," easily below their majority at fourteen, transcending visible fleshy Lauragais reality. A trio of grown Lauragais men believed these boys to be *amicx de Dieu*, even if these little good men were themselves blasé about, or unaware of, the intensely passive holiness emanating from them. Or, perhaps, one is merely seeing a glimpse of how a group of adult male *crezens* in one village practiced and confirmed their beliefs about the universe through two children.

Adult *bons omes*, though, do seem to have often gone out of their way in a conscious effort at getting children to like them and, as a consequence, so they seem to have hoped, at making boys and girls into, if not ardent believers, then at least sympathizers. For instance, Guilhem Julian of Auriac had a fond memory of the *bons omes* giving out bread to all the boys of the village when he was a child. He did not know at the time, somewhere around 1230, that taking this bread was bad, because all the other children were doing it too.[41] Bernart Recort *junior*, who had eaten some blessed bread from the good men around 1242, did not confess this to Guilhem Arnaut and Esteve de Saint-Thibéry when they were at Fanjeaux, "because I was a boy and didn't know anything about heresy."[42] The youthful Peire Faure of Mas-Saintes-Puelles, thinking back to 1238 when he was a small boy, recalled the *bons omes* Donat and Arnaut Pradier asking him, in front of the *crezens* Peire and Sussana Cap-de-Porc, whether "I would like to go with them." As an incentive to induce him to leave his family, "they would teach me to be literate"; the good men held out this promise of learning "because they disapproved of guarding cows," which was what the boy did. In an instant, "I wanted to go with the heretics," Peire Faure as a man confessed about himself as a lad. Unfortunately for the impressionable boy and the impressive *bons omes*, his mother na Mateuz Faure would have none of this, and, while giving her son a tongue-lashing, "she dragged me away by the hair of my head" from Peire Cap-de-Porc's house. Interestingly, and somewhat ironically, Peire Faure went on to become a tonsured *clericus*.[43]

The promise of the heretics to Peire Faure takes one straight into the exercises and teachings that a man or a woman had to go through to become a *bon ome* or *bona femna*, outside of becoming a "friend of God" in the moments before death. As with so much else about the faith of the good men and good women, the testimonies transcribed at Saint-Sernin lack a certain lucidity, coherence—in short, detailed evidence—concerning how healthy men, women, boys, and girls were made into *bons omes* and *bonas femnas*. The friar-inquisitors were not interested in such details, but then there does not seem to be, as with the *melhoramen*, a truly systematic method by which a person became an *amic de Dieu*. Unquestionably, this divine metamorphosis involved an individual's receiving the *consolamen* in life, rather than the more common consolation when dying, and though the steps that led to this conversion varied from place to place, as well as from one decade to another, it was still a transformation theoretically available to anyone (adult or child) in a Lauragais village. One of the most informative confessions, if only because of the hasty list of habits it included, was given by Audiardis Ebrarda of Villeneuve-la-Comptal, with Arnaut Auriol and her village priest Raines as interrogators, in which she stated that, after the *bon ome* Izarn de Castres had made her a girl *bona femna* in 1206, "I stayed in the sect of the heretics for a year, praying, fasting, adoring heretics, hearing their preaching, and doing other things which heretics do and understand must be observed."[44] Despite this impression of a fairly regular routine, and so the reinforcement of a holy manner upon a young life, Audiardis Ebrada left the heretics and, like previously mentioned child good women, quickly took a husband (though the bishop of Toulouse still gave her the penance of yellow crosses in 1236).[45] In 1220, while Peire Amielh was a youth at Mas-Saintes-Puelles, he left his father's house with Izarn de Castres and stayed with the heretics at Laurac for two months. "But," he stressed for Bernart de Caux on Saturday, 13 May 1245, "I wasn't made a clothed heretic [*hereticus indutus*], nor did I fast, pray, or abstain from those things from which the heretics abstain." After these two months at Laurac he returned to his father at Mas-Saintes-Puelles.[46] In the years before the Peace of Paris-Meaux, as Peire Amielh's confession recalled, sometimes the good men and good women deliberately dressed in dark or plain cloth when they became *bons omes* and *bonas femnas.* This concern for sartorial blandness—similar to the desire for imitating Christ that dressed the Waldensians, Franciscans, and Dominicans—possessed for the *amicx de Dieu* a much more somber and deathly quality, where the very fabric enshrouding their Devil-made bodies visibly proclaimed their amicability with God. After 1230 such divine affability was no longer fashionable.[47]

Raimona Jocglar in her first testimony on Saturday, 20 January 1246, before Bernart de Caux, Guilhem Pelhisson, and Arnaut Auriol, told how, three years earlier, "my father banished me from his house on account of heresy and," as though one naturally went with the other, "because he thought I was a slut." Fortunately, five Saint-Martin-de-la-Lande women, who all seem to have been *crezens,* if not *bonas femnas,* and whom Raimon Jocglar did not frighten, gladly comforted the girl. Then, without fully explaining how or why, Raimona Jocglar ended up staying with some good women in two houses at Laurac, which were no longer *domibus propriis hereticorum* but the dwellings of sympathetic *crezens,* and, even though she wanted to give herself to the heretics, the *bon ome* Fanjaus "didn't wish to hereticate me until I could be properly instructed, according to mores of the heretics, and undergo three fasts, each lasting forty days." After a month, however, all the Laurac *bons omes* and *bonas femnas* decided to leave for Montségur, and, though Raimona Jocglar wanted to go with them, the good men and good women refused because "I wasn't thoroughly instructed or entirely firm in the sect of the heretics." A Laurac youth came to Raimona Jocglar's rescue and secretly led her to a lord at Gaja-la-Selve, whose name she did not know; this nobleman then escorted her from his house at night to a nearby wood where he left her with two *bonas femnas,* one of whom was his mother. Unfortunately, these three heretical women were soon captured, despite their hiding place, and the two good women were burnt at Toulouse in 1243. Raimona Jocglar, condemned to the flames as well, though not a *bona femna,* at least in the view of other good women, converted at the sight of the flaming pyre.[48]

In the same year that Raimon Jocglar cast out his daughter, the barber, *barbitonsor,* Peire Fornier booted two *bons omes,* Raimon Rigaut and a companion, from his house at Fanjeaux. This practioner of cures was himself gravely sick from an illness that would eventually kill him. It was for this reason that Peire Fornier had originally invited the *bon ome* Raimon Rigaut to his house. The dying man wanted the good men to make him a *bon ome.* Raimon Rigaut, however, did not wish to, because, rather interestingly, the deathbed bequest of Peire Fornier's parents had never reached the *bons omes.* Peire Fornier then offered a pledge of twenty-six measures of wine on behalf of himself and his deceased parents. Still, Raimon Rigaut would not make Peire Fornier a "friend of God," as his pledge was, so the good man told him, not their custom. It was this surprising rigidity on the part of the *bons omes* that so exasperated Peire Fornier and caused him to expel, cursing all the way, Raimon Rigaut and his friend. Arnaut Auriol and Bernart de Caux heard about this incident on Tuesday, 8 May 1246, from the very old Bernart Gasc, easily in his late seventies, because, by sheer coincidence, this elderly man had wandered into Peire Fornier's house to get—and this is a wonderful insight into village existence—a candle lit. No one, by the way, adored the heretics.[49]

Particularly striking about the fates of Peire Fornier and Raimona Jocglar are the rather hard-and-fast rules that the good men and good women chose to adopt in a time of turmoil and persecution. Such inflexibility was rarely remembered by individuals who saw the *bons omes* and *bonas femnas* living publicly at beginning of the thirteenth century. Undoubtedly, the good men and good women were not taking risks with anyone in whom they did not have complete confidence once the friar-inquisitors had begun their investigations. Yet, as seems to have been the case with the *melhoramen*—concerning which the friar-inquisitors objectified a style of highly contingent politeness into the classifiable form of *adoratio,* so that it forced people to see their past and future nods and benedictions as much more formulaic than they ever were—a reciprocal sharpness of vision was produced within the good men and good women themselves. Admittedly, though such precision seems more mechanical than inspired, a *bon ome* or a *bona femna* now possessed a new clarity of purpose about what he or she might or might not do in his or her, let alone everyone else's, imagination.

# 14

## NOT QUITE DEAD

AT Avignonet in 1231 Bertran de Quiders was very ill. His mother, Blanca de Quiders, an incredibly fervent *crezen*, "frequently admonished and pleaded that I love the good men, and, if I should happen to die, that I would entrust myself to them." Blanca de Quiders then had Raimon Sans, a deacon of the good men, visit her son in his sickroom; though not a *medicus*, "he took my pulse and said that I should regain my health." After this happy diagnosis, Raimon Sans and his companion preached, though no one adored them. Bertran de Quiders, at the instigation of his mother, along with two other *crezens* at his bedside, all promised the good men "that I would be entrusted into their hands, if I should happen to die." Indeed, immediately acting upon these morbid thoughts, Bertran de Quiders bequeathed fifty shillings to the *bons omes*, which his mother would pay after his death.[1] It is worth knowing that Bertran de Quiders' confession of his mother's faith in the good men was a melancholic memory for him because, when the *bayle* Macip de Tolosa seized *bons omes* living in three Avignonet houses in 1237, Blanca de Quiders blamed her son for telling the *bayle* where to look. "Although it wasn't true," Bertran de Quiders' mother believed in his treachery, and so, he ruefully told the inquisition, she "wept all the time and hated me."[2]

The *consolamen* was the ritual by which a *crezen* ended his or her life. A person was made into, for all intents and purposes, a *bon ome* or a *bona femna*. Once more, the notion that holiness was something that all men and women could, and would, one day experience suffused the expectation, and performance, of this necessary ritual. Guilhem Cabi Blanc, of Labécède, emphasized the necessity of becoming a "friend of God" before death for Bernart de Caux and Arnaut Auriol on Tuesday, 4 July 1245, by recollecting how some good men had once told him that a person's soul, without the *consolamen*, immediately left the body and entered an ass, becoming trapped there, braying and lamenting for salvation.[3] The *consolamen* also assumed that the sensation of sanctity lay outside the visible restrictions of time and space, in that being made a good man in the last moments of life was exactly the same as having lived ten, twenty, thirty years as a *bon ome*.

Unlike adoration, which involved both *bons omes* and *bonas femnas*, the one hundred and fifty instances remembered at Saint-Sernin of "heretication," as the friar-inquisitors labeled this transformative act, deathbed or otherwise, were all performed by men and, until the years after 1230, only by *bons omes* designated as deacons.[4] Once more, the procedures at Saint-Sernin, the words spoken, the words written down, and the words used by friar-inquisitors and witnesses shifted and altered in the process of confession. Undoubtedly, a recollected *consolamen*, especially if given no formal description by the person confessing, frequently became a "heretication" through scribal transcription. Yet just as common, and this has to taken into account, numerous men and women deliberately chose to say "heretication" or to describe someone as "hereticated" in their testimonies, well aware, as was not the case with the more hazily defined "adoration," of what it meant to the inquisition to become an *amic de Dieu*. Unlike the courtesy of the *melhoramen*—which, to most men and women in the Lauragais apart from the two friar-inquisitors, was only a passing confirmation of previously existing communal habits—the transformation of a person into a *bon ome* or *bona femna* on his or her deathbed consciously attempted to create profoundly new relations, deep intimacies unlike anything in life, in short, a friendship with God.

Moreover, this newly forged relationship with the holy had to be terrestrially fleeting, even if it left discernible patterns (to friar-inquisitors, if to no one else) in the lives of those who knew the dead *bon ome* or *bona femna*, because the man or woman newly transformed into an *amic de Dieu* had to die without delay. To be made a good man or good woman through the *consolamen*, an individual had to be so ill that there was no chance of recovery; though, as Bernarta Fabre of Saint-Martin-de-la-Lande observed in her testimony to Bernart de Caux, a person could not be so sick as to be unable to speak.[5] Raimon Sans, when he took Bernart de Quiders' pulse, demonstrated the necessity of attempting to get the moment just right when a person could become a "friend of God." No significant interval of time must elapse before death; otherwise the bedside work of a good man might be destroyed. The dying notary Azemar de Avinhos, for instance, was given chicken soup by Folquet de Marselha, the bishop of Toulouse, after having been hereticated and so immediately ceased to be possessed of the docile holiness of a *bon ome*. Azemar de Avinhos, overcoming the active corruption of the chicken soup, managed to live long enough to be remade a good man.[6] Bernart Blanc, of Cambon, gladly accepted the *consolamen* from the good men Pons and Bernart Gitbert when he was about to die in 1206; nine days later this new "friend of God" was, much to his surprise, well again, and Bernart Blanc, regretting his decision to be a *bon ome*, was given the penance of fasting on feast days for a year by Folquet de Marselha.[7] An odd contrast to all this was something the *bon ome* and knight Pagan de Beceda said to Peire Rigaut in 1228 when the latter wondered about a friend who had stopped being a good man and converted to Catholicism.

"Nothing," and the noble Pagan de Beceda was adamant about this, "breaks the promise that you made to the Lord!"[8]

This constant observation of the sick and dying by the good men, their judging an individual ill enough to be become one of them, was undoubtedly why Bernart de Caux and Jean de Saint-Pierre were so interested in testimonies that mentioned heretics as *medici*, or, to put it another way, why so many people thought the two friar-inquisitors would like to know such things. Consequently, Peire Pis of Avignonet admitted to Bernart de Caux and Arnaut Auriol on Friday, 4 May 1246, that he once carried his sick son into a wood near Caraman in 1230. He wanted the *bons omes* Arnaut and Pons Faure, who lived there, to heal his boy. As to why he chose them, it was because Pons de Saint-Germier had told him that these two good men "were the best practitioners," *optimi medici erant*. Peire Pis, although further confessing that he did give the good men seven shillings of Toulouse for what they had done for his son, still made it very clear for the friar-inquisitors that he never adored the Faure brothers, or heard them preach, or ever thought of himself as a *crezen*.[9] Arnaut Faure's interest in healing, incidentally, seems to have been quite learned, or at least based on study as well as practice, because he once deposited a *liber medicine* with a *crezen* at Auriac. Pons Esteve, the man who on Monday, 22 January 1246, offered the inquisition this fact, or rather this piece of village hearsay, while noting that Arnaut Faure had recently been burnt, still thought, and once more he relied on gossip, that the heretic's medical book remained safely ensconced at Auriac.[10]

Three years after the healing of Peire Pis' boy, a man at Mas-Saintes-Puelles, Raimon Bernart, had an annoying ailment in his shin bone. A friend, Guilhem de Canast, told him that he should go and seek out the *bon ome* Arnaut Faure for a cure. So he and Guilhem de Canast went in search of Arnaut Faure. They first went to les Cassés, a good morning's walk, or limp in Raimon Bernart's case, and found a "house of heretics" there. Unfortunately, Arnaut Faure was nowhere to be found. After staying at les Cassés long enough to eat a meal with the good men, the two friends retraced their steps toward Mas-Saintes-Puelles and, in a hut hidden in a wood near Lanta, rather than Caraman, they discovered Arnaut Faure. "And," without ever explaining to Bernart de Caux how he knew about Arnaut Faure's cabin, Raimon Bernart ended his medicinal travelogue with the succinct "[T]hen the heretic gave me herbs to heal the ailment."[11] Interestingly, even though Raimon Bernart kept swearing that he was not a *crezen*, someone (perhaps Bernart de Caux as a reminder to himself) still scribbled in the margin next to his rather damning confession, "He is said to be a Catholic," *Hic dictus esse catholicus*.[12]

Guilhem Deumer of Scaupon, a hamlet north of Toulouse along the river Tarn, had a less benevolent memory of a good man as *medicus*. In

1231, "when I was gravely hurt from a wound, and all the practitioners [*medici*] had given up on me," he began his testimony on Friday, 22 December 1245, with Guilhem Pelhisson and Bernart de Caux listening, "it was said to me that, at Vaux, there was a practitioner [*medicus*] who could cure me, if I took myself to him." So, in desperation, he followed this advice and had himself carried to Vaux, a village about halfway between les Cassés and Auriac. "And there I found this practitioner, and he was a heretic, but I don't recollect his name," a curious admission, as Guilhem Deumer stayed in the care of this *medicus* for a whole month. This nameless good man, throughout these weeks of healing, "asked me many times that I make myself a heretic, but that I didn't want to do." Eventually, the good man gave up trying to make Guilhem Deumer a *bon ome*, and, with the patient obviously healed and so no longer needing any deathbed transformation, the *medicus* "didn't wish to have me in his care, so he threw me out."[13]

"I often instructed the sick to send me either a belt or a shirt or buttons or some shoes," the young *divinatrix* (*devina*) Alisson acknowledged about herself on Monday, 3 July 1245, at Saint-Sernin. "Now, when I had the belts, the linen shirts, and the shoes, I questioned a lead crystal. Then I would say: 'You make the following of plasters or the following of herbs.' " As to why Alisson did all this, "so I could have money." This rationale she repeated once more to the two friar-inquisitors and, a crucial judgment about her ability to predict the future, to anticipate certain causes from the effects of her crystal, "I believed no virtuous powers dwelt in the lead." Alisson also noted that another woman from Mas-Saintes-Puelles, na Garejada de Jular, frequently questioned lead for the sick, but unlike this older matron, the young *divinatrix* never "gave people to understand that with conjured lead they were being freed from sickness."[14]

The mistake here would be to assume that Alisson confessed all this because Bernart de Caux and Jean de Saint-Pierre, like later inquisitors, were interested in magic or other supernatural doings. In fact the two friar-inquisitors did not concern themelves with such things unless, as with any piece of evidence collected at Saint-Sernin, it specifically related to the problem of the *bons omes* and the *bonas femnas*—whom, in the common admission of someone her age, Alisson had never seen except captured. Indeed, prediction and telling the future, accepting the passage of time, trying to know what would happen and so change it, would have been anathema to the holiness of a good man or a good woman. Also, unlike the case of a dying person becoming a good man or a good woman through the *consolamen*, it seems that the *divinatrix* Alisson did not necessarily have to be in the same room as the person for whom she conjured. In any case, Alisson's testimony was a pointed exercise in making sure the friar-inquisitors clearly understood why she did what she did in life. She may have taken gifts, she may have occasionally been at the bedside of dying or desperate people, but she was definitely not a *bona femna* or even a believer in them. It was not for nothing that Alisson, when questioned a second time at Saint-Sernin, though on the same day as her first interrogation, now chose to call herself a *medica*, as if to state unequivocally that what she did was not secretive or similar to the actions of heretics.[15]

Alisson's renaming is significant in more ways than one because, though the Faure brothers were *medici* and Guilhem Deumer traveled a fair way to meet a *bon ome* who was also one, the good men, though able to discern the onset of death, never seem to have actually recommended any cures for a person they had decided would not die. Undoubtedly, being a *medicus* while a "friend of God" must have given a good man better forensic skills, fine-tuning his judgments of imminent demise. Also, a good man known as a healer clearly had more access to the dying and, as with Guilhem Deumer, could make the ill into *bons omes* before they died. The desperately argumentative Raimon Bru confirmed this impression of the heretical *medicus* discussing errors with his patients, while at the same time healing them, by remembering the *mala verba* he and Arnaut Faure had in the house of a sick friend at Avignonet in 1235.[16] Nevertheless, Alisson's self-definition as *medica* rather than youthful *devina* does suggest that practitioners of healing were not in themselves suspicious characters.[17] Rather, and here is another example of inquisitorial objectification, the relationships realized through sickness and death possessed a disturbing similarity to heretical habits, in that the effect of a disease at Mas-Saintes-Puelles, like the outcome of a life at Laurac, all too often ended in the *consolamen*.

In any event, the last thing a good man really wanted to do, was expected to do, was to heal the corruptible body, to mend the Devil's physical creation, to involve himself in the visible world of the flesh. A *bon ome* like Arnaut Faure was the exception and not the rule. Normally, a good man was indifferent to the causes of a specific disease, being concerned only with the last-minute effects of an illness, and so he was never skilled enough to truly make the sick well. Indeed, the dead and dying must have possessed a general sameness for the *bons omes* that, probably, was all the knowledge they needed for a diagnosis. Such stock insights into the last moments of a person's life were clearly potent tools in a good man's repertoire of wisdom. This must have been part of the reason that Guilhem Deumer never wanted to be a made a *bon ome* by the good man *medicus* at Vaux, because to accept such an act, to acquiesce in becoming a "friend of God," was the same as admitting that one was about to die. The ability to say with conviction that death, and so heaven, were near at hand was obviously a powerful demonstration of the close friendship a *bon ome* had with God.[18] Occasionally, however, a good man could be way off the mark.

Petrona Fizela of Laurac witnessed a remarkable example of two *bons omes* not particularly talented in knowing a dead man when they saw one. The flawed diagnosis she had in mind occurred just before her interrogation on Wednesday, 12 July 1245, and involved the youthful and somewhat sickly Joan Afailer. Petrona Fizela, for reasons she did not go into, was one of eleven people, including two unknown *bons omes*, who crowded inside a hut near Laurac to participate in the heretication (as it would clearly have been understood to be) of the ill Joan Afailer. "Will you receive me?" Joan Afailer asked the good men. "No," they replied, "because you're too young," and, by implication, healthy. This made the not-quite-dead Joan Afailer somewhat angry, and so, as Petrona Fizela alone observed, the youth mischievously "closed his eyes as if dead." The trick seemed to work, as the good men then placed a New Testament above Joan Afailer's head and made him into a *bon ome*, even though the lad obviously could not talk. The good men were then adored before they left the hut, none the wiser, it seems, about the pretense of Joan Afailer.[19] This, quite simply, was a *consolamen*, even down to the earnest desire of Joan Afailer to be a made an *amic de Dieu*, except that the perception of death was so wonderfully wrong. Nevertheless, one detail was missing, which the elderly lawyer Raimon Venercha remembered with legalistic precision about the time his sister Condors became a *bona femna* in 1236—namely, as she lay dying, she repeated the Lord's Prayer three times.[20]

Despite the comic overtones of Joan Afailer's apparent demise, the act of making someone a "friend of God" was usually a rather somber occasion, more like the death of Raimon Venercha's sister, with, it seems, a tendency on the part of the *bons omes* to frown upon any overt displays of emotion, especially by women. Alazaïs, former wife of the lord of Mireval Roger de Turre, and now the spouse of Raimon de Cantes from Gibel, recalled being asked by two anonymous *bons omes* to leave the deathbed of her first husband in 1234 because of her lamentations and inability to calm down. Moreover, despite Roger de Turre's being made a good man, Alazaïs had him buried the next day in the grounds of the Hospitalers at Pexiora.[21] Asking a hysterical wife to leave while her husband became a "friend of God" might seem a sensible thing to do, and yet one cannot escape thinking that extreme emotion was, at least for the good men, a reminder of something inherently human, feminine, and so terrestrial. In 1216, for instance, na Mabilia de Mortario recalled being removed from a house at Conques by some *bons omes* when her first husband Uc de Vilhaigle lay dying, on account of her sadness and, one clearly resembling the other for the good men, because she was pregnant.[22]

The death and heretication of Roger de Turre in 1234, even without the crying of his wife, was a loud, raucous, and very public affair in the village of Mireval. In the last moments of Roger de Turre's life, just as he was about to be made a good man, the noble Joan Aldabert burst into the room and contemptuously bellowed at the two *bons omes* by the lord of Mireval's bedside, "What kind of villains are those?" Joan Aldabert, making it theatrically obvious what he thought of the "friends of God," and these good men do not appear to have been servile *vilans* like the *homines proprii* of Jordan Sais, was then violently thrown out of Roger de Turre's house by four knightly *crezens*. It is not easy to tell how serious Joan Aldalbert was in his boisterous mockery of the good men, let alone the reason behind his wild desire to disrupt a village lord's dying moments, or even what he thought the inquisition would make of his swaggering contempt for the habits of his village. Joan Aldabert was, after all, the same jocular fellow who apparently took communion with some special tree leaves during sunsets and eclipses, or so his boastful son, Peire, told that chatty schoolboy from Mireval, Amielh Bernart *junior*.[23]

As to what Arnaut Godera heard through the porous stone walls of his Montferrand house in 1242 when Peireta Rei was made a *prodome*, it was this lucidly remembered rogation that Raimon Marti, Raimon Rei, and Arnaut de Fajac recited to a lone good man: "Truly approve of us, because this *prodome* [*probus homo*] is to be received by the *prodomes* [*probis hominibus*], and, similarly, truly approve of us, because we will be present during his heretication." The remarkable choice of the term "heretication" by a good man was either a profound acknowledgment of how much the world had changed by 1242, in that the *bons omes* now consciously incorporated their secretive existence as heretics into their rituals, or, and this seems more likely, Arnaut Godera, helped by a friar-inquisitor, reworded some of the noise heard through Peireta Rei's stone wall. Arnaut Godera also noted, after he went outside and used his eyes, that the corpse of Peireta Rei was immediately buried.[24] Where Peireta Rei's body now lay, Arnaut Godera did not say.

Despite Roger de Turre's interment with the Hospitalers, secrecy played a large part in the burial of men and women who had been hereticated after 1230, especially individuals who had lived their entire lives as *amicx de Dieu*, because friar-inquisitors and *bayles* systematically sought out the graves of heretics so that their remains might be burnt.[25] "We decree," so Bernart de Caux and Jean de Saint-Pierre wrote in their manual about dead heretics, "that his or her bones be exhumed from the cemetery, if they can be distinguished from others, and burned in detestation of so heinous an offense."[26] On account of such attitudes, Guilhem de la Grassa of Avignonet covertly buried in 1232 a *bona femna* late one night in a garden he owned outside the village.[27] One curious memory about the burial of a hereticated person was confessed by a certain Raimon Novell who, in 1229, just so happened to glance through an open door in Fanjeaux and see a man he knew to be a murderer receiving the *consolamen* from two good men. Raimon Novell did not know the *bons omes*, but he did add that the murderer was about to be buried alive for his crime.[28]

"The heretics had a cemetery at Montesquieu," sometime around 1206, the elderly Esteve Joan remembered on Tuesday, 15 May 1246, for Bernart de Caux and Robert, the priest of Montesquieu, "and they buried there Balandrau, Bernart de Montesquieu, Guilhem de Vilela, his brother n'Estotz, his son n'Inauz, Raimon Ninau, lord of Montesquieu, Arnaut de Laia," and, Esteve Joan kept on counting, "Bernart de la Greuleth, Arnaut de Gardoh, and his brother Azemar, Arnaut Raimon Gota, and Guilabert de Gardoh, also the brother of Arnaut de Gardoh," before he drew a breath and added, "[T]hey were all hereticated in death and then buried in the cemetery."[29] It is interesting that Montesquieu's cemetery for *bons omes*, apparently not at all secretive, and once outside the village walls, seemed to be only for dead men. Esteve Joan's own mother, Sobraseria, a "clothed heretic" also around 1206, does not seem to have been buried with the good men of Montesquieu; or, perhaps, despite never having been a *crezen* himself, Esteve Joan nevertheless did not wish his mother's body to be unearthed and burnt. Still, "there were six houses in the village, both for male heretics and for female heretics," to repeat Arnaut Picoc's memory of Montesquieu in 1215, and thus it may be the case that there were cemeteries for both good men and good women as well.[30]

Sometimes sick people were forced by friends or relatives to be hereticated even if they did not want to be. Pons de Beauteville recalled having to yell "No!" in 1230 to his brother, *in potestate sua*, when asked, because he was very ill, "if I wished myself to be made a heretic."[31] Marti de Cesalles, the *quondam* priest of Auriac, repeated to Bernart de Caux what Aimersent Viguier had informed him about na Austorga de Resengas's attempt to hereticate her dying husband, Peire de Resengas *senior*. Marti de Cesalles had no idea exactly when na Austorga de Resengas delivered two *bons omes* to the Cambiac bedside of her noble husband, but the priest did know, or rather Aimersent Viguier knew, that when the sickly Peire de Resengas was asked by his wife to immediately give himself to the good men, "he replied, angrily, that he didn't want them!"[32] Peire Izarn from Saint-Martin-de-la-Lande stressed for the friar-inquisitors that, though he subsequently learned that his uncle had him made into a good man in 1232 when he was gravely sick, "I was out of my mind."[33]

The vehement responses of Pons de Beautville and Peire de Resengas may have been provoked by the same fear that kept Guilhem Deumer alive, in that hearing relatives urge you to become a *bon ome*, seeing the faces of good men by the bedside, could mean only imminent, and far from welcome, death. Yet, as with Peire Izarn, it is more likely that an ardent *crezen* in the family wished, in those last moments, to finally introduce an individual, reluctant in life to become a true believer, into the circle of God's friends. It is also fascinating how the healthy Peire Izarn, in not remembering his own heretication, in feeling that he had no control over his will while sick, therefore considered it to be no part of his biography, and so this incident should not be seen by the inquisition as something accountable within his life. One may also assume that Peire Izarn ate meat, drank chicken soup, and slept with his wife after his unremembered transformation into a *bon ome*.

Around 1225, Pons de Gibel, a merchant who had moved from the tiny village of his birth to Castelnaudary some years earlier, lay dying in the house of Dulcia Ferreira at Narbonne. He was away from home on business, along with some other men from Castelnaudary, including his nephew Bernart Peire. One of his fellow travelers, knowing Pons de Gibel to be a *crezen*, arranged, apparently quite easily, for two good men to visit his bedside. Yet "Pons de Gibel wasn't hereticated in death," so Raimon Arrufat, another *mercator* from Castelnaudary lodging at Dulcia Ferreira's house, told Bernart de Caux on Saturday, 17 February 1246; "[H]e didn't wish to be hereticated from the said heretics because," though Pons de Gibel was a *crezen*, the unknown *bons omes* "weren't of the faith of the heretics of Toulouse." It was not so much that Pons de Gibel did not want to become a *bon ome* in death: he never yelled abuse at the good men, as did Peire de Resengas, and, unlike Peire Izarn, he knew he was dying, but he also knew that the reticent holiness of the *bons omes* was intensely localized. Pons de Gibel did not necessarily think that the Narbonne good men were unable to transform him into one of them, though that may have weighed on his mind; it was simply that they did not have the particular and precise friendship with God that a Lauragais and Toulousain *bon ome* had for a Lauragais and Toulousain *crezen*. Consequently, with no good man having the local divine touch that Pons de Gibel needed in his final moments, this *crezen*, according to Raimon Arrufat, chose another path to salvation, where the source of consolation was more certain, and where the last-minute ritual of the *consolamen* was unnecessary. Pons de Gibel, remembering the landscape of his youth, sent for the Cistercian monks of Boulbonne Abbey, holy men living on the other side of the river Hers from the village of Gibel, and so gave his body to them.[34]

The *consolamen*—through involving so many people, many of whom were not always ardent *crezens*, and this often included the dying individuals—instantly made households, family, and acquaintances potentially guilty of heresy for Bernart de Caux and Jean de Saint-Pierre. The friar-inquisitors saw attendance at a *consolamentum* not as the creation of fleeting relationships among the individual who died, his family, and a good man, all of which were often dissipated by death, but as the confirmation of habits that must have been there all along. All the years prior to a person's heretication, as well as the subsequent lives of his or her friends and relatives in attendance, were implicated in the *consolamen*. A heretication, in the friar-inquisitors' view, was, in a sense, both the cause and the effect of relations with heretics: it was merely the realization of something that people must have anticipated all their lives.

# 15

## ONE FULL DISH OF CHESTNUTS

AIMERSENT, the wife of Bernart Mir Arezat, the lord of Saint-Martin-de-la-Lande, remembered a gift her husband did not give to the *bon ome* Bernart Marti in 1231 or 1232. She had gone to the house of Guilhem de Sant-Nazari with another *crezen*, na Cerdana, specifically to meet the good man. Already in the house were Bernart Marti and a number of other men and women, all of them knights and ladies, all of them *crezens*. One of these men, Guilhem de Canast, carried a full dish of chestnuts on behalf of Aimersent Mir as a gift to be given to Bernart Marti. "Nevertheless," Aimersent Mir confessed to Bernart de Caux (and Silurus, chaplain of Verfeil, Arnaut d'Astarac, chaplain of Puylaurens, and Guilhem Pelhisson) on Monday, 11 June 1246, "Guilhem de Canast said to Bernart Marti, heretic, that Bernart Mir Arezat had sent the chestnuts." As to why Guilhem de Canast lied to the good man about the origin of the chestnuts, "he said he did it at the request and instigation of Raimon Mir, my husband's nephew." The young nobleman excused this falsehood by telling his aunt that all he wanted to do was "cause humor and lightheartedness." Still, Raimon Mir's little jest was far from being a piece of whimsy; instead, it was intended to annoy his uncle by implicating him in heresy, "because," and this was the real reason why the nephew made Guilhem de Canast lie, "Bernart Mir didn't love the heretics."[1]

The gift of the chestnuts, and the circumstances in which it took place, suggest that the original intention of Aimersent Mir had been to honor (and feed) Bernart Marti. And the gift may have fulfilled these intentions, for we do not know whether the good man was himself aware of the deception; indeed, he went on to give a very long sermon after receiving the chestnuts.[2] On the other hand, if Bernart Marti was aware of Raimon Mir's intentions, then what went on in Guilhem de Sant-Nazari's house was a rather public joke, which would quickly spread through the village, at the expense of the lord of Saint-Martin-de-la-Lande. In any event, Raimon Mir's sense of humor plays up the significance that even the simplest gift had for the good men, the good women, and their believers. Yet, more important, the dish of chestnuts is a reminder of the cometlike tails that gifts possess within a society, forever leaving traces of themselves within communal time and space. Thus the anticipation of giving and receiving gifts, let alone the gifts themselves, was a powerful realization of what it meant to be a *crezen*, at once causing one's relations with *bons omes* and *bonas femnas* and simultaneously being the effect of such relationships.[3] In this way, the nephew's needling implication of his uncle in the respectful habits of noble *crezens* was an unwitting prediction of how, a decade later, any gift given, or known to have been given, would be a potent indicator of complicity with the *boni homines* and *bone femine* for the inquisition at Saint-Sernin.

Consequently, thirteen days before his wife's testimony, Bernart Mir Arezat attempted to second-guess what the friar-inquisitors might already know, or eventually hear, about him and the heretical chestnuts. So, though the year was now remembered as 1236 and no nasty nephew was involved in the gift, Bernart Mir Arezat testified that "my wife sent Bertran Marti, heretic, one full dish of chestnuts, under my name, of which I was utterly ignorant."[4] As in so many confessions, husbands and wives, parents and children, frequently adopted seemingly contrasting paths to salvation, and while this calculus of the various ways of accessing the divine is important to an understanding of the appeal of the *bons omes* and *bonas femnas*, such familial tolerance, if that is what it is, simply conveyed the potential for evil to one of the friar-inquisitors. Interestingly, four days after his wife's confession, that is, on Friday, 15 June 1246, Bernart Mir Arezat was called back for further questioning; though he did not then talk about chestnuts given to a *bon ome* in 1236 or 1232, he did recall how in 1211, "when I was a boy and the heretics lived openly, they gave me nuts and made me genuflect and to say 'bless us.' "[5] That same day Guilhem de Canast was interrogated by Guilhem Pelhisson, and, though he swore that he had never believed in the heretics, he did admit to the incident of the chestnuts at Guilhem de Sant-Nazari's house, despite dating the gift to 1230 and making no mention of Raimon Mir.[6]

Chestnuts and nuts, the little and the large, the present and the past, fiction and reality were clearly in the thoughts of Bernart Mir Arezat and his interrogators at Saint-Sernin, and even though the two gifts were separated by two decades and very different circumstances, both were now integral parts of Bernart Mir Arezat's life, whether he liked it or not, because his worth as a Christian was being judged on such edible things. Whatever continuities had once allowed Bernart Mir Arezat to recognize something similar about himself from one year to next—that the six-year-old boy in 1211 really did resemble the forty-one-year-old man in 1246—were now, for all intents and purposes, shattered and rebuilt by the two friar-inquisitors. This Lauragais noble was made to rethink habits, memories, childish behavior, things he had not even done, and which he clearly thought innocent, ephemeral, nothing more than gossamer in his life. The inquisition at Saint-Sernin, through making a man see that anything in his past, no matter how mundane, could have profound ramifications, now or in the future, let alone in the way the past itself was understood, profoundly changed the way in which Bernart Mir Arezat remembered, thought about, and imagined himself. A final note about chestnuts, and one that must have must struck Bernard Mir Arezat as bitterly ironic, was that "I wouldn't give the value of a nut," *no doneren d'una notz lo valent,* and "not worth a chestnut," *prezan pas per forsa une castanha,* were common thirteenth-century Toulousain and Lauragais proverbs about a person or thing transparently worthless, forgettable, mere fluff.[7]

Bernart Mir Arezat was, as already stated, made to wear two yellow crosses because of things and actions such as a gift of chestnuts never given.[8] As for Aimersent Mir Arezat, with whom the troublesome chestnuts originated, she was sentenced by Bernart de Caux and Jean de Saint-Pierre on Sunday, 8 July 1246, only four weeks after her confession, to perpetual imprisonment for the crimes of having heard the heretics preach, believing in their errors, and giving them gifts.[9] A week later, the two friar-inquisitors also sent Guilhem de Sant-Nazari to prison for life for having received heretics into his house.[10] Two years later, on Sunday, 29 March 1248, Bernart de Caux and Jean de Saint-Pierre would punish another woman, a certain Esclarmonte de Sauzet of Sainte-Apollonie, whose interrogation does not survive, with perpetual incarceration for, among the usual crimes of a *credens,* baking some bread for the *boni homines* and *bone femine.*[11]

"The clerks and the Friars Preachers have deserved ill," the troubador Guilhem de Montanhagol cynically, but insightfully, sang in 1233 or 1234 with the new *inquisitiones heretice pravitatis* in mind, "because they forbid that which does not suit them, namely, that people should, out of a sense of honor, bestow gifts or offer help."[12] A decade later, this concern about how the lives of things implicated the lives of people for the inquisition, that any gift possessed a potentially incriminating life after giving, permeated thousands of testimonies at Saint-Sernin. For instance, Raimon Taffanel of Villepinte recalled having in 1195 given, on behalf of a certain Saurimunda from Laurac, some eels to the good men in his village, even though "I never believed in them, or adored, or gave, or sent, or heard their preaching."[13] In 1240, the *crezen* Bernart Benedict of Montgaillard remembered passing on three fishes from Bernart de Rocovila to Raimon de Rocovila before, finally, the gift reached the *bon ome* Peire Got and his companion hiding in a nearby wood known as Gomervila.[14] Arnaut d'En Terren of Fanjeaux often presented the gift of incense, on behalf of the *crezens* Veziata Bernart and Aimergart d'En Rioter, to a certain Brunissent, a good woman hiding near the village in 1242. Interestingly, later that year on Christmas Day, Arnaut d'En Terren would carry some freshly baked bread from the secretive Brunissent to Longabruna, the wife of Peire Raimon de Tonenx, and this bread, made by a good woman, was then blessed by some good men.[15] Na Pagana Torrier of Maurens, definitely not a *crezen*, but clearly thinking about such moral continuities in the movement of things, made sure the friar-inquisitors knew that when she sold seven measures of wine to Bernart de Messall in 1242, she did not know, as she heard it said afterward, that the wine had been bought for heretics.[16]

This argument could not be made by a man like Guilhem Cabi Blanc, who carried a dish of fish to some *bons omes* in the woods near his village in 1231; though this was not a gift, in that the good men paid him five shillings of Melgueil for the food, a subtle economic and ethical point at best, he still brought suspicion upon himself by admitting that he had adored the good men before leaving.[17] Similarly, Raimon Pinaut from Mas-Saintes-Puelles, confessing at Saint-Sernin before Arnaut Gaillart, the prior of his village, admitted having been given four pence of Toulouse by the *bons omes* Peire Guilhem and Donat in 1234 for leading and accompanying them through the territory around the *castrum*. Also, like Guilhem Cabi Blanc, Raimon Pinaut recalled adoring the good men only when he left them.[18]

In contrast to the above purchases, Guilhem Helias of Montesquieu acknowledged that in 1211, when there were ten houses of heretics (*.x. mansiones hereticorum*) in the village, he sold another one to some un-named *bons omes* for forty shillings of Toulouse. This sale was not a prob-lem for Guilhem Helias, even though "I've never believed in the heretics, adored them, heard their preaching, given or sent them anything, or led them anywhere."[19] Guilhem Helias, somewhat overdoing his orthodoxy thirty-five years later, and so creating an impossibly pristine image of his day-to-day village existence, still does not seem to have ever been a *crezen*. Unlike the anonymous buyers in Guilhem Helias' memory, the *bons omes* Bernart de la Font and Peire Beneg, according to Jordan de Quiders, purchased a *domus* at Mas-Saintes-Puelles from the sometime *crezen* Pons Magrefort in 1210.[20] Incidentally, the house Guilhem Helias sold the good men must have been either quite small or rather cheap, because, even when inflation and higher urban prices are taken into account, a *domus* four meters wide and twenty-one meters long was worth two hundred shillings in Bernard Gui's tally of properties acquired by the Dominicans between 1248 and 1263, while houses so small that they did not even rate having their measurements recorded cost only forty-six shillings.[21]

All the past "houses of heretics," remembered by men like the noble Bernard Mir Arezat or the cobbler Arnaut Picoc (who confessed on the same day as Guilhem Helias), and which existed quite openly in the early decades of the thirteenth century, that is, before the crusaders came, were undoubtedly acquired in similar, very ordinary, buying-and-selling ways. Peire de Mazerolis, the lord of Gaja-la-Selve, even had a memory of a house at Toulouse simply loaned temporarily. The *crezen* Estotz de Rocovila did this for Peire de Mazerolis' aunt Braida and a number of other noble good women, including his own wife Girauda, *in tempus guerre*, that is, during the Albigensian Crusade.[22]

A problem, however, arises here that is similar to the scribal writing of *hereticus* when a person said *bon ome* at Saint-Sernin, or the deliberate and self-conscious effort by many of those interrogated to speak and think of formerly commonplace things and habits as heretical. It is more than likely that many structures called *domus hereticorum* at Saint-Sernin were not always houses deliberately set aside for groups of *bons omes* and *bonas femnas*; rather, many *domus* renamed as "houses of heretics" when recollected at Saint-Sernin must simply have been dwellings where men like Jordan Sais' serfs and Arnaut Picoc's cobblers lived. The elderly Bernart Gasc, for example, remembered that he and his mother, Marqueza, once lived in a house at Fanjeaux for about a year in 1176, "near the *domus* of Guilhem de Carlipac, heretic," and, thinking of his innocent appetite as a child, he also recalled, "I ate there often, as he gave me bread, wine, and nuts." Bernart Gasc then contrasted this memory, easily the oldest heard at Saint-Sernin, of one house occupied by one friendly good man with the recollection that his village, thirty years later in 1206, possessed a number of what he specified as *domus hereticorum*.[23]

Unquestionably, there were houses before the crusaders came, no doubt often quite tiny, where the good men and good women lived together, as so many confessions at Saint-Sernin testify (even when the twists of scribal wordplay are taken into account). These houses, at least in the memories of those confessing, seem to be particularly associated with women, young and old, and *bonas domnas*, noble ladies, at that. Many of the previously discussed girl *bonas femnas* were clearly deposited in these houses because they came from noble families that, like so many in the Lauragais, were not particularly wealthy. The already-mentioned Covinens Mairanel was rudely left with some older good women in 1212 by her *crezen* brother Peire Coloma when she was around twelve years old, that is, the age of her majority, the time when she could be married and so provided with a dowry.[24] Still—this cannot be emphasized enough—these heretical houses should never be seen as analogous to monasteries or *Frauenkonvente*.[25] The gifts and donations of *crezens* to the good men and good women, for one thing, never equal those given to more orthodox establishments throughout the Lauragais and the Toulousain.[26] Then again, these houses of good women were not meant to compete with Catholic institutions; on the contrary, they, like so much else in the Lauragais before the inquisitors came, were the stone manifestations of the normal contingent patterns of the holy in a village, where the choice between a monastery and a "house of heretics" for a young girl often depended more on local practice than on fervent heretical belief.

Covinens Mairanel did not mention whether her brother left any monies with the *bonas molhers,* but the Vaudreville knight Guilhem Airoart did make such an admission. In 1215, Guilhem Airoart and his brother Pons paid for the expenses of their mother Bernarta Airoart when she left their *hospitum,* after she became a *bona domna,* for another *hospitum* in the village.[27] The noble Guilhem Airoart's slightly pompous and deliberate use of *hospitum,* which was gaining popularity with the Toulousain and Lauragais nobility in the early thirteenth century as a term describing their residences, was a rather grand way of differentiating his house, and so the house his mother retired to, from other houses in the village.[28] The *hospitum* Bernarta Airoart moved to, and presumably died in, was, more than likely, a dwelling with other noble good women like herself, unmarried and elderly, but her architecturally proud son never called his mother's new *hospitum* a "house of heretics." Guilhem Airoart also stressed for the two friar-inquisitors that this was the only time he gave the heretics anything throughout his entire life.[29]

Also, though many girls were sent to houses with older good women, and then made into child *bonas femnas,* there really is no implication that such a transformation of these infants into diminutive examplars of the passively holy was necessarily for life. In many ways an infant's entering a house of *bonas femnas* was no different from the little migrations to live with an older woman, almost always an aunt or grandmother, that all Lauragais girls seem to have undertaken in the years before their majority at twelve. It was not so much that a girl was turned into a good woman—that is to concentrate on the beginning of the journey; the point was, rather, that the aunt or grandmother who was to receive her was a *bona molher* in a house of similar matronly women, and so the girl, for the duration of her visit in a *domus* of older unmarried women, had to be a *bona molher* too.

Already, a number of confessions have shown this common occurrence of young girls' traveling to live with old women, and, moreover, within these testimonies there has been the implication that the expected length of the visit, variable from weeks to years, frequently determined whether or not the child was made into a good woman. Crivessent Pelhicier, for instance, the Plaigne woman who told Bernart de Caux about the mutilation of the inquisitor Guilhem Arnaut, began her confession by immediately recalling how in 1205, at the age of four, she went to Laurac to live with her grandmother and the old woman's friends, some elderly *bonas molhers.* Crivessent Pelhicier stayed with her grandmother, whom she never called a heretic, for five years in that Laurac *domus*, which she never called a "house of heretics" either, and though she ate, drank, and slept in the same house as these good women, neither did she adore them nor was she made a good woman herself.[30]

The houses in which the good men lived, before the coming of the *crucesignati*, never seem to have been anything at all like the houses within which old women and young girls quietly dwelt. For a start, the *domus* of the good men seem to have been, quite literally, open houses. In 1216, when Peire Serni traveled from Mas-Saintes-Puelles to Laurac, with six other men, to build a new stone gate for this village, all of them ate, by the mandate of the *vila*, in the *domus* of Izarn de Castres, a deacon of the *bons omes*. In this house Peire Serni saw two other good men, but neither he nor his laboring mates ever adored or saw others adore the *bons omes*.[31] This is, perhaps, an intriguing demonstration of one community's believing that a good man's house was a focal point, a safe *domus*, a separate space, where working men not from the village could eat and stay without disturbing the tempo of Laurac. The good men, just as physically caught within the walls of nearness, closeness, and perpetual immediacy as anyone else in a village, created in their public and open houses, in their blatant acceptance that all things could be seen and heard, in their deep acquiescence in what was most traumatic in communal life, exhilarating pockets of grand insouciance toward the everyday world. Bernart Mir Arezat, in his first testimony, still remembered how the *bon ome* Raimon Bernart, embodying this studied disinterest in earthly affairs, was able to solve a dispute over a debt that the lord of Saint-Martin-de-la-Lande had with two other knights in 1226.[32] Sanctity, in men and buildings, was achieved through a sort of nonchalance toward visible reality, toward the Devil-made constraints of village existence.

"Fifteen days ago," said Guilhem Calvet of Montmaur on Friday, 8 June 1246, before Arnaut, the chaplain of Saint-Paulet, and the scribe Bernart de Ladignac, "Guilhem Calvet, my nephew, sick and depressed, said to me that he thought he'd die soon, and, if he could, he wished the heretics to have all his goods." Guilhem Calvet then asked his nephew how he should go about this, and the sick Guilhem Calvert told his uncle about Peire Marti and Raimon Amelii in the nearby parish of Airoz, who would lead him to the *bons omes*. The uncle went in search of these two men, found them, and then explained what he wanted. Peire Marti and Raimon Amelii still had to check Guilhem Calvet's story; once they had, a clandestine meeting was arranged at night in a field belonging to Guilhem Alazaïs. Guilhem Calvet, in an interesting mix of courtroom honesty and avuncular anguish, told his interrogators how he, Peire Marti, and Raimon Amelii waited all night in anticipation of the good men's arrival, "yet they didn't come, and we wondered a great deal, but, through the grace of God, we soon found them." Guilhem Calvet ended his testimony by saying that his nephew wanted some pennies to give to the *bons omes*, and, as far as the uncle knew, these coins found their way into the hands of the heretics.[33]

Guilhem Calvet's testimony captures the profound shift in the habits of *crezens, bons omes,* and *bonas femnas* that occurred with the end of the Albigensian Crusade and the beginning of the inquisitions into the Lauragais. In almost every testimony recalling these years before 1230, whether by a *crezen* or not, a person can name each good man and good woman individually, something that happens very rarely after this time, when so many *bons omes* and *bonas femnas* become anonymous figures merely populating the nighttime landscape outside a village. Guilhem Calvet's recent activities also emphasize that the source of most of the monies which the good men and good women possessed, particularly after 1230, came from deathbed bequests. Curiously, as far as goods and gifts were concerned, deathbed or otherwise, the memories recorded at Saint-Sernin from this time show the good men and good women to have been quite interested in, if not greedy for, money and things.

Peire Devise, *clericus* of the priest of Auriac, even confessed on Monday, 19 March 1246, with no friar-inquisitor listening, that a year earlier, when two *bonas femnas* were locked in a wooden cage next to the house of Auriac's priest, "I wrote a regulation of their testament," before the good women were taken to Toulouse. The two imprisoned women told Peire Devise that they wished to give this piece of parchment, this "testament, that is, a regulation of their affairs," to a certain Andreva de Auriac, who, in turn, would give it to some "believers of the heretics" with whom the *bonas femnas* had left a small amount of money. Peire Devise hastily scribbled out, more than likely in abbreviated Latin, the final wishes of the good women (which, far from being otherwordly, appear to have been totally financial) and gave the testament to Andreva de Auriac. Unfortunately, the priest of Auriac at the time, the tenacious Marti de Cesalles, immediately found out about this parchment scrap; though Andreva de Auriac quickly hid it between her breasts with an innocent "What document, Lord?" when the priest confronted her outside Auriac's church, this angry and agitated prelate, knowing full well what was going on, simply put his hand down her dress and extracted it. "My Lord, I swear to God I have nothing to do with this!" exclaimed Andreva de Auriac, somewhat surprised and shocked, before she quickly tried to explain away her guilt by saying that she had found the testament only by chance, by coincidence, outside the heretics' makeshift gaol.[34]

Further, confessions about gifts given in the third and fourth decades of the thirteenth century always evoked at Saint-Sernin the shadow world that the good men and good women now occupied, whether in woods or other secret places, throughout the Lauragais. The Auriac youth Bernart Aurussa had only ever met, adored, given a gift to, or heard the preaching of the *bons omes* in the dark of night amid the tangle of woods. In 1239, for instance, Bernart Aurussa and five other male *crezens* went to meet the *bon ome* Haimon Forz at night "beneath the chestnut trees near Auriac."[35] Moreover, if the *bons omes* and the *bonas femnas* were to survive this twilight existence from one day to the next, *ductores*, men who led them, *receptatores*, individuals who were willing to receive them, and *nuncii*, men who traveled with them so as to arrange lodgings, were crucial. Or, at least, desperately important to Bernart de Caux and Jean de Saint-Pierre, who chose all these words to describe individuals helping the good men and good women. It was almost as if all the qualities that had once made the *bons omes* and *bonas femnas* appear to be possessed of a holiness worthy of respect—their common involvement in, and placid retreat from, village routine—became, through fear and danger, enhanced by the unavoidable peripatetic habits that they now had to undertake. Marqueza de Columbiac of Lavaur, however, did recall that an old *crezen* knight named Raimon de Castlar wanted nothing to do with the new fugitive *bons omes*, "because all are dead that were good."[36]

Indeed, as the nature of the good men and good women changed, as they left the intimacy of villages for the intimacy of vineyards and woods, as their relationship to the Lauragais became even more stark, so the essence of being a *crezen* took on a precision it never had before—as in the Fanjeaux fund-raising scramble the former *crezen* Bernart de Cailhavel narrated on Monday, 15 May 1245, only a couple of weeks after Bernart de Caux and Jean de Saint-Pierre began their inquisition. Bernart de Cailhavel began by telling the two friar-inquisitors about the time in 1233 when the *bayles* of Fanjeaux, Ainart and Guilhem Ugon, captured four *bons omes* in the house of Bernart Forner. Incidentally, Bernart Marti, who had eaten that full dish of chestnuts only a year or so earlier at Saint-Martin-de-la-Lande, was one of the good men caught. Anyhow, after the arrest of the *bons omes*, Bernart Forner's wife, Causida, immediately went to Bernart de Cailhavel and made him come with her to the workshop of a certain Peitavin Armier, also a *crezen*. It was here that Causida Forner informed Bernart de Cailhavel and Peitavin Armier that the four good men could be freed for three hundred shillings of Toulouse.[37]

"Guilhem de Palarac, twenty-five shillings of Toulouse, Bernart Fabre, cutler, five shillings, Guilhem Martel, ten shillings," and so on, as Bernart de Cailhavel confessed twelve years later, with surprisingly precision, the inventory of all the shillings and pence that the *crezens* of Fanjeaux, rich and poor, struggled throughout the night to collect. Bernart Marti and his fellow good men were released the next day; the *crezens* of Fanjeaux, no doubt bankrupting themselves, had found the money.[38] This reflected a very different understanding from what it had meant to believe in the good men only a few years earlier, and it was a frightening realization that to believe in the *bons omes* now possessed a new and dangerous kind of clarity. A more modest example of this reevaluation of what a *crezen* did, or thought he could do, was recalled by Giraut Durant when he talked about visiting two *bonas femnas* in a wood near Auriac in 1244, and how a friend of his, Peire Guilhem, gave the good women a gift of some cabbages that he had stolen from a garden. "I didn't give them anything," Giraut Durant confessed his poverty, "because I didn't have anything."[39] In this new world of attempted subterfuge, clandestine meetings, stolen vegetables, and perpetual fear, even "God was a fugitive," or so Giraut Durant recalled hearing the good women say.[40]

As the behavior of *crezens* became more self-consciously obvious in the Lauragais, so too did the reactions of men and women who wanted nothing to do with the heretics. Raimon Jocglar from Saint-Martin-de-la-Lande, testifying on the same day as Bernart Mir Arezat's second confession and Guilhem de Canast's first, began by describing how three years previously in 1243 he had journeyed to a place called la Peira, near Beaupuy, and so left his daughter Raimona and his son Raimon behind. Unfortunately, when he came back, he found inside his house two *bonas femnas*. "I then asked my son and daughter who'd sent these heretics," and though the son chose to stay quiet, Raimona confessed that Izarn Gibel had persuaded her to let the good women stay. Indeed, she went on to tell her father that this *ductor* and *receptator* had promised her "great good," *magnum bonum*, if she received the good women. This seems to have been too much for Raimon Jocglar, and, in a fit of almost theatrically violent anger, he cursed his daughter, beat her, and "I threw her from the house, naked, without any clothes." Raimon Jocglar then went around to Izarn Gibel's house and threatened this *crezen* and his wife. Finally, after all this, now that his position on heresy was clearly known throughout the village, he expelled the *bonas femnas* from his house. And yet, almost as if to make sure it was publicly understood who was the *crezen* and who was the Catholic that day, he deliberately led the good women to Izarn Gibel's *domus*. "And then," Raimon Jocglar added, as if he did not really care one way or other, "my daughter made herself a heretic, though I never saw her afterward, but I did hear it said that she's converted." As in all testimonies, though here it might seem rather unnecessary, Raimon Jocglar still noted that he did not adore the good women or see anyone else adore them.[41]

Guilhem Guasc, not at all a *crezen*, found two good men in a wood near Saint-Germier called Rivala de Bigons when he went there one day to work in the winter of 1242. He did not realize that they were *bons omes* until they followed him about "asking me to love them," and declaring "that I should listen to the Epistles and the Evangelist." The good men lived in the wood for half a year until the summer of 1242, but "I didn't attempt to go back into the wood," Guilhem Guasc confessed on Tuesday, 4 July 1245, "on account of the heretics." Guilhem Guasc, even though he told the heretics to leave him alone and mentioned that he had a brother who was a *clericus*, was still hesitant to enter the wood for six months because it might be thought that he was a heretical sympathizer. He was frightened not so much of the heretics themselves as of all the connotations that heresy and woods, particular times and places, hidden men and seasons of the year, now had in the Lauragais.

At dusk one day in 1241 Guilhem de Rival unexpectedly found two *bons omes* and three *crezens* secretly meeting in a vineyard near Lagarde. This discovery was not at all deliberate; it was simply a coincidence, in that Guilhem de Rival was actually searching for some cows.[42] Similarly, it was a coincidence, an incident totally unanticipated, when those two intuitive cowherds Arnaut del Faget and Guilhem Vezat found heretics in the woods near Maurens in 1243. Indeed, Arnaut del Faget stressed the unintended nature of this discovery by saying that all he had done was follow the barking of his dogs—so, in fact, his knowledge of the heretics was once removed to begin with. Arnaut del Faget even went on to tell the inquisition about how fifteen days later he came back to those woods with the *bayle* of Lavaur to capture these two men. Unfortunately, the two supposed heretics were nowhere to be found.[43] Likewise, Peire Alaman of Mas-Saintes-Puelles testified that the only reason he saw the *bon ome* Bertran de Maireville in 1235 was "because I found him by accident when I went hunting with my dogs."[44]

The woods, fields, streams, vineyards, seasons, even the day and night of the Lauragais were all transfigured by the inquisition into spaces, times, sounds, sensations of light that could no longer be taken for granted, that could no longer be experienced without a second thought. Why a man or a woman happened to be somewhere at some time, whether beneath a tree or in a street at night, was now something that always needed to be explained. People, food, clothing, an empty hut, anything discovered among trees or blurred by darkness were all suspicious, were all obviously marked by the residue of heresy. This is one of the most remarkable aspects of the model of consequentiality imposed upon the Lauragais by Bernart de Caux and Jean de Saint-Pierre, in that these two mendicants, simply through their questions, managed to transform, or to finally confirm, how thousands of men and women saw, felt, heard, and understood landscape and light in their lives.

Bernart de Quiders, the lord of Mas-Saintes-Puelles, had to argue for unanticipated consequences, and so his innocence, when Bernart de Caux called him back on Monday, 3 July 1245, to explain why in 1220, according to Peire Raimon Prosat's testimony, "Bernart de Quiders, in the workshop of [the scribe] Peire Gauta, with other men of Mas-Saintes-Puelles present, acting of his own volition, urinated on my tonsure" ("I'm an acolyte," he mentioned, in a quick aside) "in opprobrium and vituperation of the whole Catholic Church."[45] Bernart de Quiders, in response to such an accusation, recollected how on that particular night, fifteen years previously, "some Mas-Saintes-Puelles fellows were playing dice in the house of Peire Gauta, and," assuming that prudery would be applauded by a friar-inquisitor, "I became annoyed because the players were cursing"; yet Bernart de Caux must have been a little amused to hear that the logical response of a middle-aged *miles* to swearing was "[S]o I climbed on a chest and urinated on the players' table." Now, Bernart de Quiders sheepishly speculated, "I think that part of the urine fell on the tonsure of Peire Raimon Crozat [*sic*] who was seated with the players, but I didn't see it or do it on purpose."[46] Despite such a straight-faced response, Bernart de Quiders, the same man who cruelly pushed meat into the mouths of his heretical mother and sister, was sentenced by the friar-inquisitors on Friday, 1 June 1246, to the penance of two yellow crosses.[47]

The importance of coincidence, and it occurs in many testimonies describing the recent Lauragais past, is that unlike the earlier decades when the heretics dwelt out in the open, and so associating with them was unavoidable, a person who saw, heard, or helped a *bon ome* or *bona femna* in the middle of the thirteenth century was now an individual who had to be completely aware of what he or she was doing. Coincidence was the only way of breaking the friar-inquisitors' consequential formula. Essentially, emphasizing that an action was unexpected, unintended, unanticipated was an attempt at separating cause and effect, as the friar-inquisitors saw such things, and so severing the sequence of complicity that went from, say, seeing a good man at dusk to being a *crezen* to being a future giver of chestnuts.

# 16

## TWO YELLOW CROSSES

BERNART de Caux and Jean de Saint-Pierre in their *Processus inqui-sitionis* outlined the punishment to be imposed on men and women who, though judged guilty of the criminal stigma of her-esy, nevertheless wished to return to the bosom of Holy Mother Church as, somewhat paradoxically, the very private penance of always having to carry a letter describing the very public penance now visibly regulating their lives. The letter, in part, told readers (and listeners) that the individ-ual who had just handed over the parchment *littere penitentiarum* had to

> wear two crosses, one on the breast and one on the shoulders, yellow in
> color, two palms in height, two in breadth, each arm three fingers in width.
> The clothing on which he [or she] wears the crosses shall never be yellow
> in color. As long as he [or she] lives, he [or she] shall attend mass and
> vespers on Sundays and feast days, as well as a general sermon if one is deliv-
> ered in the village where he [or she] is, unless some impediment without
> fraud prevents it. He [or she] shall follow processions for so many years,
> bearing large branches in his [or her] hand, walking between the clergy and
> the people, in each procession in which he [or she] is displaying him- [or
> her-] self in such aspect that he [or she] reveals to the people that he [or
> she] is doing penance there because of acts he [or she] committed against
> the faith.[1]

In the two hundred and seven known sentences that the two friar-inquisitors pronounced in a series of general sermons given, largely at Saint-Sernin, between Sunday, 18 March, and Sunday, 22 July 1246, only twenty-three did not involve having to wear yellow crosses. Instead, these twenty-one men and two women who had "shamefully offended God and the Church" were all punished with perpetual incarceration in a "decent and humane prison."[2] Further, no property was directly confiscated as a result of the inquisition at Saint-Sernin, and, as far as we know, no man or woman was ever burnt by Bernart de Caux and Jean de Saint-Pierre for heresy.[3]

These absurdly small figures make one awfully reticent about drawing too many conclusions simply based upon the sentences of Bernart de Caux and Jean de Saint-Pierre themselves. This must seem somewhat of an anticlimax, as if the last page has been rudely torn from a murder mystery. Nonetheless, what has survived seems to accord with much that has been suggested about the two Dominicans and their inquisition into the Lauragais, in that the friar-inquisitors' preference—if that is not too strong a word, given the paucity of information—for distributing yellow crosses, for forcing men and women to visibly alter their habits, and so allowing their fellow villagers to see such shifts in routine, is in keeping with a detective model that understood individuals as existing only through their relationships with other people. If such collective relations were the causes of individual heresy, then a sprinkling of crosses would be its communal undoing.

As a person was guilty through his or her complicity with others, and vice versa, so the penance of the yellow crosses was an equally complicit model, affecting not only the individuals being punished but also the men and women who did not dress in crosses. It was a punishment that played upon, and in a sense enhanced, that oppressive intimacy of the village that the *bons omes* and *bonas femnas* had sought to evade. Moreover, many Lauragais communities already had, or supposedly had, men and women walking through village squares displaying their yellow crosses. Around 1209, Dominic Guzman made Guilhema Marti wear crosses for two years at Fanjeaux because, as a girl, she gave bread and nuts to the heretics for the "love of God." Apart from the crosses, so Guilhema Marti told Bernart de Caux on Monday, 15 March 1246, "I couldn't eat meat except at Christmas, Easter, and Pentecost." She also had some letters of penance from Dominic Guzman, but these were lost when, in the first year of the Albigensian Crusade, "Fanjeaux was burnt by the Count of Montfort." The widow Arnauta de Fremiac, also from Fanjeaux and confessing on the same Monday as Guilhema Marti, compelled by her uncle Izarn Bola into being a child *bona femna* in the first decade of the thirteenth century, was made to wear two yellow crosses by Dominic Guzman until she found herself a husband. She wore them for a year until her marriage to the late Arnaut de Fremiac. Soon after, though, the abbot of Saint-Papoul imposed another cross-wearing penance upon Arnauta de Fremiac, but these strips of yellow fabric stayed stitched to her clothes for only two months. "Why did you throw away the crosses?" Bernart de Caux wanted to know. "Everyone else marked with crosses threw their crosses away, so I got rid of mine," Arnauta de Fremiac remembered her individual reasoning, based on communal example, from three decades earlier.[4]

At Mas-Saintes-Puelles, the elderly Ermengart Aichard, a *bona femna* for only six weeks in 1195, was given the penance of two yellow crosses by Folquet de Marselha, the bishop of Toulouse, just before the crusaders came, "and I wore them openly, though one of the crosses fell in the street."[5] Na Comdors Heuna from the same village, forced by her mother to be a good woman for nine months in 1200 at the age of ten, was also decorated with crosses by Folquet de Marselha around the same time as

Ermengart Aichard, and "though I carried them under my pelisse in winter, I wore them outside all the other times."[6] Guilhema Gaufreza, again dressed in crosses by Folquet de Marselha, and a girl *bona femna* for two years at the end of the twelfth century, did not even attempt to wear her yellow penitential markers outside her Mas-Saintes-Puelles house.[7] The constant observation of these women tagged with crosses—bright saffron yellow and hard to miss—by everyone in their village must have been quite unbearable. Indeed, "I never made fun of those marked with crosses from the inquisitors," a Mas-Saintes-Puelles man, Guilhem Pellissa, simply had to tell Bernart de Gaus, the inquisitorial scribe who questioned him.[8] Guilhem Pellissa's somewhat overdone confession of tolerance toward those doing penance for heresy at Mas-Saintes-Puelles does imply, quite deliberately of course, just how terrible the manner of some people must have been in the village.

As for those twenty-three people condemned to imprisonment, permanently removing them from the life of a village—that can only be an admission on the part of the friar-inquisitors that the habits of these people could never be changed, could never be altered through yellow crosses. Instead, by imprisonment, such men and women ceased to exist. If people were understood as individuals who derived their identity from past actions and relations, and from the anticipation that such habitual forms would be repeated, then imprisonment, by severing all ties, all relations, made men like Peire Guilhem de Rocovila and women like Aimersent Mir Arezat simply stop living, as far as the friar-inquisitors were concerned.

Popes, however, could change what two Dominicans might have intended. For instance, Pons Barrau, "richer than anyone else in Mas-Saintes-Puelles," and sentenced by Bernart de Caux and Jean de Saint-Pierre on Sunday, 18 August 1247, to perpetual incarceration for his crimes as a *credens*, was, after sixteen months in the Château Narbonnais, released by Innocent IV in a special papal penitentiary on Thursday, 24 December 1248.[9] The reason for Pons Barrau's release, which had nothing specifically to do with the Lauragais inquisitions, had everything to do with the struggle between the papacy and the Friars Preachers over who should continue the work of the inquisitors in Languedoc in the last half of the thirteenth century.[10] Everyone else condemned by Bernart de Caux and Jean de Saint-Pierre to permanent imprisonment stayed, it seems, in prison for life.

It should be stressed, and the scarcity of evidence about what happened to all those interrogated by the two friar-inquisitors necessitates such emphasis, that the very process of bringing so many people to Saint-Sernin to be questioned, and making them confess, was in itself a penitential exercise for the men and women of the Lauragais. There should be no doubt that Bernart de Caux and Jean de Saint-Pierre, and those they questioned, were well aware of this aspect of the inquisition. The whole procedure, from beginning to end, functioned as a form of spiritual inoculation, if somewhat time-delayed in a few cases, against the disease of heresy. Saint-Sernin was a laboratory in which the practice of confession, in and of itself, as the only form of *penitentia* necessary to a Christian, was tried and tested. In this way, the habit of confessing that would eventually dominate the thoughts and lives of all medieval (indeed, all modern) men and women, and all the implications that confession had (and has) for individual and communal identity, can already be vividly perceived in the testimonies collected from the Lauragais.[11]

Three years after the Lauragais inquisition, Raimon VII, count of Toulouse, died at the age of seventy on Monday, 27 September 1249. Twenty-one years later, the fifty-six-year-old Louis IX, king of France, weak, ill, and defeated, died while on crusade outside Tunis on Monday, 25 August 1270. A year after the death of Louis IX, his brother Alphonse de Poitiers, who had become the count of Toulouse in 1249, died at fifty-one. Alphonse de Poitiers had unexpectedly had no children with Joanna de Tolosa; his vast properties as count of Toulouse, which he visited, all in all, for only about a month in twenty-odd years, were, following the 1229 Peace of Meaux-Paris, now absorbed by the *regnum* of France.[12] In 1281 the body of Bernart de Caux was exhumed, twenty-nine years after the Dominican had died, and reburied beneath a grander tomb that better accommodated, according to Bernard Gui, the affection of pilgrims for this "hammer of heretics."[13] Two years earlier at Paris, Philip III, the king of France after Louis IX, issued during August 1279 an amnesty for two hundred and seventy-eight men and women from the Toulousain and the Lauragais whose properties had been confiscated because of involvement in heresy and other crimes.[14]

Fifty-seven of the persons named in the royal pardon of 1279 had, three decades earlier, been interrogated and punished by Bernart de Caux and Jean de Saint-Pierre. One of the fifty-seven, for instance, was na Austorga de Resengas, the mother of the fervent *crezen* Orbria, that chaste wife of the *crezen* Guilhem Sais, callous lord of Cambiac and the man who stuffed poor Aimersent Viguier into a wine barrel in 1245.[15] Na Austorga de Resengas had been condemned to perpetual imprisonment on Sunday, 25 March 1246, by the two friar-inquisitors in the cloister of Saint-Sernin because of her errors as a *credens*, not the least of which was her attempt to hereticate her dying husband Peire de Resengas against his will.[16] These fifty-seven names in the amnesty of 1279 were the last faint echo of the thousands of voices heard by Bernart de Caux and Jean de Saint-Pierre in those two hundred and one days of questioning at Saint-Sernin.

As faith in the "friends of God" started disappearing in the middle of the thirteenth century, as Lauragais men and women stopped seeing holiness in the *bons omes* and *bonas femnas*, those who still believed in the heretics now did so with a new awareness about themselves: a self-consciousness that was, ironically, made precise and clear through the very men who wished to punish them, that is, through the two friar-inquisitors. In never giving any relationship the benefit of a doubt, in always seeing deliberate implications in the accidental, Bernart de Caux and Jean de Saint-Pierre made every person who answered their questions think about, if only for a moment, how what an individual did, or would do, related to what he or she did, or would, think. Yet, and this can never be stressed enough, even with this severely consequential model shaping interrogations and the analysis of testimonies, no elaborate international heretical organization was discovered by the two Dominicans, nor, no matter how many times manuscript 609 is read, will a "Cathar Church" be found by modern historians—on the contrary, an intimate, intensely local, and deliberately unadorned way of living with the holy will be discerned. It was this mundane experience of a quiet sanctity in the Lauragais that the two friar-inquistors reshaped, transformed, and so eliminated.

This does not mean that the thousands questioned by Bernart de Caux and Jean de Saint-Pierre immediately forgot what constituted the holiness of the good men and good women. Such an understanding did not vanish overnight, even with yellow crosses in village streets and squares; what vanished was merely the reasons for adopting that understanding in practice. For without the constant entrenchment of adoption, understanding will eventually fade and disappear. That is why within any society there will always be fuzzy spots where the mortise work which supports a culture, that subtle carpentry of metaphor and matter, has begun to slip. In the end, as these seams separate further, the reasons for remembering why something is done or thought dissipate. As men and women no longer believed in the *bons omes* and *bonas femnas*, as they no longer gave gifts to them, as they no longer felt the imprint of their relationships with each other, and with the holy, in day-to-day rituals of greeting, then, and only then, would the good men and good women truly disappear from the memory of the Lauragais. Societies really do forget as easily as they remember.

# 17

## LIFE AROUND A LEAF

BERNART de Caux and Jean de Saint-Pierre, through their two hundred and one days of questioning at Saint-Sernin, through making individuals think about certain continuities in their lives, through demanding that a particular style of truth be understood even by those who wished to resist it, forever changed the way in which men and women thought about themselves in the Lauragais. A polite nod given without a second thought in a doorway at Laurac, but seen by someone else or innocently remembered, now took on such significance that the subsequent relations a person had, and was anticipated to have, were so different in meaning and intention from what they would have been without the perceived consequences of a quickly given courtesy that essentially a new man or a woman was created.

This taking apart of a world and causing it to be remade, quickly and so very differently from what had been there before, is what is so fascinating and frightening about the great inquisition of Bernart de Caux and Jean de Saint-Pierre. The world of the Lauragais, recast in the consequential determinism of the two friar-inquisitors, where past actions were forever anticipating future deeds, meant that men or women who adored a *bon ome* in 1247 not only knew why they were doing it, because of relationships buried in time already lived, but also knew they would go on doing it, because the present act was a prediction of time yet to unfold. The confessional model of reality through which Bernart de Caux and Jean de Saint-Pierre questioned, judged, and punished the Lauragais became, paradoxically, the very method by which thousands of men and women now understood their existence in the world, now understood their lives within, and around, village streets, dark woods, tiny houses, and all those smudged leaves of inquisitorial parchment and paper.

# NOTES

## ABBREVIATIONS

AD                        Archives départementales.

AN                        Paris, Archives nationales.

Doat                      Paris, Bibliothèque nationale, Collection Doat.

*HGL*                     Claude Devic and Joseph Vaissette, *Histoire Générale de Languedoc avec des notes et les pièces justificatives*, ed. Auguste Molinier, 2d ed., 16 vols. (Toulouse: Édouard Privat, 1882–1904).

*Layettes*                Alexandre Teulet et al., *Layettes du Tresor des chartes*, 5 vols. (Paris: H. Plon, 1863–1909).

MS 609                    Toulouse, Bibliothèque municipale, MS 609.

*PL*                      J. P. Migne, ed., *Patrologiae cursus completus: Series latina* (Paris: Garnier, 1844–1904).

*RHGF*                    M. Bouquet et al., *Recueil des historiens des Gaules et de la France*, 24 vols. (Paris: [imprint varies], 1738–1904).

*Sacrorum conciliorum*    J. D. Mansi, ed., *Sacrorum conciliorum nova et amplissima collectio*, 54 vols. (1759–1798; Paris: H. Welter, 1901–1927).

## CHAPTER 2
### THE DEATH OF ONE CISTERCIAN

1.  Pierre des Vaux-de-Cernay, *Historia Albigensis*, ed. Pascal Guébin and Ernest Lyon, Société de l'Histoire de France (Paris: Librairie Ancienne Honoré Champion, 1926), 1:54, §59, where he reproduced the letter of Pope Innocent III, issued on 10 March 1208, that specified the manner in which Peire de Castelnau was killed. Guilhem de Tudela, *La Chanson de la Croisade Albigeoise*, ed. and trans. Eugène Martin-Chabot, Les Classiques de l'Histoire de France au Moyen Age (Paris: Société d'édition «Les Belles Lettres», 2d ed., 1960) 1:14, laisse 4, noted the complexion of the assassin's heart but, unlike Pierre des Vaux-de-Cernay, sang that Peire de Castelnau was killed by a sharp sword's being driven into his spine. Pierre des Vaux-de-Cernay has been translated by W. A. and M. D. Sibly as *The History of the Albigensian Crusade* (Woodbridge: The Boydell Press, 1998); while Janet Shirley has translated the *canso* of Guilhem de Tudela and his anonymous continuator as *The Song of the Cathar Wars: A History of the Albigensian Crusade* (Aldershot: Scolar Press, 1996).

All personal names, if the origin of the individual is known, are given in medieval Occitan rather than the more common, and frequently misleading, modern French or English. To avoid confusion, however, I give Lauragais and Toulousain villages and towns their modern spellings. I have, throughout, always attempted consistency and clarity.

2.  It is in *La Chanson de la Croisade Albigeoise*, 1:15, laisse 4, that the unnamed assassin's family are said to have come from Beaucaire.

3. Peire de Castelnau's murder was also described by Guilhem de Puylaurens, *Chronica Magistri Guillelmi de Podio Laurentii*, ed. and trans. Jean Duvernoy, Sources d'Histoire Médiévale (Paris: Éditions du Centre National de la Recherche Scientifique, 1976), p. 52. On the various prejudices and talents of Pierre des Vaux-de-Cernay, Guilhem de Puylaurens, and Guilhem de Tudela, see the excellent introduction and notes of the Sibleys in *The History of the Albigensian Crusade*, pp. xix–xlvi; Shirley in *The Song of the Cathar Wars*, pp. 1–10; Duvernoy in *Chronica*, pp. 1–20; Michel Roquebert, *L'épopée Cathare*, vol. 1, *1198–1212: L'invasion* (Toulouse: Privat, 1970), 211–19; and Yves Dossat, "La croisade vue par les chroniqueurs," *Cahiers de Fanjeaux: Paix de Dieu et guerre sainte en Languedoc au XIII$^e$* 4 (1969): 221–259. More generally, and concerned only with troubadours, see William Paden, "The Troubadours and the Albigensian Crusade: A Long View," *Romance Philology* 49 (1995): 168–191, and Michael Routledge, "The Later Troubadours . . . noels gigz de nova maestria . . . ," in *The Troubadours: An Introduction*, ed. Simon Gaunt and Sarah Kay (Cambridge: Cambridge University Press, 1999), pp. 99–112.

4. *PL* 215, cols. 1354–1358; *Layettes*, vol. 1, no. 841; and *Historia Albigensis*, 1:51–65, §§55–65, quoted the letter verbatim.

5. *La Chanson de la Croisade Albigeoise*, 1:14, laisse 4, and *Historia Albigensis*, 1:30–31, §27 [*The History of the Albigensian Crusade*, p. 21 n. 35].

6. Innocent III to Count Raimon VI of Toulouse, 29 May 1207, *PL* 215, cols. 1166–68, and *RHGF* 13:140.

7. *PL* 215, cols. 1354–1358; *Layettes*, vol. 1, no. 841; and *Historia Albigensis*, 1:64–65, §64.

8. Cf. Achille Luchaire, *Innocent III: La Croisade des Albigeois* (Paris: Libraire Hachette, 1911), pp. 119–122.

9. *La Chanson de la Croisade Albigeoise*, 1:14, laisse 4, "Per so qu'el agues grat del comte an avant." Guilhem de Tudela, ibid., p. 4 and n. 1, laisse 1, said that he was in the entourage of Baudui, the youngest son of Count Raimon V of Toulouse and Constance, sister of King Louis VII of France. In May 1211 Baudui left his brother Raimon VI to fight with Simon de Montfort (ibid., pp. 176–188, laisses 73–77). Raimon VI hanged Baudui from a walnut tree outside Montauban in February 1214 (*Historia Albigensis*, 2:186–193, §§495–500, and *The History of the Albigensian Crusade*, p. 121 n. 13).

10. On the lands and titles of Raimon VI in Languedoc, see Walter L. Wakefield, *Heresy, Crusade and Inquisition in Southern France 1100–1250* (London: George Allen & Unwin, 1974), pp. 50–64, and Auguste Molinier, "Étude sur l'administration féodale dans le Languedoc," *HGL* 7, cols. 132–212.

11. Innocent III had sent Philip II Augustus a copy of his widely circulating letter of 10 March 1208. See n. 4. The pope also sent the king a personal letter of 3 February 1209, *PL* 215, col. 1545. Philip II Augustus, in a curt and dismissive letter—April 1208, *HGL* 8, col. 558—instructed the pope that legally, *de jure*, no one could seize the lands of Raimon VI unless the count of Toulouse was formally condemned for heresy. Moreover, these lands belonged (at least in principle) to the domain of France, and it was only the king of France who could proclaim them open to conquest and seizure. Philip II Augustus ended his lesson in the law by saying that, so far as he knew, the papal *curia* had not officially judged

Raimon VI to be a heretic, and, until that happened, the king of France, busy in warfare against King John of England, would not move against his vassal the count of Toulouse.

12. May 1208, *HGL* 8, cols. 563–564.

13. *La Chanson de la Croisade Albigeoise*, 1:24, laisse 8. Pierre des Vaux-de-Cernay, *Historia Albigensis*, 1:81–84, §82 [*The History of the Albigensian Crusade*, p. 47 and nn. 5–11], proudly noted that, apart from the duke of Burgundy and the count of Nevers, there were, among the noble and powerful *crucesignati*, Pierre, the archbishop of Sens, Gautier, Robert, and Guillaume, the bishops of Autun, Clermont, and Nevers, Gaucher de Châtillon, the count of Saint Pol, Milo IV, the count of Bar-sur-Seine, Guichard IV de Beaujeu, Guillaume des Roches, seneschal of Anjou, Gaucher de Joigny, lord of Châteaurenard, Simon de Montfort, a baron from the Ile-de-France and titular earl (through his mother) of Leicester, and Arnaud Amalric, abbot of Cîteaux and the papal legate appointed to lead the crusade.

14. *La Chanson de la Croisade Albigeoise*, 1:36, laisse 12.

15. Wakefield, *Heresy, Crusade and Inquisition in Southern France*, p. 112 n. 1. See, for example, *La Chanson de la Croisade Albigeoise*, 1:38, laisse 13, where he tallied up twenty thousand crusading knights and two hundred thousand other followers.

16. *Historia Albigensis*, 1:67, § 68 [*The History of the Albigensian Crusade*, p. 39 n. 51]. It is a pun on "Tolosanus dolosanus."

17. The reconciliation of Raimon VI, along with what was expected of him, was recorded in the *Processus negotii Raymundi Comitis Tolosani* in *PL* 216, cols. 89–98. On the count's taking up the cross, see *PL* 216, col. 95. The reaction of Innocent III in a letter of 27 July 1209, surprisingly warm and foreseeing no further difficulties between the Church and the count, is in *PL* 216, col. 100.

18. *La Chanson de la Croisade Albigeoise*, 1:44–47, laisse 15, and *Historia Albigensis*, 1:85–86, §83.

19. *La Chanson de la Croisade Albigeoise*, 1:52, laisse 18, and *Historia Albigensis*, 1:90–91, §89 [*The History of the Albigensian Crusade*, p. 50 and n. 28].

20. *La Chanson de la Croisade Albigeoise*, 1:54, laisse 19.

21. Ibid., p. 56, laisse 20.

22. Ibid., p. 58, laisse 21.

23. Ibid., p. 60, laisse 22, for the cry of "A foc! a foc!" and *Historia Albigensis*, 1:91, §90, for the term "ribauds" [*The History of the Albigensian Crusade*, p. 50 and n. 30].

24. Arnaud Amalric to Innocent III, August 1209, *PL* 216, col. 139.

25. See, especially, Appendix B in *The History of the Albigensian Crusade*, pp. 289–293, for a thoughtful analysis of the massacre at Béziers. William Chester Jordan, *The French Monarchy and the Jews: From Philip Augustus to the Last Capetians* (Philadelphia: University of Pennsylvania Press, 1989), pp. 122–124, has some interesting observations concerning Languedocian Jews, Raimon-Roger Trencavel, and the massacre at Béziers.

26. Wakefield, *Heresy, Crusade and Inquisition in Southern France*, pp. 100–103, 112 n. 4.

27. Yves Dossat, *Les crises de l'Inquisition Toulousaine au XIIIᵉ siècle (1233–1273)* (Bordeaux: Imprimerie Bière, 1959), p. 155, and idem, "Une figure d'inquisiteur: Bernard de Caux," *Cahiers de Fanjeaux: Le Crédo, la Morale, et l'Inquisition* 6 (1971): 253–254, where it is argued that Bernart de Caux came, more than likely, from Agen rather than the diocese of Béziers.

28. *Historia Albigensis*, 1:95–96, §§94–95.

29. Ibid., pp. 96–98, § 96, and *La Chanson de la Croisade Albigeoise*, 1:66–68, laisse 25.

30. *La Chanson de la Croisade Albigeoise*, 1:74–76, laisse 30, and *Chronica*, p. 62.

31. *Historia Albigensis*, 1:101–102 and 105, §§101 and 105, for the use of *peregrini* to describe the crusaders [*The History of the Albigensian Crusade*, pp. 55–56 nn. 60–65, and p. 57 n. 70]; *La Chanson de la Croisade Albigeoise*, 1:84, laisse 34; and Arnaud Amalric to Innocent III, August 1209, *PL* 216, col. 140, where he used the term *communi consilio* regarding Simon de Montfort's acquisition of the lands of Raimon-Roger Trencavel. See Simon de Montfort's letter to Innocent III, *PL* 216, cols. 141–142, and the pope's replies in two letters of 11 and 12 November, *PL* 216, cols. 151–153. On Simon de Montfort, see Yves Dossat, "Simon de Montfort," *Cahiers de Fanjeaux: Paix de Dieu et guerre sainte en Languedoc au XIIIᵉ* 4 (1969): 288–298. Cf. Roquebert, *L'épopée Cathare*, 1:279–290, on Simon de Montfort's motives.

32. *Historia Albigensis*, 1:105–106, §105.

33. Ibid., pp. 112–113, §108.

34. *HGL* 5, col. 36, and *La Chanson de la Croisade Albigeoise*, 1:94, laisse 37, where the poet was adamant, against the rumors of murder, that Raimon-Roger Trencavel had died of dysentery.

35. *La Chanson de la Croisade Albigeoise*, 1:100, laisse 41, and *Historia Albigensis*, 1:120–122, §§116–117 [*The History of the Albigensian Crusade*, pp. 64–65 and n. 105]. See also Simon de Montfort's letter to Innocent III, *PL* 216, cols. 141–142.

36. *Historia Albigensis*, 1:122–124, §§118–120.

37. Ibid., pp. 117–118, §113 [*The History of the Albigensian Crusade*, pp. 62–63 and n. 102].

38. *La Chanson de la Croisade Albigeoise*, 1:96–98, laisse 39, and the details of this delegation were given in a letter to Pere II of Aragon by the Toulousains of July 1211, *HGL* 8, cols. 612–619. See also *The History of the Albigensian Crusade*, pp. 74–75 n. 42.

39. *La Chanson de la Croisade Albigeoise*, 1:98–101, laisse 40.

40. *Historia Albigensis*, 1:211 and n. 1, §212 [*The History of the Albigensian Crusade*, p. 108 n. 38]. Three Languedocian ecclesiastical councils—Saint-Gilles in the late summer of 1210, Narbonne starting around 22 January 1211, and Montpellier a month later—refused any reconciliation with Raimon VI. *Historia Albigensis*, 1:167–168, 196–197, 210–211, §§164, 195, 212 [*The History of the Albigensian Crusade*, pp. 88–89 nn. 59–62, 101–102 n. 9, 108 n. 38]; *La Chanson de la Croisade Albigeoise*, 1:140–154, laisses 58–61; and Wakefield, *Heresy, Crusade and Inquisition in Southern France*, pp. 104–105.

41. *PL* 216, cols. 410–411.

42. *Historia Albigensis*, 1:131–132, §127.

43. Ibid., pp. 147–149, §142. Cabaret itself was taken soon after by Simon de Montfort, not only because knights from this *castrum* were harassing his supply lines but because, in a cruel irony, any crusader caught near the village was being disfigured by blinding and the removal of his nose. See also *The History of the Albigensian Crusade*, p. 92 n. 81.

44. *Historia Albigensis*, 1:214–230, §§215–230 [*The History of the Albigensian Crusade*, pp. 111–118 and especially n. 9]

45. *Historia Albigensis*, 1:227–228, §227 [*The History of the Albigensian Crusade*, p. 117 and n. 44]; *Chronica*, pp. 66–71, said that three hundred heretics were burnt; and *La Chanson de la Croisade Albigeoise*, 1:164–166, 172–174, laisses 68, 71, described how ninety-four heretical "traitors" were discovered in a tower in the castle.

46. *Historia Albigensis*, 1:230–231, §231 [*The History of the Albigensian Crusade*, p. 119 and n. 3].

47. *The History of the Albigensian Crusade*, p. 119 n. 4.

48. *Historia Albigensis*, 1:232–233, §233 [*The History of the Albigensian Crusade*, p. 120 and n. 7]; *Chronica*, p. 72, which gave the same figure of sixty; and *La Chanson de la Croisade Albigeoise*, 1:200–202, laisse 84.

49. *La Chanson de la Croisade Albigeoise*, 1:190, laisse 79.

50. For example, ibid., p. 112, laisse 47.

51. Ibid., pp. 190–191 and n. 1, laisse 79.

52. *Historia Albigensis*, 1:243–251, §§243–251.

53. Ibid., pp. 252–283, §§253–285; Roquebert, *L'épopée Cathare*, 1:440–448; and Wakefield, *Heresy, Crusade and Inquisition in Southern France*, p. 106.

54. *Historia Albigensis*, 1:283–293, §§286–300, 2:1–61, §§301–361 [*The History of the Albigensian Crusade*, pp. 143–169]; *La Chanson de la Croisade Albigeoise*, 1:246–288, laisses 111–130; and Wakefield, *Heresy, Crusade and Inquisition in Southern France*, pp. 106–109.

55. *Historia Albigensis*, 2:62–64, §§362–363 [*The History of the Albigensian Crusade*, pp. 170–171], and *La Chanson de la Croisade Albigeoise*, 1:280–284, laisse 127. See Pierre Timbal, *Un Conflit d'annexion au Moyen Age: L'Application de la coutume de Paris au pays d'Albigeois* (Toulouse: Edouard Privat, 1949), Appendix, pp. 177–184, for a Latin edition of Simon de Montfort's statutes, and *The History of the Albigensian Crusade*, Appendix H, pp. 320–329, for an English translation.

56. *Historia Albigensis*, 2:65–66, §367 [*The History of the Albigensian Crusade*, pp. 172–173 nn. 1–2]. See Wakefield, *Heresy, Crusade and Inquisition in Southern France*, pp. 106–108.

57. Derek Lomax, *The Reconquest of Spain* (London: Longman, 1978), pp. 124–128, and John France, *Western Warfare in the Age of the Crusades, 1000–1300* (Ithaca: Cornell University Press, 1999), pp. 137, 166–167.

58. *Historia Albigensis*, 2:67–85, 97–111, 128–134, §§368–388, 399–419, 438–441 [*The History of the Albigensian Crusade*, pp. 173–180 nn. 4–39, 185–193 nn. 1–42].

59. *Historia Albigensis*, 2:85 and n. 1, §389 [*The History of the Albigensian Crusade*, p. 180 n. 40]. The oaths of allegiance are given in *PL* 216, cols. 845–849. See Michel Roquebert, *L'épopée Cathare*, vol. 2, *1213–1216: Muret ou la dépossession* (Toulouse: Privat, 1977), 90–168, for the general history of these events, and

John W. Baldwin, *The Government of Philip Augustus: Foundations of French Royal Power in the Middle Ages* (Berkeley and Los Angeles: University of California Press, 1986), pp. 360–361, for the meaning of *regnum* in the early thirteenth century.

60.  *La Chanson de la Croisade Albigeoise*, 2:12–36, laisses 135–141; *Historia Albigensis*, 2:138–179, §§446–486 [*The History of the Albigensian Crusade*, pp. 203–219 nn. 1–90]; and *Chronica*, pp. 78–86 [trans. as Appendix I in *The History of the Albigensian Crusade*, pp. 330–333]. On Muret, see France, *Western Warfare in the Age of the Crusades*, pp. 167–169; Wakefield, *Heresy, Crusade, and Inquisition in Southern France*, pp. 109–112; Roquebert, *L'épopée Cathare*, 2:187–233; and Jonathan Sumption, *The Albigensian Crusade* (London: Faber and Faber, 1978), pp. 164–169.

61.  *La Chanson de la Croisade Albigeoise*, 2:40–89, laisses 143–152; *Historia Albigensis*, 2:259–263, §§570–572 [*The History of the Albigensian Crusade*, pp. 253–255 nn. 40–57]; and *Chronica*, pp. 92–94. The judgment of Innocent III at the Fourth Lateran Council was set out in a papal letter of 14 December 1215, *RHGF* 19:598–599 and *HGL* 8, col. 681. See also *The History of the Albigensian Crusade*, pp. 311–312, for a translation of the letter.

62.  On Bouvines, see Georges Duby, *Le Dimanche de Bouvines, 27 juillet 1214* (Paris: Gallimard, 1973) [trans. by Catherine Tihanyi as *The Legend of Bouvines: War, Religion, and Culture in the Middle Ages* (Berkeley and Los Angeles: University of California Press, 1990)]; Baldwin, *The Government of Philip Augustus*, pp. 207–219; and France, *Western Warfare in the Age of the Crusades*, pp. 235–241.

63.  *La Chanson de la Croisade Albigeoise*, 2:32–36, laisse 141, and *Historia Albigensis*, 2:242–247, §§550–553 [*The History of the Albigensian Crusade*, pp. 246–248 nn. 1–11]. On this crusade undertaken by Prince Louis, see Charles Petit-Dutaillis, *Étude sur la vie et le règne Louis VIII (1187–1226). Thèse présenté à la Faculté des Lettres de Paris* (Paris: Librairie Émile Bouillon, 1894), pp. 184–193.

64.  *Historia Albigensis*, 2:264–265, §573 [*The History of the Albigensian Crusade*, pp. 255–256 n. 58]. On Philip II Augustus and the homage of Simon de Montfort, see Roquebert, *L'épopée Cathare*, 2:345–397, and Baldwin, *The Government of Philip Augustus*, pp. 336–339.

65.  *La Chanson de la Croisade Albigeoise*, 2:91–262, laisses 153–180; *Historia Albigensis*, 2:266–293, §§574–599 [*The History of the Albigensian Crusade*, pp. 257–270 nn. 1–80]; and *Chronica*, pp. 94–96.

66.  *La Chanson de la Croisade Albigeoise*, 2:274, laisse 182.

67.  Ibid., p. 276.

68.  Ibid., 2:208, laisse 172.

69.  Ibid., p. 276, laisse 182.

70.  Ibid., p. 280, laisse 183.

71.  Ibid., p. 282, "«A, lassa!», so ditz ela, «tant be m'anava ier!»"

72.  Ibid., pp. 284–308, laisses 183–186, 3:8–16, laisse 187, and *Historia Albigensis*, 2:296–299, §§ 601–603 [*The History of the Albigensian Crusade*, pp. 270–271 nn. 83–94].

73.  *La Chanson de la Croisade Albigeoise*, 3:86, laisse 194 [cf. translation in *The Song of the Cathar Wars*, p. 147], "E el camp de Montoliu es plantatz us jardis, / Que tot jorn nais e brolha, e es plantatz de lis, / Mas lo blanc el vermelh, qu'i grana e floris, / Es carn e sanc e glazis e cervelas gequis. / Entr'esperitz e armas

e pecatz e mercis / Novelament i pobla iferns e paradis." On this *jardin*, see Wakefield, *Heresy, Crusade and Inquisition in Southern France*, p. 120. Generally, on the siege of Toulouse and the death of Simon de Montfort, see Michel Roquebert, *L'épopée Cathare*, vol. 3, *1216–1229: Le Lys et La Croix* (Toulouse: Privat, 1986), 70–147.

74. *La Chanson de la Croisade Albigeoise*, 3:204, laisse 205. The anonymous *canso*-continuator, ibid., pp. 8–226, laisses 187–207, devoted almost two thousand lines to the siege of Toulouse. Somewhat shorter descriptions occur in the *Historia Albigensis*, 2:298–320, §§603–617, and the *Chronica*, pp. 100–104. On the siege, see Sumption, *Albigensian Crusade*, pp. 192–198; Wakefield, *Heresy, Crusade and Inquisition in Southern France*, pp. 118–122; and France, *Western Warfare in the Age of the Crusades*, pp. 110–111, 122–124.

75. *La Chanson de la Croisade Albigeoise*, 3:110, laisse 196.

76. Ibid., pp. 206–208, laisse 205; *Historia Albigensis*, 2:315, §612315; and *Chronica*, pp. 102.

77. *La Chanson de la Croisade Albigeoise*, 3:226, laisse 207. *Chronica*, p. 104, noted that Simon de Montfort was buried *more gallico*. On such northern burial habits, see *La Chanson de la Croisade Albigeoise*, 3:226–227 n. 5.

78. *La Chanson de la Croisade Albigeoise*, 3:234, laisse 208. Roquebert, *L'epopée cathare*, 3:144–162, and Wakefield, *Heresy, Crusade and Inquisition in Southern France*, p. 122.

79. Honorius III to Philip II Augustus, urging the king to send his son on crusade, *Regesta Honorii papae III*, ed. Petrus Pressutti (1888; reprint, Hildesheim: Georg Olms Verlag, 1978), 1:263, no. 1578, and another letter of 5 September to both Philip Augustus and Louis, ibid., p, 264, no. 1583.

80. Honorius III in *RHGF* 19:669–670 and *Regesta Honorii papae III*, 1:312–313, nos. 1891–1892. Baldwin, *The Government of Philip Augustus*, pp. 337–338, is good on the efforts of Honorius III at involving Philip II Augustus in the southern crusade.

81. Petit-Dutaillis, *Étude sur la vie et le règne Louis VIII*, pp. 196–197; Wakefield, *Heresy, Crusade and Inquisition in Southern France*, pp. 122–123; and Baldwin, *The Government of Philip Augustus*, p. 338.

82. *La Chanson de la Croisade Albigeoise*, 3:284, laisse 212, and *Chronica*, pp. 106–108.

83. *La Chanson de la Croisade Albigeoise*, 3:290, laisse 212.

84. Petit-Dutaillis, *Étude sur la vie et le règne Louis VIII*, pp. 198–199, and Wakefield, *Heresy, Crusade and Inquisition in Southern France*, p. 123.

85. *Chronica*, p. 108. Cf. Petit-Dutaillis, *Étude sur la vie et le règne de Louis VIII*, pp. 200–201.

86. *Chronica*, p. 112. See Petit-Dutaillis, *Étude sur la vie et le règne de Louis VIII*, p. 202.

87. Baldwin, *The Government of Philip Augustus*, pp. 389–392.

88. Wakefield, *Heresy, Crusade and Inquisition in Southern France*, pp. 124–125, and Roquebert, *L'épopée Cathare*, 3:229–237.

89. *Chronica*, pp. 112–116.

90. *HGL* 8, no. 241, cols. 815–816. Now, see Wakefield, *Heresy, Crusade and Inquisition in Southern France*, p. 125; and Michael Costen, *The Cathars and the Albigensian Crusade* (Manchester: Manchester University Press, 1997), p. 153.

91. *HGL* 8, no. 261, cols. 858–859.

92. Petit-Dutaillis, *Étude sur la vie et le règne de Louis VIII*, pp. 279–296, and Wakefield, *Heresy, Crusade and Inquisition in Southern France*, p. 125.

93. *Chronica*, pp. 118–120.

94. Ibid., pp. 121–124. See Petit-Dutaillis, *Étude sur la règne de Louis VIII*, pp. 297–328, on the 1226 crusade and death of Louis VIII.

95. Guilhem Figueira, "D'un sirventes far en est son que m'agenssa," in *Los Trovadores: Historia y Textos*, ed. Martín de Riquer (Barcelona: Editorial Planeta, 1975), 3:1274.

96. *Chronica*, esp. pp. 124–128, for the massacre of the population at Labécéde, a small village in the Lauragais, in 1227.

97. Pierre Belperron, *La Croisade contre les Albigeois et l'union de Languedoc à la France (1209–1249)* (Paris: Perrin, 1967), pp. 405–406, and Wakefield, *Heresy, Crusade and Inquisition in Southern France*, pp. 126–127.

98. *HGL* 8, no. 270, cols. 878–883, for the preliminary articles accepted at Meaux, and no. 271. cols. 883–893, for the Peace of Paris. Alexandre Teulet also edited the treaty between Raimon VII and Louis IX in *Layettes*, vol. 2, no. 1992, pp. 147–152.

99. Jacques Le Goff, *Saint Louis* (Paris: Gallimard, 1996), pp. 108–109.

100. *HGL* 8, no. 271, col. 885. Jordan, *The French Monarchy and the Jews*, pp. 105–127, is excellent about Jews and the Albigensian Crusade.

101. On the term *faidit*, see *The History of the Albigensian Crusade*, p. xlii.

102. Belperron, *La Croisade*, pp. 407–41; Wakefield, *Heresy, Crusade and Inquisition in Southern France*, pp. 127–128; Roquebert, *L'épopée Cathare*, 3:374–420; and Joseph Strayer, *The Albigensian Crusades. With a New Epilogue by Carol Lansing* (1971; Ann Arbor: University of Michigan Press, 1992), pp. 136–137.

103. Sumption, *Albigensian Crusade*, pp. 224–225, and Roquebert, *L'épopée Cathare*, 3:423–426.

104. Le Goff, *Saint Louis*, p. 108, and Strayer, *The Albigensian Crusades*, pp. 137–138.

105. *HGL* 8, no. 271, col. 884, and Dossat, *Les crises de l'Inquisition Toulousaine au XIII$^e$ siècle*, p. 110.

106. On the many uses of the Albigensian Crusade in southern French life, past and present, see, for example, Robert Gildea, *The Past in French History* (New Haven: Yale University Press, 1994), pp. 208–213; Susan Carol Rodgers, "Good to Think: The 'Peasant' in Contemporary France," *Anthropological Quarterly* 60 (1987): 56–63; Vera Mark, "In Search of the Occitan Village: Regionalist Ideologies and the Ethnography of Southern France," *Anthropological Quarterly* 60 (1987): 64–70; Winnie Lem, "Identity and History: Class and Regional Consciousness in Rural Languedoc," *Journal of Historical Sociology* 8 (1995): 198–220; and idem, *Cultivating Dissent: Work, Identity, and Praxis in Rural Languedoc* (Albany: State University of New York Press, 1999), p. 81.

## CHAPTER 3
### WEDGED BETWEEN CATHA AND CATHAY

1. *Encyclopædia Britannica*, 11th ed. s.v. "Cathars."

2. Ibid. When Conybeare published *The Key of Truth: A Manual of the Paulician Church of Armenia* (Oxford: Oxford University Press, 1898), he argued on pp. lv–lvi that the Paulicians were the direct ancestors of the Cathars. Indeed, he included a translation on pp. 160–170 of the Provençal Cathar ritual edited by Leon Clédat in *Le Nouveau Testament traduit au XIIIᵉ siècle en langue provençale, suivi d'un rituel cathare* (Paris: E. Leroux, 1897), pp. 470–82. John Bagnall Bury discussed this work of Conybeare's, and agreed with his notion of Paulician ancestry for the heretics of Languedoc, in an appendix to his edition of Edward Gibbon's *The History of the Decline and Fall of the Roman Empire* (London: Methuen & Co., 1898), 5:543. Gibbon himself, 5:124–125, thought the Cathars (or Albigensians, as he called them) were descended from the Paulicians as well. Conybeare's other publications that mentioned the Cathars—"A Hitherto Unpublished Treatise against the Italian Manicheans," *American Journal of Theology* 3 (1899): 704–28, and, with F. P. Badham, "Fragments of an Ancient (? Egyptian) Gospel Used by the Cathars of Albi," *Hibbert Journal* 11 (1913): 805–818—argued for similar continuities. Now, see Walter L. Wakefield's comments on Conybeare in "Notes on Some Antiheretical Writings of the Thirteenth Century," *Franciscan Studies* 27 (1967): 285–321, esp. p. 285 n. 4.

3. See, for example, Charles Schmidt, *Histoire et Doctrine des Cathares* (1849; Bayonne: Jean Curutchet les Éditions Harriet, 1983), esp. pp. 1–54, and Henry Charles Lea, *A History of the Inquisition of the Middle Ages* (New York: Harper & Brother, 1887), vol. 1, esp. pp. 89–92, who argued for a broad chain of ideas, through time and over space, in a manner similar to Conybeare's. On Schmidt, see Yves Dossat, "Un initiateur: Charles Schmidt," *Cahiers de Fanjeaux: Historiographie du catharisme* 14 (1979): 163–184, and Bernard Hamilton, "The State of Research: The Legacy of Charles Schmidt to the Study of Christian Dualism," *Journal of Medieval History* 24 (1998): 191–214. On Lea, see Edward Peters, "Henry Charles Lea (1825–1909)," in *Medieval Scholarship. Biographical Studies on the Formation of a Discipline*, vol. 1, *History*, ed. Helen Damico and Joseph B. Zavadil, Garland Reference Library of the Humanities, 1350 (New York: Garland Publishing, 1995), pp. 89–100.

4. In the far-from-illustrious *New Encyclopædia Britannica*, Micropædia, 15th ed., the anonymous author of the half-page entry on the "Cathari" (now smothered between "catgut" and "catharis") says almost exactly the same as Conybeare did eighty years earlier—but without the latter's erudition or flair.

5. For some of the ideas adopted (and adapted) in this chapter, see especially Mary Douglas, "Rightness of Categories," in *How Classification Works: Nelson Goodman among the Social Sciences*, ed. idem and David Hull (Edinburgh: Edinburgh University Press, 1992), pp. 239–271; idem, *In the Wilderness: The Doctrine of Defilement in the Book of Numbers*, Journal for the Study of the Old Testament Supplement Series, 158 (Sheffield: Sheffield Academic Press, 1993), pp. 26–29; idem, "Comment: Hunting the Pangolin," *Man*, n.s., 28 (1993): 161–164; Pierre Bour-

dieu, *Le sens pratique* (Paris: Les Éditions de Minuit, 1980) [trans. and condensed by Richard Nice as *The Logic of Practice* (Cambridge: Polity Press, 1990)]; and Marilyn Strathern, *The Gender of the Gift: Problems with Women and Problems with Society in Melanesia*, Studies in Melanesian Anthropology, 6 (Berkeley and Los Angeles: University of California Press, 1990). Two much-cited anthropological justifications of the intellectualist approach to religion (and so heresy) are Robin Horton, "African Conversion," *Africa* 41 (1971): 85–108, and Clifford Geertz, "Religion as a Cultural System," in his *The Interpretation of Cultures: Selected Essays* (New York: Basic Books, 1973), pp. 87–125.

6. This view was explicitly stated by Herbert Grundmann throughout his influential *Religiöse Bewegungen im Mittelalter. Untersuchungen über die geschichtlichen Zusammenhänge zwischen der Ketzerei, den Bettelorden und der religiösen Frauenbewegung im 12. und 13. Jahrhundert und über die geschichtlichen Grundlagen der deutschen Mystik*, 2d ed. (1935; Hildesheim: Georg Olms, 1961), esp. pp. 396 ff., 503 [*Religious Movements in the Middle Ages: The Historical Links between Heresy, the Mendicant Orders, and the Women's Religious Movement in the Twelfth and Thirteenth Century, with the Historical Foundations of German Mysticism*, trans. Steven Rowan (Notre Dame: University of Notre Dame Press, 1995), and see esp. Robert E. Lerner, "Introduction," ix–xxv]. By contrast, it is implicit, for example, in Jean Duvernoy, *Le catharisme: la religion des cathares* (Toulouse: Privat, 1976); idem, *Cathares, Vaudois et Beguins, dissidents du pays d'Oc*, Domaine Cathare (Toulouse: Privat, 1994); René Nelli, *La philosophie du catharisme: le dualisme radical au XIII^e siècle*, (Paris: Payot, 1978); and Anne Brenon, *Le vrai visage du Catharisme* (Portet-sur-Garonne: Éditions Loubatières, 1988). Now, see Jeffrey Burton Russell, "Interpretations of the Origins of Medieval Heresy," *Medieval Studies* 25 (1963): 34, where he emphasized over thirty years ago that most modern writers, especially Grundmann, favored intellectual or moral reasons for medieval heresy and implicitly rejected any thesis that took account of the material world. The irony here is not only that Russell's observation is still correct but that the somewhat older Russell, in works such as *Lucifer: The Devil in the Middle Ages* (Ithaca: Cornell University Press, 1984), is just as intellectualist, ahistorical, and moralizing as the historians his younger self had once criticized.

7. This attitude governed Arno Borst's important *Die Katharer*, Schriften der Monumenta Germaniae Historica (Deutsches Institut für Erforschung des Mittelalters), 12 (Stuttgart: Anton Hiersemann Verlag, 1953) [trans. into French by Charles Roy as *Les Cathares*, Bibliothèque Historique (Paris: Payot, 1978)], and, under the confessed influence of Borst, Malcolm Lambert's revised *Medieval Heresy: Popular Movements from the Gregorian Reform to the Reformation*, 2d ed. (1977; Oxford: Blackwell Publishers, 1992), esp. p. 126 n. 126. This guiding assumption caused Borst, *Die Katharer*, p. 49, to refer, rather weirdly, to Austin Evans' not especially outlandish arguments about heresy as being based upon a "sozialistische These"—simply because Evans thought that there was some relation between the society in which heretics lived and their beliefs. See Evans, "Social Aspects of Medieval Heresy," in *Persecution and Liberty: Essays in Honor of George Lincoln Burr* (New York: Columbia University Press, 1931), pp. 93–116, and John H. Mundy, *The Repression of Catharism at Toulouse*, Studies and Texts, 74 (Toronto: Pontifical Institute of Medieval Studies, 1985), p. 57 n. 49. See also Borst's discus-

sion of the life and work of Herbert Grundmann (it reveals much about both men) in "Herbert Grundmann (1902–1970)," in *Herbert Grundmann Ausgewählte Aufsätze. Teil 1 Religiöse Bewegungen*, Schriften der Monumenta Germaniae Historica, 25 (Stuttgart: Anton Hiersemann Verlag, 1976), pp. 1–25.

8. Steven Runciman's *The Medieval Manichee: A Study of the Christian Dualist Heresy* (Cambridge: Cambridge University Press, 1947; reprint, 1982) is a famous illustration of this assumption that original religious intent can be inferred despite the passage of millennia and alterations of landscape. Yuri Stoyanov, *The Hidden Tradition: The Secret History of Medieval Christian Heresy* (London: Arkana, 1994), assumes the same ability to follow dualist thought, whether Mahayana Buddhism or Bogomilism, through time and space.

9. The Cistercian Caesarius of Heisterbach in his early-thirteenth-century *Dialogus Miraculorum*, ed. Joseph Strange (Cologne: H. Lempertz & Co., 1851), 1.5.21, pp. 300–303, in the chapter *De haeresi Albiensium*, compared the heretical tenets of the Languedocian heretics with the heresies of the Manichees. The Benedictine Wibald of Corvey, writing to Manegold of Paderborn in 1147, deftly stated the guiding principle of this explanatory technique (medieval and modern) when he noted—in Ep. 167, *Monumenta Corbeiensia*, ed. Philip Jaffé, Bibliotheca Rerum Germanicarum (Berlin: Weidmann, 1864), 1:278—that so much had already been written "that it is impossible to say anything new [ut nichil iam possit dici novum]," and that even heretics "do not invent new things but repeat old ones [non nova inveniunt, set vetera replicant]." Three or four years earlier, Eberwin, the prior of Steinfeld's Premonstratensian abbey, in a letter (Ep. 472, *PL* 182, col. 679) to Bernard of Clairvaux, described a group of dualist heretics (usually labeled as Cathars) seized in Cologne who, when brought to trial, defended their beliefs by saying that their heresy had "lain concealed from the time of the martyrs even to our own day," and, intriguingly, they went on to say that these hidden philosophies had apparently "persisted so in Greece and certain other lands [. . . hanc haeresim usque ad haec tempora occultatam fuisse a temporibus martyrum, et permansisse in Graecia et quibusdam aliis terris]."

10. See, for example, in the nineteenth century, Jules Michelet, *Histoire de France: Moyen Age* (Paris: Ernest Flammarion, 1869), 2:317–319; Célestin Douais, *Les Albigeois. Leurs origines, action de l'église au XII^e siècle* (Paris: Didier et C^ie, 1879), pp. 1–216; Lea, *A History of the Inquisition of the Middle Ages*, vol. 1, esp. p. 92. In the twentieth century, see, for example, Hans Söderberg, *La Religion des Cathares: Étude sur le Gnosticisme de la Basse Antiquité et du Moyen âge* (Uppsala: Almqvist & Wiksells Boktr, 1949), passim, esp. p. 6; Heinrich Sproemberg, "Die Enstehung des Manichäismus im Abendland," in *Mittelalter und demokratische Geschichtsschreibung*, ed. Heinrich Sproemberg and Manfred Unger, Ausgewählte Abhandlungen, Forschungen zur mittelalterlichen Geschichte, 18 (Berlin: Akademie-Verlag, 1971), pp. 85–102; Armand Abel, "Aspects sociologiques des religions 'manichéennes,' " in *Mélanges offerts à René Crozet*, ed. René Crozet, Pierre Gallais, and Yves Jean Rion (Poitiers: Société d'études Médiévales, 1966), 1:33–46; Roger French and Andrew Cunningham, *Before Science: The Invention of the Friars' Natural Philosophy* (Aldershot: Scolar Press, 1996), p. 103, asserting that the "derivation of Catharism from Manicheeism is almost certainly correct, and on its long journey, chronologically and geographically, the heresy has developed variations"; Lutz

Kaelber, *Schools of Asceticism: Ideology and Organization in Medieval Religious Communities* (University Park: Pennsylvannia State University Press, 1998), p. 175; and Hamilton, "The State of Research: The Legacy of Charles Schmidt to the Study of Christian Dualism," pp. 194–195, where he implies that a continuity may still be established between the Manichaeans and the Cathars. Interestingly, Schmidt, *Histoire et Doctrine des Cathares*, p. 253, thought that there was no connection between the Cathars and the Manichees.

11. See, for example, Dimitri Obolensky, *The Bogomils: A Study in Balkan Neo-Manichaeism* (Cambridge: Cambridge University Press, 1948), passim, and Antoine Dondaine, "Aux origines de l'hérésie médievale," *Rivista di Storia della Chiesa in Italia* 6 (1952): 78, ". . . les Cathares occidentaux étaient fils des Bogomils, eux-mêmes héritiers du lointain Manichéisme."

12. On the Bogomils, see Franjo Šanjek, *Les chrétiens bosniaques et le movement cathare XII^e–XV^e siècles*, Publications de la Sorbonne, NS Recherches, 20 (Brussels: Editions Nauwelaerts-Diffusion Vander Oyez, 1976); idem, "Dernières traces de catharisme dans les Balkans," *Cahiers de Fanjeaux: Effacement du Catharisme? (XIII^e– XIV^e S.)* 20 (1985): 119–134; Jaroslav Šidak, *Studije o "Crkvi Bosanskoj" i Bogumilstvu*, Biblioteka Znanstvenih Radova (Zagreb: Sveucilisna naklada Liber, 1976); Dimitar Angelov, "Der Bogomilismus in Bulgarien," *Bulgarian Historical Review* 2 (1975): 34–54; idem, "Ursprung und Wesen des Bogomilentums," in *The Concept of Heresy in the Middle Ages (11th–13th C.). Proceedings of the International Conference, Louvain May 13–16, 1973*, ed. W. Lourdaux and D. Verhelst, Medievalia Lovaniensia, Series I—Studia IV (The Hague: Leuven University Press–Martinus Nijhoff, 1976), pp. 144–156; and John V. A. Fine, Jr., *The Early Medieval Balkans: A Critical Survey from the Sixth to the Late Twelfth Century* (Ann Arbor: University of Michigan Press, 1983), pp. 171–79, esp. 179, where this thought-provoking observation is made: "[I]f we are analyzing Bulgarian history as a whole and significant movements and causes of historical developments in Bulgaria, Bogomilism's importance has been tremendously exaggerated in all historical works. In fact . . . one would be justified in writing a history of medieval Bulgaria without the Bogomils at all. . . ."

13. See, for example, the arguments for Bogomil influence in western Europe before the twelfth century by Borst, *Die Katharer*, pp. 71–80; Runciman, *The Medieval Manichee*, pp. 117–18; Dondaine, "Aux origines de l'hérésie médievale," 43–78; Malcolm Lambert, *Medieval Heresy: Popular Movements from Bogomil to Hus* (London: Edward Arnold, 1977), pp. 24–36, 343–348; Jean-Pierre Poly and Eric Bournazel, *La Mutation féodale, x^e–xii^e* (Paris: Presses Universitaire de France, 1980), pp. 382–427 [trans. Caroline Higgitt as *The Feudal Transformation, 900–1200* (New York: Holmes and Meier, 1991), pp. 272–308]; Heinrich Fichtenau, *Ketzer und Professoren: Häresie un Vernunftglaube im Hochmittelalter* (Munich: C. H. Beck'sche Verlagsbuchhandlung, 1992), pp. 17–53 [trans. Denise A. Kaiser as *Heretics and Scholars in the High Middle Ages: 1000–1200* (University Park: Pennsylvania State University Press, 1998), pp. 13–51]. Robert Moore, in "Heresy, Repression, and Social Change in the Age of Gregorian Reform," in *Christendom and Its Discontents: Exclusion, Persecution, and Rebellion, 1000–1500*, ed. Scott L. Waugh and Peter D. Diehl (Cambridge: Cambridge University Press, 1996), pp. 19–46, and "The Birth of Popular Heresy: A Millennial Phenomenon?" *Journal of Reli-*

*gious History* 24 (2000): 8–25, repeats his nuanced opposition—first articulated in "The Origins of Medieval Heresy," *History* 55 (1970): 21–361—to these opinions. Other important arguments against Bogomil influence in the early Middle Ages were made by Raffaello Morghen, *Medioevo Cristiano* (Bari: Laterza, 1953), pp. 212–86; idem, "Problèmes sur l'origine de l'hérésie au moyen-âge," *Revue historique* 336 (1966): 1–16; Henri-Charles Puech, "Catharisme médieval et bogomilisme," in his *Sur le Manicheisme et autres essais*, Idees et Recherches (Paris: Flammarion, 1979), pp. 395–427; Raoul Manselli, *L'eresia del male* (1963), 2d ed. (Naples: Morano, 1980), pp. 118–38; Brian Stock, *The Implications of Literacy: Written Language and Models of Interpretation in the Eleventh and Twelfth Centuries* (Princeton: Princeton University Press, 1983), pp. 98–99, 102–103; and Guy Lobrichon, "The Chiaroscuro of Heresy: Early Eleventh-Century Aquitaine as Seen from Auxerre," in *The Peace of God: Social Violence and Religious Response in France around the Year 1000*, ed. Thomas Head and Richard Landes (Ithaca: Cornell University Press, 1992), pp. 80–103. Richard Landes, in his *Relics, Apocalyse, and the Deceits of History: Ademar of Chabannes, 989–1034* (Cambridge: Harvard University Press, 1995), pp. 188–189, argues, somewhat inconclusively, that heretics in the early Middle Ages suffered from this "Manichaean scapegoating" because such scapegoating "made sense of a confusing and disappointing world." Hamilton, "The State of Research: The Legacy of Charles Schmidt to the Study of Christian Dualism," pp. 196–198, while not openly suggesting Bogomil missionaries before the twelfth century, still condemns what he calls "reductionist" arguments that dismiss the possibility of such Balkan visitors to western Europe. Furthermore, searches within the handful of reported (and persecuted) incidents of heresy in western Europe before the middle of the twelfth century for pre-Catharism or proto-Catharism that simply unearth what appear to be dualist images, or recognize an inherent sameness about heretical anticlericism between one century and the next, are exercises more in the quixotic than in quiddity. Jean Duvernoy, "Le problème des origines du catharisme," in his *Cathare, Vaudois et Beguines, dissidents du pays d'Oc*, pp. 39–52; Anne Brenon, "Les heresies de l'an mil: nouvelles perspectives sur les origines du catharisme," *Heresis* 24 (1995): 21–36; and idem, "The Voice of the Good Women: An Essay on the Pastoral and Sacerdotal Role of Women in the Cathar Church," in *Women Preachers and Prophets through Two Millennia of Christianity*, ed. Beverly Mayne Kienzle and Pamela J. Walker (Berkeley and Los Angeles: University of California Press, 1998), esp. pp. 115–116, who lean heavily toward searching for, and believing in, proto-Catharism in earlier European heresies.

14. Gerhard Rottenwöhrer, *Der Katherismus*, vol. 3, *Die Herkunft der Katharer nach Theologie und Geschichte* (Bad Honnef: Bock and Herchen, 1990), pp. 74–114, 570–571; Fichtenau, *Ketzer und Professoren*, pp. 70–119 [*Heretics and Scholars*, pp. 70–126]; Bernard Hamilton, "Wisdom from the East: The Reception by the Cathars of Eastern Dualist Texts," in *Heresy and Literacy, 1000–1530*, ed. Peter Biller and Anne Hudson, Cambridge Studies in Medieval Literature, 23 (Cambridge: Cambridge University Press, 1994), pp. 38–60; and Malcolm Lambert, *The Cathars* (Oxford: Blackwell, 1998), pp. 29–59, are all good, as well as nuanced, summaries of the evidence (and scholarship) for missionary and doctrinal connections between the Cathars and the Bogomils. Janet and Bernard Hamilton's

*Christian Dualist Heresies in the Byzantine World c. 650–c. 1450*, Manchester Medieval Sources Series (Manchester: Manchester University Press, 1998), is a remarkable collection of translated sources on dualism and has a useful "Historical Introduction," pp. 1–55. The visit by the supposed Bogomil bishop of Constantinople, *papa* Nicetas, to Saint-Félix-de-Caraman in the Lauragais happened in 1167. The document that records Nicetas' journey is lost and exists only as an appendix to Guillaume Besse's *Histoire des ducs, marquis et comtes de Narbonne, autrement appellez Princes des Goths, Ducs de Septimanie, et Marquis de Gothie. Dedié à Monseigneur l'Archevesque Duc de Narbonne* (Paris: Antoine de Sommaville, 1660), pp. 483–486. This document, given to Besse by "M. Caseneuue, Prebendier au Chapitre de l'Eglisle de Sainct Estienne de Tolose, en l'an 1652," p. 483, is probably (at best) a mid-thirteenth-century forgery by some *bons omes* or *crezens* rather than a seventeenth-century forgery. Bernard Hamilton, "The Cathar Council of S. Félix Reconsidered," *Archivum Fratrum Praedicatorum* 48 (1978): 23–53, is generally assumed to have proven the validity of Besse's appendix—I remain unconvinced. In support of Hamilton, see, for example, Pilar Jimenez, "Relire la Charte de Niquinta—1) Origine et problématique de la Charte," *Heresis* 22 (1994): 1–26; idem, "Relire la Charte de Niquinta—2) Sens et portée de la charte," *Heresis* 23 (1994): 1–28; and Lambert, *The Cathars*, pp. 45–59. Cf. Yves Dossat, "A propos du concile cathare de Saint-Félix: les Milingues," *Cahiers de Fanjeaux: Cathares en Languedoc* 3 (1968): 201–214, where it is argued that Besse's document was a seventeenth-century forgery (and probably forged by Besse). It has also been argued that Bogomil dualism was secretly carried back by crusaders returning from twelfth-century Outremer. On such heretical transmissions from the Levant, Christine Thouzellier, "Hérésie et croisade au XII$^e$ siècle," *Revue d'histoire ecclésiastique* 49 (1954): 855–872, was the first to strongly suggest the importation of dualist beliefs by returning crusaders. Along similar lines, Karl Heisig, in "Ein gnostische Sekte im abendländischen Mittelalter," *Zeitschrift für Religions und Geistesgeschichte* 16 (1964): 271–74, suggested that crusaders brought ancient Gnostic practices back from the East to the Rhineland.

15. See, for example, Samuel Roffey Maitland, *Facts and Documents Illustrative of the History, Doctrine, and Rites of the Ancient Albigenses and Waldenses* (London: C.J.G. and F. Rivington, 1832), esp. p. 92, who thought that the southern French Albigensians were Paulician immigrants. The great Frederic Maitland wrote a very revealing letter about his grandfather Samuel Roffey in *The Letters of Frederic William Maitland*, ed. C.H.S. Fifoot (Cambridge Harvard University Press, 1965), No. 98, To Selina Maitland, 22 Nov. 1891, p. 98. On the Paulicians, see, especially, Nina Garsoïan, *The Paulician Heresy: A Study of the Origin and Development of Paulicianism in Armenia and the Eastern Provinces of the Roman Empire* (The Hague: Mouton & Co., 1967), esp. pp. 18–21, where she argues against Paulician influence in western Europe in the Middle Ages. Garsoïan, pp. 186–230, also strongly rejects the Paulicians as descendants of Manichees; rather, she considers the original Paulicians to have been nothing more than Armenian Old Believers—an argument that is perhaps as unconvincing, and certainly just as unprovable, as the one she rejects. Bernard Hamilton cannot let go of the notion that there must be some connection between the Paulicians and the Cathars, despite the dearth of evidence, in his "The Origins of the Dualist Church of Drugunthia,"

*Eastern Churches Review* 6 (1974): 115–124, his "Wisdom from the East," pp. 50–51, and his *Christian Dualist Heresies in the Byzantine World c. 650–c. 1450*, pp. 5–25.

16. Searching for what seems similar over the *longue durée*, or between *les vastes espaces*, can never account for former predictive or inductive practices. Any two things can have properties in common. Similarities are ubiquitous, while meanings are always elusive. So two apparently similar Indo-European symbols, two popular *mentalités*, two diasporic myths, two heretical discourses prove nothing conclusive in themselves about the past. See Nelson Goodman, "Seven Strictures against Similarity," in his *Problems and Projects* (Indianapolis: Hackett Publishing Company, 1972), pp. 437–446. See also idem, "The New Riddle of Induction," in his *Fact, Fiction, and Forecast*, 4th ed. (Cambridge: Harvard University Press, 1983), pp. 59–83; idem, *Of Mind and Other Matters* (Cambridge: Harvard University Press, 1984); Catherine Z. Elgin and Nelson Goodman, *Reconceptions in Philosophy and Other Arts and Sciences* (Indianapolis: Hackett Publishing Company, 1988). See also the collected (philosophical) essays on the problem of "grue" put forward in *Grue! The New Riddle of Induction*, ed. Douglas Stalker (Chicago: Open Court, 1994), esp. Ian Hacking, "Entrenchment," pp. 193–224, and the collected (historical, philosophical, anthropological) essays in *How Classification Works: Nelson Goodman among the Social Sciences*, ed. Mary Douglas and David Hull (Edinburgh: Edinburgh University Press, 1992).

17. For example, Ernst Werner, *Pauperes Christi. Studien zu sozial-religiösen Bewegungen im Zeitalter des Reformpapsttums* (Leipzig: Kochler & Amelang, 1957); Martin Erbstösser and Ernst Werner, *Ideologische Probleme des Mittelalterlichen Plebejertums: Die freigeistige Häresie und ihre sozialen Wurzeln*, Forschungen zur mittelalterlichen Geschichte, 7 (Berlin: Akademie-Verlag, 1960); Gottfried Koch, *Frauenfrage und Ketzertum in Mittelalter*, Forschungen zur mittelalterlichen Geschichte, 9 (Berlin: Akademie-Verlag, 1962); Bernhard Töpfer, *Das kommende Reich des Friedens; zur Entwicklung chiliasticscher Zukunftshoffnungen im Hochmittelalter*, Forschungen zur mittelalterlichen Geschichte, 11 (Berlin: Akademie-Verlag, 1964); Martin Erbstösser, *Ketzer im Mittelalter* (Stuttgart: Kohlhammer, 1984) [trans. Janet Fraser as *Heretics in the Middle Ages* (Leipzig: Edition Leipzig, 1984)]; and Martin Erbstösser and Ernst Werner, *Ketzer und Heilige: Das religiöse Leben im Hochmittelalter* (Vienna: Böhlaus, 1986). On this (especially former East German, especially Karl-Marx University of Leipzig) way with history that, despite the Marxist materialism, had many affinities with the medieval vision of a Jules Michelet, see Andreas Dorpalen, *German History in Marxist Perspective: The East German Approach* (Detroit: Wayne State University Press, 1985), esp. pp. 74–76, 91–92; Werner Malecsek, "Le ricerche eresiologiche in area germanica," in *Eretici ed eresie medievali nella storiografia contemporanea: atti del XXXII Convegno du studi seilla Riforma e i movimenti religiosi in Italia*, ed. Grado Giovanni Merlo, Bolleltino della Societa di Studi Valdesi, 174 (Torre Pellice: Societa di Studi Valdesi, 1994), pp. 64–93, esp. 68–75; Peter Biller, "Cathars and Material Women," in *Medieval Theology and the Natural Body*, ed. Peter Biller and Alastair J. Minnis, York Studies in Medieval Theology, 1 (Woodbridge: York Medieval Press–Boydell & Brewer, 1997), pp. 75–81; Fichtenau, *Ketzer und Professoren*, pp. 110–113 [*Heretics and Scholars*, pp. 115–119]; and Kaelber, *Schools of Asceticism*, pp. 196–202. It was also this

East German treatment of medieval heresy and spirituality that Borst and Grund-mann, sincere anti-Marxists and West Germans, consciously reacted against with their overt intellectualist arguments. An informed commentary on this issue is made by Lerner in his introduction to Grundmann, *Religious Movements in the Middle Ages*, pp. xxii–xxv. Interestingly, James Given, stepping outside of this his-toriographic debate, has adopted a subtle neo-Marxist approach in his *Inquisition and Medieval Society: Power, Discipline, and Resistance in Languedoc* (Ithaca: Cornell University Press, 1997). This paragraph has benefited from the wise observations of Edward Peters.

18. See, for example, Emmanuel Le Roy Ladurie, *Montaillou, village occitan de 1294 à 1324* (1975; Paris: Gallimard, 1993) [trans. and condensed by Barbara Bray as *Montaillou: Cathars and Catholics in a French Village 1294–1324* (Harmonds-worth: Penguin Books, 1981)], where a tendency to romanticize life in the Occi-tan countryside, and to see it as possessing unchanging qualities, is crucial to his brillant evocation of rural existence from a late-thirteenth/early-fourteenth-century inquisitorial register. The same is true for Carlo Ginzburg's remarkable, but supremely ahistorical, *Storia Notturna* (Turin: Giulio Einaudi Editore, 1989) [translated by Raymond Rosenthal, *Ecstasies: Deciphering the Witches' Sabbath* (Harmondsworth: Penguin Books, 1991)]. Perry Anderson, "Nocturnal Enquiry: Carlo Ginzburg," in his *A Zone of Engagement* (London: Verso, 1992), pp. 207–229, thoughtfully, but severely, reviews Ginzburg's unchanging rural world and the curious materialist assumptions such an idea embraces. William Chester Jordan in his *The Great Famine: Northern Europe in the Early Fourteenth Century* (Princeton: Princeton University Press, 1996), p. 13, has attacked the gener-al prevalence of such timeless notions about the tempo of rural life in the Middle Ages.

19. Aron Gurevitch, for instance, has expressed these views in his *Categories of Medieval Culture*, trans. G. L. Campbell (London: Routledge & Kegan Paul, 1985), p. 98, and *Medieval Popular Culture: Problems of Belief and Perception*, trans. János Bak and Paul Hollingsworth (Cambridge: Cambridge University Press, 1992), p. 99. Cf. James Fentress and Chris Wickham, *Social Memory* (Oxford: Blackwell, 1992), p. 100, who dismiss such views of time and memory in rural communities.

20. W. H. Auden, "The Poet and the City," in his *The Dyer's Hand and Other Essays* (1962; New York: Vintage, 1989), p. 74.

21. See, out of a vast and extremely popular literature, especially Déodat Roche, *Etudes Manichéennes et Cathares*, Editions des Cahiers d'Etudes Cathares (Paris: Librairie Véga-Institut d'Etudes Occitanes, 1952), and René Nelli, *Histoire Secrète du Languedoc* (Paris: Albin Michel, 1978). Roche was the founder of a neo-Cathar group at the turn of this century and of the journal *Cahiers d'Etudes Ca-thares*. On Roche, see Jean-Louis Biget, "Mythographie du Catharisme," *Cahiers de Fanjeaux: Historiographie du catharisme* 14 (1979): 308–310. Roche also had a curious, and still unpublished, correspondence with Simone Weil; for example, the latter once wrote—as is cited by Jean Duvernoy, "Albigeisme ou Catharisme," in his *Cathare, Vaudois et Beguines, dissidents du pays d'Oc*, p. 15—that Catharism was "la denière expression vivante de l'antiquité pré-romaine. . . . " Weil had more to say about Catharism and Occitanism in her "L'agonie d'une civilisation vue à travers une poème épique" and "En quoi l'inspiration occitanienne," in *Ecrits*

*historiques et politiques* (Paris: Gallimard, 1960), pp. 66–74 and 75–84. On Weil, see for example, Peter Winch, *Simone Weil: "The Just Balance"* (Cambridge: Cambridge University Press, 1989), p. 369, where he considers Weil's notion that Catharism was a descendant of late antique neo-Platonic Christianity to be historically correct; he even argues for Catharism to be the offspring of Gnosticism because (and this is his only evidence) "of a similarity of ideas." Arthur Guirdham, *The Cathars and Reincarnation: The Record of a Past Life in Thirteenth Century France* (London: Quest, 1970), even documents a fascinating case of an Englishwoman who was convinced that she had experienced a past life as a *crezen* in the early-thirteenth-century Lauragais. A southern French travelogue, heavily laced with Cathar fact and fancy, is Rion Klawinski, *Chasing the Heretics: A Modern Journey through the Medieval Languedoc* (St. Paul: Hungry Mind Press, 1999). As for Catharism and the Holy Grail, see Michel Roquebert, *Les Cathares et le Graal* (Toulouse: Privat, 1994). On the innumerable (and usually rather odd) theories about courtly love, *amour courtois*, and the Cathars, see the excellent critical survey of Roger Boase, *The Origin and Meaning of Courtly Love: A Critical Study of European Scholarship* (Manchester: Manchester University Press; Totowa: Rowman and Littlefield, 1977), pp. 77–81. Today, the Centre d'Études Cathares at Carcassonne, under the direction of Anne Brenon, still keeps the neo-Cathar flame alive. The Centre d'Études Cathares also publishes the serious and learned journal *Heresis*. See Duvernoy, "Albigeisme ou Catharisme," pp. 15–38, and Biller, "Cathars and Material Women," pp. 80–81.

22. Jean Duvernoy, for one, basically sees the Cathars as proto-Protestants, in "Cathares et vaudois sont-ils des précurseurs de la Réforme?" in his *Cathare, Vaudois et Beguines, dissidents du pays d'Oc*, pp. 53–62. In the seventeenth and eighteenth centuries, not surprisingly, such views were quite common among Catholic and Protestant thinkers. On these early modern ideas about the Cathars, see Arno Borst, "Neue Funde und Forschungen zur Geschichte der Katharer," *Historische Zeitschrift* 174 (1952): 17; Henri Duranton, "Les Albigeois dans les histoires générales et les manuels scolaires du XVIe au XVIIIe siècle," *Cahiers de Fanjeaux: Historiographie du catharisme* 14 (1979): 85–118; and Abraham Friesen, "Medieval Heretics or Forerunners of the Reformation: the Protestant Rewriting of the History of Medieval Heresy," in *The Devil, Heresy, and Witchcraft in the Middle Ages: Essays in Honor of Jeffrey B. Russell*, ed. Alberto Ferreiro (Leiden: Brill, 1998), pp. 165–190. Interestingly, under "Albigenses," the first edition of the *Encyclopædia Britannica or, A Dictionary of Arts and Sciences* (Edinburgh: A. Bell and C. Macfarquhar, 1771), 1:75, noted this: "They [the Albigenses] are ranked among the grossest heretics, the Manicheans, by Roman Catholics; from which charge Protestants generally acquit them, though with some limitations. . . . At the time of the Reformation, those of the Albigenses who remained embraced Calvinism."

23. Eckbert of Schönau, *Sermones contra Catharos*, PL 195, col. 31, "Catharos, id est mundos." See Robert Moore, *The Origins of European Dissent* (London: Allen Lane, Penguin Books, 1977), pp. 176–182.

24. According to Borst, *Die Katharer*, p. 240, Eckbert of Schönau was the first to give the etymology.

25. Alain de Lille had this to say in his *De fide catholica contra hereticos libri IX*, PL 210, col. 366: "These persons are called 'Cathars'—meaning those who are

dissolved through vice, from *catha*, that is, a purifying flow; or, with the meaning 'chaste,' because they make themselves out to be chaste or righteous. Or 'Cathars,' from 'cat,' because, it is said, they kiss the hinder parts of a cat, in whose likeness, so they say, Lucifer appears to them." See Christine Thouzellier, *Catharisme et Valdéisme en Languedoc à la fin du XIIe et au début du XIIIe siècle: Politique pontificale—Controverses*, Publications de la Faculté des Lettres et Sciences Humaines de Paris. Série «Recherches», 27 (Paris: Presses Universitaires de France, 1966), pp. 81–106.

26. Canon 27 (*De hæreticis*), *Sacrorum Conciliorum*, vol. 22, col. 231.

27. Rainer Sacconi, *Summa de Catharis et Pauperibus de Lugduno*, is in the preface of Antoine Dondaine's edition of *Un Traité néo-manichéen du XIIIᵉ Siècle: Le Liber de duobus principiis suivi d'un fragment de rituel cathare* (Rome: Istituto Storico Domenicano, 1939), pp. 64–78, esp. 77 [trans. Walter Wakefield and Austin Evans in their *Heresies of the High Middle Ages: Selected Sources Translated and Annotated*, Records of Western Civilization (New York: Columbia University Press, 1991), pp. 329–346, esp. p. 345. Now, see Thouzellier, *Catharisme et Valdéisme en Languedoc*, pp. 19–26, and the more general discussion of Italian heresy (and one that assumes a strong, and obvious, connection to the heretics of Languedoc) in Carol Lansing, *Power and Purity: Cathar Heresy in Medieval Italy* (New York: Oxford University Press, 1998), esp. 4–5, 15–16, 37–39, 188–190.

28. *Historia Albigensis*, 1:13–14, §13 [*The History of the Albigensian Crusade*, p. 12 n. 39], and §§14–15, p. 15–16.

29. Jean Duvernoy, "L'acception: 'haereticus' (*iretge*) = 'parfait cathare' en Languedoc au XIIIᵉ siècle," in *The Concept of Heresy in the Middle Ages (11th–13th C.): Proceedings of the International Conference, Louvain, May 13–16, 1973*, ed. W. Lourdaux and D. Verhelst, Medievalia Lovaniensia, Series I—Studia IV (The Hague: Leuven University Press–Martinus Nijhoff, 1976), pp. 198–210. See, for example, MS 609, fol. 110v, where Peire Pausa from Gardouch noted: "De Poncio Guilabert credit quod sit credens hereticorum. . . ."

30. On this point about Cathars and Waldensians, see Peter Biller, "Words and the Medieval Notion of 'Religion,' " *Journal of Ecclesiastical History* 36 (1985): esp. 365 ff.

31. See, for example, *Historia Albigensis*, 1:3–4 and n. 3.

32. See the discussions in *HGL* 7:33–37; Borst, *Die Katharer*, p. 249 n. 5; Louis de Lacger, "L'Albigeois pendant la crise de l'albigéisme," *Revue d'histoire ecclésiastique* 29 (1933): 276–283; Lambert, *The Cathars*, p. 69; and Wakefield and Evans, *Heresies of the High Middle Ages*, p. 720 n. 1.

33. Arnold Fitz-Thedmar, *De antiquis legibus liber. Cronica maiorum et vicecomitum Londoniarum*, ed. Thomas Stapleton, Camden Society, 34 (London: The Camden Society, 1846), p. 3, "Hoc anno concrematus est quidam Ambigensis apud Londonias."

34. Peter Biller, "William of Newburgh and the Cathar Mission to England," in *Life and Thought in the Northern Church c. 1100–c. 1700: Essays in Honour of Claire Cross*, ed. Diana Wood (Woodbridge: The Ecclesiastical History Society–The Boydell Press, 1999), p. 27, not only says conclusively that "Albigensian" always means "Cathar" but that Arnold Fitz-Thedmar's single sentence, so many years later, helps demonstrate an early-thirteenth-century Cathar mission to England—

neither of these statements is obvious or conclusive. See also Borst, *Die Katharer,* p. 103 and n. 20.

35. On the meaning of *Albigenses,* see Christine Thouzellier, *Hérésie et Héretiques: Vaudois, Cathares, Patarins, Albigeois,* Storia e Letteratura, Raccolta di Studi e Testi, 116 (Rome: Edizioni di Storia e Letteratura, 1969), pp. 223–262.

36. Paul Daniel Alphandéry, "Albigenses," *Encyclopædia Britannica,* 1:505–506. Alphandéry (ibid., 14: 587–596) also wrote the balanced and learned entry on "Inquisition, The." Now, see Paul Daniel Alphandéry, *Les idées morales chez les hétérodoxes latins au début du XIIIe siècle* (Paris: E. Leroux, 1903), and idem, *La chrétienté et l'idée de croisade. Texte établi par Alphonse Dupront* (Paris: A. Michel, 1954).

37. Alphandéry, "Albigenses," 1:505.

38. Ibid. Conybeare's wonderful ability to see the Cathars everywhere he looked, no matter the time or place, found further expression in the eleventh edition of the *Encyclopædia Britannica* (indeed only 397 pages after Alphandéry's Albigenses) when he stylishly summarized the sixteenth-century zeal of the "Anabaptists" (ibid., 1:903–905), who apparently possessed "an affinity to the Cathari and other medieval sects" (p. 904).

## CHAPTER 4
## PAPER AND PARCHMENT

1. On *les armées du crime, déchristianisation,* and the pillaging of Toulouse by *révolutionaires,* see Richard Cobb, *Les Armées Révolutionnaires: Instrument de la Terreur dans les Départements. Avril 1793–Floréal An II,* Société et Idéologies, Première Série, École Pratique des Hautes Études-Sorbonne (Paris: Mouton & Co., 1963), 2:635–694, esp. 686–687, and pp. 695–734, esp. 704–705. See also Charles Molinier, *L'Inquisition dans le Midi de la France au XIII<sup>e</sup> et au XIV<sup>e</sup> siècle: Étude sur les sources de son histoire* (Paris: Librairie Sandoz et Fischbacher, 1880), pp. 21 ff., and Dossat, *Les crises de l'Inquisition Toulousaine au XIII<sup>e</sup> siècle,* 29–37.

2. Auguste Molinier, in the *Catalogue général des manuscrits des Bibliothèques Publiques des Départments publié sous les auspices du Ministre de l'Instruction Publique,* vol. 7, *Toulouse-Nîmes* (Paris: Imprimerie Nationale, 1885), p. 358, where MS 609 (second series) is the new classification of what was formerly known as MS 155 (first series). Charles Molinier, for example, in his *L'Inquisition dans le Midi de la France au XIII<sup>e</sup> et au XIV<sup>e</sup> siècle,* pp. 163–195, uses the older classification of MS 155 1<sup>re</sup>. Oddly enough, the manuscript is given no designation in Léopold Delisle's *Notice sur les Manuscrits de Bernard Gui* (Paris: Imprimerie Nationale, 1879), p. 351 n. 1. See the more recent catalog of Charles Samaran and Robert Marichal, *Catalogue des manuscrits en écriture Latine. Portant des indications de date, de lieu ou de copiste,* Comité International de Paléographie, 4, Bourgogne, Centre, Sud-Est et Sud-Ouest de la France (Paris: Éditions de Centre National de la Recherche Scientifique, 1968), p. 415. The estimated dates for the creation of MS 609 come from the knowledge that Guilhem Bernart de Dax ended his inquisitorial activity in 1263 to became prior of the Dominican convent in Toulouse, and the presence of an isolated testimony copied into the manuscript from 1258. See Dossat, *Les crises de l'Inquisition Toulousaine au XIII<sup>e</sup> siècle,* pp. 57 and 192.

3. For example, MS 124 (formerly Dominicans 85 H) of the Archives départ-mentales of the Haute-Garonne consists of five double parchment folios of two inquisitions, and of two different scribes and registers, from 1254 and 1256. The first leaves, fols. 71–76 and 89–90, come from a register of Raimon Respland and Arnaut de Gouzens. The other folios, originally marked ?–103, 144–145, 196–201, are testimonies from converted *bons omes* from a register of Jean de Saint-Pierre and Renaud de Chartres. They were found in the mid–nineteenth century by the archivist Guy Belhomme in the binding of a *cahier* of the Contrôle des exploits of the Salles-sur-l'Hers of 1674 and were refoliated as 1–4 (fols. 71–76, 89–90) and 5–10 (?–103, 144–145, 196–201). Belhomme edited fols. 71, 76, and 196–201 with an appalling lack of precision in *Documents inédits concernant les hérétiques bons hommes de la secte des Albigeois* (Toulouse: Imprimerie d'Augustin Manavit, 1850), pp. 133–146; and in a pamphlet drawn from "Documents inédits sur l'hérésie des Albigeois," *Mémoires de la Société archéologique du Midi de la France* 6 (1847, 1848, 1849, 1850, and 1852): 133–146. There is a flawless transcription of just fol. 196—which is very faded and difficult to read—in Annie Cazenave's "Les cathares en Catalogne et en Sabarthès d'après les registres d'Inquisition: la hiérarchie cathare en Sabarthès après Montségur," in *Les relations franco-espagnoles jusqu'au XVIIᵉ siècle.* Bulletin philologique et historique (jusqu'à 1610) du Comité des travaux historiques et scientifiques. Année 1969, Actes du 94ᵒ Congrès na-tional des Sociétés savantes tenu à Pau (Paris: Bibliothèque Nationale, 1972), 1:429–436. See also Molinier, *L'Inquisition dans le Midi de la France au XIIIᵉ et au XIVᵉ siècle*, pp. 237–246, and Dossat, *Les crises de l'Inquisition Toulousaine au XIIIᵉ siècle*, p. 39. It should be mentioned that a double folio, marked fols. 106 and 117, and apparently from the register of Jean de Saint-Pierre and Renaud de Chartres, was discovered by Henri Blaquière in the binding of a *cahier* of the Bureau de l'Enregistrement de Salles-sur-l'Hers of 1674–1675. Blaquière pub-lished an edition in 1968, and these folios are now MS 202 in the Archives départ-mentales of the Haute-Garonne. See Henri Blaquière and Yves Dossat, "Les ca-thares au jour le jour, Confessions inédites de cathares quercynois," *Cahiers de Fanjeaux: Cathares en Languedoc* 3 (1968): 259–298.

4. On Colbert's commission and Doat's copying, see Léopold Delisle, *Le Cabi-net des Manuscrits de la Bibliothèque Impériale*, Histoire Générale de Paris (Paris: Imprimerie Impériale, 1868), 1:441–442; Henri Omont, "La Collection Doat à la Bibliothèque Nationale: Documents sur les recherches de Doat dans les archives du sud-ouest de la France de 1663 à 1670," *Bibliothèque de l'Ecole des Chartres* 77 (1916): 286–336; Lothar Kolmer, *Ad Capiendas Vulpes. Die Ketzerbekämpfung in Süd-frankreich in der ersten Hälfte des 13. Jahrhunderts und die Ausbildung des Inquisi-tionsverfahrens*, Pariser Historische Studien, 19 (Bonn: Ludwig Röhrscheid Verlag, 1982), pp. 12–15; idem, "Colbert und die Entstehung der Collection Doat," *Francia* 7 (1979): 463–489; and the less learned but still useful Gustave Brunet, "Jean-Baptiste Colbert," *Le Bibliophile Français. Gazette Illustrée des amateurs de livres, d'estampes et de haute curiosité* 4 (1869): 9. See also Dossat, *Les crises de l'Inquisition Toulousaine au XIIIᵉ siècle*, pp. 30–37; and Molinier, *L'Inquisition dans le Midi de la France au XIIIᵉ et au XIVᵉ siècle*, p. 34. On early medieval manuscripts and transcrip-tions in Colbert's library, see Rosamund McKitterick, "The Study of Frankish

History in France and Germany in the Sixteenth and Seventeenth Centuries," *Francia* 8 (1991): 556–572.

5. The inquisitions of the thirteenth century fill volumes 21–26 of the Collection Doat. The *Interrogatio Johannis* and *Tractatus de diversis predicabilibus* are both in Doat 36 at fols. 26v–35r for the first and then fols. 35v–66 for the second. Doat's commission worked in Toulouse and Carcassonne between September and October 1669. See Delisle, *Le Cabinet des Manuscrits de la Bibliothèque Impériale*, 1:441, and Dossat, *Les crises de l'Inquisition Toulousaine au XIII^e siècle*, pp. 29–55.

6. See Molinier's description of the Collection Doat in his *L'Inquisition dans le Midi de la France au XIII^e et au XIV^e siècle*, pp. 34–48.

7. Dossat, *Les crises de l'Inquisition Toulousaine au XIII^e siècle*, pp. 29–55.

8. Ibid., p. 61; Molinier, *Catalogue général des manuscrits des Bibliothèques Publiques*, p. 358; and Samaran and Marichal, *Catalogue des manuscrits en écriture Latine*, p. 415. On archival "treasuries," see Michael T. Clanchy, *From Memory to Written Record: England 1066–1307*, 2d ed. (Oxford: Blackwell, 1994), pp. 162–163.

9. Dossat, *Les crises de l'Inquisition Toulousaine au XIII^e siècle*, p. 56. Cf. the uncertainty of Molinier, *L'Inquisition dans le Midi de la France au XIII^e et au XIV^e siècle*, pp. 34–48.

10. Dossat, *Les crises de l'Inquisition Toulousaine au XIII^e siècle*, pp. 56 and 61.

11. Ibid., p. 62.

12. I have estimated the size of the original sheets from the charts and diagrams of J. Peter Gumbert, "Sizes and Formats," in *Ancient and Medieval Book Materials and Techniques (Erice, 18–25 september 1992)*, ed. Marilena Maniaci and Paola F. Munafò, Studi e Testi, 357 (Vatican City: Biblioteca Apostolica Vaticana, 1993), 1:227–263. See also idem, "Ruling by Rake and Board: Notes on Some Medieval Ruling Techniques," in *The Role of the Book in Medieval Culture: Proceedings of the Oxford International Symposium, 26 September–1 October 1982*, ed. Peter Ganz, Bibliologia. Elementa ad librorum studia pertinentia, 3 (Turnhout: Brepols, 1986), 1:41–54.

13. On paper in the Middle Ages, especially before the fourteenth century, see Charles-Moïse Briquet, "Recherches sur les premiers papiers employés en Occident and en Orient du X^e au XIV^e siècle," *Mémoires de la Société nationale des antiquaires de France* 46 (1886): 132–205; Jean Irigoin, "Les papiers non filigranés état présent des recherches et perspectives d'avenir," in *Ancient and Medieval Book Materials and Techniques (Erice, 18–25 september 1992)*, ed. Marilena Maniaci and Paola F. Munafò, Studi e Testi, 357 (Vatican City: Biblioteca Apostolica Vaticana, 1993), 1:265–312; and Carla Bozzolo and Ezio Ornato, *Pour une histoire du livre manuscrit au Moyen Age. Trois essais de codicologie quantitative*, Equipe de Recherche sur l'humanisme française des XIV^e et XV^e siècles, Textes et Etudes. 2 (Paris: Éditions du Centre Nationale de la Recherche Scientifique, 1980), pp. 123–215. On Catalonian and Andalusian paper, see Simona di Zio, Paul Canart, Lucina Polistena, and Daniela Scialanga, "Une enquête sur le papier de type 'Arabe Occidental' ou 'Espagnol non filigrané,' " in *Ancient and Medieval Book Materials and Techniques (Erice, 18–25 september 1992)*, ed. Marilena Maniaci and Paola F. Munafò, Studi e Testi, 357 (Vatican City: Biblioteca Apostolica Vaticana, 1993), 1:313–393; Oriol Valls i Subira, *The History of Paper in Spain X–XIV Centuries* (Ma-

drid: Empresa Nacional de Celulosas, S.A., 1978), vol. 1, esp. pp. 98–100, 170–171 and 226–227; and Olivia Remie Constable, *Trade and Traders in Muslim Spain: The Commercial Realignment of the Iberian Peninsula 900–1500*, Cambridge Studies in Medieval Life and Thought, 4th ser., 24 (Cambridge: Cambridge University Press, 1994), pp. 194–196.

14. Dossat, *Les crises de l'Inquisition Toulousaine au XIII^e siècle*, p. 56. The earliest paper documents, for example, in the English medieval archives are letters sent from Italy to the Riccardi, the bankers of Edward I, and they date from 1296–1303. On paper in medieval England, see Clanchy, *From Memory to Written Record*, p. 120.

15. Dossat, *Les crises de l'Inquisition Toulousaine au XIII^e siècle*, pp. 56–70.

16. Peter the Venerable, *Adversus iudeorum*, ed. Yvonne Friedman, Corpus Christianorum: Continuatio Mediaevalis, 58 (Turnhout: Brepols, 1981), p. 130, and Johannes Trithemius, *De laude scriptorum*, ed. and trans. Klaus Arnold (Lawrence, Kans.: Coronado Press, 1974), p. 63. On the abbot of Cluny's disgust at books made of paper, especially some Jewish ones he saw in Toledo, see Subira, *The History of Paper in Spain*, p. 100, and Constable, *Trade and Traders in Muslim Spain*, p. 195. On the abbot of Sponheim's contempt for the brief life of paper (despite his owning some paper manuscripts himself) as opposed to the immortality of parchment, see Clanchy, *From Memory to Written Record*, p. 196.

17. This roll is now cataloged as J 330 b, no. 59 in the Archives nationale in Paris. This roll was awkwardly (but not badly) edited by Edmund Cabié, "Compte des inquisiteurs des Diocèses de Toulouse, d'Albi et de Cahors, 1255–1256," *Revue du Tarn*, 2d ser., 22 (1905): 110–133, 215–229.

18. See Clanchy, *From Memory to Written Record*, pp. 114–117.

19. Dossat, *Les crises de l'Inquisition Toulousaine au XIII^e siècle*, pp. 66–67 and 81, esp. n. 147.

20. Ibid. The oblong of vellum reads: "Here are two volumes of confessions from the books of Friar Bernart de Caux transcribed: namely of the Lauragais and of many other places in the diocese of Toulouse: by Friars Guilhem Bernart and Renaud de Chartres, inquisitors." The verso of the last folio of the flyleaf reads: "Confessions of the fifth book of the Lauragais—of Friar Bernart de Caux, copied in this book up to folio 173. Likewise, after this, from the fourth book."

21. MS 609, fol. 43v. Also, in the margin next to the testimony of Esteve Dejean, from Montesquieu, fol. 99r, is written: "Continetur Na Sapta, W. de Casal, in confessione Willelme Concriburde de Montesquieu, in X° libro, XXII." See Dossat, *Les crises de l'Inquisition Toulousaine au XIII^e siècle*, p. 227 n. 72.

22. Dossat, *Les crises de l'Inquisition Toulousaine au XIII^e siècle*, p. 66.

23. Mary A. and Richard H. Rouse, *Authentic Witnesses: Approaches to Medieval Texts and Manuscripts*, Publications in Medieval Studies, 17 (Notre Dame, Ind.: University of Notre Dame Press, 1991), p. 244. MS 609 is foliated in the upper right of the recto until fol. 111, then both sides for fols. 111 and 112; for fols. 113 to 173 the foliation is on the verso upper right; after that the numbering returns to the upper right of the recto. On this easily overlooked new attitude to the page, as far as MS 609 is concerned, see Dossat, *Les crises de l'Inquisition Toulousaine au XIII^e siècle*, p. 66. In the middle of the nineteenth century the departmental archivist of the Haute-Garonne renumbered the folios correctly in Arabic

numerals. On this, see Molinier, *L'Inquisition dans le Midi de la France au XIIIe et au XIVe siècle*, p. 169, and Célestin Douais, *Documents pour servir à l'histoire de l'Inquisition dans le Languedoc* (Paris: Librairie Renouard and Société de l'Histoire de France, 1900), 1:cliij.

24. Dossat, *Les crises de l'Inquisition Toulousaine au XIIIe siècle*, p. 62.

25. Ibid., pp. 64 and 84.

26. Ibid., p. 63.

27. The testimonies of Bernart des Plas and of Adalaïs of Auriac, 10 June 1245, are copied in MS 609 on fol. 87r and then repeated at fol. 95r. The testimony of na Aimengart of Gaja, wife of Peire de Mazerolles, given on 30 November 1245, is incomplete in MS 609 at fols. 123r–124r but complete at fol. 196r–v. See also Dossat, *Les crises de l'Inquisition Toulousaine au XIIIe siècle*, p. 81.

28. Specifically, Dossat, *Les crises de l'Inquisition Toulousaine au XIIIe siècle*, p. 64, and, more generally, the remarkable Malcolm Beckwith Parkes, *Pause and Effect: An Introduction to the History of Punctuation in the West* (Aldershot: Scolar Press, 1992), pp. 41–44. See also Nicholson Baker's clever discussion of punctuation, as well as a perceptive review of Parkes, in his *The Size of Thoughts: Essays and Other Lumber* (New York: Random House, 1996), pp. 70–88.

29. MS 609, fol. 48r.

30. On this research tool, see Dossat, *Les crises de l'Inquisition Toulousaine au XIIIe siècle*, p. 80, and Rouse and Rouse, *Authentic Witnesses*, p. 244.

31. For example, MS 609 fol. 172r, where the testimony of Guilhema, wife of Azemar de Avinhos, heard on 1 July 1245, ended with the formula " . . . P. Ariberti, publicus notarius, qui hoc scripsit qui recepit instrumentum." On the medieval notariate of Toulouse, see John H. Mundy, *Liberty and Political Power in Toulouse 1050–1230* (New York: Columbia University Press, 1954), pp. 115–121. For a slightly later period, see Jean L. Laffont, "A propos de l'historiographie notariale du Midi toulousain," in *Visages du notariat dans l'histoire du Midi toulousain XIVe au XIXe siècles*, ed. idem (Toulouse: Presses Universitaires du Mirail, 1992), pp. 62–78; Jean-Michel Minovez, "Notaires et société en Midi toulousain. L'exemple de Montesquieu-Volvestre, du XIVe au XIXe siècle," in *Visages du notariat dans l'histoire du Midi toulousain XIVe au XIXe siècles*, ed. Jean L. Laffont (Toulouse: Presses Universitaires du Mirail, 1992), pp. 23–62; and Marie-Claude Marandet, "L'approche du milieu social: le notariat en Midi toulousain au XIVe siècle," in *Visages du notariat dans l'histoire du Midi toulousain XIVe au XIXe siècles*, ed. Jean L. Laffont (Toulouse: Presses Universitaires du Mirail, 1992), pp. 81–109.

32. See especially Mundy, *Liberty and Political Power in Toulouse 1050–1230*, pp. 118–119; Dossat, *Les crises de l'Inquisition Toulousaine au XIIIe siècle*, pp. 58–59 and 249; and Given, *Inquisition and Medieval Society*, pp. 26–28. Now, see Jean L. Laffont, "Histoire du notariat ou histoire notariale? Eléments pour une réflexion épistémologique," in *Notaires, Notariat et Société sous l'Ancien Régime. Actes du colloque de Toulouse, 15 et 16 décembre 1989, Université des Sciences Sociales de Toulouse, Centre d'Histoire Contemporaine des Institutions*, ed. idem (Toulouse: Presses Universitaires du Mirail, 1990), pp. 51–60, and Françoise Hildesheimer, "Les archives du notaire: de la protection à la connaissance de l'intime," in *Notaires, Notariat et Société sous l'Ancien Régime. Actes du colloque de Toulouse, 15 et 16 décembre 1989, Université des Sciences Sociales de Toulouse, Centre d'Histoire Contemporaine des Institu-*

*tions,* ed. Jean L. Laffont (Toulouse: Presses Universitaires du Mirail, 1990), pp. 19–49.

33. For example, MS 609, fols. 37r and 49v, where a cross is used as the *signe de renvoi.*

34. An example of this fidelity to the original—though a somewhat back-handed compliment—is a marginal reference on 41v guiding the reader to testimonies from Mas-Saintes-Puelles at folio 32r; a correct reference in the original, whereas in the copy these testimonies actually occur at folio 30r. Dossat, *Les crises de l'Inquisition Toulousaine au XIII^e siècle,* p. 60.

35. See Dossat's list of marginalia in *Les crises de l'Inquisition Toulousaine au XIII^e siècle,* pp. 67 ff. n. 82, and Walter L. Wakefield's thoughtful insights on the implications of marginal notes in "Inquisitor's Assistants: Witnesses to Confessions in Manuscript 609," *Heresis* 20 (1993): 57–65.

36. MS 609, fol. 16v: "Iste et uxor eius Saurimunda sunt pejores omnibus de Vauro [corr. Manso] ut dicitur." See Walter L. Wakefield, "Heretics and Inquisitors: The Case of Le Mas-Saintes-Puelles," *Catholic Historical Review* 69 (1983): 221–222.

37. MS 609, fol. 21v: "Hec ad murum retineatur."

38. Ibid.

39. Ibid., fol. 22r, ". . . et Frater B., Inquisitor, legit."

40. A. Baudouin, the nineteenth-century departmental archivist of the Haute-Garonne, inserted at the beginning of MS 609 two sheets of paper listing the parishes under the title "Table alphabétique des localités visitées par les inquisiteurs de 1245 à 1253." See Dossat, *Les crises de l'Inquisition Toulousaine au XIII^e siècle,* p. 69.

41. The error in the marginal note at MS 609, fol. 41v, arose only because the scribe erred in not keeping all of the confessions and abjurations of Mas-Saintes-Puelles together—as they would have been in the original.

42. Twenty-five confessions and nine abjurations from Mas-Saintes-Puelles at MS 609, fols. 8–9v, 18v, and 23r; seven confessions from Renneville at 56r–57r; one confession and twenty-five abjurations from Baziège at 58r and 59r; four confessions and five abjurations from Goudourville at 62r; five confessions from Lavaur at 63v–64r; three confessions and five abjurations from Mauremont at 82r–82v; sixty abjurations from La-Bastide-de-Beauvoir at 82v–83r; fourteen abjurations from Auriac at 96r–96v; five confessions from Juzès at 230r; twenty-one abjurations from Saint-Martin-de-Massac at 247r. See Wakefield's discussion of this partculiar day in "Inquisitor's Assistants: Witnesses to Confessions in Manuscript 609," 63–65.

43. Dossat, *Les crises de l'Inquisition Toulousaine au XIII^e siècle,* p. 83.

44. On the *enquêteurs* of Louis IX, with some reference to Alphonse of Poitiers, see William Chester Jordan, *Louis IX and the Challenge of the Crusade: A Study in Rulership* (Princeton: Princeton University Press, 1979), esp. 135–181, 236–246. On philosophers, theologians, and librarians, see Rouse and Rouse, *Authentic Witnesses,* pp. 221–255, esp. 236–237. Cf. Given, *Inquisition and Medieval Society,* p. 35, and idem, "The Inquisitors of Languedoc and the Medieval Technology of Power," *American Historical Review* 94 (1989): 347 n. 40.

45. Célestin Douais, *Acta capitulorum provincialium ordinis fratrum Praedicatorum* (Toulouse: Edouard Privat, 1894), p. 23, "Item, libri Inquisitionis non portentur."

46. Jean Duvernoy, ed., *Le Registre d'Inquisition de Jacques Fournier, évêque de Pamiers (1318–1325)*, Bibliothèque Méridionale, ser. 2, 41 (Toulouse: Édouard Privat, 1965, and additional *Corrections*, 1972) 1:7–22. Jacques Fournier's register is now shelved as MS lat. 4030 in the Biblioteca Apostolica Vaticana; the bishop-inquisitor became one of the popes at Avignon, Benedict XII, in 1334. These last words are on the last folio (115v of MS lat. 4030 and 3:549 in *Le Registre d'Inquisition de Jacques Fournier*) of the transcription: ". . . vice cuius ego Iohannes Iabbaudi, clericus de Tholosa, ea de originali transcripsi fideliter et correxi." One tiny village in particular from this manuscript, Montaillou, has been famously evoked by Emmanuel Le Roy Ladurie in *Montaillou*.

47. Dossat, *Les crises de l'Inquisition Toulousaine au XIII^e siècle*, pp. 57–58.

48. For example, the sentences pronounced by Bernard Gui between 1308 and 1323 in the diocese of Toulouse, once thought lost, exist as Add. MS 4697 in the Department of Manuscripts of the British Museum. Molinier assumed that this document was lost, in *L'Inquisition dans le Midi de la France au XIII^e et au XIV^e siècle*, p. 6; as did Douais, *Documents pour servir à l'histoire de l'Inquisition dans le Languedoc*, 1:cciv; also Dossat, *Les crises de l'Inquisition Toulousaine au XIII^e siècle*, p. 40; and most recently Duvernoy, in *Le Registre d'Inquisition de Jacques Fournier*, 1:15. They all assumed that it had survived only in the transcription published by Philip van Limborch, *Historia Inquisitionis, cui subjungitur Liber Sententiarum Inquisitionis Tholosanae ab anno Christi 1307 ad annum 1323* (Amsterdam: Henri Wetsten, 1692). Limborch's *Historia* was translated and modified—the *Liber Sententiarum* was left out—early in the eighteenth century as *The History of the Inquisition translated in English by Samuel Chandler in Two Volumes* (London: J. Gray, 1731). (Chandler's preface, esp. pp. xi–xvii, is wonderfully witty about the lot of the historian in the eighteenth century.) M.A.E. Nickson cleared the muddle up about Bernard Gui and Limborch (and reminded us of John Locke's abiding interest in the medieval inquisition) in "Locke and the Inquisition of Toulouse," *British Museum Quarterly* 36 (1971–1972): 83–92. See Edward Peters, *Inquisition* (New York: The Free Press, 1988), pp. 166–167, on Limborch, Locke, Chandler, toleration, and the Inquisition.

49. Molinier, *L'Inquisition dans le Midi de la France au XIII^e et au XIV^e siècle*, pp. 35–39; Dossat, *Les crises de l'Inquisition Toulousaine au XIII^e siècle*, pp. 50–51; Given, "The Inquisitors of Languedoc," p. 351.

50. MS 609, fols. 250r–253v.

51. The same doubts are raised by villages like Lavaur with only nineteen testimonies (MS 609, fols. 235r–237v), or Maurens with eight (MS 609, fols. 117r–118r), or Mireval-Lauragais with three (MS 609, fol. 198r–v), or Mayreville with one (MS 609, fol. 177r). See Dossat, *Les crises de l'Inquisition Toulousaine au XIII^e siècle*, p. 79.

52. MS 609, fols. 232r (19 February 1254), 253v–254r (22 February 1254) have "Magister S" alone; fol. 254r–v (1 December 1253); fol. 215r (because the date is given as *IIII marcii*, it is either 26 February or 4 March or 12 March 1254) has Raimon Respland alone; and 253v (18 November 1253) has them together. Dossat, *Les crises de l'Inquisition Toulousaine au XIII^e siècle*, pp. 178–179.

53. MS 609, fol. 127r.

54. Ibid., fols. 126r–v, 127r.

55. Ibid. Dossat, *Les crises de l'Inquisition Toulousaine au XIII<sup>e</sup> siècle*, pp. 192–193.

56. Leonard E. Boyle, "Montaillou Revisited: *Mentalité* and Methodology," in *Pathways to Medieval Peasants*, ed. J. A. Raftis, Papers in Medieval Studies (Toronto: Pontifical Institute of Medieval Studies, 1981), 2:120–121, specifically criticizes Le Roy Ladurie in his *Montaillou* for being vague about the fact that Jacques Fournier's surviving register is only one of two books. Boyle then goes on to fault Le Roy Ladurie for some of his speculations about medieval *mentalités*—speculations that, perhaps, could be proven wrong if the other book were ever found.

57. Richard Abels and Ellen Harrison, "The Participation of Women in Languedocian Catharism," *Medieval Studies* 61 (1979): 241. On men's introducing court cases for women, before *enquêteurs* and other judges, see Jordan, *Louis IX and the Challenge of the Crusade*, pp. 236–246.

58. Douais, *Documents pour servir àl'histoire de l'Inquisition dans le Languedoc*, 1:ccxlviij–cclxvj, and Dossat, *Les crises de l'Inquisition Toulousaine au XIII<sup>e</sup> siècle*, p. 250.

59. Jean-Jacques Percin, *Monumenta conventus Tolosani ordinis F.F. Praedicatorum primi, ex vetustissimis manuscriptis originalibus transcripta, et S.S. Ecclesiæ Patrum Placitis Conventûs per annos distribuitur; Refertur Totius Albigensium facti narratio: Agiturque de Captibus hæresos, de LXI Conciliis contra eos habitis: De justa eorum poena, & de bello quo profligati sunt. De sanctæ Inquisitionis Officii Institutione, & perpetuo exercito, De Rosario, de Academia Tolosania. De primis Sanctæ Inquisitionis Martyribus F.F. Prædicatoribus & Minoribus, nec-non Ecclesiæ Metropolitanæ Tolosæ Canonicis, De Translatione Corporis Sancti Thomæ .V. Ecclesiæ Doctoris, [authore F. Raymundo Hugonis]. Et tandem de Nobilioribus Tolosæ familiis Aliisque plurimis, in ejus Ecclesia sepultis. Quarum Genealogia, Gentilitiaque scuta, referuntur, &c. Superiorum Jussu, & Regio Privilegio* (Toulouse: Jean & Guillaume Pech, 1693), p. 54. Percin supervised a commission doing research on the canonization of the "martyrs" of Avignonet. Some notes (quite neat and in a dark black ink) from this commission can still be found in the margins of MS 609. The commission's research was gathered as "Acta Romam missa pro fratribus inquisitoribus et eorum adjutoribus Avinioneti occisis anno 1242, transcripta anno 1700, die junii" and is now cataloged as Dominicans 112 H 7 in the departmental archives of the Haute-Garonne. Dossat, *Les crises de l'Inquisition Toulousaine au XIII<sup>e</sup> siècle*, p. 69 n. 93.

60. Dossat, *Les crises de l'Inquisition Toulousaine au XIII<sup>e</sup> siècle*, p. 249, and Douais, *Documents pour servir à l'histoire de l'Inquisition dans le Languedoc*, 1:cclij, where he stresses that this *aide-mémoire* was drafted "vraisemblement sous les yeux de Bernart de Caux et de Jean de Saint-Pierre."

61. Douais has edited these sentences in *Documents pour servir a l'histoire de l'Inquisition dans le Languedoc*, 2:1–89. Cf. Wakefield, *Heresy, Crusade and Inquisition in Southern France*, p. 240 n. 1, who counted 192 people sentenced in fifty-two general sermons.

62. The abbé Magi wrote a note in the margin of fol. 151r (now renumbered as fol. 2) from MS lat. 9992 that reads: "1781. Cayer que j'ai retiré de chez un

libraire qui s'en servait pour couvrir des alphabets. Morceau très-rare." See Molinier, *L'Inquisition dans le Midi de la France au XIIIᵉ et au XIVᵉ siècle*, p. 57; Douais, *Documents pour servir a l'histoire de l'Inquisition dans le Languedoc*, 1:ccliij; and Dossat, *Les crises de l'Inquisition Toulousaine au XIIIᵉ siècle*, p. 36.

63. MS 609, Peire Barot, fol. 210v: "Ad recipiendum penitentiam perpetui carceris vel exilii," and Estotz de Rocovila, fol. 65r: "Fuit convictus apud villamum et reddidit se ad murum coram Episcopo." See Dossat, *Les crises de l'Inquisition Toulousaine au XIIIᵉ siècle*, pp. 36, 72.

64. For example, AA 34 3 of the Archives municipales of Toulouse. It is a vidimus of the Royal Amnesty of August 1279 dated 1 February 1313. John Mundy has edited and exhaustively annotated this document in *The Repression of Catharism at Toulouse*, esp. pp. 43–44, where he observes that fifty-seven condemnations of Bernart de Caux and Jean de Saint-Pierre are to be found in the amnesty (though only forty-nine match those published by Douais from Paris: BN lat. MS 9992).

65. Dossat, *Les crises de l'Inquisition Toulousaine au XIIIᵉ siècle*, esp. pp. 56–86, where he describes MS 609 in two elegant and immensely detailed chapters.

66. Rouse and Rouse, *Authentic Witnesses*, pp. 216–217 and 249–251.

67. Bruno Dusan, "De Manso Sanctarum Puellarum," *Revue Archéologique du Midi de la France: Recueil de notes, mémoires, documents relatifs aux monuments de l'histoire et des Beaux-Arts dans les Pays de Langue d'Oc* 2 (1868–1869): Appendix, separate pagination from volume, 1–12. In the departmental archives of the Haute-Garonne there is an odd little manuscript labeled MS 167; it is a blue nineteenth-century schoolbook with the first thirty folios of MS 609 written out by the archivist A. Baudouin; it probably formed the basis for Dusan's appendix.

68. New York, Columbia University, Austin Evans to Merriam Sherwood, 23 January 1934, Folder 1, John H. Mundy Papers.

69. The mid-thirties was a time when, for instance, a live-in maid in New York earned roughly eight dollars a week; the average weekly wage was fifteen dollars for a worker employed by the New Deal's Civil Works Administration. On wages and dollars, see the uneven but interesting Robert S. McElvaine, *The Great Depression: America, 1929–1941* (New York: Times Books, 1984), pp. 153 and 183.

70. New York, Columbia University, Austin Evans to Nelson C. McCrea, 21 December 1933, Folder 1, John H. Mundy Papers.

71. Ibid.

72. Peter Biller, "Heresy and Literacy: Earlier History of the Theme," in *Heresy and Literacy, 1000–1530*, ed. Anne Hudson and Peter Biller, Cambridge Studies in Medieval Literature, 23 (Cambridge: Cambridge University Press, 1994), p. 16, and idem, "La storiografia intorno all'eresia medievale negli Stati Uniti e in Gran Bretagna (1942–92)," in *Eretici ed eresie medievali nella storiografia contemporanea: atti del XXXII Convegno du studi seilla Riforma e i movimenti religiosi in Italia*, ed. Grado Giovanni Merlo, Bolletino della Societa di Studi Valdesi, 174 (Torre Pellice: Societa di Studi Valdesi, 1994), pp. 39–63, esp. 44–49.

73. The letters between Sherwood and Evans about publishing MS 609, stored in the John H. Mundy Papers, continue for eighteen years between 1934 and 1952. Columbia University still possesses some of their notes on (and transcriptions of) MS 609, but they are uncataloged (and the transcriptions, often student

exercises from half a century or more ago, vary in accuracy). Rather poignantly, the first footnote of Sherwood's "Mélanges et Documents: Un registre de la cour criminelle de Mireval-Lauragais au quatorzième siècle," *Annales du Midi* 53 (1941): 78 n. 1, confidently suggests that the register will be appearing in the immediate future—unfortunately, the entry of the United States into the Second World War delayed such projects. Interestingly, the document edited in the article was found in a parish church while Sherwood was walking through the Lauragais familarizing herself with the physical landscape mentioned in MS 609. Now, see John H. Mundy, *Society and Government at Toulouse in the Age of the Cathars*, Studies and Texts, 129 (Toronto: Pontifical Institute of Medieval Studies, 1997), p. ix, for his memories of Sherwood (who, sadly, died shortly after retiring to southern France).

74. New York, Columbia University, Merriam Sherwood to Austin Evans, 28 November 1934, Folder 1, John H. Mundy Papers.

75. The small holes from humidity in MS 609 are at fols. 35, 37, 38, 43, 44, 47r where the fifth line is completely blurred, 52, 56, 58, 95, 98, 99, 100, and 101.

76. The unreadable blurring in MS 609 is at fols. 26r and 42r.

77. The scribes cut through MS 609 at fols. 26, 60, and 116; the rips have scarred fols. 40 and 45.

78. Georges Duby, *L'Histoire Continue* (Paris: Éditions Odile Jacob, 1991), p. 35 [trans. Arthur Goldhammer as *History Continues* (Chicago: University of Chicago Press, 1994), p. 17]. For scholars experiencing similar sensations, but not with medieval documents, see Richard Cobb's sharply idiosyncratic and joyfully lyrical *A Second Identity: Essays on France and French History* (London: Oxford University Press, 1969), pp. 1–50, esp. 53–63 where he expresses his annoyance that most French archivists are medievalists with a disdain for anything beyond the fifteenth century, and Arlette Farge's almost sensual *Le goût de l'archive*, La Librairie du XX*ᵉ* *Siècle* (Paris: Éditions du Seuil, 1989).

79. Duby, *L'Histoire Continue*, p. 35, ". . . le parfum de vies depuis longtemps éteintes."

## CHAPTER 5
### SPLITTING HEADS AND TEARING SKIN

1. MS 609, fol. 140v: "Requisitus quare interesse nec dictorum inquisitorum. Respondit quod credebat, et dicebatur ab aliis, quod negotium inquisitionis esset extinctum, et tota terra esset liberata, et non fieret de cetero inquisitio."

2. Ibid., fol. 5v, ". . . etiam quod ipse testis non interfuit morti inquisitorum nec scivit, sed in crastinum scivit apud Falgairat et audivit Austorgam, uxor Petrus de Resengas, dicentem, 'Totum est liberatum, et estor,' et vir ipsius dixit, 'Totus est mortuus.' "

3. Ibid., fol. 85v, ". . . Guillelmus dixit quod ipse abscidit linguam fratri Guillelmo Arnaldi inquisitori."

4. Na Faiz de Plaigne, 18 March 1244, Doat 22, fols. 248–258. The murders of Guilhem Arnaut and Esteve de Saint-Thibéry are mentioned many times throughout MS 609. Two testimonies in particular, however, are quite detailed: Guilhem Arnaut of Saint-Martin-de-la-Lande, fol. 37r–v, who testified on 19 June

1245; and the already-mentioned Bertran de Quiders of Avignonet, fols. 139v–140v, who testified on 6 February 1246. On the importance of the assassinations, see especially Yves Dossat, "Le massacre d'Avignonet," *Cahiers de Fanjeaux: Le Credo, la Morale et l'Inquisition* 6 (1971): 343–359.

5. Jordan, *Louis IX and the Challenge of the Crusade,* pp. 15–16; Wakefield, *Heresy, Crusade, and Inquisition in Southern France,* pp. 153–158; and Roquebert, *L'épopée Cathare,* 4:287–311.

6. Jordan, *Louis IX and the Challenge of the Crusade,* p. 16, and Roquebert, *L'épopée Cathare,* 4:316–322.

7. Roquebert, *L'épopée Cathare,* 4:323–347, and Wakefield, *Heresy, Crusade, and Inquisition in Southern France,* pp. 158–161.

8. Pacts of submission were forced on the Lusignans (*Layettes,* vol. 2, nos. 2980–2981), on Raimon VII (*Layettes,* vol. 2, nos. 2995–2996, 3013), on Amalric, *vescomte* of Narbonne (*Layettes,* vol. 2, no. 3014), and Roger, count of Foix (*Layettes,* vol. 2, no. 3015). By contrast, written pledges were extracted, for example, from Raimon Trencavel (*Layettes,* vol. 3, no. 3616; *HGL* 8, cols. 1212–1214), Bertran, brother of Raimon VII (*Layettes,* vol. 2, no. 3057), Raoul, bishop of Angoulême, and Guilhem, abbot of Corona (*Layettes,* vol. 2, n. 3110). See, especially, Jordan, *Louis IX and the Challenge of the Crusade,* p. 16 and n. 10.

9. *Layettes,* vol. 3, nos. 3625, 3651, and *HGL* 6, col. 788. Also see Jordan, *Louis IX and the Challenge of the Crusade,* pp. 41–42.

10. The excommunication of the inquisitors is in *Layettes,* vol. 2, no. 2976, and that of the archbishop of Narbonne is in *HGL* 8, cols. 1090–1091. See especially Dossat, *Les crises de l'Inquisition Toulousaine au XIII^e siècle,* p. 150.

11. Mundy has recently edited this oath in his *Society and Government at Toulouse,* pp. 368–384 (Appendix 3).

12. On Montségur, see Yves Dossat, "Le «bûcher de Montségur» et les bûchers de l'inquisition," *Cahiers de Fanjeaux: Le Credo, la Morale, et l'Inquisition* 6 (1971): 361–378; Roquebert, *L'épopée Cathare,* 4:348–437, 417–426; and Lambert, *The Cathars,* pp. 165–170.

13. MS 609, fol. 97v: "Item dixit quod ipse testis fuit captus apud Tholosam et stetit in castro Narbonensi captus per tres septimanas pro heresi, et fuit cruce signatus in fronte cum ferro calido. . . ."

14. Ibid., fol. 121v., ". . . ad domum ipsius testis apud Castrum Bren juxta Gajanum Raimundam de Banheras hereticam quam ipse testis receptavit per tres septimanas . . . et postmodum dicta heretica fuit capta in domo ipsius testis et combusta apud Lauracum, et propter hoc ipse testis fuit cauterizatus in fronte et amisit omnia que habebat. . . ."

15. Ibid., fol. 94v: "Dicit etiam quod ipse aufugit de terra pro timore ballivorum Comitis."

16. Ibid., fol. 40r.

17. Ibid., fol. 246r.

18. Jordan, *Louis IX and the Challenge of the Crusade,* pp. 161–165.

19. MS 609, fol. 44r.

20. Dossat, *Les crises de l'Inquisition Toulousaine au XIII^e siècle,* pp. 89–92, and Given, *Inquisition and Medieval Society,* p. 194.

21. Dossat, *Les crises de l'Inquisition Toulousaine au XIII^e siècle,* p. 91.

22. Given, *Inquisition and Medieval Society,* p. 197. Dossat, *Les crises de l'Inquisition Toulousaine au XIII^e siècle,* p. 93, has the figure of 800 pounds, 14 shillings. Cabié, "Compte des inquisiteurs des Diocèses de Toulouse, d'Albi et de Cahors, 1255–1256," p. 220, where the parchment roll itself gives the figure of 832 pounds, 19 shillings, 3 pence.

23. Given, *Inquisition and Medieval Society,* p. 196.

24. Doat 27, fols. 112v–118r.

25. AN: J 330 b, no. 59, ". . . pro una aumucia de anniculis pro fratre Johanne." Dossat, *Les crises de l'Inquisition Toulousaine au XIII^e siècle,* pp. 93–99, is very good on the cornucopia purchased by Jean de Saint-Pierre and Renaud de Chartres

26. Guilhem Pelhisson, *Chronique (1229–1244) suivie du récit des troubles d'Albi (1234),* ed. Jean Duvernoy (Paris: CNRS Éditions, 1994), p. 72–81. See Wakefield, *Heresy, Crusade and Inquisition in Southern France,* pp. 146–149.

27. Richard Kieckhefer, "The Office of Inquisition and Medieval Heresy: The Transition from Personal to Institutional Jurisdiction," *Journal of Ecclesiastical History* 46 (1995): 36–61, esp. 56–57, and Henry Ansgar Kelly, "Inquisition and the Prosecution of Heresy: Misconceptions and Abuses," *Church History* 58 (1989): 439–451. On the use of the word *inquisitor* by a thirteenth-century cleric with no implication that he represented an institutional Inquisition or that his inquiries had anything to do with heresy, see AD: Tarn-et-Garonne, G 722 bis (dated October 1253 to May 1254), where Guilhem de Bessenco styled himself "a domino papa judux unicus seu inquisitor constitutus" (line 7 in a roll of five parchment sheets) in his summons of 29 October 1253 to Peire de Dalbs, onetime prior of the Daurade in Toulouse, later abbot of Lézat. Guilhem de Bessenco was investigating irregularities at Lézat. See John H. Mundy, *Men and Women at Toulouse in the Age of the Cathars,* Studies and Texts, 101 (Toronto: Pontifical Institute of Medieval Studies, 1990), pp. 195–212, for his discussion of this inquisition.

28. Dossat, *Les crises de l'Inquisition Toulousaine au XIII^e siècle,* pp. 211–215.

29. *Bullarium diplomatum et privilegiorum sanctorum romanum pontificum,* ed. Charles Cocquelines, 25 vols. (Turin: Dalmazzo, 1857–1872), 3:552–8. See Dossat, *Les crises de l'Inquisition Toulousaine au XIII^e siècle,* p. 214; Piero Fiorelli, *La tortura guidiziaria nel diritto comune,* 2 vols. (Milan: Guiffre, 1953), 1:80; Helmut Walther, "Ziele und Mittel päpstlicher Ketzerpolitik in der Lombardei und im Kirchenstaat 1184–1252," in *Die Anfänge der Inquisition im Mittelalter, mit einem Ausblick auf das 20. Jahrhundert und einem Beitrag über religiöse Intoleranz im nichtchristlichen Bereich,* ed. Peter Segl, Bayrether Historische Kolloquien, 7 (Cologne: Böhlau Verlag, 1993), p. 127; and Edward Peters, *Torture: Expanded Edition* (Philadelphia: University of Pennsylvania Press, 1996), pp. 62–67, and pp. 236–237 where the relevant part of *Ad extirpanda* is translated.

30. Dossat, *Les crises de l'Inquisition Toulousaine au XIII^e siècle,* pp. 214 ff., and Peters, *Torture,* pp. 65 ff.

31. Doat 31, fols. 196v–197r. Dossat, *Les crises de l'Inquisition Toulousaine au XIII^e siècle,* p. 214, and Peters, *Torture,* p. 65. Also see Kenneth Pennington, *The Prince and the Law, 1200–1600: Sovereignty and Rights in the Western Legal Tradition* (Berkeley and Los Angeles: University of California Press, 1993), pp. 157–164, and Edward Peters, "Destruction of the Flesh—Salvation of the Spirit: The Paradoxes of Torture in Medieval Christian Society," in *The Devil, Heresy, and Witchcraft in the*

*Middle Ages: Essays in Honor of Jeffrey Burton Russell,* ed. Alberto Ferreiro (Leiden: Brill, 1998), pp. 131–148.

32. MS 609, fol. 38r, ". . . et ipse dictus P. de Vinhalet respondit ipsi testi quod confessus fuerat et quod nihil dixerat inquisitoribus de hiis que fecerat cum dicto Willelmo de Sancto Nazario de facto heresis, nec confiteretur alicui si deberet findi per medium capitis."

33. Ibid., fol. 98v, ". . . immo erant plures de Auriaco qui non proponebant dicere veritatem si Fratres excoriarent ipsos."

34. Walter L. Wakefield, "Heretics and Inquisitors: The Case of Auriac and Cambiac," *Journal of Medieval History* 12 (1986): 229, implies that Fabrissa Artus was talking about a genuine fear of torture.

35. Ibid., fol. 41r, ". . . et ipsa testis, ducta usque ad ignem, timore ignis convertit ad fidem catholicam." On heretics who converted from fear of death, and who should still be imprisoned lest they corrupt others, see the Council of Toulouse, 1229, in *Sacrorum conciliorum,* vol. 23, col. 196.

36. On defining torture in the modern world, see, for example, Peters, *Torture,* pp. 183–289; *A Glimpse of Hell: Reports in Torture Worldwide,* ed. Duncan Forrest (London: Cassell and Amnesty International, 1996); and *Torture: Human Rights, Medical Ethics and the Case of Israel,* ed. Neve Gordon and Ruchama Marton (London: Zed Books, 1995).

37. Dossat, *Les crises de l'Inquisition Toulousaine au XIIIᵉ siècle,* p. 214, and Mundy, *Men and Women at Toulouse,* p. 124. Indeed, it has been argued—by Given, "The Inquisitors of Languedoc," 343–347, and his *Inquisition and Medieval Society,* esp. pp. 78–84, for instance—that the inquisitors were the first to use imprisonment systematically in the Middle Ages—a point demonstrated by the common inquisitorial punishment of lifelong incarceration for heresy. See the lucid discussion of medieval prisons by Edward Peters, "Prison before the Prison: The Ancient and Medieval Worlds," in *The Oxford History of the Prison: The Practice of Punishment in Western Society,* ed. Norval Morris and David J. Rothman (New York: Oxford University Press, 1995), pp. 3–47.

38. Edward Peters has elegantly tracked the literary history of this cruel animal in his *Inquisition,* passim. See also Bernard Schimmelpfennig, "*Intoleranz und Repression.* Die Inquisition, Bernard Gui und William von Baskerville," in "*. . . eine finstere und fast unglaubliche Geschichte*"? *Mediävistische Notizen zu Umberto Ecos Mönchroman "Der Name der Rose*", ed. Max Kerner (Darmstadt: Wissenschaftliche Buchgesellschaft, 1987), pp. 191–215, where he notes that Bernard Gui was not at all like the ogre-inquisitor of Umberto Eco's *The Name of the Rose.*

39. Kieckhefer, "The Office of Inquisition and Medieval Heresy," passim. Bernard Hamilton, for example, in his *The Medieval Inquisition,* (New York: Holmes & Meier, 1981), argues for the existence of a medieval Inquisition. Even Henry Charles Lea admitted that there was no comprehensive institutional "Inquisition" throughout the European Middle Ages. Lea's admission is in his *A History of the Inquisition of the Middle Ages* (New York: Harper & Brothers, 1887), 1:397 ff. On Lea's thoughts about the medieval inquisition, see Peters, "Henry Charles Lea (1825–1909)," pp. 89–100, and idem, *Inquisition,* pp. 287–292. A good examination of the differences between not only the early and the later medieval inquisition, but also between France and Spain, is Teófilo F. Ruiz's "The Holy Office in

Medieval France and in Late Medieval Castile: Origins and Contrasts," in his *The City and the Realm: Burgos and Castile 1080–1492* (Aldershot: Variorum, 1992), pp. 33–51. Giovanni Gonnet's "Bibliographical Appendix: Recent European Historiography on the Medieval Inquisition," in *The Inquisition in Early Modern Europe: Studies on Sources and Methods,* ed. Gustav Henningsen and John Tedeschi with Charles Amiel (DeKalb: Northern Illinois University Press: 1986), pp. 198–223, is also helpful on defining Inquisitions, medieval and early modern. John Tedeschi, in his *The Prosecution of Heresy: Collected Studies on the Inquisition in Early Medieval Italy,* Medieval & Renaissance Texts & Studies, 78 (Binghamton: Medieval & Renaissance Texts & Studies, 1991), also carefully discusses many different aspects of the early modern Inquisition. It is a lack of historical nuance about the inquisition in the Middle Ages that, for example, ultimately discredits Kathleen Biddick's "The Devil's Anal Eye: Inquisitorial Optics and Ethnographic Authority," in her *The Shock of Medievalism* (Durham, N.C.: Duke University Press, 1998), pp. 105–134.

40. Joseph Strayer states this view quite succinctly in his *On the Medieval Origins of the Modern State* (Princeton: Princeton University Press, 1970). Robert Moore's *The Formation of a Persecuting Society* (Oxford: Oxford University Press, 1987) also clearly depends upon a Weberian model for its argument (despite some influence from anthropologists like Emile Durkheim and Mary Douglas). For an interesting and critical discussion of Weber, Moore, institutions, and persecuting societies, see Bob Scribner, "Preconditions of Tolerance and Intolerance in Sixteenth-Century Germany," in *Tolerance and Intolerance in the European Reformation,* ed. Ole Peter Grell and Bob Scribner (Cambridge: Cambridge University Press, 1996), pp. 32–47. See also Alexander Murray, "The Medieval Inquisition: An Instrument of Secular Politics?" *Peritia: Journal of the Medieval Academy of Ireland* 5 (1986): 161–200. On the resemblance between modern totalitarian states and the Inquisition, see Bernhard Schimmelpfennig, "Des Großen Bruders Großmutter. Die christliche Inquisition als Vorläuferin des modernen Totalitarismus," in Segl, *Die Anfänge der Inquisition im Mittelalter,* pp. 258–296. On one specific democracy's imitating the Inquisition, see Avigdor Feldman, "The Modern Inquisition State," in *Torture: Human Rights, Medical Ethics and the Case of Israel,* pp. 85–89. Mary Douglas examines institutions in general in her *How Institutions Think* (London: Routledge, 1987).

### CHAPTER 6
### SUMMONED TO SAINT-SERNIN

1. Henry James, *A Little Tour in France* (1884; London: Sidgewick & Jackson, 1987), p. 140. In the reprinted preface from the illustrated edition of 1900, p. 6, James modestly wrote that his book should be understood as a collection of word "sketches on 'drawing-paper' and nothing more."

2. Raymond Rey, "Le cloître de Saint-Sernin et l'inquisition à Toulouse au XIII$^e$ siècle," *Bulletin Monumental* 110 (1952): 63–69.

3. Célestin Douais, introduction to his edition of the *Cartulaire de l'abbaye de Saint-Sernin de Toulouse (844–1200)* (Paris: Alphonse Picard; Toulouse: Édouard Privat, 1887), p. xxxvii.

4. Michèle Eclache, "L'église et ses abords: topographie et urbanisme," in *Saint-Sernin de Toulouse. Trésors et Métamorphoses. Deux siècles de restaurations 1802–1989. Toulouse, Musée Saint-Raymond, 15 septembre 1989–14 janvier 1990* (Toulouse; Musée Saint-Raymond, 1990), pp. 50–51.

5. Prosper Mérimée, *Notes d'un voyage dans le Midi de la France*, in *Notes de Voyages*, ed. Pierre-Marie Auzas (Paris: Librairie Hachette, 1971), pp. 233–235.

6. Marcel Durliat, "Saint-Sernin et ses métamorphoses," in *Saint-Sernin de Toulouse. Trésors et Métamorphoses. Deux siècles de restaurations 1802–1989. Toulouse, Musée Saint-Raymond, 15 septembre 1989–14 janvier 1990* (Toulouse; Musée Saint-Raymond, 1989), p. 21, and his *Saint-Sernin de Toulouse* (Toulouse: Eché, 1986).

7. Francis Salet, "Viollet-le-Duc et Mérimée," *Les Monuments Historiques de la France* 11 (1965): 19–32.

8. On Viollet-le-Duc's restoration of Saint-Sernin, see Louis Peyrusse, "Viollet-le-Duc à Saint-Sernin ou le génie de la restauration," in *Saint-Sernin de Toulouse. Trésors et Métamorphoses. Deux siècles de restaurations 1802–1989. Toulouse, Musée Saint-Raymond, 15 septembre 1989–14 janvier 1990* (Toulouse: Musée Saint-Raymond, 1989), pp. 109–119. For a general discussion of Viollet-le-Duc's architectural theories, see Millard Fillmore Hearn, "Viollet-le-Duc: A Visionary among the Gargoyles," in his *The Architectural Theory of Viollet-le-Duc: Readings and Commentary* (Cambridge: MIT Press, 1990), pp. 1–19, and Yves-Marie Froidevaux, "Viollet le Duc restaurateur et son influence," in *Actes du Colloque International Viollet le Duc, Paris 1980*, ed. Pierre-Marie Auzas (Paris: Nouvelles Editions Latines, 1982), pp. 145–151.

9. Durliat, "Saint-Sernin et ses métamorphoses," p. 22, for the "de-restoration" work on Saint-Sernin.

10. Cf. Quitterie Cazes, "Le cloître Saint-Etienne de Toulouse sous la Révolution et le Premier Empire," *Mémoires de la Société Archéologique de Midi de la France* 49 (1989): 191–206, for another cloister destroyed at the same time as Saint-Sernin's.

11. Mundy, *The Repression of Catharism at Toulouse*, pp. 155–167, esp. 156–157, gives a detailed history of the de Capdenier family in the twelfth and thirteenth centuries. AD: Haute-Garonne, Toulouse, Saint-Bernard 138, fols. 91r, 93r, and 94r, contain the original sale of the town house to Pons de Capdenier by Saint-Sernin in October 1225. AM: Toulouse, AA 1 100, August 1240, noted not only the sale of the storerooms but also how the storerooms had, for far too long, obstructed movement around Saint-Sernin. See also Mundy, *Society and Government at Toulouse*, pp. 118 and 151.

12. Mundy, *Liberty and Political Power in Toulouse 1050–1230*, p. 62, called Pons de Capdenier "the Croesus of late twelfth and thirteenth century Toulouse." Aurimunda de Capdenier (according to Mundy, *The Repression of Catharism at Toulouse*, p. 156) died sometime after December 1251, though no later than March 1254. Pelhisson, *Chronique* [trans. into English by Wakefield in his *Heresy, Crusade and Inquisition in Southern France*, pp. 207–236], pp. 38–41, and Bernard Gui, *Bernardus Guidonis de fundatione et prioribus conventuum provinciarum Tolosanae et Provinciae ordinis predictorum*, ed. P. A. Amargier, in *Monumenta ordinis fratrum praedictorum historica* 24 (Rome: Institutum historicum fratrum praedicatorum, 1961),

pp. 32–33. On the growth of the city and the bourg, see Mundy, *Liberty and Political Power in Toulouse 1050–1230*, pp. 43–92.

13. Pelhisson, *Chronique*, pp. 41–43, and Gui, *De fundatione*, p. 42. On Pons de Capdenier as "patron of the house" for the Dominicans in Toulouse, see Marie-Humbert Vicaire, "Le développement de la province Dominicaine de Provence (1215–1295)," *Cahiers de Fanjeaux: Les mendiants en pays d'Oc au XIIIᵉ siècle* 8 (1973): 52–54, and Mundy, *Society and Government at Toulouse*, p. 207 and n. 34.

14. Dossat, *Les crises de l'Inquisition Toulousaine au XIIIᵉ siècle*, pp. 118–121 and his edition of both bulls on pp. 325–329. See also Wakefield, *Heresy, Crusade and Inquisition in Southern France*, pp. 140–141, and Kolmer, *Ad Capiendum Vulpes*, pp. 126–127.

15. Apart from the numerous recollections of these previous inquisitions in MS 609, some of the original testimonies survive, for example, in the seventeenth-century copying of Doat 21, fols. 151r–159v for the inquiries of Guilhem Arnalt and Esteve de Saint-Thibéry. Only a double folio of Ferrer's Lauragais inquisition now exists. It was published by Paul Cayla in "Fragment d'un registre de l'Inquisition," *Mémoires de la Société des Arts et des Sciences de Carcassonne*, 3d ser., 6 (1941–1943): 282–289. See also Dossat, *Les crises de l'Inquisition Toulousaine au XIIIᵉ siècle*, pp. 220–226.

16. Dossat, *Les crises de l'Inquisition Toulousaine au XIIIᵉ siècle*, p. 220.

17. MS 609, fol. 187r, na Gerdana remembered that "homines de Sancto Martino fuerunt citati ut comparerent coram fratribus Willelmo Arnaldi et socio, olim inquisitoribus apud Castrum Novum, pro confessione de heresi facienda. . . ."

18. Dossat, *Les crises de l'Inquisition Toulousaine au XIIIᵉ siècle*, p. 227, observed that all we know about the archdeaconries of Lanta and Vieilmorez in the thirteenth century, including their very existence, comes from MS 609.

19. Dossat, *Les crises de l'Inquisition Toulousaine au XIIIᵉ siècle*, pp. 146–151, 238–239. Cf. Lea, *A History of the Inquisition of the Middle Ages*, 2:45, who missed the significance of Saint-Sernin's cloister for the inquisition of Bernart de Caux and Jean de Saint-Pierre. Lea's error (and he really made very few) was to assume that the two Dominicans, like earlier inquisitors, had actually traveled throughout the Lauragais in their pursuit of heresy.

20. A bull from Innocent IV, 4 February 1248—Doat 31, fol. 105v and *HGL* 8, cols. 1239–1240—called upon the inquisitors to avenge these deaths. See Dossat, *Les crises de l'Inquisition Toulousaine au XIIIᵉ siècle*, p. 169.

21. Doat 22, fols. 1–29v, 31–32v, 56v–62r, 69–74.

22. Ibid., fols. 29v–31, 32v–44, 46v–56, 62–69.

23. Doat 24, fols. 240–286. Jean Duvernoy edited these investigations in "Le registre de l'inquisiteur Bernard de Caux, Pamiers, 1246–1247," *Bulletin de Société ariégeoise Sciences, Lettres, et Arts* 45 (1990): 5–108.

24. Douais edited all the testimonies concerning Peire Garcias, originally in Doat 22, fols. 89–106, in his *Documents pour servir à l'histoire de l'Inquisition dans le Languedoc*, 2:90–114. Wakefield has translated Guilhem Cogot's testimony, and a small part of Déodat de Rodez's confession, in his *Heresy, Crusade and Inquisition in Southern France*, p. 242–249.

25. Dossat, *Les crises de l'Inquisition Toulousaine au XIIIᵉ siècle*, p. 167.

26. Dossat, "Une figure d'inquisiteur," 269 ff.

27. Dossat, *Les crises de l'Inquisition Toulousaine au XIII<sup>e</sup> siècle*, p. 192.

28. Ad. Tardif edited the *Processus inquisitionis* (from MS 53 at the Biblioteca universitaria de Madrid) in "Document pour l'histoire du *processus per inquisitionem* et de l'*inquisitio heretice pravitatis*," *Nouvelle revue historique du droit français et étranger* 7 (1883): 669–678 [trans. into English by Wakefield in his *Heresy, Crusade and Inquisition in Southern France*, pp. 250–258].

29. Yves Dossat, "Le plus ancien manuel de l'inquisition méridionale: le *Processsus inquisitionis* (1248–1249)," *Bulletin philologique et historique (jusqu'à 1715), années 1948–1949–1950* (1952): 33–37, and idem, *Les crises de l'Inquisition Toulousaine au XIII<sup>e</sup> siècle*, p. 167. Antoine Dondaine, by contrast, in his "Le Manuel de l'Inquisitor (1230–1330)," *Archivum Fratrum Praedicatorum* 17 (1947): 97–101, argued that the *Processus*, which is number two on his list of manuals, was the work of the inquisitors of Narbonne, the Dominicans Guilhem Raimon and Peire Durant. Kolmer, *Ad Capiendas Vulpes*, pp. 13–203, accepted Dondaine's attribution of the *Processus*. Dossat convincingly demonstrated this judgment to be mistaken. Wakefield, *Heresy, Crusade and Inquisition in Southern France*, p. 250, also accepts that the *Processus* was written by Bernart de Caux and Jean de Saint-Pierre. Cf. Given, *Inquisition and Medieval Society*, p. 45, where he attributes the *Processus* to no particular inquisitor, though he does emphasize that it was the earliest manual.

30. Dossat, *Les crises de l'Inquisition Toulousaine au XIII<sup>e</sup> siècle*, pp. 232–234. Ramon de Peñafort had already written a guide for inquisitors in the Kingdom of Aragon around 1242, and though he sets out an approach for making inquiries into heresy, his manual lacks the tone of experience that pervades the *Processus* and reads more like the handbook of an early-thirteenth-century confessor than one for an inquisitor. Nevertheless, Bernart de Caux and Jean de Saint-Pierre had probably read Ramon de Peñafort's pamphlet before writing their own manual. On Ramon de Peñafort's manual, see Dondaine, "Le Manuel de l'Inquisitor," 96–97. Célestin Douais edited the manual in his *L'Inquisition: Ses Origines—Sa Procédure* (Paris: Librairie Plon, 1906), pp. 275–288.

31. Tardif, "Document pour l'histoire du *processus per inquisitionem*," 671.

32. *Sacrorum conciliorum*, vol. 23, col. 716, for the Council of Béziers in 1246 on the suitability of a place for conducting an inquisition: "Nos volentes eisdem insidiis obviare, citandi dictos hereticos vel suspectos de heresi pro audiendis eorum confessionibus et penitentiis injungendis ad loca vobis tuta concedimus facultatem." Innocent IV—*Les régistres d'Innocent IV*, ed. Elie Berger, Bibliothèque des écoles françaises d'Athens et de Rome, 2d ser. (Paris: Ernest Thorin, 1884), vol. 1, no. 317—confirmed this decision in a bull of 19 November 1247.

33. Tardif, "Document pour l'histoire du *processus per inquisitionem*," 671.

34. MS 609, fol. 221v, ". . . et dimisit illam credulitatem ultimo in festo Asscentionis [sic], quando audivit fratrem Bernardem de Cautio predicantem." In Douais, *Documents pour servir à l'histoire de l'Inquisition dans le Languedoc*, 2:18–19, on 17 May 1246 Bernart de Caux condemned seven people to perpetual imprisonment ". . . in claustro Sancti Saturnini . . . in generali scrmone. . . ."

35. Tardif, "Document pour l'histoire du *processus per inquisitionem*," 671.

36. Ibid., 673.

37. Ibid., 671. See *Les régistres d'Innocent IV*, 1, no. 317, and *Sacrorum conciliorum*, vol. 23, col. 716: "Assignato eis termino competenti, quod tempus gratie vocare soletis, quibus tamen alias hujusmodi gratia non est facta; infra quem terminum venientes poenitentes et dicentes, immurationis, exilii et confiscationis bonorum."

38. Tardif, "Document pour l'histoire du *processus per inquisitionem*," 671.

39. Mundy, *Men and Women at Toulouse*, pp. 80–82, and his *Society and Government at Toulouse*, pp. 136–143.

40. Mundy, *Society and Government at Toulouse*, pp. 139–142, esp. 142 where it is observed that by the end of the thirteenth century twenty, rather than twenty-five, seems to have become the mean age for men to start acting independently of their families in Toulouse. See also Mireille Castaing-Sicard, *Les contrats dans le très ancien droit Toulousain—Xe–XIIIe siècle* (Toulouse: M. Espic, 1959), pp. 409–411. Occasionally, fatherless adolescent males were thought fit to manage their affairs as young as fourteen. In January 1243, for example, a certain Peire Marti from Toulouse, whose father had recently died, was judged in a charter (AD: HG Malta 15 133) to have reached a "legitimate and perfect age" at fourteen and so to be able to control his transactions with other men, "perfecte legitime hetatis .xiiii. annorum et amplius. . . ." On Peire Marti, see Mundy, *Society and Government at Toulouse*, p. 138.

41. Mundy, *Society and Government at Toulouse*, p. 138.

42. MS 609, fol. 174r. There are a few confessions from Villeneuve-la-Comtal on fols. 143r–144r that are dated 15 April 1245, *XVII kal. maii*. Dossat, *Les crises de l'Inquisition Toulousaine au XIII⁰ siècle*, p. 227 n. 77, argued that this should read *XVII kal. iunii*, 16 May 1245, and that it was probably a scribal error in the writing of the original register. Also, there are ten testimonies after 1 August 1246, nine from Barsa on 13 December 1246, fol. 197v, and one from Castelnaudary on 9 September 1247, fol. 253v. On the rigid dating of the year from 1 April adopted by the public notariate of Toulouse sometime in the 1190s, see Mundy, *Society and Government at Toulouse*, p. 386.

43. MS 609, fol 98r: "Item dixit quod nuperrime, quando ipsa testis fuit citata, fuit locuta cum Fabrissa uxore Geraldi Artus et dixit ei quod multum timebat de Fratribus Inquisitoribus et quod Deus vellet quod injungerent sibi bonam poenitentiam. . . ."

44. Ibid., fol. 63v, Bernart de Caux had "tamen promissum fuit ei quod si meram et plenam diceret veritatem reciperetur in tempore gratie . . . , " and fol. 215r where in the margin next to Peire de Valères' confession the scribe has written, "Huic fuit promissa impunitas carceris et exilii." See, on the "time of grace," Dossat, *Les crises de l'Inquisition Toulousaine au XIII⁰ siècle*, p. 233 and nn. 91–93. Cf. Douais, *Documents pour servir à l'histoire de l'Inquisition dans le Languedoc*, 1:cliv.

45. Ibid., fol. 195r: "Ar. Faber loquitur de Lauraco, gratis venit et non citatus," and fol. 210r where in the margin next to Guilhem Gasc, from Rojols (near Varennes), the scribe wrote, "Hic venit non citatus." See Dossat, *Les crises de l'Inquisition Toulousaine au XIII⁰ siècle*, p. 233.

46. Douais, *Documents pour servir à l'histoire de l'Inquisition dans le Languedoc*, 2:61, ". . . non venit tempore gratie coram aliis inquisitoribus pro confessione de heresia facienda." In MS 609 the testimonies from Villeneuve-la-Comptal occur at fols. 143r–144r, 183v–184v. No one mentioned the crimes of Algaia de Villeneuve-la-Comptal.

47. MS 609, fol. 228r.

48. On disease metaphors for heresy, see Robert Moore, "Heresy as Disease," in *The Concept of Heresy in the Middle Ages (11th–13th C.): Proceedings of the International Conference, Louvain May 13–16, 1973*, ed. W. Lourdaux and D. Verhelst, Medievalia Lovaniensia, Series I—Studia IV (The Hague: Leuven University Press-Martinus Hjhoff, 1976), pp. 1–11.

49. Tardif, "Document pour l'histoire du *processus per inquisitionem*," 673.

50. Given, *Inquisition and Medieval Society*, p. 39.

51. MS 609, fol. 242r.

52. There is some uncertainty about how many testimonies manuscript 609 actually contains. This mathematical vagueness is due to witnesses' being referred to by different names in different places throughout the manuscript. For example, Dossat, *Les crises de l'Inquisition Toulousaine au XIII^e siècle*, p. 232, gives the figure of 5,471; Douais, *Documents pour servir à histoire de l'Inquisition dans le Languedoc*, 1:cliii, has 5,600; Molinier, *L'Inquisition dans le Midi de la France au XIII^e et au XIV^e siècle*, p. 190, argued for somewhere between 8,000 and 10,000; Abels and Harrison, "The Participation of Women in Languedocian Catharism," 220, counted 5,604; Wakefield, "Inquisitor's Assistants," 57, opts for 5,600; while Given, *Inquisition and Medieval Society*, p. 39, decided on 5,518. After a number of attempts at counting the witnesses, I have come to accept Dossat's slightly more modest figure.

53. Wakefield, "Inquisitor's Assistants," 57–65.

54. MS 609, fols. 12r, 48r, 57v.

55. Wakefield, "Inquisitor's Assistants," 60 ff.

56. Ibid., 62 ff.

57. Ibid.

58. Ibid., 61 ff.

59. Ibid.

60. MS 609, fol. 75v: "Archipresbiter de Lauragues dicit quod R. Bartha miles suspendit duos servientes suos quia ceperunt matrem dicti Ramundi at alias VI hereticas."

61. Ibid., fol. 76r.

62. Ibid., fol. 108r, ". . . et fuit confessa fratri Stephano inquisitori apud Montem Esquivem qui venit ibi de mandato fratris Willelmi Arnaldi inquisitoris ad audiendum confessiones mulierum pregnantium, et infirmorum."

63. Ibid., fols. 2r, 76r, 143r.

64. Ibid., fol. 165v: "Dixit tamen quod ante confessionem vidit pluries hereticos. . . ."

65. Ibid., fol. 108v, and fol. 101v, for the testimony of Peire Raimon Gros on 12 May 1246. On the lady Marqueza de Montesquieu, see Dossat, *Les crises de l'Inquisition Toulousaine au XIII^e siècle*, p. 234.

66. For example, MS 609, fols. 14v and 20r.

67. Ibid., fol. 144v: "Item dixit quod hodie Bernardus de na Sibilia et P. Bauguel de Monte Ferrando dixerunt ipsi testi in via extra Tholosam, in strata publica, dum venieret Tholosam, quod non diceret veritatem Inquisitoribus."

68. *Locke's Travels in France 1675–1679*, ed. John Lough (New York: Garland Publishing, 1984), p. 242. Locke's interest in the Inquisition, among other things, was powerfully transformed in his brillant and profound *Epistola de Tolerantia [A Letter Concerning Toleration]: Latin and English Texts Revised and Edited with Variants* (1689), ed. Mario Montuori (The Hague: Martinus Nijhoff, 1963).

69. MS 609, fols. 66v, 201v, and 206r. See also John H. Mundy, "Village, Town, and City in the Region of Toulouse," in *Pathways to Medieval Pathways*, ed. J. A. Raftis, Papers in Medieval Studies (Toronto: Pontifical Institute of Medieval Studies, 1981), 2:153.

70. MS 609, fols. 193v–194r.

71. Ibid., fol. 226v, ". . . Poncius Rogerii intravit Tholosam ad addiscendum artem pellicere. Et ibi fecit se hereticum. . . ."

72. On the problem of estimating the population of Toulouse in the thirteenth century, see Mundy, *The Repression of Catharism at Toulouse*, p. 48, and his *Society and Government at Toulouse*, p. 9.

73. Pelhisson, *Chronique*, p. 72–81. See also Wakefield, *Heresy, Crusade and Inquisition in Southern France*, pp. 146–149.

74. Pelhisson, *Chronique*, pp. 7–12, and Wakefield, *Heresy, Crusade and Inquisition in Southern France*, p. 207.

75. Pelhisson, *Chronique*, p. 34, "scripsit manu sua que sequuntur in papiro. . . ."

76. Puylaurens, *Chronica*, p. 113, and *HGL* 6, pp. 548 ff. Now, see Charles Molinier, "La question de l'ensevelissement du comte de Toulouse Raimond VI en terre sainte (1222–1247). Etude accompagne de pièces inédites du XII$^e$ et du XIII$^e$ siècle," *Annales de la Faculté des Lettres de Bordeaux* 7 (1885): 1–38, esp. 32–34.

77. John H. Mundy, "The Farm of Fontanas at Toulouse: Two Families, a Monastery, and a Pope," *Bulletin of Medieval Canon Law*, n.s., 11 (1981): 29–40, esp. 32–40 for the publication of documents from the municipal archives of Toulouse relating to the de la Claustra family (named after the Close of Saint-Sernin) properties in Toulouse. Bernarta, the mother of Guilhem and Aycard de la Claustra, did manage, however, through the help of Saint-Sernin's abbot, to have the house torn down carefully, so that the wood and stone could be resold.

78. See, for example, Pelhisson, *Chronique*, pp. 42 ff., for a description of the destruction of the Waldensian Galvan's house by Dominicans in 1231. See Mundy, *The Repression of Catharism at Toulouse*, pp. 65–66, for a general discussion of inquisitorial damage to property in Toulouse.

79. *Les régistres de Grégoire IX (1227–1241), Recueil des bulles de ce pape*, ed. Lucien Auvray, Bibliothèque des écoles françaises d'Athenes et de Rome, 2d ser., 9 (Paris: A. Fontemoing, 1907), 2:1245, no. 4758 (June 1236), ". . . tam nobilem civitatem ruinis non deceat deformari, maxime cum non res sed homines peccaverunt. . . ."

## CHAPTER 7
## QUESTIONS ABOUT QUESTIONS

1. Tardif, "Document pour l'histoire du *processus per inquisitionem*," 672. In MS 609, for example, see the beginning of Pons de Beatueville's testimony on 16 June 1246 at fol. 129r, ". . . requisitus de veritate dicenda de se et de aliis, tam vivis quam mortuis, super crimine heresis et valdesie, testis juratus, dixit quod. . . ."

2. Tardif, "Document pour l'histoire du *processus per inquisitionem*," 672.

3. See, for example, Raimon Bru's response to these questions at MS 609, fol. 130v.

4. See, for example, the testimony of Peire Jouglar (MS 609, fol. 120r), where the question was actually written into the confession: "Requisitus si, postquam dimisit sectam hereticorum, vidit hereticos, dixit quod plures vidit stantes apud La Besseda."

5. Bernard Gui, *Practica inquisitionis heretice pravitatis*, ed. Célestin Douais (Paris: Alphonse Picard, 1886), esp. pt. 5, pp. 235–355. See Annette Pales-Gobilliard, "Bernard Gui inquisiteur et auteur de la *Practica*," *Cahiers de Fanjeaux: Bernard Gui et son monde* 16 (1981): 253–264.

6. Dondaine, "Le Manuel de l'Inquisitor," 115–117; Pales-Gobilliard, "Bernard Gui inquisiteur et auteur de la *Practica*," 255 ff.; Jacques Paul, "La mentalité de l'inquisiteur chez Bernard Gui," *Cahiers de Fanjeaux: Bernard Gui et son monde* 16 (1981): 286–292; and Given, *Inquisition and Medieval Society*, pp. 44–51.

7. Cf. Jean-Louis Biget, "L'extinction du catharisme urbain: les points chauds de la répression," *Cahiers de Fanjeaux: Effacement du Catharisme? (XIIIᵉ–XIVᵉ S.)* 20 (1985): 305–340.

8. *Practica inquisitionis heretice pravitatis*, p. 237, ". . . item conversorum ex Judeis ad fidem Christi qui redeunt ad vomitum Judaysmi. . . ."

9. Ibid.

10. Ibid., esp. pp. 237–239 ("De erroribus Manicheorum moderni temporis") and 239–241 ("De modo et ritu vivendi ipsorum Manicheorum"). On Gui's methods as an inquisitor, see James Given, "A Medieval Inquisitor at Work: Bernard Gui, 3 March 1308 to 19 June 1323," in *Portraits of Medieval and Renaissance Living: Essays in Memory of David Herlihy*, ed. Samuel K. Cohn Jr. and Steven A. Epstein (Ann Arbor: University of Michigan Press, 1996), pp. 207–232.

11. For example, Mundy, "Village, Town, and City in the Region of Toulouse," pp. 141 ff., and Wakefield, "Heretics and Inquisitors: The Case of Auriac and Cambiac," pp. 225 ff. Both scholars (with Le Roy Ladurie's *Montaillou* in mind) imply this about the Lauragais interrogations.

12. Carlo Ginzburg, "The Inquisitor as Anthropologist," in his *Myths, Emblems, Clues*, trans. John and Anne Tedeschi (London: Hutchinson Radius, 1986), pp. 156–164. See also Renato Rosaldo's thought-provoking comparison of Le Roy Ladurie's *Montaillou* with Edward Evans-Pritchard's *The Nuer* in "From the Door of His Tent: The Fieldworker and the Inquisitor," in *Writing Culture: The Poetics and Politics of Ethnography*, ed. James Clifford and George E. Marcus (Berkeley and Los Angeles: University of California Press, 1986), pp. 77–97. Claire Sponsler, "Medieval Ethnography: Fieldwork in the European Past," *Assays: Critical Approaches to Medieval and Renaissance Texts* 7 (1992): 1–30, and Biddick, "The Devil's

Anal Eye," pp. 105–134, both use the ethnographic analogy, and though each of them overtly attempts to be provocative, especially the latter, in the end they demonstrate very little.

13. On the questions used by medieval inquisitors, and some of the problems this causes when scholars use inquisitorial registers, see the helpful comments of Herbert Grundmann, "Ketzerverhöre des Spätmittelalters als quellenkritisches Problem," *Deutsches Archiv* 21 (1965): 519–575; Grado Giovanni Merlo, *Eretici e inquisitori nella società piemontese del Trecento: con l'edizione dei processi tenuti a Giaveno dall'inquisitore Alberto De Castellario (1335) e nelle Valli di Lanzo dall'inquisitore Tommaso Di Casasco (1373)* (Turin: Claudiana, 1977), pp. 11–15; Dossat, *Les crises de l'Inquisition Toulousaine au XIII<sup>e</sup> siècle,* pp. 239–240; and Kolmer, *Ad capiendas vulpes,* pp. 92–95, 97, 159, 171–175, 182–185, 204. See also the thoughtful discussions about questions by Douglas, "Rightness of Categories," pp. 258–259; Susanne K. Langer, *Philosophy in a New Key: A Study in the Symbolism of Reason, Rite, and Art,* 3d ed. (Cambridge: Harvard University Press, 1979), esp. pp. 3–9; and Nicholas Jardine, *The Scenes of Inquiry: On the Reality of Questions in the Sciences* (Oxford: Clarendon Press, 1991), passim.

14. MS 609, fol. 117v, where Arnaut del Faget says about himself and Guilhem Vezat, ". . . et perpenderunt in animo suo quod heretici erant."

15. Étienne de Bourbon, *Anecdotes Historiques. Légendes et Apologues tirés du recueil inédit d'Etienne de Bourbon, Dominicain du XIII<sup>e</sup> siècle,* ed. Richard Albert Lecoy de la Marche (Paris: Librairie Renouard, 1877), pp. 34–35.

16. Guillaume de Auvergne in his *De Universo—Opera Omnia* (Paris: Andreas Pralard, 1674; reprint, Frankfurt: Minerva, 1963), 1055—written around 1235, clearly stated this persuasive thirteenth-century forensic notion. On the related problem of defining and understanding the causes of medieval wonder, see Caroline Walker Bynum's "Wonder," *American Historical Review* 102 (1997): 1–26, esp. 7–11.

17. Caesarius of Heisterbach, *Dialogus Miraculorum,* 1:302, col. 21, distinctio 5.

18. See, for example, ibid., 2:217, col. 1, distinctio 10, where Caesarius of Heisterbach had this to say about miracles and nature: "NOVICIUS: Quid est miraculum? MONACHUS: Miraculum dicimus quicquid fit contra solitum cursum naturae, unde miramur."

19. Wendy Davies and Paul Fouracre, "Conclusion," in *The Settlement of Disputes in Early Medieval Europe,* ed. Wendy Davies and Paul Fouracre (Cambridge: Cambridge University Press, 1986), pp. 207–240, strongly argue against assuming simplistic notions of proof, procedure, and truth in the centuries before the twelfth and thirteenth.

20. Pennington, *The Prince and the Law,* pp. 132–135.

21. Antonio García y García, *Constitutiones Concilii quarti Lateranensis una cum commentariis glossatorum,* Monumenta iuris canonici. Series A. Corpus glossatorum 2 (Vatican City: Biblioteca Apostolica Vaticano, 1981), pp. 66–68, and *Sacrorum conciliorum,* vol. 22, cols. 1006–10.

22. On the *ordo iudiciarius,* see esp. Linda Fowler-Magerl, *Ordo iudiciorum vel ordo iudiciarius: Begriff und Literaturgattung,* Repertorien zur Frühzeit der gelehrten Rechte (Frankfurt am Main: V. Klostermann, 1984), and Pennington, *The Prince and the Law,* pp. 135–164.

23. On the judicial ordeal, see Peter Brown, "Society and the Supernatural: A Medieval Change," in his *Society and the Holy in Late Antiquity* (Berkeley and Los Angeles: University of California Press, 1982), pp. 302–332; Dominique Barthélemy, "Présence de l'aveu dans le déroulement des ordalies (IXème–XIVème) siècles," in *L'Aveu: Antiquité et moyen-âge: Actes de la table ronde organisée par l'Ecole française de Rome avec le concours du CNRS et de l'Université de Trieste, Rome 28–30 mars 1984* (Rome: Ecole française de Rome, 1986), pp. 315–340; Robert Bartlett, *Trial by Fire and Water: The Medieval Judicial Ordeal* (Oxford: Oxford University Press, 1986), pp. 4–12, and esp. 42–43 for his criticism of Brown; Pennington, *The Prince and the Law*, pp. 132–134, for his criticism of Bartlett; and John W. Baldwin, "The Crisis of the Ordeal: Literature, Law, and Religion around 1200," *Journal of Medieval and Renaissance Studies* 24 (1994): 327–353.

24. On *imitatio Christi*, see Giles Constable, *Three Studies in Medieval Religious and Social Thought: The Interpretation of Mary, the Ideal of the Imitation of Christ, the Orders of Society* (Cambridge: Cambridge University Press, 1995), pp. 143–248.

25. Cf. John W. Baldwin, "The 1996 York Quodlibet Lecture: From the Ordeal to Confession. In Search of Lay Religion in Early Thirteenth Century France," in *Handling Sin: Confession in the Middle Ages*, ed. Peter Biller and A. J. Minnis, York Studies in Medieval Theology, 2 (Woodbridge: Boydell & Brewer; York: York Medieval Press, 1998), pp. 191–209.

26. Cf. Laura A. Smoller's analysis of questions and investigative procedures in her "Defining Boundaries of the Natural in Fifteenth-Century Brittany: The Inquest into the Miracles of Saint Vincent Ferrer (d. 1419)," *Viator* 28 (1997): 333–359. Two longer studies with thoughtful discussions on the asking of questions are Rebbeca Redwood French, *The Golden Yoke: The Legal Cosmology of Buddhist Tibet* (Ithaca: Cornell University Press, 1995), passim, and Elizabeth Lunbeck, *The Psychiatric Persausion: Knowledge, Gender, and Power in Modern America* (Princeton: Princeton University Press, 1994), esp. pp. 133–144.

27. Anthony Kenny and Jan Pinborg, "Medieval Philosophical Literature," in *The Cambridge History of Later Medieval Philosophy: From the Rediscovery of Aristotle to the Disintegration of Scholasticism 1100–1600*, ed. Norman Kretzmann, Anthony Kenny, and Jan Pinborg (Cambridge: Cambridge University Press, 1990), pp. 26–28 ff.

28. Incidentally, the *studium* of Toulouse was, after a remarkable grant of Gregory IX in 1233, considered the equal of Paris in all privileges, including the provision that any student awarded the *licentia docendi* in Toulouse could freely *regere ubique*, that is, teach wherever he chose without any further examinations. On the Toulouse *universitas* of masters and scholars, see Yves Dossat, "Université et Inquisition à Toulouse: la foundation du Collège Saint-Raimond (1250)," in *Actes du 95ᵉ Congrès national des Sociétés savantes*, Reims, 1970. Section de philologie et d'histoire jusqu'à 1610 (Paris: Comité des travaux historiques et scientifiques, 1975), 1:227–238, esp. pp. 227 ff.; Marie-Humbert Vicaire and Henri Gilles, "Rôle de l'université de Toulouse dans l'effacement du catharisme," *Cahiers de Fanjeaux: Effacement du Catharisme? (XIIIᵉ–XIVᵉ S.)* 20 (1985): 257–276; Paolo Nardi, "Relations with Authority," in *A History of the University in Europe*, ed. Hilde de Ridder-Symoens (Cambridge: Cambridge University Press, 1992), 1:89, 94; and, with reservations, French and Cunningham, *Before Science*, pp. 156–160.

29. On the dialogue form in the Middle Ages, see Peter von Moos, "Literatur- und bildungsgeschichtliche Aspekte der Dialogform im lateinischen Mittelalter. Der Dialogus Ratii des Eberhard von Ypern zwischen theologischer disputatio und Scholaren-Komödie," in *Tradition und Wertung. Festschrift für Franz Brunhölzl zum 65. Geburtstag*, ed. Günter Bernt, Fidel Rädle, and Gabriel Silagi (Sigmaringen: Jan Thorbecke, 1989), pp. 165–209, and his "Rhetorik, Dialektik und 'civilios scientia' im Hochmittelalter," in *Dialektik und Rhetorik im früheren und hohen Mittelalter: Rezeption, überlieferung und gesellschaftliche Wirkung antiker Gelehrsamkeit vornehmlich im 9. und 12. Jahrhundert*, ed. Johannes Fried, Schriften des Historischen Kollegs, Kolloquien 27 (Munich: R. Oldenburg, 1997), pp. 133–156.

30. "Del tot vey remaner valor," in *Les Poésies de Guilhem de Montanhagol: Troubadour Provençal du XIII*$^e$ *Siècle*, ed. and trans. Peter T. Ricketts (Toronto: Pontifical Institute of Medieval Studies, 1964), p. 44, 1.19–20, "Ar se son fait enqueredor / e jutjon aissi com lur plai."

31. Ibid., 1.21–24, "Pero l'enquerre no·m desplai, / anz me plai que casson error / e qu'ab bels digz plazentiers ses yror, / torno·ls erratz desviatz en la fe." See Catherine Léglu, "Moral and Satirical Poetry," in *The Troubadours: An Introduction*, ed. Simon Gaunt and Sarah Kay (Cambridge: Cambridge University Press, 1999), p. 63, and Routledge, "The Later Troubadours . . . noels gigz de nova maestria . . . ," p. 103.

32. Richard W. Emery, *Heresy and Inquisition in Narbonne* (New York: Columbia University Press, 1941), p. 83.

33. Ibid., p. 81. On what is known of Friar Ferrer's life, see Walter L. Wakefield, "Friar Ferrier, Inquisition at Caunes, and Escapes from Prison at Carcassonne," *Catholic Historical Review* 68 (1972): 220–237, and his "Friar Ferrier, Inquisitor," *Heresis* (1986): 33–41.

34. Pelhisson, *Chronique*, p. 80. The prior was Pons de Saint-Gilles.

### CHAPTER 8
### FOUR EAVESDROPPING FRIARS

1. Douais edited all the testimonies concerning Peire Garcias, originally in Doat 22, fols. 89–106, in his *Documents pour servir à l'histoire de l'Inquisition dans le Languedoc*, 2:90–114. Wakefield has translated Guilhem Cogot's testimony, and a small part of Déodat de Rodez's confession, in his *Heresy, Crusade and Inquisition in Southern France*, p. 242–249.

2. For example, see Douais, *Documents pour servir à l'histoire de l'Inquisition dans le Languedoc*, 2:90, for Guilhem Cogot's opening comments.

3. Ibid., where Guilhem Cogot said, ". . . erat superius inter tectum et ipsos in loco de quo poterat ipsos audire et videre"; while Peire de Sant-Barti, p. 108, another eavesdropping friar, who gave his short testimony alone on 26 August 1247, described the hiding place as ". . . inter tectum et ipsos super quodam tabulato, de quo poterat ipsos videre et audire."

4. Ibid., p. 104, Guilhem Garcias admitted that he knew ". . . eos esse in dicto loco, et vidit eos ibidem." The familial relationship between Guilhem and Peire (despite the assumption of Douais, *Documents pour servir à l'histoire de l'Inquisition dans le Languedoc*, 1:cclxvii, that they were brothers) is unclear from the evidence.

Wakefield, *Heresy, Crusade and Inquisition in Southern France*, p. 247 n. 1, is especially good on this point.

5. For example, Déodat de Rodez in Douais, *Documents pour servir à l'histoire de l'Inquisition dans le Languedoc*, 2:95, said, ". . . frater Guillelmus Garcias requireret a dicto Petro Garcia si ipse crederet in sua fide quod esset unus Deus benignus qui creasset omnia, cum hoc inveniretur in Scripturis. . . ."

6. Ibid., pp. 95–96, ". . . respondit ipse Petrus quod hoc non credebat nec crederet; sed erat unus Deus benignus qui creavit incorruptibilia et permansura, et alius Deus erat malignus qui corruptibilia et transitoria [creavit]."

7. Ibid., p. 90, ". . . quod audivit Petrum Garcia[m] . . . dicentem, cum interrogaretur a fratre Guillelmo Garcia de ordine [fratrum] Minorum utrum essent duo dii, quod cum eo cum quo disputaverat per medium annum de hoc non potuit habere certitudinem usque modo."

8. Ibid., p. 102, ". . . quesivit ipse testis a dicto Petro utrum essent duo dii; et Petrus respondit quod sic, unus benignus et alius malignus." See also Arnaut Daitz, another Franciscan hidden above the common room, who testified four months later on 10 December 1247, ". . . et tunc dictus Petrus dixit, ad requisitionem predicti fratris Guillelmi, quod duo dii erant, unus bonus qui fecerat invisibilia, et alius malus qui fecerat visibilia."

9. Ibid., p. 91, where Guilhem Cogot remembered "Deus qui sanctificat circumcisionem." A misquotation of Romans 3:30—"Deus qui justificat circumcision"—which the other Franciscans did not make.

10. Ibid., p. 96.

11. Ibid., p. 92: "Sine ipso factum est nichil."

12. Ibid., ". . . ipse dixit quod illud nichil supponebat pro rebus visibilibus, que sunt nichil."

13. Ibid., ". . . hominem esse peccatum et nichil."

14. Ibid., ". . . si ille qui fuerat positus in cruce fecisset hec visibilia. . . ."

15. Ibid., ". . . respondit dictus Petrus quod non, quia ipse erat optimus, et nichil istorum visibilium est bonum. Ergo nichil horum fecit."

16. Ibid.: "In ipso condita sunt universa que in celis et in terra sunt, visibilia et invisibilia."

17. Ibid., ". . . dixit idem Petrus quod sic debebat exponi: visibilia corde, et invisibilia oculis carnalibus."

18. Ibid., p. 93: "Item, [Guilhem Cogot] audivit dictum Petrum Garcia[m] dicentem quod omnes angeli et soli qui ceciderant de celo salvabuntur."

19. Ibid., p. 103, ". . . et quod omnes qui non erant heretici fecerat diabolus in corpore et anima."

20. Ibid., p. 105, ". . . audivit ipse testis dictum Petrum Garcia[m] dicentem quod de guta caja qui credit quod illi spiritus qui de novo creantur sint creati a Deo."

21. Ibid., p. 100: "Dixit etiam idem Petrus quod si teneret illum Deum qui de mille hominibus ab eo factis unum salvaret et omnes alios damnaret, ipsum dirumperet et dilaceraret unguibus et dentibus tanquam perfidum, et spueret in faciem ejus, addens: de gutta cadat ipse."

22. Ibid., ". . . dixit idem Petrus quod tantum angeli qui ceciderunt salvabuntur, set non omnes ut principales et assessores, set simplices tantum; ita quod de mille non dampnabitur unus."

23. Ibid., ". . . dixit idem P. quod purgatorium non erat, et quod eleemosine facte a vivis non prosunt mortuo, et quod nullus salvatur nisi perfecte fecerit penitentiam ante mortem, et quod spiritus qui in uno corpore non poterat facere penitentiam, si deberet salvari, transibit in aliud corpus ad complendum penitentiam."

24. Ibid., p. 93, ". . . audivit dictum Petrum Garcia[m] dicentem, cum dictus frater Guillelmus Garcias requireret ab eo si caro resurgeret ostendens ei manum suam, dixit quod caro non resurgeret nisi sicut postis, percussiens postem cum manu."

25. Ibid., ". . . [Guilhem Cogot] audivit dictum P. Garcia[m] dicentem quod Christus et Beata Virgo et beatus Johannes Evangelista descenderent de celo et non erant de ista carne."

26. Ibid., p. 103.

27. Ibid., pp. 96–99, "et quod matrimonium erat purum meretricium, et quod nemo poterat salvari in matrimonio habendo rem cum uxore . . . [et] quod illud quod Ecclesia Romana conjundebat, virum scilicet et mulierem, ut se et uxorem suam Aymam, [est meretricium]: nullum est matrimonium nisi inter animam et Deum."

28. Ibid., p. 99: "Dixit etiam idem Petrus quod non jacuerat carnaliter cum uxore sua duo anni erunt in Pentecoste. . . ."

29. Ibid., p. 102 n. 1.

30. Ibid., p. 99, Déodat de Rodez recalled, ". . . set erat bestia sicut ipse frater Guillelmus." Friar Imbert, p. 106, simply remembered, ". . . et quod stulta erat."

31. Ibid., p. 99, ". . . de miraculis quod nullum miraculum quod possit videri aliquid est. . . ."

32. Ibid., p. 97.

33. Ibid., p. 103, ". . . et quod Johannes Baptista fuit unus de majoribus diabolis qui unquam fuissent."

34. Ibid., ". . . quod Dominus Jhesus neminem extraxit de inferno."

35. Ibid., p. 94, ". . . quod non erat missa celebrata in Ecclesia usque ad tempus beati Silvestri, nec Ecclesia habuerat possessiones usque ad illud tempus. . . ."

36. Ibid., pp. 97–99, ". . . quod omnes illi qui ululabant in ecclesia cantando voce non intelligibili decipiebant populum simplicem. . . . Et de quadam ecclesia sibi ostensa dixit illam non esse ecclesiam, set domum in qua dicuntur falsitates et tricharie."

37. Ibid., p. 99, ". . . et vocavit Ecclesiam Romanam meretricem dantem venenum et potestatem veneo [in] omnes credentes in ea."

38. Ibid., p. 94, ". . . et quod Ecclesia deficiet citra XX annos. . . ."

39. Ibid., p. 100: "Item, dampnavit idem Petrus Garcias omnem ordinem praeter ordinem fratrum Minorum. Dixit tamen quod ille ordo nichil valebat, quia predicabat Crucem."

40. Ibid., pp. 99–100, ". . . quod non erat bonum cruce signatos ire contra Fredericum nec contra Sarracenos, vel contra aliquod castrum simile Montise-

curo quando erat contra Ecclesiam, vel contra aliquem locum ubi mors posset fieri."

41. Ibid., pp. 100–101: "Dixit etiam idem P. quod pater et mater ejus, et Petrus Cauzit et pater Guillelme de Montaigo docuerunt eum talia."

42. Ibid., p. 94, ". . . quod nullo modo est facienda justicia condempnando aliquem ad mortem."

43. Ibid.: "Item, [Guilhem Cogot] audivit dictum Petrum Garcia[m] dicentem quod si officialis judicaret aliquem hereticum et ille occideretur tanquam hereticus, quod officialis erat homicida."

44. Ibid.: "Item, cum esset dictus [Peire Garcias] sepe adjuratus et requisitus a dicto fratre Guillelmo Garcia si ita crederent sicut dicebat de predictis, respondit jurando per fidem suam quod ita credeban ut dixerant."

45. Ibid., p. 74.

46. Lansing, *Power and Purity*, pp. 87–88, where it is assumed that the four Franciscans must have recounted Peire Garcias' views correctly. Also, the recollected beliefs of Peire Garcias are used too easily, too unreflectively, and so inappropriately, to explain what an early-thirteenth-century Italian heretic might have thought.


## CHAPTER 9
## THE MEMORY OF WHAT WAS HEARD

1. On tachygraphy, see Malcolm Beckwith Parkes, "Tachygraphy in the Middle Ages: Writing Techniques Employed for Reportations of Lectures and Sermons," in his *Scribes, Scripts and Readers: Studies in the Communication, Presentation and Dissemination of Medieval Texts* (London: The Hambledon Press, 1991), pp. 19–33.

2. Perhaps such recollections were too difficult to quickly render on parchment in any other way—or it was a very clear way of letting a reader differentiate between words spoken in past conversations and words spoken in the present interrogation.

3. The questions may first have been asked in Latin, then translated, but this seems unlikely. Cf. Dossat, *Les crises de l'Inquisition Toulousaine au XIII^e siècle*, p. 203 n. 109 on friar-inquisitors' giving sermons in Latin and then having them translated.

4. On the frequency of Occitan words, see Dossat, *Les crises de l'Inquisition Toulousaine au XIII^e siècle*, p. 75. On translation in general, see the thoughtful discussion in Tim Parks, *Translating Style: The English Modernists and Their Italian Translations* (London: Cassell, 1998).

5. See, for example, Walter Ong, "Orality, Literacy and Medieval Textualization," *New Literary History* 16 (1984): 5.

6. Parkes, "Tachygraphy in the Middle Ages," p. 27.

7. MS 609, fol. 127v.

8. Ibid.

9. Ibid. Another example is a series of six testimonies from Labécède, ibid., fol. 119r, where one after the other they consist of only ". . . dixit idem quod predictus Ramundus Fort." Raimon Fort's earlier confession was also nothing

more than the standard ". . . quod nunquam vidit hereticos, nec credidit, nec adoravit, nec dedit, nec misit. Et fuit confessus aliis inquisitoribus."

10. Ibid., fol. 95r.

11. Ibid., fol. 127v.

12. On Lauragais *notarii* and *scriptores*, see Mundy, "Village, Town, and City in the Region of Toulouse," pp. 162, 182, and Biller in *Heresy and Literacy, 1000–1530*, pp. 63–64.

13. MS 609, fols. 54v, 66r, Avignonet; 98v, Auriac; 81r, Saint-Michel-de-Lanès; and 208v, Bazèges.

14. Ibid., fol. 232v. Mundy, "Village, Town, and City in the Region of Toulouse," p. 182 n. 58, notes, "Anciently *causidicus* had meant judge and even notary, but it had come to mean lawyer, although, by 1245/1246 . . . it was an old fashioned term even for that." This archaic term might have been the choice of the inquisitorial scribe rather than Raimon de Venercha's self-description, though, of course, Raimon de Venercha would have heard this word read out when he confirmed the truth of his testimony.

15. MS 609, fol. 45v: " 'Fili, dictum est mihi quod tu es datus bonis hominibus, id est, hereticis.' "

16. Ibid.

17. Ibid., fol. 135r, ". . . dixit ipsi testi quod ibi erant boni homines qui vocantur heretici. . . ."

18. Tardif, "Document pour l'histoire du *processus per inquisitionem*," 672–673.

19. For example, MS 609, fol. 68v, ". . . postea recognovit quod adoravit hereticos sicut in confessione quam fecit fratri Arnaldo et socio suo, inquisitoribus, continetur . . ."; fol. 108r, ". . . fuit ei similiter recitata antica confessio in qua continetur quod adoravit hereticos et concessit illam esse veram . . ."; and fol. 192r: "Recognovit lecta sibi confessione qum fecit aliis inquisitoribus quod vidit pluries hereticos et adoravit et comedit cum eis."

20. Steven Justice, in his *Writing and Rebellion: England 1381*, The New Historicism: Studies in Cultural Poetics, 27 (Berkeley and Los Angeles: University of California Press, 1994), esp. pp. 140–254, is particularly helpful on the nuances of this relationship.

21. John Mundy, in all his extraordinary work and research on the Toulousain and the Lauragais, especially *Society and Government at Toulouse*, demonstrates the sheer depth of this simple observation many times over.

22. MS 609, fol. 140v, ". . . et tunc habuit .viii. solidos a predicto heretico pro quadam libro qui fuerat inquisitorium interfectorum. . . ."

23. Christine Thouzellier, "La Bible de Cathares languedociens et son usage dans la controverse au début au XIII$^e$ *siècle*," *Cahiers de Fanjeaux: Cathares en Languedoc* 3 (1968): 42–58, and Peter Biller, "The Cathars of Languedoc and Written Materials," in *Heresy and Literacy, 1000–1530*, ed. Anne Hudson and Peter Biller, Cambridge Studies in Medieval Literature, 23 (Cambridge: Cambridge University Press, 1994), p. 74.

24. MS 609, fol. 34r, ". . . et tunc dictus hereticus [Raimon Peire] fregit archam mariti ipsius testis et abstraxit de dicta archa quasdam cartas que erant Bernardus Petri, viri ipsius testis. Sed non adoravit, nec vidit adorare."

25. Duvernoy, "Le registre de l'inquisiteur Bernard de Caux, Pamiers, 1246–1247," 30, "Dixit etiam quod habet quemdam librum scriptum in latino et romano quem nobis promisit reddere."

26. *Conciliorum oecumenicorum decreta,* ed. Giuseppe Alberigo et al., 3d ed. (Bologna: Istituto per le scienze religiose, 1973), p. 245. On *Omnis utriusque,* see Mary Mansfield, *The Humiliation of Sinners: Public Penance in Thirteenth-Century France* (Ithaca: Cornell University Press, 1995), pp. 66–68, and Alexander Murray, "Confession as an Historical Source in the Thirteenth Century," in *The Writing of History in the Middle Ages: Essays Presented to Richard William Southern,* ed. Ralph Henry Carless Davis and John Michael Wallace-Hadrill (Oxford: Clarendon Press, 1981), pp. 279 ff.

27. This word of warning was strongly urged by Mansfield in her *The Humiliation of Sinners,* pp. 76–77.

28. According to na Baretges in a testimony given to Bernart de Caux on 16 February 1245 in Doat 22, fol. 43v: "Requisita si scivit quando frater W. Arnaldi et socius ejus venerunt apud Castrum Sarracenum pro inquisitione. . . . Dixit tamen quod confessio sua non fuit scripta, quia inquisitores noluerunt scribere confessionem ejus."

29. The same caution should also be extended to confession and inquisition manuals—in that the techniques recommended for an inquisitor should never be read into the role of a confessor. Cf. Annie Cazenave, "Aveu et contrition: Manuels de confesseurs et interrogatoires d'Inquisition en Languedoc et en Catalogne," in *La piété populaire au Moyen Age, Actes du 99ᵉ Congrès national des sociétés savantes, Besançon, 1974,* Philologie et histoire jusqu'à 1610, 1 (Paris: Comité des travaux historiques et scientifiques, 1977), pp. 333–349. The decree of the Council of Toulouse, 1229, is in *Sacrorum conciliorum,* vol. 23, col. 197.

30. Cf., for example, Gabriel Spiegel, *Romancing the Past: The Rise of Vernacular Prose Historiography in Thirteenth-Century France* (Berkeley and Los Angeles: University of California Press, 1993), p. 68.

31. For example, see Caesarius of Heisterbach, *Dialogus Miraculorum,* 1:144, col. 27, distinctio 3, which has the chapter heading "De eo quod non sufficiat scripto confiteri, nisi in necessitate" [How it is not enough to make a confession in writing except in case of necessity]. See Carla Casagrande and Silvana Vecchio, *I peccati della lingua. Disciplina ed etica della parola nella cultura medievale,* Bibliotheca Biographica: Sezione Storico-Antropologica (Rome: Istituto della Enciclopedia Italiana fondata da Giovanni Treccani, 1987), pp. 103–229.

32. Pelhisson, *Chronique,* p. 70, ". . . confessiones de heresi receperunt et in libris memorie commendaverunt."

## CHAPTER 10
### LIES

1. MS 609, fols. 239v–240r, ". . . et dictus Willelmus Saicius dixit ipsi testi quod nullo modo diceret veritatem de hiis que viderat fieri ab ipsis de facto heresis inquisitoribus . . . et tunc ipsa testis respondit eis quod ipsa diceret veritatem de hiis que faciebat, et tunc dictus W. Saicius cepit ipsam testem et posuit in quadam tonella et filium [*sic*] ipsius testis similiter, quia manutenebat eam dicendo et

'Garcifer, vultis vos juvare vetulam istam que vult nos destruere omnes' . . . et stetit in dicta tonella per unam noctem et in crastino redimit se de dictis dominis de Cambiaco III sol. et VII den." Dossat, *Les crises de l'Inquisition Toulousaine au XIII^e siècle*, p. 242; Wakefield, "Heretics and Inquisitors: The Case of Auriac and Cambiac," esp. 233; and Biller, "Cathars and Material Women," esp. pp. 61–63, discuss Aimersent Viguier.

2. MS 609, fol. 88r.

3. Ibid., fol. 239v. Douais, *Documents pour servir à l'histoire de l'Inquisition dans le Languedoc*, 2:97–98 n. 1, has edited this part of Aimersent Viguier's confession.

4. MS 609, fols. 239v–240r.

5. Ibid., fol. 240r, ". . . Sais similiter, qui fecit omnes alios predictos jurare et condicere inter se ne revelarent fratribus inquisitoribus, scilicet Ber. de Cautio et Johanni de Sancti Petro, quod ipsi dederant bladum ecclesie hereticis. . . ."

6. Ibid., fol. 234r.

7. Ibid., fol. 166v, ". . . et hoc fecit propter timorem, quia dictus P. Recordi dixerat ipsi testi quod bene posset capud amittere si nominaret eos fratri Ferrario in confessione."

8. Ibid.: "Ramundus Recordi, sutor, consanguineus Petri Recordi, immura-ti. . . ."

9. Ibid., fol. 161v: "Dixit etiam quod de dicta hereticatione matris ipsius testis non fuit confessa Fratri Willelmo Arnaldi. Requisita quare celavit, dixit quod propter timorem mortis."

10. Ibid., fol. 98r–v, ". . . et tunc dicta Fabrissa dixit ipsi testi: 'Et Geralda, et dixisti ei sic veritatem?' Et ipsa testis respondit quod sic. Et tunc dicta Fabrissa dixit ipsi testi quod mortua erat quia dixit veritatem inquisitoribus. Et tunc ipsa testis peciit a dicta Fabrissa si non dixit ipsa veritatem inquisitoribus, et ipsa Fabrissa respondit quod non. Immo erant plures de Aurico qui non proponebant dicere veritatem si Fratres excoriarent ipsos"

11. Ibid., fol. 144v.

12. Ibid., fol. 148r.

13. Ibid., fol. 215v.

14. Ibid., fols. 49r–v, 185r–v.

15. For example, ibid., fols. 88v, 94r (Auriac), and fols. 33r–v, 38r (Saint-Martin-de-la-Lande).

16. Ibid., fol. 142r: "Item dixit quod, in quadragesima proximo preterita fuit annus, quod dictus W. Gras bajulus congregavit populum de Mont Auriol, quando debebant ire apud Concas confiteri inquisitoribus, dixit quod dictus W. Gras populo: 'Caveatis quod nullus loquatur mala de alio quia, si ego scirem quod faceretis, ego caperem illum qui faceret et publicarem omnia bona sua,' et nullus dixit veritatem coram fratre Ferrario de hiis que viderat cum hereticis, preter ipsum testem qui omnia que tunc fecerat cum dictis hereticis dixit fratri Ferrario tunc."

17. Ibid., fol. 223r. Cf. Pons Esteve's memory of Raimon de Auriac's advive to him about the inquisition of Guilhem Arnaut at fol. 94r: "Item dixit quod, cum Frater W. Arnaldi faceret inquisitionem, Ramundus de Auriaco Carchassonensi, quod, quando inquireretur ad inquisitoribus, ad omnia responderet eis 'nodum,' quia sic condixerant inter se omnes homines de Auriaco de dicta responsione

cum essent coram dictis inquisitoribus, et tunc ipse testis respondit dicto Ra- mundo de Auriaco quod ullo modo diceret 'nodum' inquisitoribus prefatis, immo diceret eis plenariam veritatem de hiis que noverat de heresi."

18. Tardif, "Document pour l'histoire du *processus per inquisitionem*," 673. Now, see Albert C. Shannon, "The Secrecy of Witnesses in Inquisitorial Tribunals and in Contemporary Secular Criminal Trials," in *Essays in Medieval Life and Thought Presented in Honor of Austin Patterson Evans*, ed. John H. Mundy, Richard W. Emery, and Benjamin N. Nelson (New York: Columbia University Press, 1955), pp. 59– 69, and Edward Peters, "Wounded Names: The Medieval Doctrine of Infamy," in *Law in Medieval Life and Thought*, ed. Edward B. King and Susan J. Ridyard (Se- wanee. Tenn.: Press of the University of the South, 1990), pp. 43–89.

19. Shannon, "The Secrecy of Witnesses in Inquisitorial Tribunals," pp. 60– 63.

20. Douais, *Documents pour servir à l'histoire de l'Inquisition dans le Languedoc*, 2:132–33, 139–40. Peire de Garda was interrogated at Villalier on 14 October 1250, while Alazaïs Barrau was questioned on 8 December 1250 at Carcassonne.

21. MS 609, fol. 2v.

22. Ibid.: "Item dixit quod P. Gauta loqutus est publice Bernado, domino del Mas, . . . in hunc modum 'Bernarde del Mas, est ne bonum quod aliquis qui detexerit vos eat vivus super terram?' et propter illa verba cum familia sua exunt de Manso."

23. Ibid., fol. 2v: "Modo apparebit quis expeditus erit citus? Vos, qui perve- nistis alios in confessione." Cf. Roger Sartre, fol. 12v, who thought he once saw Bernart Cogota at a heretication, *ut credit.*

24. Ibid., fol. 125r, ". . . et quod fecerat destrui villam de Gaiano."

25. Ibid., fol. 55v: "Item dixit quod P. Baussa de Gardog dixit ipsi testi . . . quando ipse testis interrogabat ipsum P. si fuerit coram inquisitoribus, et dictus P. Baussa respondit quod manserat coram proditoribus, et cavi mihi ne dicerem aliquid de vicinis meis."

26. On the sacerdotal delinquent known as the *proditor confessionum*, see Mur- ray, "Confession as an Historical Source in the Thirteenth Century," pp. 282– 283.

27. Ibid., fol. 98r, ". . . quod quadam die, dum ipsa testis veniret de fonte obvia- vit Alazais d'Auri uxori P. Manent immo timore perterrite. Et tunc ipsa testis peciit a dicta Alazais quare erat ita perterrite, et tunc dicta Alazais respondit quod Arnaldus Garriga hereticus, qui erat captus in Castro Narbonnese, erat conversus. Et tunc ipsa peciit a dicta Alazais quare timebat propter hoc, et hunc dicta Alazais respondit quod ipsa viderat predictum Arnaldum de Garriga in domo Geraldi Artus, ubi dictus Arnaldus et socii sui heretici fecerat consilium suum. Et dixit ipsi testi quod ipsa testis et Geralda Artus et Fabrissa uxor dicti Geraldi et Bertranda mater dicte Fabrisse et Ademarius de Monte Maur miles interfuerat dicto consilio. Et sunt .iiii. anni vel circa."

28. Useful discussions of the physical layout of the medieval Lauragais village specifically, and Languedoc more generally, can be found in Fredric Cheyette, "The Castles of the Trencavels: A Preliminary Aerial Survey," in *Order and Innova- tion in the Middle Ages: Essays in Honor of Joseph R. Strayer*, ed. William Chester Jordan, Bruce McNab, and Teófilo Ruiz (Princeton: Princeton University Press,

1976), pp. 255–272; Michel Dauzat, "Les mottes castrales du Lauragais: notes préliminaires," in *Le Lauragais: Histoire et Archéologie, Actes du LIV<sup>e</sup> Congrès de la Fédération historique du Languedoc méditerranéen et du Roussillon et du XXXVI<sup>e</sup> Congrès de la Fédération des Sociétés académiques et savantes de Languedoc-Pyrénées-Gascogne (Castelnaudary, 13–14 juin 1981)*, ed. Jean Sablou and Philippe Wolff (Montpellier: Fédération historique du Languedoc méditerranéen et du Roussillon Université Paul-Valéry, 1983), pp. 73–88; Jean-Paul Cazes, "Un village castral de la plaine lauragais: Lasbordes (Aude)," *Archéologie du Midi Medieval* 8–9 (1990–1991): 3–25; Charles Higounet, "Structures sociales, '*castra*' et castelnaux dans le Sud-Ouest aquitain (X<sup>e</sup>–XII<sup>e</sup> siècle)," in *Villes, Sociétés et économies Médiévales: Recueil d'articles de Charles Higounet*, ed. Robert Étienne, Études et Documents d'Aquitaine (Bordeaux: La Nef et Fédération Historique du Sud-Ouest, 1992), pp. 257–262; and the remarkable research to be found within Marie-Geneviève Colin et al., *La maison du castrum de la bordure méridionale du Massif Central*, Archéologie du Midi médiéval Supplément N° 1 (Carcassonne: Centre d'archéologie médiéval du Languedoc, 1996).

29. MS 609, fol. 144r, ". . . quod .iiii. annis citra Peireta Rex de Monte Ferrando fuit hereticatus in morte a quodam heretico, filio Ademari. Et hoc audivit ipse testis de domo sua, que domus est juxta domum dicit P. Regis."

30. See Marie-Élise Gardel, "Le bâtiment III du *castrum* de Cabaret," in *La maison du castrum de la bordure méridionale du Massif Central*, ed. Marie-Geneviève Colin et al., Archéologie du Midi médiéval Supplément N° 1 (Carcassonne: Centre d'archéologie médiéval du Languedoc, 1996), pp. 165–166, on a quite large *domus* from Cabaret.

31. *La Chanson de la Croisade Albigeoise*, 1:216, laisse 92.

32. Mundy, *Society and Government at Toulouse*, pp. 146–147, where this information from Gui's *De fundatione*, pp. 338–339, is summarized.

33. Cf. Mundy, *Society and Government at Toulouse*, pp. 146–154, and Gardel, "Le bâtiment III du *castrum* de Cabaret," p. 165. See also Ronnie Ellenblum, *Frankish Settlement in the Latin Kingdom of Jerusalem* (Cambridge: Cambridge University Press, 1998), pp. 86–102, for an excellent discussion on stone houses and the *castra* of twelfth-century Outremer.

34. MS 609, fol. 24v.

35. Colin et al., *La maison du castrum de la bordure méridionale du Massif Central*, p. 68, and foundation walls were fractionally thicker again.

36. Ibid., p. 73.

37. Ibid. The highest door measured in excavations at Cabaret was quite high, at 154 centimeters.

38. Cazes, "Un village castral de la plaine lauragais: Lasbordes (Aude)," 24.

39. Colin et al., *La maison du castrum de la bordure méridionale du Massif Central*, p. 74.

40. Dossat, *Les crises de l'Inquisition Toulousaine au XIII<sup>e</sup> siècle*, p. 98.

41. Jean Chapelot and Robert Fossier, *The Village and House in the Middle Ages*, trans. Henry Cleere (Berkeley and Los Angeles: University of California Press, 1985), pp. 313–320, and Gardel, "Le bâtiment III du *castrum* de Cabaret," p. 165.

42. Mundy, *Society and Government at Toulouse*, pp. 144–145, notes the same use of *domus* in Toulouse.

43. MS 609, fol. 200r–v.

44. See Martha L. MacFarlane, "Medievalism in the Midi: Inventing the Medieval House in Nineteenth-Century France," in *Medievalism in Europe II*, ed. Leslie J. Workman and Kathleen Verduin (Cambridge: D. S. Brewer, 1997), pp. 125–155, for an interesting discussion about the nineteenth-century invention of the "medieval house" that still attracts people to go live in southern France.

45. Jean-Paul Cazes, "Structures agraires et domaine comtal dans la bailie de Castelnaudary en 1272," *Annales du Midi* 99 (1987): 453–477.

46. AN: JJ 25, *Liber Reddituum Serenissimi Domini Regis Francie* [550 folios], fol. 197, for Mas-Saintes Puelles, and Cazes, "Structure agraires et domaine comtal dans la bailie de Castelnaudary en 1272," 457.

47. *Liber Reddituum*, fols. 188–189, for Saint-Martin-de-la-Lande, and Cazes, "Structures agraires et domaine comtal dans la bailie de Castelnaudary en 1272," 457. On *ferragines*, or *ferratjals*, which were usually situated close to dwellings, walls, or stables, and specific to the agriculture of Languedoc, see Aline Durand, *Les paysages médiévaux du Languedoc, Xe–XIIe siècles* (Toulouse: Presses Universitaires du Mirail, 1998), pp. 100, 124, 128, 138, 263, 290, 343.

48. Cazes, "Structures agraires et domaine comtal dans la bailie de Castelnaudary en 1272," 458–461, and Durand, *Les paysages médiévaux du Languedoc*, pp. 130–133.

49. Georges Jorré, *Le Terrefort Toulousain et Lauragais: Histoire et Géographie agraire* (Toulouse: Edouard Privat, 1971), esp. 69–105; Pierre Portet, "Permanences et mutations dans un terroir du Lauragais de l'après-croisade: Fanjeaux, vers 1250–vers 1340," *Annales du Midi* 99 (1987): 479–493; Marc Bompaire, "Circulation et vie monétaire dans le Tarn médiéval (XIe–XIVe siècles)," *Bulletin de la Société des Sciences, Arts et Belles-Lettres du Tarn*, n.s., 45–46 (1991–1992): 479–491; Victor Allegre, "Caractères généraux des vieilles églises du Lauragais," *Mémoires de la Société Archeologique du Midi de la France* 31 (1965): 75–94. Jean Ramière de Fortanier, *Recueil de Documents relatifs à l'Histoire du Droit Municipal en France des origines à la Révolution: Chartes de Fránchises du Lauragais*, Société d'Histoire du Droit (Paris: Librairie du Recueil Sirey, 1939), esp. his introductions to each set of village charters. On heresy and the Lauragais economy, see Georgi Šemkov, "Le contexte socio-économique du catharisme au Mas Sainte Puelles dans la première moitié du XIIIe siècle," *Heresis* 2 (1984): 34–55. Cf. the difference in monastic holdings, in that they were grouped together, as shown by Monique Bourin-Derruau in her "Un exemple d'agriculture monastique en Lauragais: Les domaines de Prouille en 1340," in *Le Lauragais: Histoire et Archéologie, Actes du LIVe Congrès de la Fédération historique du Languedoc méditerranéen et du Rousillon et du XXXVIe Congrès de la Fédération des Sociétés académiques et savantes de Languedoc-Pyrénées-Gascogne (Castelnaudary, 13–14 juin 1981)*, ed. Jean Sablou and Philippe Wolff (Montpellier: Fédération historique du Languedoc méditerranéen et du Roussillon Université Paul-Valéry, 1983), pp. 115–125.

50. Mundy, *Society and Government at Toulouse*, pp. 130–133.

51. Laurence Sterne, Letter 31, To Mr Foley in Paris, in *The Works of Laurence Sterne* (Philadelphia: Grigg and Elliot, 1834), p. 348.

52. MS 609, fol. 144v: "Et recognovit quod male fecit, quia nuper, in judicio constitutus, juratus, et requisitus, negavit predicta coram Fratre Bernardo inquisitore."

53. Ibid., fol. 49r–v, ". . . dixit dolet et penitet, quia, esterna die, in judicio constituta, jurata et requisita, negavit ea que sequentur. . . ."

54. For example, ibid., fol. 142r, about halfway through the testimony of Pons Aigra: "Et dolet et penitet, quia nuper, in judicio constitutus coram Fratre Bernardo, inquisitore, hoc [having once adored heretics] scienter negavit."

55. Dossat, *Les crises de l'Inquisition Toulousaine au XIII<sup>e</sup> siècle*, p. 233.

56. On the importance for the friar-inquisitors of collecting all the name variations that an individual would go (or be called) by, see Walter L. Wakefield, "Pseudonyms and Nicknames in Inquisitorial Documents of the Middle Ages," *Heresis* 13 (1990): 9–22. Mundy, *Society and Government at Toulouse*, pp. 158–176, is very good on the use of names in the Toulousain and the Lauragais. Cf. Stephen Wilson, *A Social and Cultural History of Personal Naming in Western Europe* (London: UCL Press, 1998), pp. 63–182, on medieval naming in general.

57. MS 609, fol. 237v: "Item, dixit ipsi testi dicta Aimersens quod dictis Petrus Arnaldi et Ramundus Vassaro et Willelmus de Manso et Petrus Vicarius mutaverunt nomina sua hoc anno coram Fratro Bernardo de Cautio, inquisitore. Et Petrus Arnaldi fecit se scribi Petrus Gitbert, et Ramundus Vassaro fecit scribi Ramundus Sicardi, et Willelmus de Manso, Willelmus Stephani, et Petrus Vicarii, Petrus Martini. Hoc fecerunt, et postea derribebant inde Fratrem B. de mutatione dictorum nominum audivit ipse testis dici ab Arnaldo Durandi, de Aurico, et a quibusdam aliis apud Auriacum qui faciebant inde suas derrisiones." Dossat, *Les crises de l'Inquisition Toulousaine au XIII<sup>e</sup> siècle*, p. 243, and Wakefield, "Heretics and Inquisitors: The Case of Auriac and Cambiac," 231, mention this deception.

58. Thomas Aquinas, *Summa contra Gentiles*, in *S Thomae Aquinas Doctoris Angelici Opera Omnia, Iussu impensaque Leonis XIII, P.M. Edita* (Leonine ed.), vol. 13 (Rome: R. Garroni, 1918), 1.59, n. 2, "Cum enim veritas intellectus sit adaequatio intellectus et rei, secundum quod intellectus dicit esse quos est vel non esse quod non est. . . ." Eilene Serene, "Demonstrative Science," in *The Cambridge History of Later Medieval Philosophy: From the Rediscovery of Aristotle to the Disintegration of Scholasticism 1100–1600*, ed. Norman Kretzmann, Anthony Kenny, and Jan Pinborg (Cambridge: Cambridge University Press, 1990), p. 504, translates this passage about truth as ". . . the conformity of the understanding with reality, such that the understanding says that what is the case is so, and that what is not is not."

59. Douais, *Documents pour servir à l'histoire de l'Inquisition dans le Languedoc*, 2:22–23, "Renominatus etiam P. Babau vidit et adoravit hereticos, audivit predicationem eorum, fecit condictum de non revelando heresim, negavit scienter coram nobis veritatem et eandem celavit aliis inquisitoribus contra proprium juramentum."

60. Ibid., p. 12. Esclarmont Bret's sentence was read out at Saint-Sernin on 13 May 1246. See MS 609, fol. 62r–v.

61. Carla Casagrande and Silvana Vecchio discuss *mendacium-periurium-falsum testimonium* in their *I peccati della lingua*, pp. 251–290. On lying in general, see John Arundel Barnes, *A Pack of Lies: Towards a Sociology of Lying*, Themes in the Social Sciences (Cambridge: Cambridge University Press, 1994), esp. 36–54, and

Perez Zagorin, "The Historical Significance of Lying and Dissimulation," *Social Research* 63 (1996): 863–912.

## CHAPTER 11
### NOW ARE YOU WILLING TO PUT THAT IN WRITING?

1. MS 609, fol. 106r: "Sibilia uxor Stephani Johannis. . . . Item dixit quod cum quadam vice ipsa testis et Willelma, uxor Poncii Tornafuilha venirent de Tholosa, dicta Willelma cecidit et tunc dixit: 'Maledictus sit magister qui fecit istam corporatam!' Et ipsa testis dixit ei: 'Et nonne fecit vos Deus?' Et ipsa respondit: 'Eamus! Vultis modo scribere mihi istud!' Et sunt .xvi. anni quod hoc fuit."

2. Mundy, *Society and Government at Toulouse*, p. 167, for the distinction between a *magister* trained in the liberal arts, where the title mostly occurred before someone's name, and a "master" in a craft, art, or trade, where the title usually came after a person's name.

3. MS 609, fol. 239v: "Et dicte heretice dixerunt ipsi testi, coram omnibus, quia erat adolescentula pregnans, quod demonium portabat in ventre. Et alii ceperunt ridere inde."

4. Ibid.: "Sed ipsa testis noluit diligere, postquam dixerunt sibi heretice quod pregnans erat de demonio." On this particular recollection of Aimersent Viguier, also see Biller, "Cathars and Material Women," pp. 61–63.

5. Ibid., fol. 117v.

6. Ibid., fol. 58v.

7. For example, ibid., fol. 18v, where Raimon de Quiders from Mas-Saintes-Puelles, testified, ". . . sed non audivit eos dicentes errores . . . sed audivit clericos exprimentes errores quos heretici dicent."

8. Ibid., fol. 235v, where Izarn Boquer, of Lavaur, noted that his knowledge about the heretical idea that God did not make visible things came from the bishop of Tolouse.

9. Ibid., fol. 110r.

10. Ibid., fol. 110r–v, ". . . credebat in eis et in fide et in operibus eorum."

11. Ibid., fol. 65v: "Item de erroribus requisita dixit quod bene audivit hereticos loquentes quod omnia visibilia facta fuerant de voluntate e vultu dei."

12. Ibid., fol. 2r: "Et audivit hereticos dicentes quod diabolus fecerat visibilia. . . ."

13. Ibid., fol. 15v, ". . . audivit hereticos dicentes quod Deus non fecit celum et terram. Et ipse credidit predicto errori."

14. Ibid., fol. 130r, ". . . et quod homo non poterat salvari cum uxore sua, habendo rem cum ea."

15. Ibid., fol. 75r, ". . . quod tantum peccam fecit homo cum uxore sua propria quantum cum alia muliere . . . et ipse testis credidit omnibus predictis erroribus. . . ."

16. Ibid., fol. 40r.

17. Ibid., fol. 161v.

18. Ibid., fol. 191r, ". . . sed ipsa testis non vidit quia iuvenis erat et nondum moratur cum ipso marito."

19. Ibid., fol. 200r.

20. Ibid., fol. 238v, Jordan Sais in his testimony mentioned a "Valencia concubina Willelmi Saissi." See fol. 240r for the reference to Valencia's husband, Pierre Valencii.

21. Ibid., fol. 238v.

22. On concubinage in the Toulousain and the Lauragais, see Mundy, *Men and Women at Toulouse*, pp. 69–79.

23. Ibid., fol. 5r, ". . . Ar. Maiestre, concubinarium ipsius testis."

24. MS 609, fols. 147r, in Guillaume Aimeric de Sant-Esteve's testimony, ". . . Willelmam, uxorem Petri Fabri, cotellier de Laurac," and 149r, in Bernard Richart's confession, ". . . Guillermam, concubinam Petri Faure, cotelher."

25. Ibid., fol. 75v, ". . . qui hereticaverunt dictam infirmam, licet primo recepisset corpus domini. Tamen ipse testis non interfuit, but audivit dici a predictis hereticis quedam verba quibus mediantibus credit dictam infirmam fuisse hereticatem."

26. Ibid., fol. 76r, ". . . et quod dictus Ramundus non credebat nisi novum testamentum et hoc audierunt Ramunda, uxor ipsius testis, et filius eius Hysarnus et Aumenzs leprosa."

27. Ibid., fol. 75v, ". . . et tunc manebat in predicta leprosaria cotidie et dissipabat omnia bona dicte domus malo velle eorum qui erant ibi."

28. On leprosaria in the Lauragais and the Toulousain, see John H. Mundy, "Hospitals and Leprosaries in Twelfth-and-Early-Thirteenth-Century Toulouse," in *Essays in Medieval Life and Thought Presented in Honor of Austin Patterson Evans*, ed. John H. Mundy, Richard W. Emery, and Benjamin N. Nelson (New York: Columbia University Press, 1955) pp. 181–205; idem, "The Parishes of Toulouse from 1150 to 1250," *Traditio* 46 (1991): 171–204; and idem, "Village, Town, and City in the Region of Toulouse," pp. 157–159.

29. MS 609, fol. 2r.

30. On the Leper's Plot, see David Nirenberg, *Communities of Violence: Persecution of Minorities in the Middle Ages* (Princeton: Princeton University Press, 1996), pp. 54–63.

31. Jean Duvernoy, *Inquisition à Pamiers: Cathares, Juifs, Lépreux . . . devant leurs juges*, 2d ed., Bibliothèque historique Privat (1966; Toulouse: Privat, 1986), esp. pp. 73–82.

32. Ibid., fol. 177r.

33. Cf. David Maybury-Lewis, "Introduction: The Quest for Harmony," and Uri Almagor, "Introduction: Dual Organization Reconsidered," in *The Attraction of Opposites: Thought and Society in the Dualist Mode*, ed. Almagor and Maybury-Lewis (Ann Arbor: University of Michigan Press, 1989), pp. 1–18, 19–32, where each one argues (under the influence of Claude Lévi-Strauss) that dualism is inherent in the human perception of the world.

34. MS 609, fol. 22r, ". . . dixit quod non credidit firmiter hereticos esse bonos homines, sed quotiens credebat ipsos esse bonos et quotiens discredebat."

35. Cf. Borst, *Die Katherer*, pp. 181–182, where he describes Catharism as possessing a *radikaler Frauenhass*. See also John M. Riddle, *Contraception and Abortion from the Ancient World to the Renaissance* (Cambridge: Harvard University Press, 1992), pp. 5, 113.

36. Cf. Jean Duvernoy, "La nourriture en Languedoc à l'époque cathare," in his *Cathares, Vaudois et Béguins: Dissidents du pays d'Oc*, Domaine Cathare (Toulouse: Privat, 1994), pp. 229–236.

37. MS 609, fol. 63v, ". . . Sabdalina, uxor Raymundi de Godervila, soror Raymundi Bret. . . . Audivit hereticos dicentes quod Deus non faciebat florere nec granare sed terra hoc faciebant per se. . . ."

38. On the morality of landscapes, see the collected essays in *The Anthropology of Landscape: Perspectives on Place and Space*, ed. Eric Hirsch and Michael O'Hanlon (Oxford: Clarendon Press, 1995).

39. MS 609, fol. 130r.

40. On the bodies of orthodox men and women emanating holiness through fasting and diet, see Caroline Walker Bynum, *Holy Feast and Holy Fast: The Religious Significance of Food to Medieval Women*, The New Historicism: Studies in Cultural Poetics, 1 (Berkeley and Los Angeles: University of California Press, 1987), esp. 189–297, and idem, *The Resurrection of the Body in Western Christianity, 200–1336*, Lectures on the History of Religions, 15 (New York: Columbia University Press, 1995), pp. 229–278.

41. MS 609, fol. 140r, ". . . vidit apud Ast in Lombardia Ramundum Hymberti de Moysiaco, hereticum, qui ivit cum ipso teste de Ast usque Alba. Et ibi cognovit ipse testis dictum Ramundum esse hereticum, quando voluerunt comedere."

42. Ibid., fols. 16v–17r, ". . . ipse testis [Bernart de Quiders] et Willelmus del Mas et Willelmus Palazis, prior del Mas frater ipsius, abstraxerunt matrem et sororem ipsorum de heresi, et dederunt eis carnes ad comedendum. Et postea iterum fecerunt se hereticas et fuerunt combuste."

## CHAPTER 12
### BEFORE THE CRUSADERS CAME

1. MS 609, fol. 198r: "Item, quod alter dictorum trutannorum dicebat quod ita bonum esset comunicare de folio arboris vel de stercus asini sicut de corpore Xristi, solummodo quod fieret bona fide. Et alius trutannus redarguebat eum. Et postea ipse testis audivit a Petro Adalberti, puero, in ecclesia de Miravalle, quod Johannes Adalberti, pater ejusdem P. Adalbert, comunicaverat de quodam folio herbe quando sol obiit seu fuit eclipsatus. Et hoc audito ipse testis narravit predicta sicut audierat a predictis trutannis presentibus Stephano Clerici, Bernardo Donati, et Morgat, scolaribus. Et sunt duo anni vel circa. . . ."

2. Ibid., ". . . Poncius Amelii senex, notarius de Miravalle, testis juratus, dixit quod vidit apud Lauracum in platea, Isarnum de Castris, hereticum, disputantem cum Bernardo Prim, Valdense, presente populo ejusdem castri."

3. Puylaurens, *Chronica*, Prologue, p. 24 and n. 2. Cf. Mundy, *Society and Government at Toulouse*, p. 84.

4. MS 609, fol. 136r: "Item dixit quod Valdenses presequebantur dictos hereticos, et multociens fecit [ipse testis] helemosinam dictis Valdensibus, quando querebant hostiatim amore dei; et quia ecclesia sustinebat tunc dictos Valdenses, et erant cum clericis in ipsa ecclesia cantantes et legentes, credebat eos esse bonos homines." Guilhema Michaela of Auriac, fol. 96v, had this interesting memory of what two Waldensian women once, she did not date it, said to her

about truth and lies: "Et audivit eos dicentes quod nemo debet jurare pro veritate vel mendatio ned condicere juste vel injuste." On Waldensians and good men, see Thouzellier, *Catharisme et Valdéisme en Languedoc.*

5. MS 609, fol. 133v: "Item apud Montem Maurum et Mirapiscem et apud Lauracum et in multis aliis locis terre vidit hereticos publice stantes, sicut ceteri homines, et predicantes. Et fere omnes homines de terra conveniebant et veniebant audire eorum et adorabant eos."

6. Ibid., fol. 57v.

7. Ibid., fol. 96v: "Petrus monachus . . . vidit . . . hereticos apud Vitrac in platea publica. . . . Et sunt .xxv. anni. Item dixit quod ipse testis disputavit ibi cum predictis hereticis de resurrectione."

8. Ibid., fol. 69v: "Item dixit quod apud Gardam vidit W. de Solario et socium suum hereticos in platea publice predicantes, et quia pigebat quosdam de villa moverunt maximas rixas catholici cum credentibus."

9. Ibid., fol. 135v, ". . . predicantes in platea, presente populo ejusdam castri."

10. Ibid., fol. 16v.

11. Ibid., fols. 109v–110r.

12. Ibid., fol. 121r, ". . . quendam librum, ubi legebat, et dicti heretici exponebant quod ipse legebat, predicando."

13. Ibid., fol. 80r: "Et dictus hereticus exponebat ibi passionem christi et dictus Guillelmus Ramundi notarius de la besoeda legebat passionem." Cf. fol. 232v, where the *miles* Guilhem Bernart (also called Sancho), from Vaudreuille, recalled this event, which he placed in 1233: ". . . Petrum Cortes et Guillelmus Ramundi, scriptores, legebant in quodam libro, et dicti heretici exponebant illud quod ipsi dicebant."

14. Ibid., fol. 252v: "Item dixit quod Willelmus Symon, frater ipsius testis, fecit se hereticum. Sed, antequam fieret hereticus abbas sancti papuli posuerat penes eum in pignus quendam bibliam pro .c. solidos tolosanos et tunc fuit factus hereticus et recessit ea." Cf. Biller, "The Cathars of Languedoc and Written Materials," p. 72.

15. MS 609, fol. 252v: "Postea venit dictus abbas ad ipsum testem et rogavit instantissime quod reciperet ab eo dictus .c. solidos et quod iret ad dictum fratrem suum, hereticum, ubi manebat apud Lauracum, et quod recuperaret dictam bibliam et quod aportaret sibi. Quod et fecit ipse testis. . . ."

16. Ibid.

17. Ibid., fol. 130v, ". . . et omnes predicti [the good men and their believers] disputaverunt cum ipso teste et cum Stephano de Boscenac et cum Willelmo Petri, capellano."

18. Ibid., fol. 130r–v.

19. Ibid., fol. 42r.

20. In MS 609, these eleven good women were Blanca *et sociae*, fol. 184v, at Castelnaudary in 1205; unknown good woman, fol. 239v, at Cambiac in 1227; Guilhema de Deime, fol. 201r, at Lanta in 1231; Guilhema de Longacamp, fol. 35v, at Saint-Martin-de-Lande in 1233; na Belengueira de Seguerville, fol. 137v, at Avignonet in 1233; na Bruna *et socia*, with Bertran Marti as deacon, fol. 35v, at Saint-Martin-de-Lande in 1234, and na Bruna with Rixenda, fols. 192v–193r, at

Laurac in 1235; Raimona Borda, fol. 76v, in 1238; Fabrissa et *socia*, fol. 41r, at Saint-Martin-de-la-Lande in 1240; Tholosana *et tres sociae*, fols. 123v and 196r, at Gaja-la-Selve in 1240; Guilhema Sicart and Arnata, fol. 204r, at Odars in 1241; and four anonymous *bonas femnas* and two *bons omes*, 72v, at Laurac in 1242. Abels and Harrison, "The Participation of Women in Languedocian Catharism," pp. 228–229, is indispensable on MS 609 and the good women of the Lauragais.

21. MS 609, fol. 184v for Dulcia Faber's testimony and fol. 72v for the confession of Guilhema Garrona.

22. Ibid., fol. 103r: "Et erant bene tunc in dicta vila .vi. mansiones, tam hereticorum quam hereticorum publice existentium."

23. Ibid., fol. 30r, ". . . dixit quod ipse vidit stare hereticos publice in castro Sancti Martini de la Landa in .x. domibus. Et vidit quod maxima pars hominum dicti castri ibat ad predicationem dictorum hereticorum."

24. Ibid., fol. 143v.

25. Ibid., fol. 180v.

26. Ibid.

27. Ibid., fol. 106r.

28. Ibid., fol. 18r, ". . . tempore quo comes fecit pacem Ecclesia."

29. Ibid., fol. 130r, where Mateuz Esteve, as one more example of many, remembered that around 1228, ". . . in pluribus aliis hospiciis Tholose, nomina quorum ignorat, vidit hereticos et hereticas."

30. Ibid., fol. 18v, as Bernart Amielh put it, ". . . ante adventum crucesignatorum, vidit hereticos publice ambulantes per carrerias. . . ."

31. Ibid., fol. 121v, ". . . tempore guerre comitis," and fol. 197r, ". . . tempore quo Carchassona fuit obsessa."

32. By contrast, the friar-*enquêteurs* of Louis IX and Alphonse of Poitiers, who specifically questioned men and women in the Lauragais and the Toulousain about, among other things, property damage caused during the war, heard a great deal about the activities of crusaders, *bayles,* and *faidits*. On this point, see Jordan, *Louis IX and the Challenge of the Crusade*, pp. 236–246.

33. MS 609, fol. 66v. Cf. Mundy, *The Repression of Catharism at Toulouse*, p. 21, who mistook Peire Guilhem's confession, and so his description of capturing the soldiers, for something his brother Estotz had said and done.

34. Monique Bourin, "Quel jour; en quelle année? A l'origine de la "révolution calendaire" dans le Midi de la France," in *Le Temps, sa mesure et sa perception au Moyen Age: Actes du Colloque, Orléans 12–13 avril, 1991*, ed. Bernard Ribémont (Caen: Paradigme, 1992), pp. 37–46, briefly discusses time and history derived from inquisitorial documents. A longer discussion about time and confession before the medieval inquisition, particularly in Languedoc, is in Alexander Murray's "Time and Money," in *The Work of Jacques Le Goff and the Challenges of Medieval History*, ed. Miri Rubin (Woodbridge: The Boydell Press, 1997), pp. 1–25.

35. Douais, *Documents pour servir à l'histoire de l'Inquisition dans le Languedoc*, 2:20.

36. *La Chanson de la Croisade Albigeoise*, 1:200, laisse 84. Cf. *Historia Albigensis*, 1:232–233, §233 [*The History of the Albigensian Crusade*, pp. 119–120 n. 8].

37. MS 609, fol. 187v, ". . . quando heretici stabant publice per terram de Lauraguesio."

38. Ibid., fols. 30v and 187v: "Alibi non vidit hereticos nisi publice. . . ."

39. Dossat, *Les crises de l'Inquisition Toulousaine au XIII° siècle*, p. 254.

40. MS 609, fol. 103v, ". . . et, quia erant sabatarii, tenebant ibi operatorium et operabantur ibi publice, et omnes homines et femine de vila veniebant et emebant ita publice. . . . Et, quia dictus testis erat sabaterius, conducebat se cum dictis hereticis ad suendum et ad operandum. . . . Requisitus si audivit hereticos dicentes errores, dixit quod audivit eos loquentes quod nichil de hiis que Deus fecerant potuerant corrumpi nec preterire. . . ." Cf. Kaelber, *Schools of Asceticism*, p. 205, for his interpretation of the Montesquieu cobblers Pons de Grazac and Arnaut Cabosz.

41. MS 609., fol. 87v: "Dixit tamen quod in tempore guerre vidit stantes publice Arnaldum Fabrum et Poncium fratres et P. Guausberti hereticos in forcia patris ipsius testis et sunt .xxv. anni et amplius. Sed neminem vidit ire ad sermones hereticorum nec adoravit nec vidit adorari."

42. Ibid., ". . . dixit quod numquam credidit hereticos esse bonos homines nec audivit errores eorum. . . ."

43. Ibid., fol. 238r, ". . . apud Auriacum vidit hereticos publice manentes in domibus eorumdem, scilicet, Petrum Gausberti, Ar. Faber, Poncium Faber. Et erant homines ipsius testis."

44. Ibid., ". . . non vidit hereticos nec credidit. . . ."

45. Dossat, *Les crises de l'Inquisition Toulousaine au XIII° siècle*, p. 256.

46. MS 609, fol. 146v: "Alibi nunquam vidit hereticos nisi captos. . . ."

47. Ibid., fol. 28v, ". . . dixit quod nunquam vidit hereticos nisi captos vel publice. . . ."

48. Ibid., ". . . excepto quod dixit quod non vidit hereticos captos."

49. Ibid., fol. 103r.

50. See, for example, ibid., fol. 239v, where Aimersent Viguier testified about heretics visiting houses at night in 1244 at Cambiac; or Raimon Gaut listening to *bons omes* preach in a field near Mas-Saintes-Puelles in 1233.

51. Doat 24, fol. 85.

52. MS 609, fol. 145v, ". . . duo homines intraverunt domum, qui statim inceperunt disputare cum Ramundo Bruni de Avinione qui erat ibi presens. Et tunc ipse testis perpendit ipsos hereticos esse."

## CHAPTER 13
### WORDS AND NODS

1. For example, see MS 609, fol. 2r, Bernart Cogota's testimony: "Benedicite, probi homines, orate Deum pro nobis." Or Pons de Rozenge's version, fol. 3v: "Benedicite, boni homines, orate Deum pro nobis." Or Pelegrina de Mont Seruer's recitation for the good women, fol. 2v: "Benedicite, bone muleres, orate Deum pro nobis."

2. For example, ibid., fol. 5r, where Guilhema Companha phrased it, ". . . et alii adoraverunt ibi dictos hereticos, ter flexis genibus, dicendo: 'Benedicite, boni homines, orate Deum pro nobis.' "

3. For example, ibid., fol. 231r, where Arnaut Ugon said, ". . . ipse testis et dictus Ramundum [Fabri] adoraverunt ibi dictos hereticos, flexis genibus, dicendo: 'Benedicite.' Et ipsi heretici respondebant: 'Deus vos benedicat.' Et audivit ibi predicationem eorum."

4. Ibid., fol. 4v, ". . . omnes et ipse testis adoraverunt ibi dictos hereticos, dicendo, quilibet per se, ter, 'Benedicite,' flexibus genibus ante ipsos et addentes, 'Domini, orate Deum pro isto peccatore, quod faciat me bonum Christianum et perducat ad bonum finem.' " See also Pons Esteve Amada from Fanjeaux, fol. 162r, who recalled saying: "Benedicite, boni homines, orate Deum pro isto peccatore."

5. Ibid., fol. 20v, ". . . et fuit hereticata et dictus Hysarnus hereticavit eam ibi. . . . Et sunt .xl. anni vel circa. Et reconciliavit eam Beatus Dominicus. . . . Et ipsa testis credidit predictas hereticas bonas mulieres et quod possent salvari per ipsas."

6. Ibid., ". . . qualibet septimana, adoravit hereticas tribus vicibus vel pluribus."

7. Ibid.: "Suspecta est ista et posset multa dicere."

8. Ibid., ". . . sed nec ipse testis nec alii adoraverunt ibi dictos hereticos . . . tamen quod ipse testis adoravit illos hereticos quando intraverunt primo domum suam."

9. Ibid.

10. Ibid., fol. 163r.

11. Ibid.

12. Ibid., fol. 163r–163v: "Interrogatus quare non dixit capellano de Fano Javis de predictis hereticis. Dixit quod propter timorem dimisit."

13. Ibid., fol. 33r.

14. Ibid.: "Et omnes adoraverunt ibi dictos hereticos, flexis genibus ter, dicendo, Benedicite, excepto ipso teste, qui non flexit genua, sed tamen inclinavit capud."

15. Ibid.: "Et recognovit quod male fecit, quia, postquam abjuravit heresim et juravit, promisit persequi hereticos, vidit hereticos, celavit et eis capud suum inclinavit."

16. Ibid., fol. 69v, ". . . et omnes supradicti adoraverunt hereticos excepto ipso teste, qui inclinavit tamen caput."

17. Ibid., fol. 58v.

18. Ibid., fol. 190r.

19. Ibid., ". . . et hoc fecerunt intentione adorandi."

20. Ibid., fol. 164v.

21. Ibid., fol. 21v, ". . . et ipsa testis et dicta Na Flors, ad preces dictorum hereticorum, adoraverunt ibi dictos hereticos et audierunt predicationem eorum."

22. Ibid., fol. 197r: "Et dicta Aimengarda dixit ipsi testi quod flecteret genua sua coram dictis hereticis, et ipsa testis respondit quod non faceret. Et tunc dicta Ermengarda compulit ipsam testem flectere genua coram predictis hereticis. . . ." See, as another example, Guilhema Forneira of Saint-Martin-de-la-Lande, fol. 32r, testifying that Andriva Faure compelled her to adore the *bons omes* Adam and Peire Arnaut in the house of Izarn de Gibel in 1239.

23. Mundy, *Society and Government at Toulouse*, pp. 60–66.

24. For example, Lambert, *The Cathars*, p. 62, misreads *bonomios sive bonosios* in Guilhem de Puylaurens' *Chronica*, p. 32, as referring to the " '*Bonosii*', that is Bosnians," and so the Cathars.

25. For example, MS 609, fol. 186v.

26. Ibid., fol. 136r.

27. Ibid., fol. 157v.

28. Ibid., fols. 95–96.

29. Ibid., fol. 67r–v, ". . . quia erat de nobili genere."

30. Ibid., fol. 216r.

31. Ibid., fol. 21r: "Item, in domo Arnaldum Godalh, vidit dictum filium suum et socius suus, hereticos, et vidit ibi cum eis ipsum Arnaldum Godalh et filium ipsius Arnaldi Poncium. Et ipsa testis adoravit eos, sed non vidit alios adorare. Et sunt .v. anni vel circa."

32. Ibid., fol. 238v: "Dixit etiam quod vidit Petrum Gausbert et Arnaldus Faure, hereticos, homines suos, in domibus ipsorum hereticorum apud Cambiac, et ipse testis, flexis genibus ter, dicendo, benedicite, adoravit ipsos hereticos. . . ."

33. Lambert, *The Cathars*, pp. 142–143.

34. MS 609, fol. 164v.

35. Ibid., fol. 140v.

36. Ibid., fol. 16v.

37. Ibid., fol. 186v.

38. Ibid., fol. 164r.

39. Ibid., fol. 110r: "Item vidit dictus testis apud Mon Esquiu quod Willelmus Petri del Lux invenit ipsum testem in platea eiusdem ville, et dixit sibi quod iret cum ipso teste usque ad domum suam, quia volebat sibi ostendere duos pueros. Et tunc testis adoravit dictos hereticos, et dictus Willelmus Petri similiter, et Petrus Ramundi Gros, miles eiusdem ville de Monte Esquivo. Non cognovit dictus testis illos hereticos."

40. Ibid., ". . . et salutavit eas, sed non adoravit eas."

41. Ibid., fol. 89r.

42. Ibid., fol. 165r.

43. Ibid, fol. 42r. Na Mateuz Faure's testimony, in which she mentions her son's youthful desires, is at fol. 29r.

44. Ibid., fol. 184r, ". . . et tenuit sectam hereticorum per unum annum, orando, jejunando, hereticos adorando, predictiones eorum audiendo, et alia faciendo que heretici faciunt et percipiunt observari. . . ."

45. Ibid., fol. ". . . et postea dimisit dictam sectam hereticorum et accepit virum. Et sunt .xl. anni."

46. Ibid., fol. 13r, ". . . sed non fuit hereticus indutus, nec jejunavit, nec oravit, nec fecit illas abstinentias quas ipsi faciebant. Et post duos menses ipsa testis rediit ad domum patris sui. Et sunt .xxv. anni vel circa."

47. Yves Dossat, "Les Cathares d'après les Documents de l'Inquisition," *Cahiers de Fanjeaux: Cathares en Languedoc* 3 (1968): 74.

48. MS 609, fol. 41r.

49. Ibid., fol. 159r–v.

## CHAPTER 14
### NOT QUITE DEAD

1. MS 609, fols. 139v–140r.

2. Ibid., fol. 140r: "Item dixit quod, cum Macip de Tholosa cepisset hereticos apud Avinionem in tribus domibus, videlicit, Tholosani de la Sala et in domo Stephani de Villa Nova et in domo Willelmi de Calhavel, exivit sonus et fama quod ipse testis reddiderat dictos hereticos, licet non esset verum. Et propter hoc dicta Blancha, mater sua, flebat sepissime et odiebat ipsum testem, quia credebat quod dictos hereticos reddidisset. Et sunt .viii. anni vel circa." On the Tolosa family see Mundy, *The Repression of Catharism at Toulouse*, pp. 268–283, esp. 280–282 for Macip de Tolosa and his brother Peire.

3. Ibid., fol. 120v.

4. Abel and Harrison, "The Participation of Women in Languedocian Catharism," 227 and n. 61, are very good on this point. In other inquisitions, only two references can be found in the surviving documentation. They are: Doat 22, fol. 77r–v, has the good woman Marqueza hereticating a dying woman, Taysseiras de Auca, in 1225; Doat 23, fol. 300r, where Guilhema den Pons Durant hereticated a sick woman at Toulouse in 1230.

5. Ibid., fol. 39v, ". . . virum ipsius testis, qui infirmabatur et non poterat loqui. Sed non hereticaverunt eum, nec legerunt aliquid super capud eius, nec predicaverunt." See also Esteve Faure of Saint-Martin-de-la-Lande, fol. 31r, ". . . et Willelmum Fabri, fratrem ipsius testis, qui jacebat infirmus. Et tunc dicti heretici volebant hereticare dictum infirmum, sed non poterat loqui."

6. Ibid., fol. 54v, ". . . et dedit ei brodium galline ad bibendum et postea fuit hereticatus alia vice."

7. Ibid., fol. 243r.

8. Ibid., fol. 252r, ". . . quod nunquam frangeret votum quod fecerat Domino."

9. Ibid., fol. 132v. Cf. Mundy, "Village, Town, and City in the Region of Toulouse," p. 161, who mistook Peire Pis' very specific reference to Arnaut and Pons Faure for an assertion that "Cathars were the best doctors."

10. Ibid., fol. 94r.

11. Ibid., fol. 9v.

12. Ibid.

13. Ibid., fol. 246r.

14. Ibid., fol. 6r: "Et postea dicebat: 'Faciatis tale emplastrum vel tale de herbis.' Et hoc totum dicebat ut posset habere denarios. Item, dixit quod multociens iecit plumbum infirmis, ut haberet denarios et nullam virtutem credebat in plumbo. Item, dixit quod na Garejada de Vilario conjuravit multociens plumbum et dedit intelligere gentibus quod cum plumbo conjurato liberabantur ab infirmitatibus."

15. Ibid., fol. 11.

16. Ibid., fol. 130v, ". . . et dictus Arnaldus Fabri, hereticus, habebat in cura sua dictum Willelmus de Borgafre, et ipse testis habuit cum eis mala verba, ita quod in nocte recesserunt dicti heretici."

17. Quite the contrary, as Bernart de Caux and Jean de Saint-Pierre heard a number of stories about the contempt that *medici* appear to have had for the *bons omes* and *bonas femnas*. For example, fol. 35r, in 1244, the *bayle* of Saint-Martin-de-la-Lande, Guilhem Faure, took two *bons omes* to the house of Pons Joan, where the *medicus* Joan Traver was looking after a sick child. One of these good women had broken her arm, and Guilhem Faure, who seems to have been a *crezen*, wanted the Catholic Joan Traver to fix it. The *medicus* adamantly refused, and the *bayle*, with the heretics, immediately left. The next day, according to Pons Joan, these two good men were caught and burnt. Similarly, on fol. 13r and in 1237, the *physicus* Guilhem Garnier showed equal distaste for two *bons omes* he accidently found in a wood near Mas-Saintes-Puelles, who had the gall to ask the *physicus* if he would talk to them. Guilhem Garnier refused to even get off his horse. Cf. Walter L. Wakefield, "Heretics as Physicians in the Thirteenth Century," *Speculum* 57 (1982): 328–331.

18. Cf. Frederick S. Paxton, "*Signa Mortifera*: Death and Prognostication in Early Medieval Medicine," *Bulletin of the History of Medicine* 67 (1993): 631–650, and Michael R. McVaugh, *Medicine before the Plague: Practioners and Their Patients in the Crown of Aragon, 1285–1345*, Cambridge History of Medicine, 13 (Cambridge: Cambridge University Press, 1993), pp. 136–138, 143–144, 213–214, 231–232.

19. MS 609, fol. 77r, ". . . tunc infirmus rogavit predictos hereticos quod reciperent ipsum, sed ipsi noluerunt ipsum recipere quia multa juvenis erat et, dum ipse infirmus audivit quod nolebant ipsum recipere, irritus, clausit occulos quasi mortuus. Et tant cito dicti heretici posuerunt librum supra caput dicti juvenis. . . ."

20. Ibid., fol. 232r, ". . . et dicta Condors dixit orationem hereticorum, scilicet Adoremus Patrem et Filium et Spiritum Sanctum, ter, et sic mortua est. . . ."

21. Ibid., fol. 141r, ". . . sed ipsa testis non interfuit dicte hereticationi, quia pre nimio dolore quem ipsa testis paciebatur, et propter lamentationem, fuit expulsa de domo . . . Et crastinum Hospitalarii de Sancto Johanne de Podio Siura receperunt dictum virum ipsius testis mortuum, sepelierunt." On the Hospitalers at Pexiora, see Maurice Berthe, "Deux commanderies hospitalières du Lauragais, Puysubran et Caignac (XIIᵉ–XIVᵉ siècles)," in *Flaran 6: Les ordres militaires, la vie rurale et le peuplement en Europe occidentale (XIIᵉ–XVIIIᵉ S.). Sixièmes Journées internationales d'histoire, 21–23 septembre 1984*, ed. Charles Higounet (Auch: Centre Culturel de l'Abbaye de Flaran, 1986), 1:207–213, and Dominic Selwood, *Knights of the Cloister: Templars and Hospitallers in Central-Southern Occitania c. 1100–c.1300* (Woodbridge: The Boydell Press, 1999), pp. 52–54.

22. MS 609, fol. 162r, ". . . ipsa testis non vidit nec interfuit dicte hereticatione, quia fecerunt eam removeri, quia erat pregnans, propter dolorem quam habebat ipsa testis."

23. Ibid., fol. 198v., ". . . cujusmodi villani essent illi?"

24. Ibid., fol. 144r–v: " 'Bene accedit nobis, quia iste probus homo est receptus a probis hominibus, et nobis similiter bene accedit, quia interfuimus hereticationi ipsius.' . . . et dictum Peireta mortuum et statim sepelierunt dictum hereticatum."

25. See, for example, Pelhisson, *Chronique*, pp. 56–57. See also Walter L. Wakefield's "Burial of Heretics in the Middle Ages," *Heresis* 5 (1985): 29–32.

26. Tardif, "Document pour l'histoire du *processus per inquisitionem*," 677.

27. MS 609, fol. 133v: "Et omnes et ipse testis portaverunt dictam hereticam mortuam de nocte usque ad quendam ortum ipsius testis extra prope villam et sepelierunt eam ibi."

28. Ibid., fol. 165r, ". . . quod ipse testis fuit custodiam ante januam cuiusdam domus dum quidam homicida, qui debebat sepeliri vivus, hereticabatur ibi."

29. Ibid., fol. 99r.

30. Ibid., fol. 103r.

31. Ibid., fol. 129r, ". . . frater ipsius testis ad eum, qui tenebat ipsum testem in potestate sua, et quesivit ab ipso teste si volebat se reddere hereticum. Et ipse testis respondit iratus quod non."

32. Ibid., fol. 238r.

33. Ibid., fol. 36v, ". . . tunc ipse testis erat extra mentem suam. Et audivit dici ab Arnaldus Ysarni, avunculo suo, quod dicti heretici hereticaverunt ipsum testem tunc, sed ipse testis non recolit de hereticis nec de dicta hereticatione."

34. Ibid., fols. 250v–251r. Also see Jean Duvernoy, "Boulbonne et le Lauragais au XIII$^e$ siècle," in *Le Lauragais: Histoire et Archéologie, Actes du LIV$^e$ Congrès de la Fédération historique du Languedoc méditerranéen et du Roussillon et du XXXVI$^e$ Congrès de la Fédération des Sociétés académiques et savantes de Languedoc-Pyrénées-Gascogne (Castelnaudary, 13–14 juin 1981)*, ed. Jean Sablou and Philippe Wolff (Montpellier: Fédération historique du Languedoc méditerranéen et du Roussillon Université Paul-Valéry, 1983), pp. 105–113.

## CHAPTER 15
### ONE FULL DISH OF CHESTNUTS

1. MS 609, fol. 35v, ". . . et Willelmus de Canast, qui portavit quendam ciphum plenum casteneis dicto Bertrando Martini, heretico, ex parte ipsius testis. Tamen ipse Willelmus de Canast dixit dicto Bertrando Martini, heretico, quod Bertrandum Mir Arezat mittebat sibi dictas castaneas. Et dictus Willelmus de Canast dixit ad preces et ad instanciam dicti Ramundi Mir, nepotis viri ipsius testis, et dictus Ramundus Mir fecit hoc dici causa ludi et solats, et quia dictus Bernardus Mir Arezad non diligebat dictos hereticos. . . . Et sunt .xiiii. anni vel .xv."

2. Ibid.: "Et omnes et ipsa testis audierunt predicationem, que fuit maxima, et adoraverunt eos."

3. On gift giving, see Strathern, *The Gender of the Gift*, esp. 268–308. See also the essays edited by Jonathan Parry and Maurice Bloch in *Money and the Morality of Exchange* (Cambridge: Cambridge University Press, 1991).

4. MS 609, fol. 30r, ". . . uxor ipsius testis, misit Bertrando Martini, heretico, unum plenum castanearum, sub nomine ipsius testis, ipso penitus ignorante."

5. Ibid., fol. 187v, ". . . cum ipse testis esset puer et heretici starent publice, dicti heretici dabant ipsi testi nuces, et faciebant ipsi testi flectere genua et dicere benedicte, et sunt .xxxv. anni vel circa, et fuit confessus aliis inquisitoribus apud Castrum Novum Darri, quam confessionem concedit esse veram." Cf. Peire de Mazerolis, the lord of Gaja-la-Selve, fol. 124r, who remembered that as a boy ". . . comedit de pane et fructibus quos heretici debat ei. Sed non adoravit nec vidit adorare nec non recolit de tempore."

6. Ibid., fol. 33v, ". . . et transmisiy eis ipse testis unam cuppam plenam casteneis, sed non adoravit, nec vidit adorare. Et sunt .xvi. anni vel circa."

7. For example, see *La Chanson de la Croisade Albigeoise*, 1:180, laisse 74, "Dels autres no doneren d'una notz lo valent," and p. 220, laisse 94, "Que no les prezan pas per forsa une castanha." Wendy Pfeffer, *Proverbs in Medieval Occitan Literature* (Gainesville: University Press of Florida, 1997), pp. 80–111, esp. pp. 93–94, is good on proverbs after the Albigensian Crusade. Nuts, incidentally, because of the region and the dietary restrictions of the good men and good women, frequently occur as gifts. For example, see Guilhem del Verselh's confession at MS 609, fol. 65r.

8. Lambert, *The Cathars*, p. 74, assumed, rather in the manner of a friar-inquisitor, that Bernart Mir Arezat was a *crezen* as an adult because he genuflected and nibbled at those nuts given to him as a boy.

9. Douais, *Documents pour servir à l'histoire de l'Inquisition dans le Languedoc*, 2:32.

10. Ibid., p. 35.

11. Ibid., p. 81, ". . . vidit et adoravit hereticos, recepit eos in domum suam, coxit eis panem. . . ."

12. "Del tot vey remaner valor," in *Les Poésies de Guilhem de Montanhagol*, p. 43, 1.5–7: "E meron mal clerc e prezicador, / quar devedon so qu'az els no·s cove,' que hom per pretz non do ni fassa be. . . ."

13. MS 609, fol. 177r.

14. Ibid., fol. 46r, ". . dixit quod Bertrandus de Rocovila, miles, de Monte Galhart, dedit ipsi testi tres pisces, ut ipse testis traderet illos pisces Ramundo de Rocovilata, qui, ex parte sua, portaret illos pisces ad hereticos. Et sun .vi. anni."

15. Ibid., fol. 154r.

16. Ibid., fol. 117r, ". . . dixit quod ipsa testis vendidit .vi. sextarios vini Bernardo de Messall, et postea audivit dici quod dictus B. de Messall emit dictum vinum ad opus hereticorum, et credit pro certo."

17. Ibid., fol. 120v.

18. Ibid., fol. 32r.

19. Ibid, fol. 103v, ". . . et tunc vendidit dictis hereticis quandam domum pro quadringentis solidorum Tholosorum. Et sunt .xxxv. anni."

20. Ibid., fol. 18v.

21. Mundy, *Society and Government at Toulouse*, p. 147.

22. Ibid., fol. 124v.

23. MS 609., fol. 159r.

24. Ibid., fol. 161v.

25. Gottfried Koch, *Frauenfrage und Ketzertum in Mittelalter* (Berlin: Akademie-Verlag, 1962), translated *domus* and *mansiones* throughout as *Frauenkonvente*. See Abels and Harrison, "The Participation of Women in Languedocian Catharism," 228–229, for their lucid criticism of Koch. Recently, Anne Brenon, in her *Les femmes cathares* (Paris: Perrin, 1992), pp. 127–133, wrote as if the heretical houses were little different from orthodox convents and monasteries.

26. John H. Mundy, "Charity and Social Work in Toulouse 1100–1250," *Traditio* 22 (1966): 203–288; idem, "The Parishes of Toulouse from 1150 to 1250"; idem, *Men and Women at Toulouse*, pp. 163–173, is excellent on this point.

27. MS 609, fol. 232r, ". . . dixit quod Bernarda Airoarda, mater ipsius testis, fuit heretica, et vidit eam pluries in hospitio ipsius testis et Poncii, fratriis sui, sed non comedit nec bibi ibi postquam fuit heretica, sed in alio hospicio ipse testis et frater eius providebant ei in expensis."

28. Mundy, *Society and Government at Toulouse*, p. 150.

29. MS 609, fol. 232r, ". . . nec dedit ned misit eis aliquid, excepto quod dictum est superius de matre sua."

30. Ibid., fol. 85v.

31. Ibid., fol. 24v, ". . . de mandato communitatis."

32. Ibid., fol. 30r.

33. Ibid., fol. 231v.

34. Ibid., fol. 94v, for an anonymous note about this incident; fol. 98v for Peire Devise; ibid., Domina Brunissent, for "Quam cartam, Domine?"; and ibid., the Carcassès knight Raimon Pons, for "E Domine, Deus j. sic valeat!"

35. Ibid., fol. 94.v.

36. Ibid., fol. 237v.

37. Ibid., fol. 152v.

38. Ibid., fol. 152v.

39. Ibid., fol. 94v.

40. Ibid.

41. Ibid., fol. 32v.

42. Ibid., fol. 69v, ". . . alia vice in fundo vinee capellanii de garda prope quadam gardam in crepusculo noctis, dum quereret quondam bovem quod non poterat invenire, vidit W. de Raissa et socium suum, hereticos, et vidit cum eis W. Johannis et W. Got et W. Baussa, et non adoravit nec vidit adorare . . . et ipse testis recessit et dimisit alios ibidem."

43. Ibid., fol. 117v, ". . . dum ipse testis et W. Vezat custodirent boves suos, audierunt quendam canem latrantem in quadam bartam. Et tunc ipse testis et W. Vezat respexerunt in predicta barta, viderunt ibi duos homines, et perpenderunt in animo suo quod heretici erant. Et tunc infra .xv. dies ipse testis et W. Vezat redierunt cum hominibus de Maurenx, et cum Bertrando Amblart, ballivo de Vauro, ad predictam cabanam, et voluerunt capere predictos hereticos, sed non invenerunt eos ibi."

44. Ibid., fol. 13r, ". . . quia casu invenerat eos dum ipse testis iret venando cum canibus."

45. Ibid., fol. 3v, and given on 22 May 1245, ". . . propria voluntate minxit supra coronam ipsius testis, qui est acolitus, in obprobium et vituperium tocius Ecclesia Catholice, ut credit ipse testis firmiter."

46. Ibid., fol. 18r, ". . . quod quadam nocte, apud Mansum in domo Petrus Gauta, ludebant quidam homines de Manso ad taxillos. Et ipse testis, provocatus quia jurabant lusores, ascendit in quandam archam et inde minxit super tabularium illorum lusorum. Et pars urine ipsius testis cecidit super coronam Petri Ramundi Crozat, qui sedebat ibi cum lusoribus, ut credit, sed non vidit nec fecit de industria nec velle suo."

47. Dossat, *Les crises de l'Inquisition Toulousaine au XIII<sup>e</sup> siècle*, p. 252.

## CHAPTER 16
## TWO YELLOW CROSSES

1. Tardif, "Document pour l'histoire du *processus per inquisitionem*," 675.

2. Ibid., p. 674. See also Dossat, *Les crises de l'Inquisition Toulousaine au XIII*<sup>e</sup> *siècle*, pp. 250–261.

3. Dossat, *Les crises de l'Inquisition Toulousaine au XIII*<sup>e</sup> *siècle*, pp. 261, 266; cf. pp. 298–299. On the lack of property confiscations, see James Given, *State and Society in Medieval Europe: Gwynedd and Languedoc under Outside Rule* (Ithaca: Cornell University Press, 1990), pp. 110–111.

4. MS 609, fol. 160r–v. On Dominic Guzman at Fanjeaux specifically and in the Lauragais more generally during the Albigensian Crusade, see Christoph T. Maier, *Preaching the Crusades: Mendicant Friars and the Cross in the Thirteenth Century*, Cambridge Studies in Medieval Life and Thought, 4th ser., 28 (Cambridge: Cambridge University Press, 1994), pp. 17–19.

5. MS 609, fol. 22v, ". . . et fuit facta heretica, et stetit heretica per .vi. septimanas. Et .L. anni vel circa. . . . Et habuit penitentiam de postandis crucibus, et portavit illas coopertas, et una de crucibus cecidit in via."

6. Ibid., fol. 20v, ". . . et portavit in hyeme cruces sub pellicio, et alias portavit illas coopertas."

7. Ibid., fol. 22v, ". . . et habuit cruces ab Episcopo Tholosano, sed semper portavit cruces coopertas extra domum."

8. Ibid., fol. 27v: "Dixit etiam quod nunquam fecit derisionem de crucesignatis ab inquisitoribus."

9. Douais, *Documents pour servir à l'histoire de l'Inquisition dans le Languedoc*, 2:45 n. 1, where he has edited Doat 31, fol. 152v, where the letter of Innocent IV was copied. See also Wakefield, "Heretics and Inquisitors: The Case of Le Mas-Saintes-Puelles," 223.

10. See Dossat, *Les crises de l'Inquisition Toulousaine au XIII*<sup>e</sup> *siècle*, passim, for all the nuances of this struggle.

11. Mansfield, *The Humiliation of Sinners*, p. 66.

12. Jordan, *Louis IX and the Challenge of the Crusade*, pp. 214–220; Le Goff, *Saint Louis*, pp. 858–897, and Mundy, *Society and Government at Toulouse*, pp. 244–249.

13. Gui, *De fundatione*, pp. 109–112, and Dossat, "Une figure d'inquisiteur," p. 270.

14. Mundy, *The Repression of Catharism at Toulouse*, esp. pp. 75–123, is indispensable on the 1279 amnesty.

15. Ibid, pp. 107–108, no. 216.

16. Douais, *Documents pour servir à l'histoire de l'Inquisition dans le Languedoc*, 2:3–4.

# BIBLIOGRAPHY OF WORKS CITED

This bibliography contains full citations for printed works cited. References to manuscript sources are given only in the notes.

Abel, Armand. "Aspects sociologiques des religions 'manichéennes.'" In *Mélanges offerts à René Crozet*, edited by René Crozet, Pierre Gallais, and Yves Jean Rion, 1:33–46. Poitiers: Société d'études Médiévales, 1966.

Abels, Richard, and Ellen Harrison. "The Participation of Women in Languedocian Catharism." *Medieval Studies* 61 (1979): 214–251.

Allegre, Victor. "Caractères généraux des vieilles églises du Lauragais." *Mémoires de la Société Archeologique du Midi de la France* 31 (1965): 75–94.

Almagor, Uri, and David Maybury-Lewis, eds. *The Attraction of Opposites: Thought and Society in the Dualist Mode*. Ann Arbor: University of Michigan Press, 1989.

Angelov, Dimitar. "Der Bogomilismus in Bulgarien." *Bulgarian Historical Review* 2 (1975): 34–54.

———. "Ursprung und Wesen des Bogomilentums." In *The Concept of Heresy in the Middle Ages (11th–13th C.). Proceedings of the International Conference, Louvain, May 13–16, 1973*, edited by W. Lourdaux and D. Verhelst, pp. 144–156. Medievalia Lovaniensia, Series I—Studia IV. The Hague: Leuven University Press–Martinus Nijhoff, 1976.

Auden, W. H. *The Dyer's Hand and Other Essays* (1962). New York: Vintage, 1989.

Baker, Nicholson. "The History of Punctuation." In his *The Size of Thoughts: Essays and Other Lumber*, pp. 70–88. New York: Random House, 1996.

Baldwin, John W. *The Government of Philip Augustus: Foundations of French Royal Power in the Middle Ages*. Berkeley and Los Angeles: University of California Press, 1986.

———. "The Crisis of the Ordeal: Literature, Law, and Religion around 1200." *Journal of Medieval and Renaissance Studies* 24 (1994): 327–353.

———. "The 1996 York Quodlibet Lecture: From the Ordeal to Confession. In Search of Lay Religion in Early Thirteenth Century France." In *Handling Sin: Confession in the Middle Ages*, edited by Peter Biller and A. J. Minnis, pp. 191–209. York Studies in Medieval Theology, 2. Woodbridge: Boydell & Brewer; York: York Medieval Press, 1998.

Barnes, John Arundel. *A Pack of Lies: Towards a Sociology of Lying*. Themes in the Social Sciences. Cambridge: Cambridge University Press, 1994.

Barthélemy, Dominique. "Présence de l'aveu dans le déroulement des ordalies (IXème–XIVème) siècles." In *L'Aveu: Antiquité et moyen-âge: Actes de la table ronde organisée par l'Ecole française de Rome avec le concours du CNRS et de l'Université de Trieste, Rome 28–30 mars 1984*, pp. 315–340. Rome: Ecole française de Rome, 1986.

Bartlett, Robert. *Trial by Fire and Water: The Medieval Judicial Ordeal*. Oxford: Oxford University Press, 1986.

Belhomme, Guy. "Documents inédits sur l'hérésie des Albigeois." *Mémoires de la Société archéologique du Midi de la France* 6 (1847, 1848, 1849, 1850, and 1852): 101–146.

———. *Documents inédits concernant les hérétiques bons hommes de la secte des Albigeois.* Toulouse: Imprimerie d'Augustin Manavit, 1850.

Belperron, Pierre. *La Croisade contre les Albigeois et l'union de Languedoc à la France (1209–1249).* Paris: Perrin, 1967.

Berlioz, Jacques. "*Exemplum* et Histoire: Césaire de Heisterbach (v. 1180–v. 1240) et la Croisade Albigeoise." *Bibliothèque de l'Ecole des Chartes* 147 (1989): 49–86.

Berthe, Maurice. "Deux commanderies hospitalières du Lauragais, Puysubran et Caignac (XIIᵉ–XIVᵉ siècles)." In *Flaran 6: Les ordres militaires, la vie rurale et le peuplement en Europe occidentale (XIIᵉ–XVIIIᵉ S.). Sixièmes Journées internationales d'histoire, 21–23 septembre 1984,* edited by Charles Higounet, 1:207–213. Auch: Centre Culturel de l'Abbaye de Flaran, 1986.

Besse, Guillaume. *Histoire des ducs, marquis et comtes de Narbonne, autrement appellez Princes des Goths, Ducs de Septimanie, et Marquis de Gothie. Dedié à Monseigneur l'Archevesque Duc de Narbonne.* Paris: Antoine de Sommaville, 1660.

Biget, Jean-Louis. "Mythographie du Catharisme." *Cahiers de Fanjeaux: Historiographie du catharisme* 14 (1979): 308–310.

———. "L'extinction du catharisme urbain: les points chauds de la répression." *Cahiers de Fanjeaux: Effacement du Catharisme? (XIIIᵉ–XIVᵉ S.)* 20 (1985): 305–340.

Biller, Peter. "Words and the Medieval Notion of 'Religion,' " *Journal of Ecclesiastical History* 36 (1985): 351–369.

———. "Heresy and Literacy: Earlier History of the Theme." In *Heresy and Literacy, 1000–1530,* edited by Anne Hudson and Peter Biller, pp. 1–18. Cambridge Studies in Medieval Literature, 23. Cambridge: Cambridge University Press, 1994.

———. "The Cathars of Languedoc and Written Materials." In *Heresy and Literacy, 1000–1530,* edited by Anne Hudson and Peter Biller, pp. 61–82. Cambridge Studies in Medieval Literature, 23. Cambridge: Cambridge University Press, 1994.

———. "La storiografia intorno all'eresia medievale negli Stati Uniti e in Gran Bretagna (1942–92)." In *Eretici ed eresie medievali nella storiografia contemporanea: atti del XXXII Convegno du studi seilla Riforma e i movimenti religiosi in Italia,* edited by Grado Giovanni Merlo, pp. 39–63. Bolletino della Societa di Studi Valdesi, 174. Torre Pellice: Societa di Studi Valdesi, 1994.

———. "Cathars and Material Women." In *Medieval Theology and the Natural Body,* edited by Peter Biller and Alastair J. Minnis, pp. 61–108. York Studies in Medieval Theology, I. Woodbridge: York Medieval Press–Boydell & Brewer, 1997.

———. "William of Newburgh and the Cathar Mission to England." In *Life and Thought in the Northern Church c. 1100–c.1700: Essays in Honour of Claire Cross,* edited by Diana Wood, pp. 11–30. Woodbridge: The Ecclesiastical History Society–The Boydell Press, 1999.

Biller, Peter, and Anne Hudson, eds. *Heresy and Literacy, 1000–1530.* Cambridge Studies in Medieval Literature, 23. Cambridge: Cambridge University Press, 1994.

Blaquière, Henri, and Yves Dossat. "Les cathares au jour le jour, Confessions iné-dites de cathares quercynois." *Cahiers de Fanjeaux: Cathares en Languedoc* 3 (1968): 259–298.

Boase, Roger. *The Origin and Meaning of Courtly Love: A Critical Study of European Scholarship.* Manchester: Manchester University Press; Totowa: Rowman and Littlefield, 1977.

Bompaire, Marc. "Circulation et vie monétaire dans le Tarn médiéval (XI*ᵉ–XIV*ᵉ *siècles)." Bulletin de la Société des Sciences, Arts et Belles-Lettres du Tarn,* n.s., 45–46 (1991–1992): 479–491.

Borst, Arno. "Neue Funde und Forschungen zur Geschichte der Katharer." *Historische Zeitschrift* 174 (1952): 17.

———. *Die Katharer.* Schriften der Monumenta Germaniae Historica (Deutsches Institut für Erforschung des Mittelalters), 12. Stuttgart: Anton Hiersemann Verlag, 1953.

———. "Herbert Grundmann (1902–1970)." In *Herbert Grundmann Ausgewählte Aufsätze. Teil 1 Religiöse Bewegungen,* pp. 1–25. Schriften der Monumenta Germaniae Historica, 25. Stuttgart: Anton Hiersemann Verlag, 1976.

Bourbon, Étienne de. *Anecdotes Historiques. Legendes et Apologues tirés du recueil inédit d'Etienne de Bourbon, Dominicain du XIII*ᵉ *siècle.* Edited by Richard Albert Lecoy de la Marche. Paris: Librairie Renouard, 1877.

Bourg, Antoine du. "Pexiora (Puysubran): Commanderie d'ordre de Saint-Jean de Jerusalem." *Mémoires de la Société Archéologique du Midi de la France,* 2d ser., 11 (1880): 399–409.

Bourin, Monique. "Quel jour; en quelle année? A l'origine de la «révolution calendaire» dans le Midi de la France." In *Le Temps, sa mesure et sa perception au Moyen Age: Actes du Colloque, Orléans 12–13 avril, 1991,* edited by Bernard Ribémont, pp. 37–46. Caen: Paradigme, 1992.

Bourin-Derreau, Monique. "Un exemple d'agriculture monastique en Lauragais: Les domaines de Prouille en 1340." In *Le Lauragais: Histoire et Archéologie. Actes du LIV*ᵉ *Congrès de la Fédération historique du Languedoc méditerranéen et du Rousillon et du XXXVI*ᵉ *Congrès de la Fédération des Sociétés académiques et savantes de Languedoc-Pyrénées-Gascogne (Castelnaudary, 13–14 juin 1981),* edited by Jean Sablou and Philippe Wolff, pp. 115–125. Montpellier: Fédération historique du Languedoc méditerranéen et du Roussillon Université Paul-Valéry, 1983.

Boyle, Leonard E. "Montaillou Revisited: *Mentalité* and Methodology." In *Pathways to Medieval Peasants,* edited by J. A. Raftis, 2:119–140. Papers in Medieval Studies. Toronto: Pontifical Institute of Medieval Studies, 1981.

Bozzolo, Carla, and Ezio Ornato. *Pour une histoire du livre manuscrit au Moyen Age. Trois essais de codicologie quantitative: I La production du livre manuscrit en France du Nord, II La constitution des cahiers dans les manuscrits en papier d'origine française et le probleme de l'imposition, III, Les dimensions des feuillets dans les manuscrits français du Moyen Âge.* Équipe de Recherche sur l'humanisme française des XIVᵉ et XVᵉ siècles. Textes et Etudes, 2. Paris: Éditions du Centre Nationale de la Recherche Scientifique, 1980.

Brenon, Anne. *Le vrai visage du Catharisme.* Portet-sur-Garonne: Éditions Loubatières, 1988.

Brenon, Anne. *Les femmes cathares.* Paris: Perrin, 1992.

———. "Les heresies de l'an mil: nouvelles perspectives sur les origines du catharisme." *Heresis* 25 (1995): 21–36.

———. "The Voice of the Good Women: An Essay on the Pastoral and Sacerdotal Role of Women in the Cathar Church." In *Women Preachers and Prophets through Two Millennia of Christianity,* edited by Beverly Mayne Kienzle and Pamela J. Walker, pp. 114–133. Berkeley and Los Angeles: University of California Press, 1998.

Briquet, Charles-Moïse. "Recherches sur les premiers papiers employés en Occident and en Orient du X*ᵉ* au XIV*ᵉ* siècle.*" Mémoirs de la Société nationale des antiquaires de France* 46 (1886): 132–205.

Brown, Peter. "Society and the Supernatural: A Medieval Change." In his *Society and the Holy in Late Antiquity,* pp. 302–332. Berkeley and Los Angeles: University of California Press, 1982.

Brunet, Gustave. "Jean-Baptise Colbert." *Le Bibliophile Français. Gazette Illustrée des Amateurs de Livres, d'Estampes et de haute curiosité* 4 (1869): 5–10.

*Bullarium diplomatum et privilegiorum sanctorum romanum pontificum.* Edited by Charles Cocquelines. 25 vols. Turin: Dalmazzo, 1857–1872.

Bynum, Caroline Walker. *Holy Feast and Holy Fast: The Religious Significance of Food to Medieval Women.* The New Historicism: Studies in Cultural Poetics, 1. Berkeley and Los Angeles: University of California Press, 1987.

———. *The Resurrection of the Body in Western Christianity, 200–1336.* Lectures on the History of Religions, 15. New York: Columbia University Press, 1995.

———. "Wonder." *American Historical Review* 102 (1997): 1–26.

Cabié, Edmund. "Compte des inquisiteurs des Diocèses de Toulouse, d'Albi et de Cahors, 1255–1256." *Revue du Tarn,* 2d ser., 22 (1905): 110–133, 215–229.

Caesarius of Heisterbach. *Dialogus Miraculorum.* 2 vols. Edited by Joseph Strange. Cologne: H. Lempertz & Co., 1851.

Casagrande, Carla, and Silvana Vecchio *I peccati della lingua. Disciplina ed etica della parola nella cultura medievale.* Bibliotheca Biographica: Sezione Storico-Antropologica. Rome: Istituto della Enciclopedia Italiana fondata da Giovanni Treccani, 1987.

Castaing-Sicard, Mireille. *Les contrats dans le très ancien droit Toulousain—Xe–XIIIe siècle.* Toulouse: M. Espic, 1959.

Cayla, Paul. "Fragment d'un registre de l'Inquisition." *Mémoires de la Société des Arts et des Sciences de Carcassonne,* 3d ser., 6 (1941–1943): 282–289.

Cazenave, Annie. "Les cathares en Catalogne et en Sabarthès d'après les registres d'Inquisition: la hierarchie cathare en Sabarthès après Montségur." In *Les relations franco-espagnoles jusqu'au XVIIᵉ siècle.* Bulletin philologique et historique (jusqu'à 1610) du Comité des travaux historiques et scientifiques. Année 1969, Actes du 94° Congrès national des Sociétés savantes tenu à Pau, 1:387–436. Paris: Bibliothèque Nationale, 1972.

———. "Aveu et contrition: Manuels de confesseurs et interrogatoires d'Inquisition en Languedoc et en Catalogne." In *La piété populaire au Moyen Age, Actes du 99ᵉ Congrès national des sociétés savantes,* Besançon, 1974, pp. 333–349. Philologie et histoire jusqu'à 1610, 1. Paris: Comité des travaux historiques et scientifiques, 1977.

Cazes, Jean-Paul. "Structures agraires et domaine comtal dans la bailie de Caste-lnaudary en 1272." *Annales du Midi* 99 (1987): 453–477.

———. "Un village castral de la plaine lauragais: Lasbordes (Aude)." *Archéologie du Midi Medieval* 8–9 (1990–1991): 3–25.

Cazes, Quitterie. "Le cloître Saint-Etienne de Toulouse sous la Révolution et le Premier Empire." *Mémoires de la Société Archéologique de Midi de la France* 49 (1989): 191–206.

Chapelot, Jean, and Robert Fossier. *The Village and House in the Middle Ages.* Translated by Henry Cleere. Berkeley and Los Angeles: University of California Press, 1985.

Cheyette, Fredric. "The Castles of the Trencavels: A Preliminary Aerial Survey." In *Order and Innovation in the Middle Ages: Essays in Honor of Joseph R. Strayer,* edited by William Chester Jordan, Bruce McNab, and Teófilo Ruiz, pp. 255–272. Princeton: Princeton University Press, 1976.

Clanchy, Michael T. *From Memory to Written Record: England 1066–1307.* 2d ed. Oxford: Blackwell, 1994.

Colin, Marie-Geneviève, et al. *La maison du castrum de la bordure méridionale du Massif Central.* Archéologie du Midi médiéval Supplément N° 1. Carcassonne: Centre d'archéologie médiéval du Languedoc, 1996.

*Conciliorum oecumenicorum decreta.* Edited by Giuseppe Alberigo et al. 3d ed. Bologna: Istituto per le scienze religiose, 1973.

Constable, Giles. *Three Studies in Medieval Religious and Social Thought: The Interpretation of Mary, the Ideal of the Imitation of Christ, the Orders of Society.* Cambridge: Cambridge University Press, 1995.

Constable, Olivia Remie. *Trade and Traders in Muslim Spain: The Commercial Realignment of the Iberian Peninsula 900–1500.* Cambridge Studies in Medieval Life and Thought, 4th ser., 24. Cambridge: Cambridge University Press, 1994.

Costen, Michael. *The Cathars and the Albigensian Crusade.* Manchester: Manchester University Press, 1997.

Dauzat, Michel. "Les mottes castrales du Lauragais: notes préliminaires." In *Le Lauragais: Histoire et Archéologie,* edited by Jean Sablou and Philippe Wolff, pp. 73–88. Actes du LIVᵉ Congrès de la Fédération historique du Languedoc méditerranéen et du Roussillon et du XXXVIᵉ Congrès de la Fédération des Sociétés académiques et savantes de Languedoc-Pyrénées-Gascogne (Castelnaudary, 13–14 juin 1981). Montpellier: Fédération historique du Languedoc méditerranéen et du Roussillon Université Paul-Valéry, 1983.

Delisle, Léopold. *Le Cabinet des Manuscrits de la Bibliothèque Impériale.* Histoire Générale de Paris. Paris: Imprimerie Impériale, 1868.

———. *Notice sur les Manuscrits de Bernard Gui.* Paris: Imprimerie Nationale, 1879.

Devic, Claude, and Joseph Vaissette. *Histoire Générale de Languedoc avec des notes et les pièces justificatives.* Edited by Auguste Molinier. 2d ed. 16 vols. Toulouse: Édouard Privat, 1882–1904).

Dondaine, Antoine. "Le Manuel de l'Inquisitor (1230–1330)." *Archivum Fratrum Praedicatorum* 17 (1947): 97–101.

———. "Aux origines de l'hérésie médievale." *Rivista di Storia della Chiesa in Italia* 6 (1952): 78.

Dondaine, Antoine, ed. *Un Traité néo-manichéen du XIII^e Siècle.* Le Liber de duobus principiis *suivi d'un fragment de rituel cathare.* Rome: Istituto Storico Domenicano, 1939.

Dorpalen, Andreas. *German History in Marxist Perspective: The East German Approach.* Detroit: Wayne State University Press, 1985.

Dossat, Yves. "Le plus ancien manuel de l'inquisition méridionale: le *Processsus inquisitionis* (1248–1249)." *Bulletin philologique et historique (jusqu'à 1715), années 1948–1949–1950* (1952): 33–37.

———. *Les crises de l'Inquisition Toulousaine au XIII^e siècle* (1233–1273). Bordeaux: Imprimerie Bière, 1959.

———. "Les Cathares d'après les Documents de l'Inquisition." *Cahiers de Fanjeaux: Cathares en Languedoc* 3 (1968): 74.

———. "A propos du concile cathare de Saint-Félix: les Milingues." *Cahiers de Fanjeaux: Cathares en Languedoc* 3 (1968): 201–214.

———. "La croisade vue par les chroniqueurs." *Cahiers de Fanjeaux: Paix de Dieu et guerre sainte en Languedoc au XIII^e* 4 (1969): 221–259.

———. "Simon de Montfort." *Cahiers de Fanjeaux: Paix de Dieu et guerre sainte en Languedoc au XIII^e* 4 (1969): 288–298.

———. "Le massacre d'Avignonent." *Cahiers de Fanjeaux: Le Credo, la Morale, et l'Inquisition* 6 (1971): 343–359.

———. "Le «bucher de Monségur» et les bûchers de l'inquisition." *Cahiers de Fanjeaux: Le Credo, la Morale, et l'Inquisition* 6 (1971): 361–378.

———. "Une figure d'inquisiteur: Bernard de Caux." *Cahiers de Fanjeaux: Le Crédo, la Morale, et l'Inquisition* 6 (1971): 253–254.

———. "Université et Inquisition à Toulouse: la foundation du Collège Saint-Raimond (1250)." In *Actes du 95^e Congrès national des Sociétés savantes, Reims, 1970.* Section de philologie et d'histoire jusqu'à 1610, 1:227–238. Paris: Comité des travaux historiques et scientifiques, 1975.

———. "Un initiateur: Charles Schmidt." *Cahiers de Fanjeaux: Historiographie du catharisme* 14 (1979): 163–184.

Douais, Célestin. *Les Albigeois. Leurs origines, action de l'église au XII^e siècle.* Paris: Didier et C^ie, 1879.

———. *Cartulaire de l'abbaye de Saint-Sernin de Toulouse (844–1200).* Paris: Alphonse Picard; Toulouse: édouard Privat, 1887.

———. *Acta capitulorum provincialium ordinis fratrum Praedicatorum.* Toulouse: Edouard Privat, 1894.

———. *Documents pour servir à l'histoire de l'Inquisition dans le Languedoc.* 2 vols. Paris: Librairie Renouard and Société de l'Histoire de France, 1900.

———. *L'Inquisition. Ses Origines—Sa Procedure.* Paris: Librairie Plon, 1906.

Douglas, Mary. *How Institutions Think.* London: Routledge and Kegan Paul, 1987.

———. "Rightness of Categories." In *How Classification Works: Nelson Goodman among the Social Sciences,* edited by Mary Douglas and David Hull, pp. 239–271. Edinburgh: Edinburgh University Press, 1992.

———. *In the Wilderness: The Doctrine of Defilement in the Book of Numbers.* Journal for the Study of the Old Testament Supplement Series, 158. Sheffield: Sheffield Academic Press, 1993.

———. "Comment: Hunting the Pangolin." *Man,* n.s., 28 (1993): 161–164.

Duby, Georges. *L'Histoire Continue.* Paris: Éditions Odile Jacob, 1991.

———. *History Continues.* Translated by Arthur Goldhammer. Chicago: University of Chicago Press, 1994.

Durand, Aline. *Les paysages médiévaux du Languedoc, Xe–XIIe siècles.* Toulouse: Presses Universitaires du Mirail, 1998.

Duranton, Henri. "Les Albigeois dans les histoires générales et les manuels scolaires du XVIe au XVIIIe siècle." *Cahiers de Fanjeaux: Historiographie du catharisme* 14 (1979): 85–118.

Durliat, Marcel. *Saint-Sernin de Toulouse.* Toulouse: Eché, 1986.

———. "Saint-Sernin et ses métamorphoses." In *Saint-Sernin de Toulouse. Trésors et Métamorphoses. Deux siècles de restaurations 1802–1989. Toulouse, Musée Saint-Raymond, 15 septembre 1989–14 janvier 1990*, pp. 17–22. Toulouse; Musée Saint-Raymond 1989.

Dusan, Bruno. "De Manso Sanctarum Puellarum." *Revue Archéologique du Midi de la France: Recueil de notes, mémoires, documents relatifs aux monuments de l'histoire et des Beaux-Arts dans les Pays de Langue d'Oc* 2 (1868–1869): Appendix, separate pagination from volume, 1–12.

Duvernoy, Jean. *Le Registre d'Inquisition de Jacques Fournier, évêque de Pamiers (1318–1325).* Bibliothèque Méridionale, ser. 2, 41 Toulouse: Édouard Privat, 1965. Additional *Corrections*, 1972.

———. "La nourriture en Languedoc à l'époque cathare." In *Cathares, Vaudois et Béguins: Dissidents du pays d'Oc*, pp. 229–236. Domaine Cathare. Toulouse: Privat, 1994.

———. "L'acception: 'haereticus' (*iretge*) = 'parfait cathare' en Languedoc au XIII*ᵉ* siècle." In *The Concept of Heresy in the Middle Ages (11th–13th C.): Proceedings of the International Conference, Louvain, May 13–16, 1973*, edited by W. Lourdaux and D. Verhelst, pp. 198–210. Medievalia Lovaniensia, Series I—Studia IV. The Hague: Leuven University Press–Martinus Nijhoff, 1976.

———. *Le catharisme: la religion des cathares.* Toulouse: Privat, 1976.

———. "Boulbonne et le Lauragais au XIIIe siècle." In *Le Lauragais: Histoire et Archéologie*, edited by Jean Sablou and Philippe Wolff, pp. 105–113. Actes du LIV*ᵉ* *Congrès de la Fédération historique du Languedoc méditerranéen et du Roussillon et du XXXVI*ᵉ* Congrès de la Fédération des Sociétés académiques et savantes de Languedoc-Pyrénées-Gascogne (Castelnaudary, 13–14 juin 1981). Montpellier: Fédération historique du Languedoc méditerranéen et du Roussillon Université Paul-Valéry, 1983.

———. *Inquisition à Pamiers: Cathares, Juifs, Lépreux . . . devant leurs juges (1966).* 2d ed. Bibliothèque historique Privat. Toulouse: Privat, 1986.

———. "Le registre de l'inquisiteur Bernard de Caux, Pamiers, 1246–1247." *Bulletin de Société ariégeoise Sciences, Lettres, et Arts* 45 (1990): 5–108.

———. *Cathares, Vaudois et Beguins, dissidents du pays d'Oc.* Domaine Cathare. Toulouse: Privat, 1994.

Eclache, Michèle. "L'église et ses abords: topographie et urbanisme." In *Saint-Sernin de Toulouse. Trésors et Métamorphoses. Deux siècles de restaurations 1802–1989. Toulouse, Musée Saint-Raymond, 15 septembre 1989–14 janvier 1990*, pp. 49–57. Toulouse; Musée Saint-Raymond, 1989.

Elgin, Catherine Z., and Nelson Goodman. *Reconceptions in Philosophy and Other Arts and Sciences.* Indianapolis: Hackett Publishing Company, 1988.

Emery, Richard W. *Heresy and Inquisition in Narbonne.* New York: Columbia University Press, 1941.

Erbstösser, Martin. *Ketzer im Mittelalter.* Stuttgart: Kohlhammer, 1984.

———. *Heretics in the Middle Ages.* Translated by Janet Fraser. Leipzig: Edition Leipzig, 1984.

Erbstösser, Martin, and Ernst Werner. *Ideologische Probleme des Mittelalterlichen Plebejertums: Die freigeistige Häresie und ihre sozialen Wurzeln.* Forschungen zur mittelalterlichen Geschichte, 7. Berlin: Akademie-Verlag, 1960.

Fichtenau, Heinrich. *Ketzer und Professoren: Häresie un Vernunftglaube im Hochmittelalter.* Munich: C. H. Beck'sche Verlagsbuchhandlung, 1992.

———. *Heretics and Scholars in the Middle Ages: 1000–1200.* Translated by Denise A. Kraiser. Pennsylvania State University Press, 1998.

Figueira, Guilhem. "D'un sirventes far en est son que m'agenssa." In *Los Trovadores: Historia y Textos,* edited by Martín de Riquer, 3:1272–1279. Barcelona: Editorial Planeta, 1975.

Fine, John V. A. *The Early Medieval Balkans: A Critical Survey from the Sixth to the Late Twelfth Century.* Ann Arbor: University of Michigan Press, 1983.

Fiorelli, Piero. *La tortura guidiziaria nel diritto comune.* 2 vols. Milan: Guiffre, 1953.

Fitz-Thedmar, Arnold. *De antiquis legibus liber. Cronica maiorum et vicecomitum Londoniarum.* Edited by Thomas Stapleton. Camden Society, 34. London: The Camden Society, 1846.

Fortanier, Jean Ramière de. *Recueil de Documents relatifs à l'Histoire du Droit Municipal en France des origines à la Révolution: Chartes de Fránchises du Lauragais.* Société d'Histoire du Droit. Paris: Librairie du Recueil Sirey, 1939.

Fowler-Magerl, Linda. *Ordo iudiciorum vel ordo iudiciarius: Begriff und Literaturgattung.* Repertorien zur Frühzeit der gelehrten Rechte. Frankfurt am Main: V. Klostermann, 1984.

France, John. *Western Warfare in the Age of the Crusades, 1000–1300.* Ithaca: Cornell University Press, 1999.

French, Roger, and Andrew Cunningham. *Before Science: The Invention of the Friars' Natural Philosophy.* Aldershot: Scolar Press, 1996.

Friesen, Abraham. "Medieval Heretics or Forerunners of the Reformation: the Protestant Rewriting of the History of Medieval Heresy." In *The Devil, Heresy, and Witchcraft in the Middle Ages: Essays in Honor of Jeffrey B. Russell,* edited by Alberto Ferreiro, pp. 165–190. Leiden: Brill, 1998.

Froidevaux, Yves-Marie. "Viollet le Duc restaurateur et son influence." In *Actes du Colloque International Viollet le Duc, Paris 1980,* edited by Pierre-Marie Auzas, pp. 145–151. Paris: Nouvelles Editions Latines, 1982.

Gardel, Marie-Élise. "Le bâtiment III du *castrum* de Cabaret." In *La maison du castrum* de la bordure méridionale du Massif Central, edited by Marie-Geneviève Colin et al., pp. 163–175. Archéologie du Midi médiéval Supplément Nᵒ 1. Carcassonne: Centre d'archéologie médiéval du Languedoc, 1996.

Garsoïan, Nina. *The Paulician Heresy: A Study of the Origin and Development of Paulicianism in Armenia and the Eastern Provinces of the Roman Empire.* The Hague: Mouton & Co., 1967.

Gildea, Robert. *The Past in French History.* New Haven: Yale University Press, 1994.

Ginzburg, Carlo. "The Inquisitor as Anthropologist." In *Myths, Emblems, Clues,* translated by John and Anne Tedeschi, pp. 156–164. London: Hutchinson Radius, 1986.

Given, James. "The Inquisitors of Languedoc and the Medieval Technology of Power." *American Historical Review* 94 (1989): 336–403.

———. *State and Society in Medieval Europe: Gwynedd and Languedoc under Outside Rule.* Ithaca: Cornell University Press, 1990.

———. "A Medieval Inquisitor at Work: Bernard Gui, 3 March 1308 to 19 June 1323." In *Portraits of Medieval and Renaissance Living: Essays in Memory of David Herlihy,* edited by Samuel K. Cohn Jr. and Steven A. Epstein, pp. 207–232. Ann Arbor: University of Michigan Press, 1996.

———. *Inquisition and Medieval Society: Power, Discipline, and Resistance in Languedoc.* Ithaca: Cornell University Press, 1997.

Gonnet, Giovanni. "Bibliographical Appendix: Recent European Historiography on the Medieval Inquisition." In *The Inquisition in Early Modern Europe: Studies on Sources and Methods,* edited by Gustav Henningsen and John Tedeschi with Charles Amiel, pp. 198–223. DeKalb: Northern Illinois University Press: 1986.

Goodman, Nelson. "Seven Strictures against Similarity." In *Problems and Projects,* pp. 437–446. Indianapolis: Hackett Publishing Company, 1972.

———. "The New Riddle of Induction." In *Fact, Fiction, and Forecast,* pp. 59–83. 4th ed. Cambridge: Harvard University Press, 1983.

———. *Of Mind and Other Matters.* Cambridge: Harvard University Press, 1984.

Grundmann, Herbert. *Religiöse Bewegungen im Mittelalter. Untersuchungen über die geschichtlichen Zusammenhänge zwischen der Ketzerei, den Bettelorden und der religiösen Frauenbewegung im 12. und 13. Jahrhundert und über die geschichtlichen Grundlagen der deutschen Mystik* (1935). 2d ed. Hildesheim: Georg Olms, 1961.

———. "Ketzerverhöre des Spätmittelalters als quellenkritisches Problem." *Deutsches Archiv* 21 (1965): 519–575.

———. *Religious Movements in the Middle Ages: The Historical Links between Heresy, the Mendicant Orders, and the Women's Religious Movement in the Twelfth and Thirteenth Century, with the Historical Foundations of German Mysticism.* Translated by Steven Rowan. Notre Dame: University of Notre Dame Press, 1995.

Gui, Bernard. *Practica inquisitionis heretice pravitatis.* Edited by Célestin Douais. Paris: Alphonse Picard, 1886.

———. *Bernardus Guidonis de fundatione et prioribus conventuum provinciarum Tolosanae et Provinciae ordinis predictorum.* Edited by P. A. Amargier. *Monumenta ordinis fratrum praedictorum historica,* vol. 24. Rome: Institutum historicum fratrum praedicatorum, 1961.

Guilhem de Tudela and Anonymous Continuator. *La Chanson de la Croisade Albigeoise.* Edited and translated by Eugène Martin-Chabot. 2 vols. Les Classiques de l'Histoire de France au Moyen Age. Paris: Société d'édition «Les Belles Lettres», 1957–1961.

———. *The Song of the Cathar Wars: A History of the Albigensian Crusade.* Translated by Janet Shirley. Aldershot: Scolar Press, 1996.

Guillaume de Auvergne. *De Universo—Opera Omnia.* Paris: Andreas Pralard, 1674. Reprint, Frankfurt: Minerva, 1963.

Gumbert, J. Peter. "Ruling by Rake and Board: Notes on Some Medieval Ruling Techniques." In *The Role of the Book in Medieval Culture: Proceedings of the Oxford International Symposium, 26 September–1 October 1982*, edited by Peter Ganz, 1:41–54. Bibliologia. Elementa ad librorum studia pertinentia, 3. Turnhout: Brepols, 1986.

———. "Sizes and Formats." In *Ancient and Medieval Book Materials and Techniques (Erice, 18–25 september 1992)*, edited by Marilena Maniaci and Paola F. Munafò, 1:227–263. Studi e Testi, 357. Vatican City: Biblioteca Apostolica Vaticana, 1993.

Gurevitch, Aron. *Categories of Medieval Culture*. Translated by G. L. Campbell. London: Routledge & Kegan Paul, 1985.

———. *Medieval Popular Culture: Problems of Belief and Perception*. Translated by János Bak and Paul Hollingsworth. Cambridge: Cambridge University Press, 1992.

Hamilton, Bernard. "The Origins of the Dualist Church of Drugunthia." *Eastern Churches Review* 6 (1974): 115–124.

———. "The Cathar Council of S. Félix Reconsidered." *Archivum Fratrum Praedicatorum* 48 (1978): 23–53.

———. *The Medieval Inquisition*. New York: Holmes & Meier, 1981.

———. "Wisdom from the East: The Reception by the Cathars of Eastern Dualist Texts." In *Heresy and Literacy, 1000–1530*, edited by Peter Biller and Anne Hudson, pp. 38–60. Cambridge Studies in Medieval Literature, 23. Cambridge: Cambridge University Press, 1994.

———. "The State of Research: The Legacy of Charles Schmidt to the Study of Christian Dualism" *Journal of Medieval History* 24 (1998): 191–214.

Hamilton, Janet, and Bernard Hamilton. *Christian Dualist Heresies in the Byzantine World c. 650–c. 1450*. Manchester Medieval Sources Series. Manchester: Manchester University Press, 1998.

Hearn, Millard Fillmore. "Viollet-le-Duc: A Visionary among the Gargoyles." In *The Architectural Theory of Viollet-le-Duc: Readings and Commentary*, pp. 1–19. Cambridge: MIT Press, 1990.

Heisig, Karl. "Ein gnostische Sekte im abendländischen Mittelalter." *Zeitschrift für Religions und Geistesgeschichte* 16 (1964): 271–74.

Higounet, Charles. "Structures sociales, 'castra' et castelnaux dans le Sud-Ouest aquitain (X*e*–XII*e* siècle)." In *Villes, Sociétés et économies Médiévales: Recueil d'articles de Charles Higounet*, edited by Robert Étienne, pp. 257–262. Études et Documents d'Aquitaine. Bordeaux: La Nef et Fédération Historique du Sud-Ouest, 1992.

Irigoin, Jean. "Les papiers non filigranés état présent des recherches et perspectives d'avenir." In *Ancient and Medieval Book Materials and Techniques (Erice, 18–25 september 1992)*, edited by Marilena Maniaci and Paola F. Munafò, 1:265–312. Studi e Testi, 357. Vatican City: Biblioteca Apostolica Vaticana, 1993.

James, Henry. *A Little Tour in France* (1884). London: Sidgewick & Jackson, 1987.

Jardine, Nicholas. *The Scenes of Inquiry: On the Reality of Questions in the Sciences*. Oxford: Clarendon Press, 1991.

Jimenez, Pilar. "Relire la Charte de Niquinta—1) Origine et problématique de la Charte" *Heresis* 22 (1994): 1–26.

————. "Relire la Charte de Niquinta–2) Sens et portée de la Charte." *Heresis* 23 (1994): 1–28.

Johannes Trithemius. *De laude scriptorum.* Edited and translated by Klaus Arnold. Lawrence, Kans.: Coronado Press, 1974.

Jordan, William Chester. *Louis IX and the Challenge of the Crusade: A Study in Rulership.* Princeton: Princeton University Press, 1979.

————. *The French Monarchy and the Jews.* Middle Ages Series. University of Pennsylvannia Press, 1989.

————. *The Great Famine: Northern Europe in the Early Fourteenth Century.* Princeton: Princeton University Press, 1996.

Jorré, Georges. *Le Terrefort Toulousain et Lauragais: Histoire et Géographie agraire.* Toulouse: Edouard Privat, 1971.

Justice, Steven. *Writing and Rebellion: England 1381.* The New Historicism: Studies in Cultural Poetics, 27. Berkeley and Los Angeles: University of California Press, 1994.

Kaelber, Lutz. *Schools of Asceticism: Ideology and Organization in Medieval Religious Communities.* University Park: Pennsylvannia State University Press, 1998.

Kelly, Henry Ansgar. "Inquisition and the Prosecution of Heresy: Misconceptions and Abuses." *Church History* 58 (1989): 439–451.

Kieckhefer, Richard. "The Office of Inquisition and Medieval Heresy: The Transition from Personal to Institutional Jurisdiction." *Journal of Ecclesiastical History* 46 (1995): 36–61.

Koch, Gottfried. *Frauenfrage und Ketzertum in Mittelalter.* Forschungen zur mittelalterlichen Geschichte, 9. Berlin: Akademie-Verlag, 1962.

Kolmer, Lothar. "Colbert und die Entstehung der Collection Doat." *Francia* 7 (1979): 463–489.

————. *Ad Capiendum Vulpes. Die Ketzerbekämpfung in Süd-frankreich in der ersten Hälfte des 13. Jahrhunderts und die Ausbildung des Inquisitionsverfahrens.* Pariser Historische Studien, 19. Bonn: Ludwig Röhrscheid Verlag, 1982.

Lacger, Louis de. "L'Albigeois pendant la crise de l'albigéisme." *Revue d'histoire ecclésiastique* 29 (1933): 276–283.

Ladurie, Emmanuel Le Roy. *Montaillou, village occitan de 1294 à 1324* (1975). Paris: éditions Gallimard, 1993.

————. *Montaillou: Cathars and Catholics in a French Village 1294–1324.* Translated and condensed by Barbara Bray. Harmondsworth: Penguin Books, 1981.

Laffont, Jean L. "Histoire du notariat ou histoire notariale? Eléments pour une réflexion épistémologique." In *Notaires, Notariat et Société sous l'Ancien Régime. Actes du colloque de Toulouse, 15 et 16 décembre 1989, Université des Sciences Sociales de Toulouse, Centre d'Histoire Contemporaine des Institutions,* edited by Jean L. Laffont, pp. 51–60. Toulouse: Presses Universitaires du Mirail, 1990.

————. "A propos de l'historiographie notariale du Midi toulousain." In *Visages du notariat dans l'histoire du Midi toulousain XIV^e au XIX^e siècles,* edited by Jean L. Laffont, pp. 62–78. Toulouse: Presses Universitaires du Mirail, 1992.

Lambert, Malcolm. *Medieval Heresy: Popular Movements from Bogomil to Hus.* London: Edward Arnold, 1977.

————. *Medieval Heresy: Popular Movements from the Gregorian Reform to the Reformation.* 2d ed. Oxford: Blackwell Publishers, 1992.

Lambert, Malcolm. *The Cathars.* Oxford: Blackwell, 1998.

Landes, Richard. *Relics, Apocalyse, and the Deceits of History: Ademar of Chabannes, 989–1034.* Cambridge: Harvard University Press, 1995.

Langer, Susanne K. *Philosophy in a New Key: A Study in the Symbolism of Reason, Rite, and Art.* 3d ed. Cambridge: Harvard University Press, 1979.

Lansing, Carol. *Power and Purity: Cathar Heresy in Medieval Italy.* 3 vols. New York: Oxford University Press, 1998.

Lea, Henry Charles. *A History of the Inquisition of the Middle Ages.* 3 vols. New York: Harper & Brother, 1887.

Léglu, Catherine. "Moral and Satirical Poetry." In *The Troubadours: An Introduction,* edited by Simon Gaunt and Sarah Kay, pp. 47–65. Cambridge: Cambridge University Press, 1999.

Le Goff, Jacques. *Saint Louis.* Paris: Gallimard, 1996.

Limborch, Philip van. *Historia Inquisitionis, cui subjungitur Liber Sententiarum Inquisitionis Tholosanae ab anno Christi 1307 ad annum 1323.* Amsterdam: Henry Wetsten, 1692.

———. *The History of the Inquisition translated in English by Samuel Chandler in Two Volumes.* London: J. Gray, 1731.

Lobrichon, Guy. "The Chiaroscuro of Heresy: Early Eleventh-Century Aquitaine as Seen from Auxerre." In *The Peace of God: Social Violence and Religious Response in France around the Year 1000,* edited by Thomas Head and Richard Landes, pp. 80–103. Ithaca: Cornell University Press, 1992.

Locke, John. *Epistola de Tolerantia [A Letter Concerning Toleration]: Latin and English Texts Revised and Edited with Variants* (1689). Edited by Mario Montuori. The Hague: Martinus Nijhoff, 1963.

*Locke's Travels in France 1675–1679.* Edited by John Lough. New York: Garland Publishing, 1984.

Luchaire, Achille. *Innocent III: La Croisade des Albigeois.* Paris: Libraire Hachette, 1911.

Maier, Christoph T. *Preaching the Crusades: Mendicant Friars and the Cross in the Thirteenth Century.* Cambridge Studies in Medieval Life and Thought, 4th ser., 28. Cambridge: Cambridge University Press, 1994.

Maitland, Samuel Roffey. *Facts and Documents Illustrative of the History, Doctrine, and Rites of the Ancient Albigenses and Waldenses.* London: C.J.G. and F. Rivington, 1832.

Malecsek, Werner. "Le ricerche eresiologiche in area germanica." In *Eretici ed eresie medievali nella storiografia contemporanea: atti del XXXII Convegno du studi seilla Riforma e i movimenti religiosi in Italia,* edited by Grado Giovanni Merlo, pp. 64–93. Bolleltino della Societa di Studi Valdesi, 174. Torre Pellice: Societa di Studi Valdesi, 1994.

Manselli, Raoul. *L'eresia del male* (1963). 2d ed. Naples: Morano, 1980.

Mansfield, Mary C. *The Humiliation of Sinners: Public Penance in Thirteenth-Century France.* Ithaca: Cornell University Press, 1995.

Marandet, Marie-Claude. "L'approach du milieu social: le notariat en Midi toulousain au XIV$^e$ siècle." *In Visages du notariat dans l'histoire du Midi toulousain XIV$^e$ au XIX$^e$ siècles,* edited by Jean L. Laffont, pp. 81–109. Toulouse: Presses Universitaires du Mirail, 1992.

McKitterick, Rosamund. "The Study of Frankish History in France and Germany in the Sixteenth and Seventeenth Centuries." *Francia* 8 (1991): 556–572.

McVaugh, Michael R. *Medicine before the Plague: Practitioners and Their Patients in the Crown of Aragon, 1285–1345.* Cambridge History of Medicine, 13. Cambridge: Cambridge University Press, 1993.

Mérimée, Prosper. *Notes de Voyages*, edited by Pierre-Marie Auzas. Paris: Librairie Hachette, 1971.

Merlo, Grado Giovanni. *Eretici e inquisitori nella società piemontese del Trecento: con l'edizione dei processi tenuti a Giaveno dall'inquisitore Alberto De Castellario (1335) e nelle Valli di Lanzo dall'inquisitore Tommaso Di Casasco (1373).* Turin: Claudiana, 1977.

Migne, J-P., ed. *Patrologiae cursus completus: Series latina.* Paris: Garnier, 1844–1902.

Molinier, Auguste. *Catalogue général des manuscrits des Bibliothèques Publiques des Départments publié sous les auspices du Ministre de l'Instruction Publique.* Vol. 7, *Toulouse-Nîmes.* Paris: Imprimerie Nationale, 1885.

Molinier, Charles. *L'Inquisition dans le Midi de la France au XIII^e et au XIV^e siècle: étude sur les sources de son histoire.* Paris: Librairie Sandoz et Fischbacher, 1880.

―――. "La question de l'ensevelissement du comte de Toulouse Raimond VI en terre sainte (1222–1247). Etude accompagne de pièces inédites du XII^e et du XIII^e siècle." *Annales de la Faculté des Lettres de Bordeaux* 7 (1885): 1–92.

Montanhagol, Guilhem de. *Les Poésies de Guilhem de Montanhagol: Troubadour Provençal du XIII^e Siècle.* Edited and translated by Peter T. Ricketts. Toronto: Pontifical Institute of Medieval Studies, 1964.

*Monumenta Corbeiensia.* Edited by Philip Jaffé. Bibliotheca Rerum Germanicarum. Berlin: Weidmann, 1864.

Moore, Robert. "The Origins of Medieval Heresy." *History* 55 (1970): 21–361.

―――. "Nicétas, émissaire de Dragovitch, a-t-il traversé les Alpes?" *Annales du Midi* 85 (1973): 85–90.

―――. "Heresy as Disease." In *The Concept of Heresy in the Middle Ages (11th–13th C.): Proceedings of the International Conference, Louvain May 13–16, 1973*, edited by W. Lourdaux and D. Verhelst, pp. 1–11. Medievalia Lovaniensia, Series I—Studia IV. The Hague: Leuven University Press-Martinus Nijhoff, 1976.

―――. "The Birth of Popular Heresy: A Millennial Phenomenon?" *Journal of Religious History* 24 (2000): 8–25.

Moos, Peter von. "Literatur- und bildungsgeschichtliche Aspekte der Dialogform im lateinischen Mittelalter. Der Dialogus Ratii des Eberhard von Ypern zwischen theologischer disputatio und Scholaren-Komödie." In *Tradition und Wertung. Festschrift für Franz Brunhölzl zum 65. Geburtstag*, edited by Günter Bernt, Fidel Rädle, and Gabriel Silagi, pp. 165–209. Sigmaringen: Jan Thorbecke, 1989.

―――. "Rhetorik, Dialektik und 'civilios scientia' im Hochmittelalter." In *Dialektik und Rhetorik im früheren und hohen Mittelalter: Rezeption, überlieferung und gesellschaftliche Wirkung antiker Gelehrsamkeit vornehmlich im 9. und 12. Jahrhundert*, edited by Johannes Fried, pp. 133–156. Schriften des Historischen Kollegs, Kolloquien 27. Munich: R. Oldenburg, 1997.

Morghen, Raffaello. *Medioevo Cristiano.* Bari: Laterza, 1953.

Morghen, Raffaello. "Problèmes sur l'origine de l'hérésie au moyen-âge." *Revue historique* 336 (1966): 1–16.

Mundy, John H. *Liberty and Political Power in Toulouse 1050–1230.* New York: Columbia University Press, 1954.

Mundy, John H. "Hospitals and Leprosaries in Twelfth-and-Early-Thirteenth-Century Toulouse." In *Essays in Medieval Life and Thought Presented in Honor of Austin Patterson Evans,* edited by John H. Mundy, Richard W. Emery, and Benjamin N. Nelson, pp. 181–205. New York: Columbia University Press, 1955.

————. "Charity and Social Work in Toulouse 1100–1250." *Traditio* 22 (1966): 203–288.

————. "Village, Town, and City in the Region of Toulouse." In *Pathways to Medieval Pathways,* edited by J. A. Raftis, 2:141–190. Papers in Medieval Studies. Toronto: Pontifical Institute of Medieval Studies, 1981.

————. "The Farm of Fontanas at Toulouse: Two Families, a Monastery, and a Pope." *Bulletin of Medieval Canon Law,* n.s., 11 (1981): 29–40.

————. *The Repression of Catharism at Toulouse.* Studies and Texts, 74. Toronto: Pontifical Institute of Medieval Studies, 1985.

————. *Men and Women at Toulouse in the Age of the Cathars.* Studies and Texts, 101. Toronto: Pontifical Institute of Medieval Studies, 1990.

————. "The Parishes of Toulouse from 1150 to 1250." *Traditio* 46 (1991): 171–204.

————. *Society and Government at Toulouse in the Age of the Cathars.* Studies and Texts, 129. Toronto: Pontifical Institute of Medieval Studies, 1997.

Murray, Alexander. "Confession as an Historical Source in the Thirteenth Century." In *The Writing of History in the Middle Ages: Essays Presented to Richard William Southern,* edited by Ralph Henry Carless Davis and John Michael Wallace-Hadrill, pp. 275–322. Oxford: Clarendon Press, 1981.

————. "The Medieval Inquisition: An Instrument of Secular Politics?" *Peritia: Journal of the Medieval Academy of Ireland* 5 (1986): 161–200.

————. "Time and Money." In *The Work of Jacques Le Goff and the Challenges of Medieval History,* edited by Miri Rubin, pp. 1–25. Woodbridge: The Boydell Press, 1997.

Nardi, Paolo. "Relations with Authority." In *A History of the University in Europe,* edited by Hilde de Ridder-Symoens, 1:77–107. Cambridge: Cambridge University Press, 1992.

Nickson, M.A.E. "Locke and the Inquisition of Toulouse." *British Museum Quarterly* 36 (1971–1972): 83–92.

Nirenberg, David. *Communities of Violence: Persecution of Minorities in the Middle Ages.* Princeton: Princeton University Press, 1996.

Obolensky, Dimitri. *The Bogomils: A Study in Balkan Neo-Manichaeism.* Cambridge: Cambridge University Press, 1948.

Omont, Henri. "La Collection Doat à la Bibliothèque Nationale: Documents sur les recherches de Doat dans les archives du sud-ouest de la France de 1663 à 1670." *Bibliothèque de l'Ecole des Chartes* 77 (1916): 286–336.

Paden, William. "The Troubadours and the Albigensian Crusade: A Long View." *Romance Philology* 49 (1995): 168–191.

Pales-Gobilliard, Annette. "Bernard Gui inquisiteur et auteur de la *Practica.*" *Cahiers de Fanjeaux: Bernard Gui et son monde* 16 (1981): 253–264.

Parkes, Malcolm Beckwith. "Tachygraphy in the Middle Ages: Writing Techniques Employed for Reportations of Lectures and Sermons." In his *Scribes, Scripts and Readers: Studies in the Communication, Presentation and Dissemination of Medieval Texts*, pp. 19–33. London: The Hambledon Press, 1991.

————. *Pause and Effect: An Introduction to the History of Punctuation in the West.* Aldershot: Scolar Press, 1992.

Parks, Tim. *Translating Style: The English Modernists and Their Italian Translations.* London: Cassell, 1998.

Paul, Jacques. "La mentalité de l'inquisiteur chez Bernard Gui." *Cahiers de Fanjeaux: Bernard Gui et son monde* 16 (1981): 286–292.

Paxton, Frederick S. "*Signa Mortifera*: Death and Prognostication in Early Medieval Monastic Medicine." *Bulletin of the History of Medicine* 67 (1993): 631–650.

Pelhisson, Guilhem. *Chronique (1229–1244) suivie du récit des troubles d'Albi (1234).* Edited by Jean Duvernoy. Paris: CNRS Éditions, 1994.

Pennington, Kenneth. *The Prince and the Law, 1200–1600: Sovereignty and Rights in the Western Legal Tradition.* Berkeley and Los Angeles: University of California Press, 1993.

Percin, Jean-Jacques. *Monumenta conventus Tolosani ordinis F.F. Praedicatorum primi, ex vetustissimis manuscriptis originalibus transcripta, et S.S. Ecclesiæ Patrum Placitis Conventûs per annos distribuitur; Refertur Totius Albigensium facti narratio: Agiturque de Captibus hæresos, de LXI Conciliis contra eos habitis: De justa eorum poena, & de bello quo profligati sunt. De sanctæ Inquisitionis Officii Institutione, & perpetuo exercito, De Rosario, de Academia Tolosania. De primis Sanctæ Inquisitionis Martyribus F.F. Prædicatoribus & Minoribus, nec-non Ecclesiæ Metropolitanæ Tolosæ Canonicis, De Translatione Corporis Sancti Thomæ .V. Ecclesiæ Doctoris, [authore F. Raymundo Hugonis]. Et tandem de Nobilioribus Tolosæ familiis Aliisque plurimis, in ejus Ecclesia sepultis. Quarum Genealogia, Gentilitiaque scuta, referuntur, &c. Superiorum Jussu, & Regio Privilegio.* Toulouse: Jean & Guillaume Pech, 1693.

Peter the Venerable. *Adversus iudeorum.* Edited by Yvonne Friedman. Corpus Christianorum: Continuatio Mediaevalis, 58. Turnhout: Brepols, 1981.

Peters, Edward. *Inquisition.* New York: The Free Press, 1988.

————. "Wounded Names: The Medieval Doctrine of Infamy." In *Law in Medieval Life and Thought*, edited by Edward B. King and Susan J. Ridyard, pp. 43–89. Sewanee, Tenn.: Press of the University of the South, 1990.

————. "Prison before the Prison: The Ancient and Medieval Worlds." In *The Oxford History of the Prison: The Practice of Punishment in Western Society*, edited by Norval Morris and David J. Rothman, pp. 3–47. New York: Oxford University Press, 1995.

————. "Henry Charles Lea (1825–1909)." In *Medieval Scholarship. Biographical Studies on the Formation of a Discipline*, vol. 1, *History*, edited by Helen Damico and Joseph B. Zavadil, pp. 89–100. Garland Reference Library of the Humanities, 1350. New York: Garland Publishing, 1995.

————. *Torture: Expanded Edition.* Philadelphia: University of Pennsylvannia Press, 1996.

Peters, Edward. ""Destruction of the Flesh—Salvation of the Spirit: The Paradoxes of Torture in Medieval Christian Society." In *The Devil, Heresy, and Witchcraft in the Middle Ages: Essays in Honor of Jeffrey Burton Russell*, edited by Alberto Ferreiro, pp. 131–148. Leiden: Brill, 1998.

Petit-Dutaillis, Charles. *Étude sur la vie et le règne Louis VIII (1187–1226). Thèse présenté à la Faculté des Lettres de Paris*. Paris: Librairie Émile Bouillon, 1894.

Peyrusse, Louis. "Viollet-le-Duc à Saint-Sernin ou le génie de la restauration." In *Saint-Sernin de Toulouse. Trésors et Métamorphoses. Deux siècles de restaurations 1802–1989. Toulouse, Musée Saint-Raymond, 15 septembre 1989–14 janvier 1990*, pp. 109–119. Toulouse: Musée Saint-Raymond, 1989.

Pfeffer, Wendy. *Proverbs in Medieval Occitan Literature*. Gainesville: University Press of Florida, 1997.

Pierre des Vaux-de-Cernay. *Historia Albigensis*. Edited by Pascal Guébin and Ernest Lyon. 3 vols. Société de l'Histoire de France. Paris: Librairie Ancienne Honoré Champion, 1926.

———. *The History of the Albigensian Crusade*. Translated by W. A. and M. D. Sibly. Woodbridge: The Boydell Press, 1998.

Poly, Jean-Pierre, and Eric Bournazel. *La Mutation féodale, $x^e$–$xii^e$*. Paris: Presses Universitaire de France, 1980.

Portet, Pierre. "Permanences et mutations dans un terroir du Lauragais de l'après-croisade: Fanjeaux, vers 1250–vers 1340." *Annales du Midi* 99 (1987): 479–493.

Puech, Henri-Charles. "Catharisme médieval et bogomilisme." In *Sur le Manicheisme et autres essais*, pp. 395–427. Idees et Recherches. Paris: Flammarion, 1979.

Puylaurens, Guilhem de. *Chronica Magistri Guillelmi de Podio Laurentii*. Edited and translated by Jean Duvernoy. Sources d'Histoire Médiévale. Paris: Éditions du Centre National de la Recherche Scientifique, 1976.

*Regesta Honorii papae III*. Edited by Petrus Pressutti. 1888. Reprint, Hildesheim: Georg Olms Verlag, 1978.

*Registres d'Innocent IV*. Edited by Elie Berger. Bibliothèque des écoles françaises d'Athens et de Rome, 2d ser. Paris: Ernest Thorin, 1884.

Rey, Raymond. "Le cloître de Saint-Sernin et l'inquisition à Toulouse au XIII$^e$ siècle." *Bulletin Monumental* 110 (1952): 63–69.

Riddle, John M. *Contraception and Abortion from the Ancient World to the Renaissance*. Cambridge: Harvard University Press, 1992.

Roquebert, Michel. *L'épopée Cathare*. Vol. 1, *1198–1212: L'invasion*. Vol. 2, *1213–1216: Muret ou la dépossession*. Vol. 3, *1216–1219: Le Lys et La Croix*. Vol. 4, *Mourir à Montségur*. Toulouse: Privat, 1970–1989.

———. *Les Cathares et le Graal*. Toulouse: Privat, 1994.

Rosaldo, Renato. "From the Door of His Tent: The Fieldworker and the Inquisitor." In *Writing Culture: The Poetics and Politics of Ethnography*, edited by James Clifford and George Marcus, pp. 77–97. Berkeley and Los Angeles: University of California Press, 1986.

Rottenwöhrer, Gerhard. *Der Katherismus*. Vol. 3, *Die Herkunft der Katharer nach Theologie und Geschichte*. Bad Honnef: Bock and Herchen, 1990.

Rouse, Mary A. and Richard H. *Authentic Witnesses: Approaches to Medieval Texts and Manuscripts.* Publications in Medieval Studies, 17. Notre Dame, Ind.: University of Notre Dame Press, 1991.

Routledge, Michael. "The Later Troubadours . . . noels gigz de nova maestria . . . ." In *The Troubadours: An Introduction,* edited by Simon Gaunt and Sarah Kay, pp. 99–112. Cambridge: Cambridge University Press, 1999.

Ruiz, Teófilo F. "The Holy Office in Medieval France and in Late Medieval Castile: Origins and Contrasts." In his *The City and the Realm: Burgos and Castile 1080–1492,* pp. 33–51. Aldershot: Variorum, 1992.

Runciman, Steven. *The Medieval Manichee: A Study of the Christian Dualist Heresy* (1947). Reprint, Cambridge: Cambridge University Press, 1982.

Russell, Jeffrey Burton. "Interpretations of the Origins of Medieval Heresy." *Medieval Studies* 25 (1963): 26–53.

Salet, Francis. "Viollet-le-Duc et Mérimée." *Les Monuments Historiques de la France* 11 (1965): 19–32.

Samaran, Charles, and Robert Marichal. *Catalogue des manuscrits en écriture Latine. Portant des indications de date, de lieu ou de copiste.* Comité Internationale de Paléographie, 4. Bourgogne, Centre, Sud-Est et Sud-Ouest et de la France. Paris: Éditions de Centre National de la Recherche Scientifique, 1968.

Šanjek, Franjo. *Les chrétiens bosniaques et le movement cathare XII<sup>e</sup>–XV<sup>e</sup> siècles.* Publications de la Sorbonne NS Recherches, 20. Brussels: Editions Nauwelaerts-Diffusion Vander Oyez, 1976.

———. "Dernières traces de catharisme dans les Balkans." *Cahiers de Fanjeaux: Effacement du Catharisme? (XIII<sup>e</sup>–XIV<sup>e</sup> s.)* 20 (1985): 119–134.

Schmidt, Charles. *Histoire et Doctrine des Cathares.* 1849. Bayonne: Jean Curutchet les Éditions Harriet, 1983.

Segl, Peter, ed. *Die Anfänge der Inquisition im Mittelalter, mit einem Ausblick auf das 20. Jahrhundert und einem Beitrag über religiöse Intoleranz im nichtchristlichen Bereich.* Cologne: Böhlau Verlag, 1993.

Selwood, Dominic. *Knights of the Cloister: Templars and Hospitallers in Central-Southern Occitania c. 1100–c.1300.* Woodbridge: The Boydell Press, 1999.

Šemkov, Georgi. "Le contexte socio-économique du catharisme au Mas Sainte Puelles dans la premiére moitié du XIII<sup>e</sup> siècle." *Heresis* 2 (1984): 34–55.

Serene, Eilene. "Demonstrative Science." In *The Cambridge History of Later Medieval Philosophy: From the Rediscovery of Aristotle to the Disintegration of Scholasticism 1100–1600,* edited by Norman Kretzmann, Anthony Kenny, and Jan Pinborg, pp. 496–517. Cambridge: Cambridge University Press, 1990.

Shannon, Albert C. "The Secrecy of Witnesses in Inquisitorial Tribunals and in Contemporary Secular Criminal Trials." In *Essays in Medieval Life and Thought Presented in Honor of Austin Patterson Evans,* edited by Benjamin N. Nelson et al., pp. 59–70. New York: Columbia University Press, 1955.

Sherwood, Merriam. "Mélanges et Documents: Un registre de la cour criminelle de Mireval-Lauragais au quatorzième siècle." *Annales du Midi* 53 (1941): 78–86, 169–182, 271–287, 408–427.

Šidak, Jaroslav. *Studije o "Crkvi Bosanskoj" i Bogumilstvu.* Biblioteka Znanstvenih Radova. Zagreb: Sveucilisna naklada Liber, 1976.

Smoller, Laura A. "Defining Boundaries of the Natural in Fifteenth-Century Brittany: The Inquest into the Miracles of Saint Vincent Ferrer (d. 1419)." *Viator* 28 (1997): 333–359.

Söderberg, Hans. *La Religion des Cathares: Étude sur le Gnosticisme de la Basse Antiquité et du Moyen âge.* Uppsala: Almqvist & Wiksells Boktr, 1949.

Spiegel, Gabriel. *Romancing the Past: The Rise of Vernacular Prose Historiography in Thirteenth-Century France.* Berkeley and Los Angeles: University of California Press, 1993.

Sproemberg, Heinrich. "Die Enstehung des Manichäismus im Abendland." In *Mittelalter und demokratische Geschichtsschreibung,* edited by Heinrich Sproemberg and Manfred Unger, pp. 85–102. Ausgewählte Abhandlungen, Forschungen zur mittelalterlichen Geschichte, 18. Berlin: Akademie-Verlag, 1971.

Stock, Brian. *The Implications of Literacy: Written Language and Models of Interpretation in the Eleventh and Twelfth Centuries.* Princeton: Princeton University Press, 1983.

Stoyanov, Yuri. *The Hidden Tradition: The Secret History of Medieval Christian Heresy.* London: Arkana, 1995.

Strathern, Marilyn. *The Gender of the Gift: Problems with Women and Problems with Society in Melanesia.* Studies in Melanesian Anthropology, 6. Berkeley and Los Angeles: University of California Press, 1990.

Strayer, Joseph R. *The Albigensian Crusades. With a New Epilogue by Carol Lansing* (1971). Ann Arbor: University of Michigan Press, 1992.

Subira, Oriol Valls i. *The History of Paper in Spain X–XIV Centuries.* 3 vols. Madrid: Empresa Nacional de Celulosas, S.A., 1978.

Sumption, Jonathan. *The Albigensian Crusade.* London: Faber and Faber, 1978.

Tardif, Ad. "Document pour l'histoire du *processus per inquisitionem* et de l'*inquisitio heretice pravitatis.*" *Nouvelle revue historique du droit français et étranger* 7 (1883): 669–678.

Thomas Aquinas. *Summa contra Gentiles.* In *S Thomae Aquinas Doctoris Angelici Opera Omnia, Iussu impensaque Leonis XIII, P.M. Edita* (Leonine ed.), vols. 13–15. Rome: R. Garroni, 1918–1930.

Thouzellier, Christine. "Hérésie et croisade au XII$^e$ siècle." *Revue d'histoire ecclésiastique* 49 (1954): 855–872.

———. *Catharisme et Valdéisme en Languedoc à la fin du XIIe et au début du XIIIe siècle. Politique pontificale—Controverses.* Publications de la Faculté des Lettres et Sciences Humaines de Paris. Série «Recherches», 27. Paris: Presses Universitaires de France, 1966.

———. "La Bible de Cathares languedociens et son usage dans la controverse au début au XIII$^e$ siècle." *Cahiers de Fanjeaux: Cathares en Languedoc* 3 (1968): 42–58.

———. *Hérésie et Héretiques: Vaudois, Cathares, Patarins, Albigeois.* Storia e Letteratura, Raccolta di Studi e Testi, 116. Rome: Edizioni di Storia e Letteratura, 1969.

Timbal, Pierre. *Un Conflit d'annexion au Moyen Age: L'Application de la coutume de Paris au pays d'Albigeois.* Toulouse: Edouard Privat, 1949.

Töpfer, Bernhard. *Das kommende Reich des Friedens; zur Entwicklung chiliasticscher Zukunftshoffnungen im Hochmittelalter.* Forschungen zur mittelalterlichen Geschichte, 11. Berlin: Akademie-Verlag, 1964.

Vicaire, Marie-Humbert. "Le développement de la province Dominicaine de Provence (1215–1295)." *Cahiers de Fanjeaux: Les mendiants en pays d'Oc au XIII$^e$ siècle* 8 (1973): 52–54.

Vicaire, Marie-Humbert, and Henri Gilles. "Rôle de l'université de Toulouse dans l'effacement du catharisme." *Cahiers de Fanjeaux: Effacement du Catharisme? (XIII$^e$–XIV$^e$ S.)* 20 (1985): 257–276.

Wakefield, Walter L. "Notes on Some Antiheretical Writings of the Thirteenth Century." *Franciscan Studies* 27 (1967): 285–321.

———. "Friar Ferrier, Inquisition at Caunes, and Escapes from Prison at Carcassonne." *Catholic Historical Review* 68 (1972): 220–237.

———. *Heresy, Crusade and Inquisition in Southern France 1100–1250.* London: George Allen & Unwin, 1974.

———. "Heretics as Physicians in the Thirteenth Century." *Speculum* 57 (1982): 328–331.

———. "Heretics and Inquisitors: The Case of Le Mas-Saintes-Puelles." *Catholic Historical Review* 69 (1983): 209–226.

———. "Burial of Heretics in the Middle Ages." *Heresis* 5 (1985): 29–32.

———. "Heretics and Inquisitors: The Case of Auriac and Cambiac." *Journal of Medieval History* 12 (1986): 225–237.

———. "Friar Ferrier, Inquisitor." *Heresis* 7 (1986): 33–41.

———. "Pseudonyms and Nicknames in Inquisitorial Documents of the Middle Ages." *Heresis* 15 (1990): 9–22.

———. "Inquisitor's Assistants: Witnesses to Confessions in Manuscript 609." *Heresis* 20 (1993): 57–65.

Wakefield, Walter L., and Austin P. Evans. *Heresies of the High Middle Ages: Selected Sources Translated and Annotated.* Records of Western Civilization. New York: Columbia University Press, 1991.

Walther, Helmut. "Ziele und Mittel päpstlicher Ketzerpolitik in der Lombardei und im Kirchenstaat 1184–1252." In *Die Anfänge der Inquisition im Mittelalter, mit einem Ausblick auf das 20. Jahrhundert und einem Beitrag über religiöse Intoleranz im nichtchristlichen Bereich,* edited by Peter Segl, pp. 103–130. Cologne: Böhlau Verlag, 1993.

Werner, Ernst. *Pauperes Christi. Studien zu sozial-religiösen Bewegungen im Zeitalter des Reformpapsttums.* Leipzig: Kochler & Amelang, 1957.

———. *Ketzer und Heilige: Das religiöse Leben im Hochmittelalter.* Vienna: Böhlaus, 1986.

Wickham, Chris, and James Fentress. *Social Memory.* Oxford: Blackwell, 1992.

Wilson, Stephen. *A Social and Cultural History of Personal Naming in Western Europe.* London: UCL Press, 1998.

Zagorin, Perez. "The Historical Significance of Lying and Dissimulation." *Social Research* 63 (1996): 863–912.

Zio, Simona di, Paul Canart, Lucina Polistena, and Daniela Scialanga. "Une enquête sur le papier de type «Arabe Occidental» ou «Espagnol non filigrané»." In *Ancient and Medieval Book Materials and Techniques (Erice, 18–25 september 1992),* edited by Marilena Maniaci and Paola F. Munafò, 1:313–393. Studi e Testi, 357. Vatican City: Biblioteca Apostolica Vaticana, 1993.

# INDEX

abbreviations: in MS 609, 22

adoration, 84, 87, 92–103; intention to adore, 94; *melhoramen* an affirmation of village habits, 95; not bending the knee, 93; saying "bless us," *benezion*, 45, 74, 92; village courtesies formalized by inquisition, 92. *See also* believers, in the good men and good women; good men; good women

Agen, Agenais, 5–6, 14, 37

Agnes de Beaupuy (nun at Brie), 79

Agout River, 3

Aimergarda Maserol (of Gaja-la-Selve), 95

Aimersent Mir Arezat (of Saint-Martin-de-la-Lande; wife of Bernart Mir Arezat), 114, 116; perpetual imprisonment of, 116, 128

Aimersent Viguier (of Cambiac; wife of Guilhem Viguier), 63, 66, 72, 74–75, 111; demon in her belly, 74–75; stuffed in a wine tun, 63, 129

Aimery de Montfort (son of Simon de Montfort), 11; ceded rights to Louis VIII, 12; fled the Midi, 12; at Marmande, 12; truces of with Raimon VII, 12

Ainart Ugon (*bayle* of Fanjeaux; brother of Guilhem Ugon), 122–123

Airoz, 120

Alain de Lille (Cistercian), 149–150n.25

Alamant de Roaix: condemned for heresy, 81

Alazaïs Barrau (of Moussoulens), 66

Alazaïs d'Auri (of Auriac), 67, 70

Alazaïs de Cales (of Gaja-la-Selve), 87, 95

Alazaïs den Plata (of Auriac), 58

Alazaïs de Turre (of Mireval; wife of Roger de Turre), 99, 109; second marriage of to Raimon de Cantes (of Gibel), 109

Albigenses, 17–19; *Ambigensis* used by Arnold Fitz-Thedmar, 19; use of word for heretics in Languedoc, 18–19

Albigensian Crusade, 4, 18, 31, 43, 48, 86–89, 118–119, 127; and the Albigenses, 17–19; *Ambigensis* used by Arnold Fitz-Thedmar, 19; and anecdote about Arnaud Amalric by Caesarius of Heisterbach, 48; attack on Carcassonne, 7;

battle of Muret, 10; burning of anonymous accused heretic at Castres, 7; burning of heretics and hanging of knights at Lavaur, 8; and *canso* of Guilhem de Tudela, 5; and count of Nevers, 5, 7, 135n.13; *crozada*, 5; crusade numbers, 5, 135n.13; and death of Louis VIII, 13; and death of na Girauda, 8; and death of Peire de Castelnau, 5; and duke of Burgundy, 5, 7; in *Encyclopædia Britannica* (11th ed.), 19; first attack on Toulouse, 8; and "good man" as a confusing label, 96; and Honorius III, 12; massacre at Marmande, 12; massacre of Béziers, 6; mutilations at Bram and Cabaret, 8, 137n.43; participants in, 5, 11; participation of Prince Louis in, 10, 12; Peace of Meaux-Paris, 13–14; and Pere II of Aragon, 7–9; and Philip II Augustus, 5–13; proclaimed by Innocent III, 4; and Raimon VI, 4–12; and Raimon VII, 10–14; and Raimon Roger Trencavel, 6–7; and Roman Frangipani, 13; royal crusade of Louis VIII, 13; same indulgence offered for as for expedition to Palestine, 4; seige of Avignon, 13; seige of Lavaur, 8; and Simon de Montfort, 7–11; Simon de Montfort's attack on Toulouse in 1218, 11, 88; and *sirventes* of Guilhem Figueira, 13; in modern southern French life, 140n. 106; and statutes of Pamiers, 9; as temporal demarcation, 87–88, 118–119

Albigeois, 8, 14

Alexander III (pope), 17

Alexander IV (pope), 32; *Ut negotium*, 32

Algaia de Villeneuve-la-Comptal (noblewoman), 40

Alice de Montfort (wife of Simon de Montfort), 11

Alisson (of Mas-Saintes-Puelles; *divinatrix* and *medica*), 107–108

Almohade Muslims, 9

alms, 54

*alphabets*, 25

Alphandéry, Paul: in *Encyclopædia Britannica* (11th edition), 19; views of on